PATRICK
OF
BON AVON

JEAN MANNERS MEFFAN

PATRICK
OF
BON AVON

FINIAL PUBLISHING

First published in 1999 by
FINIAL PUBLISHING

First published in paperback in 1999 by
FINIAL PUBLISHING

ISBN 1-900467-06-2

Typeset in 12 on 13pt Perpetua
by Finial Publishing & Printing Services
15 Hoburne Road, Swanage, Dorset BH19 2SL
Telephone/fax: 01929 423980
e-mail: mail@finial.co.uk

Printed by The Dorset Press, Dorchester, Dorset DT1 1HD

Cover drawing by Andrew Maltman

CONTENTS

PART I

IN THE BEGINNING

PART II

A NEW ERA

PART III

SLAVERY

PART IV
THE ROAD TO PRIESTHOOD

EPILOGUE

INTRODUCTION

The Irish have many stories about their patron saint. The facts, rather than the fiction, are taken from Patrick's own 'confession' or biography, which he wrote when he was very old.

He said that his name was Maun and that he was born in a village named Bonavon Tibernae. Some writers spell his name Maewyn and his village Bannaven Taburniae, which are merely phonetic spellings of the first.

He also said that his father was called Calpurnius and that his grandfather was Potitus. Of the name Potitus, I have doubts, for it sounds more like a title than a forename. A title given to a high ranking and respected official, which Calpurnius's father was.

In his biography, there are several hundred quotations from scripture, quite an achievement for a man who constantly bemoaned his lack of education and ignorance.

The original document was faded and damaged, some of it lost forever, but we are very fortunate that so much was rescued and translated. Over the years, many translators have had to guess what the missing words were, which is clear by the slight variations.

In the 70 years of his long life spent performing miracles so powerful that his name is indelibly printed in the consciousness of mankind, yet he never mentions one, is an example of his modesty, for Patrick would never claim credit for anything he believed was the work of God.

Unlike Patrick, I have never entered an orthodox church, except as a tourist or wedding guest. But, like him, I do not think that I can take the credit for writing 'Patrick of Bon Avon', this new book on his early life. The story seemed to be placed in my path and questions asked were mysteriously answered.

Whatever your faiths or beliefs, or your lack of either, I hope you will enjoy reading 'Patrick of Bon Avon'.

JEAN MANNERS MEFFAN
1 September 1999

SAINT PATRICK

AND

DUNBARTONSHIRE'S ANCIENT HISTORY

In the 12th Century, there lived a priest, scholar and gatherer of legends, called Geoffrey of Monmouth, who is famous for writing in 1136 the *Historia Regum Brittanniae* (History of British Kings), from the earliest - King Brut - to Cadwallen, a Welsh king who died in 689.

Somewhere between these two, Geoffrey wrote of the romantic exploits of King Arthur and his beautiful Queen Guinevere; Merlin the Magician and the Knights of the Round table.

There is one story amongst Geoffrey's many writings which differs from the others, for it is about a 'Prince Arthur'. It seems that the Prince so loathed the Saxons for daring to invade his country, that he vowed to kill as many of them as he could. He was not alone and thus he was able to amass a great Army. They gathered at Exeter and travelling north, killed everyone who even looked like a Saxon; leaving behind them a grisly trail of mangled, slaughtered bodies.

That was until they reached the most northerly part of Britain, which was the Clyde valley.

At that time, there was no England or Scotland, for it would be another 200 years and more before the Irish King Kenneth Mac Alpine of the Scottis tribe laid claim to the land south of the Clyde - calling it Scotland - and before the Saxon population had spread far enough to call southern Britain, England.

From the south coast to the Clyde had been Roman Britain and Arthur believed that this was now his future kingdom.

Geoffrey's *Historia* informs us that when Prince Arthur's forces reached land, just south of Loch Lomond, they suddenly changed tactics, deciding not to use their swords or daggers to kill the inhabitants. Instead, they herded them into the loch to either drown or swim to the islands - a strange thing for a blood-thirsty army to do! Geoffrey then goes on to relate how several bishops arrived and managed to persuade Arthur to turn around and ride south.

This story has a few puzzles and the author anticipates that of the many people who have previously read it, most will have discarded it as a 'fictitious flight of fancy', for the area south of Loch Lomond - known as the Vale of Leven - does not now warrant the presence of one bishop!

It is known that Patrick was born in a village called 'Bonavon Tibernae' somewhere in Dunbartonshire, but since there is no record of such a village, the exact location has remained a mystery.

In this book, the author claims that 'Bonavon Tibernae' is not so much a village as a river - 'Avon' being the Roman word for river.

When the Romans first arrived in the Clyde Valley and surveyed the land, they were fascinated by this river that had its source in the beautiful mountains that surround the loch. They were also amazed at the volume of water that gushed from its only outlet and which hurtled through the valley at tremendous speed.

They likened it to their own river Tiber, for that too had its source in the mountains and raced through the countryside. Both rivers travelled in a north-to-south direction and were at that time unnavigable.

However, there was one big difference - their length. The Tiber was several hundred miles long, whereas this little river was about five. But, to the surveyors, this river was of enormous strategic importance, for it was five miles of natural defence system that protected the native British-Celts from the West Highland and Irish tribes. Because of this, they named it 'The Tibernae' (the little Tiber).

The prefix 'bon' is an old British name for a 'beacon'. We are familiar with 'bon' (as in bonfire) and in days long ago, that is what 'bonhill' was, 'A Beacon Hill'. The village grew between the hill and the river.

To return to Geoffrey's story of Arthur, given that this series of events took place less than 100 years after Patrick's death, it is possible that an Abbey of some importance was built there and that it became the scene of a vast religious complex.

This would certainly put some flesh on the bones of Geoffrey's story. It would explain why 'Arthur's forces' were reluctant to kill the inhabitants as instructed, for they may have been reluctant to personally kill monks or priests and so chose instead to drown them in the fashion of a firing squad of more recent times, where people could be killed without the perpetrators feeling blame or guilt. Then there was the plurality of bishops with enough clout to convince Arthur and his Army to turn around and ride south.

Today, the remains of Bonavon Tibernae, lie buried deep below the ruins of an old dye works in an area of Bonhill called 'Dalmonach', which translated means 'the place of the monks'.

NAMES OF MAIN CHARACTERS

PART I

HOEL (Boat builder and his two sons CALIM and HARRAN)
LEELAN (Labourer working for Hoel)
CALPURNIUS (Roman soldier)
PETRUS (Wine merchant and his daughter RHONA)
OLD MISSIONARY

PART II

GAIUS *pronounced Guyus,* (Roman Army Commander)
SERGAEUS (Gaius's Adjutant)
CLODUS (Gaius's Recruiting Officer)
CALPURNIUS (Calim's son)
JOSEPH (Priest)
CONCHESSA (Joseph's daughter)
PAULUS (Joseph's adopted son)
ALANA (Conchessa's companion)
ELINOR (Harran's wife)
JULIA and PORTIA (Harran's daughters)
MAUN (became PATRICK)
CEDI and ERIC (Farm workers)

PART III

BRUNER (Captain of *The Old Sweat Rag*)
CHIEF (Second-in-Command)
EVAN (Crew member)
BARNEY (Trader)
MORA (Barney's daughter)
HANNO (Patrick's scribe)
REUBAN (Elder)
HAMMISH (Elder)
AMYOTT (Abbot)
PORTEOUS (A grateful grandfather)
ILSA (Porteous's wife)
HELEN (Julia's daughter)

PART IV

JESS (Flavia's mother)
FLAVIA (Patrick's companion)
MARGARETTA (Evan's wife)
ADAM and KARL (Evan's sons)
JOSHUA, MAX and ANTONIUS (Roman soldiers)
POPE CELESTINE and SAINT PAULINIUS
REBECCA (Hanno's wife)
KEVEN and SHERAN (Patrick's faithful companions)

PART I

IN THE BEGINNING

ROMAN BRITON
345A.D.

The war had been over for three years and the people of the little Roman British settlement of Dunbriton on the Clyde had returned to something akin to a normal way of life, at least on the outside. What trauma and pain they held hidden in their souls, no one would ever know.

The war had come about when a war-like tribe from over the sea in Hibernia learned that the Roman Army was being recalled to Gaul to put down an uprising in another part of the empire. They were already packing their weapons and ammunition and had orders to take every able bodied man with them. This was the opportunity their enemies had been waiting for. Both the Hibernians and the Picts of the Highlands and Islands had their eyes fixed on what seemed to them to be magic earth, for the Romans knew a thing or two about agriculture. They had to. With thousands of men and horses to feed they were able to produce a variety of crops year after year without fail.

By the time the army was ready to leave, the Hibernians and the Picts had joined forces and were ready to attack. They had clear instructions to wipe out the remaining population and lay claim to the land.

The Army had marched about a third of the way towards Hadrian's Wall, when they encountered a fog bank and so decided to set up camp for the night and hope that it would clear by the next day.

Next morning, a lone rider caught up with them and gave them the grim news of the invasion. The Army had no choice, but to disobey orders and turn around and get back as quickly as they could, for the land of Strathclyde was their home, the only one most of them had ever known. Their wives, children and parents were there. They got back in record time and fought the battle of their lives, chasing the enemy back to where they came from, but not quick enough to prevent the slaughter of fifteen thousand men, women and children.

Four thousand of the enemy were also killed. No prisoners were taken.

The land still belonged to the Roman Brits. The Hibernians and the Picts had gained nothing. Later on a pact of peace was signed between the three nations. It was reported that the King of the Hibernian tribe, the King of the Picts and the Legate for the Roman British met and that the Legate paid their enemies in precious jewels to leave the Britons alone.

The people of Dunbriton looked forward to many years of peace.

CHAPTER I

THE BOAT BUILDERS

When the war began, there was a man named Hoel, an old soldier who had retired from the Army when a fall from his horse rendered him lame. He made a good living for his wife and two sons building boats.

On the day of the invasion, he was in his boatyard by the river near Dunbriton's harbour, with two labourers and his young sons, when they spotted the arrival of the strange ships and the even stranger men who poured out of them. They were screaming, shouting and waving banners. Hoel had no time to think before the door of his yard was kicked open and a gang of these tribesmen entered. Being an old warrior himself, he grabbed a long pole and lashed out at them knocking them to the ground. His men also picked up weapons and attacked. They had almost got the better of their enemies, when another man barged his way in. He was a giant of a man. Seeing that his men were being beaten, he made for Hoel, grabbed him by the neck of his shirt, swung him around to face him, then drew a short dagger from his belt. He was about to plunge it into Hoel's stomach, when suddenly he stopped and stared into space as though he was seeing 'the fires of hell'. He slumped to the floor. Hoel stood looking down at him in amazement before turning to see that his young sons had been responsible. Seeing their father about to be killed, they had both picked up sharp wood cutting tools and with as much power as they could muster, they had stuck them into the giant. Hoel picked up the dagger which the fatally injured giant had dropped and quickly put him out of his misery. Thinking quickly, he ordered his workmen, "Quick. Take off your clothes and put them on the dead men, then put on theirs. If we drag them outside, their tribesmen will think it is us and not come in". That done, they climbed into the shell of the boat they had been working on and hid themselves. They could hear in the distance the pitiful screams of their fellow countrymen. It was a hellish and terrifying experience and one they could not envisage an end to.

The men were anxious to find out if their wives had survived, so when darkness fell, Hoel put on the giant's headgear and crept outside. He made his way to their homes. On checking each one, he encountered scenes of horror too terrible to describe. Sufficient to tell that his beloved wife had her throat cut from ear to ear. He quickly doused his oil lamp and hurried back to their hiding place. On the way he kept an eye out for any kind of food, but there was nothing, it had all been taken.

"Are you sure they were dead?", asked Leelan, one of his men.

"Yes I am sure", said Hoel looking up. His eyes were red raw but the rest of his face was deathly white. "There is no doubt."

For several days they survived, going out at night to get water from the river and anything that would pass for food.

Several more days passed. They could still hear the noise of battle, but further away in the distance. It was clear that the enemy had moved further inland believing that the villages along the coast had been conquered, which meant they were safe for a while. They ventured out of their hiding place, but still had to be vigilant. It was a relief for them to leave their cramped conditions, but were wary of the slightest sound. They went to their homes and buried their wives and Leelan's children, then returned to the safety of their hiding place. Several more days passed. Again they heard the sounds of battle and hid even further into the hull of the boat, but were puzzled when nothing else happened. Suddenly, they heard the approach of a horse. The door of the boatyard creaked open and a voice called out, "Is there anyone in here?". They did not answer for fear it was a trick. The voice called out again, as it moved towards the boat. Then the owner of the voice climbed up and peeped over the side. Hoel caught sight of the plume of a Roman helmet and breathed a deep sigh of relief.

"I had a strong feeling you were in here, call it intuition. I have come to tell you that the war is over. Captain Calpurnius at your service." He helped them out of the boat. "I am to take you to a safe house where all the survivors are gathering and where you can have a good meal."

Hoel was a strong man, but on this occasion he wept openly and unashamedly. Calpurnius patted his shoulder in an effort to comfort him. He then lifted the two boys on to the back of his horse and bade them to hold on tight, then led them to the house of Petrus, a wine merchant. His house had been ransacked and his furniture ruined, but the family and servants were safe hiding in the cool underground wine cellar and the house was still intact.

Petrus had two sons of his own, both a little older than Hoel's boys. He also had a little daughter who clung around his neck, afraid to let go. She was a beautiful child, with hair like spun platinum and a face so gentle, with blue eyes that looked both sorrowful and frightened. Petrus introduced her as 'his little angel' then said to her, "Say hello to Mr Hoel, Rhona". But, Rhona looked away and hid her face in her father's shoulder. "Even the little ones have suffered", said Petrus and he shook his head in despair.

Hoel wondered why there was only one officer here - where were his troops? His unspoken question was answered when Calpurnius approached them and said he would have to leave to check on his men. He had left them for too long. Petrus asked him if they were burying all of the bodies in a single grave, or were they going to burn them?

Only then did Hoel remember his wife and the dreadful discovery he had made on the night of the invasion. Anger was now taking over from the fear and grief that had absorbed him.

How dare they come here and ruin our lives. "Who are they to commit crimes so diabolical against our wives and children?"

Petrus witnessed the expression on Hoel's face. He thought, 'If I don't do something quickly, Hoel will go mad'. He picked up a bowl of food and took it over to him. "The good Captain tells me that you are a builder of boats."

Hoel looked up at him as though he had not understood a word, but after a moment's thought he began to comprehend what Petrus had said. "Yes I do build boats, that is my trade."

Petrus sat down beside him. "I am very pleased about that, for when this war; this mess, is cleared up, we - you and I - and every man among us will have to begin again and the first thing I will need is a ship."

Hoel was staring at him in wonder. "Are you saying that you want me to build a ship?"

Petrus looked around him, then commented, "Well my friend, I don't see any other ship builders around - do you?". Petrus was pleased that his idea had worked. He could see Hoel's mind working and now concentrating along more positive lines. "Excuse me for one moment", said Petrus. He walked towards his wife and gave her the now sleeping Rhona. When he returned, he told Hoel, "There are not many men left to rebuild our town, the future of our children is in the hands of men like us".

Hoel was feeling bucked up by what he'd heard. Ideas of the kind of ships he could build filled his mind. He stood up and looked out of the window. Calpurnius was there with the children, giving them rides on his horse. In the distance he could see some of Calpurnius's men returning, followed by more survivors. He then noticed his surroundings, even with the damage, it was still a splendid home. He realised for the first time what a terrible hovel he had provided for his wife and family. His mind began to fill with ideas for the future. His children were going to have a house to live in, even better than this one. Hoel found strength in his plans, for now he had a way to fight back.

CHAPTER II

CALIM AND HARRAN

In the harbour at Dunbriton, Hoel's sons Calim and Harran - now aged thirteen and twelve - sat on the quay, their feet barely touching the cold water of the Clyde below. Their boots lay carelessly beside them.

They were not at all happy, for since the day the war ended three years before, their father had changed. He was no longer the easy going and carefree builder of small craft. He had become a ruthless businessman, who thought only of making money. He hired the finest craftsmen, bought the very best tools and built great ships fit to sail on the high seas. He had become extremely rich and was planning to build the biggest and finest house in Strathclyde, in the style of a Roman villa. Yet, Calim and Harran were obliged to work long hours sweeping up sawdust and chippings and sharpening the tools used by the ships' carpenters.

It was hard, never-ending work, for no sooner had one tool been sharpened, than another blunt one was tossed into the box placed between them.

Today had been especially bad, for while they worked, they overheard two of their fellow workmen talk about their father. One had said to the other, "Why does old Hoel make his sons do menial work here? For sure, if I had all his money I would send my sons to school to be educated, maybe to become a doctor or an artist".

The other worker replied "I don't know why he treats them like slaves, it can't be to earn more money for he owns all that already". Then they laughed at their own joke.

So, as they sat there eating their bread and cheese and throwing some crumbs to the seagulls, they were feeling humiliated and not a little resentful.

They were quite unaware of a small foreign trader that passed in front of them and tied up a little further along the quay. An old man the only passenger amongst the freight had noticed the boys sitting there as the trader passed in front of them and when it tied up and he disembarked, he made towards them. "Good-day to you. I have only now arrived in your most beautiful country and I wonder if you could direct me to the nearest inn?"

Calim and Harran looked up at the quaint old man with the strange and funny accent. He was tall and thin. His long white hair and skimpy beard came to a point on his sunken chest. He wore a gown in a sandy colour and a dark woollen cloak was slung over his bony shoulders. Calim was about to point in the direction of the inn, when suddenly the old man said "Why do you young boys have such glum faces. The sun is shining. It is a beautiful day and God is in his heaven. So what ails you both so much?". He dropped his cloak on the ground beside them and sat down. Calim and Harran did not know why, but felt compelled to confide in him. He seemed harmless and had a warm sympathetic smile. They told him everything and showed him the scars made by the sharp tools.

"I see", said the old man. "Tell me, do you have a mother?"

"No", answered Calim. "She was killed in the war."

The old man nodded sadly. "Does your father beat you or starve you?"

The boys expressed horror. "Oh no sir, our father would never ever hurt us and he provides good food."

"Well", said the old man, "Why are you so angry with him? Do you think he makes you work only to acquire more money?".

"Well sir, we did not use to think so, but on hearing what the other workers said about him, we began to wonder and are now unsure."

The old man made himself even more comfortable and cleared his throat. "Do you know what I think?" He looked from one to the other, then without waiting to hear their reply, he continued. "If I were a man with no wife and two handsome sons like you whom I held dear, I would have a terrible dilemma. Who would care for them whilst I was about my business? I would have to think very hard on how to protect them from the evils that abound in the world. Where could I leave them where they would be safe and free from harm? Why, of course, I would leave them in the care of a trusted employer, one I knew would watch over them." The old man glanced along the quay towards the large boathouse and sure enough, Leelan was standing by the door watching them. The old man smiled and nodded as his guess was confirmed.

"We do understand", said Harran. "But why do we have to work so hard? You have seen the scars of our injuries."

The old man searched their faces. "Tell me my young friends. If you were not at work what would you be doing? Would you go fishing, or swimming, or would you go rambling among the hills? Oh no, no, no. That would never do. You would have to be somewhere where your guardian could watch over you all the time. Don't you see how much your father loves you both and is trying to protect you the only way he knows how. He has placed you under the protection of a trusted employee and friend."

The old man made sense, but they asked him if they would not be equally as safe in the care of a tutor? "Your father is rich?" questioned the old man. "I expect he earned his money working as you do now. It is unlikely he knows of a tutor let alone one he can trust. No, my young friends, he wants you both to learn what it is like to do hard work. He knows that people seldom place value on what comes too easily. As for not paying you for your labour, it is my understanding that a man does not gather wealth for himself, but to build an inheritance for his children. There is no doubt that your father loves you both very much and instead of grumbling you should be grateful."

The boys were happier now. "What you say sir is true and it is what we believed, until we heard what his workers were saying about him."

"My friends", said the old man. "Pay no heed to the jealous mumbling of others. Allow me to give you some advice. Set your own high standards of behaviour. Aim to be good honest sons of your Father in heaven as well as your earthly one. Do not allow others less worthy to goad you into actions that you might regret and if you have a problem, don't give up easily. Look at it from all angles. Turn it on its head and examine it. Very often the problem will disappear, or even better it could become an asset."

Just then Leelan called out. "Calim, Harran, back to work!"

The boys started to put on their boots. As they began to lace them up, the old man asked them, "Have either of you heard of a man named Jesus?".

"I have", answered Calim. "He's a religious leader." Before the old man could say another word Calim continued. "My father says religion is a fraud. It never put a denarius into a poor man's money pouch nor a crust on the table of a starving one."

The old man nodded in agreement. "Your father could be right about that, so I fear you might not understand what I am about to tell you. There are some things more important than money or food."The boys looked at him in disbelief. "Yes my young friends. Your thoughts are more important, for there never was a man that did a kind or foul act that was not first conceived in his thoughts. The quality of a man, woman or a child's soul is indicated by what they think. Jesus was only a carpenter, yet his thoughts of compassion and kindness are influencing thousands of people to create better lives for themselves. Full of hope and faith." Leelan called to them again. He was standing by the shipyard gate with hands on his hips and tapping his foot in postures of impatience.

The boys ran, but Calim looked back smiling and called out. "See you soon again."

The old man called back. "Yes my children, I will be here."

Later that day, Hoel turned up with his horse and buggy to collect his sons. He was surprised to find them in a pleasant mood and not complaining, as they usually were at the end of a hard day. He wondered what had happened to cheer them up, but decided not to inquire in case they had just forgotten. As they drove away, they passed the old man by the roadside, but did not notice that he had not travelled far. The old man saw them and taking a Cross of Christ from around his neck, he looked at it for a moment, then kissed it. "My blessed Lord, I do try, I do try. Tomorrow is another day and I will try again."

PART II

A NEW ERA

CHAPTER III

30 YEARS ON

Dunbriton has become a thriving industrious town. Thirty years of peace has allowed its population to grow and prosper. The extended port is a busy one. Ships of the Roman fleet arrive frequently bringing supplies for the Army and civilian ships bring luxury goods from more exotic parts of the world.

The town is a popular place to live, having plentiful supplies of fresh fish and soil that has received well the seeds of fruits and vegetables from distant parts of the Empire. No one goes hungry.

Peace is kept by the Army. A six thousand strong Legion of well trained and disciplined tough fighting men led by their Commander Antonius Gaius. He is a man of strong will and determination. Tall and handsome, but in a rough sort of way and a voice cultivated to reach to all ranks on parade and beyond.

Gaius believes wholeheartedly in 'peace through strength' and that power shared is power diluted. He also believes that many opinions only lead to confusion.

A thorn in the flesh of Gaius is 'The Legate'. That Ambassador from Rome, whose duty it is to liaise with the cream of the civilian population. The manufacturers, builders, exporters of goods and selected from amongst them, Decurians, respected men who will represent Rome and collect taxes from the rest of the people, each Decurian being given a district to collect from.

Gaius dislikes the Legate intensely, the reason being that he outranked him and could tell him what he could and could not do. Warnings of his annual visit is enough to make Gaius unbearable. Gaius's orders are to: keep the peace, guard and protect the ships of the fleet on the Clyde and patrol the border between the Highlands and the furthermost corner of the Roman Empire, these things are meticulously carried out. Indeed, the joke being passed around by the civilian men and women, is "Pity any poor cat or dog who unwittingly stray across the border. It will find itself being interrogated and put in jail".

Gaius's adjutant is Major Sergaeus, a young man who has been with him for two years, ever since they arrived in Strathclyde from Gaul. There had been bets made amongst the officers as to how long Sergaeus would last in his job before having a nervous breakdown, as several young officers before him had done. But, much to their surprise, Sergaeus showed remarkable powers of survival and hidden strength.

It was Sergaeus who had to remind his boss when the Legate's next visit was due. He would simply place the memo between other more mundane information, then retreat to his own outer office to await Gaius's outburst of obscenities. On this occasion, however, it did not happen for the Legate was too busy to make his regular visit, but he had a request.

A Christian priest was on his way from Gaul to open a mission and school on the borders between the Highlands and Roman Briton. The Legate requested that the Army take responsibility for the priest's safety and provide him and his helpers with suitable accommodation, until such times as they could find their own. The Legate was concerned that this priest, who was the half brother of the respected 'Bishop of Tours' and a distant relative of his own, would find this assignment extremely difficult due to lack of experience, hence the special request.

Gaius's headquarters are situated within an imposing building, with pillars on either side of a double door and large shuttered windows. The rooms within are large and uncluttered. Besides Gaius's office and Sergaeus's outer one, there is a large conference hall where once a week, fifty of the most senior officers meet to report on their own departments of responsibility, in order to co-ordinate their duties.

On this occasion, the officers have sat through long hours of discussion on transport, food supplies, weapons, boots, recruitment and 'public relations' (one of the Legate's bright ideas).

The latter has been a problem of late. Some recruits have been going into town and getting drunk on the local brew of fermented barley and cheap wine. The complaints have been many. Brawling, using foul language, being sick in public places and chasing the young women, to name but a few.

The civilian men have organised a vigilante group to patrol the streets and pick up the drunks before the trouble starts. They throw them into a cart usually reserved for moving rubbish and dump them at the camp gates, very much the worse for wear. The vigilantes have complained as a group. It would not be wise to reveal their names to Gaius, for they know his reputation and his opinion of civilians. Much better to remain anonymous, even if right is on your side.

After a quick run through of the complaints, they agree on a curfew on the recruits and an increase in the number of military police.

The conference over, Gaius is about to dismiss his officers, when Sergaeus reminds him of the Legate's request that had arrived that day all the way from Eboracum. "Wait please. There is one more item on our agenda to discuss." The men were tired, hot and thirsty and were in no mood to wait any longer, but they ungraciously sat back in their seats with a resigned sigh and waited.

"We have today received a communique from Our Beloved Legate" (this was spoken with heavy sarcasm). Gaius continued. "Our Beloved Legate" - he paused, waiting for his mens' expected reaction to his wit - "has requested that we receive and welcome a Christian missionary and that we find him and his fellow missionaries suitable accommodation".

One of the officers asked, "Was this some kind of a joke?".

"It is no joke", said Gaius. "It appears that this priest is the half brother to the Bishop of Tours and a distant relative of the Legate himself. He believes that the priest is unable to cope without some help, therefore, he has given us the task of looking after him. He requires us, not only to find property suitable for a house and schoolroom, but that we protect him, at least until he establishes his school. His orders from his superiors are to convert the natives."

The Officers are becoming even more irritable. It has been a long, boring day and they are not too pleased at this added item using up their valuable drinking time. Gaius himself has had enough and decides to dismiss his men by telling them to think it over and come up with suggestions, when a young officer at the back of the room stood up and announces himself as Captain Clodus. "Sir", he said, "Why do you think they want another Christian school here when we already have a perfectly good one in Dunbriton?" Every face turned to glare at Clodus.

There was stony silence for a moment. Gaius's lips twitched as he struggled to find words. Then he yelled, "Do we indeed. And why may I ask have you kept this information to yourself?".

"Sir", said Clodus. "As recruitment officer, I came to hear of it when new men came to me who could speak Latin fluently. This was unusual. So I asked them where they learned to speak so well and they told me of the Christian mission school."

"I am going to dismiss the men", said Gaius. "You wait here. I have a few words to say to you." Clodus was embarrassed and red faced. He wished with all his might that he'd kept his mouth tightly closed. Sergaeus, who had been taking notes, felt sorry for Clodus, but he had just broken some unwritten rules. Never speak until you are spoken to, never voice an opinion, or draw attention to yourself for to do so is to volunteer.

When the room was empty, save Gaius, Sergaeus and Clodus, Gaius sat on the edge of his desk and asked, "What exactly do you do, Clodus?". This question surprised Clodus, for it was Gaius himself who had given him the appointment. But, then Gaius said, "I don't want to know your rank and title. I want to know how you actually spend your day?".

"Well Sir. I, with one other of my men search the countryside for suitable recruits. I then have them seen by the Medical Officer and if fit they are instructed in regulations."

"Do you do all of this yourself?", asked Gaius.

"No Sir. I delegate my subordinates and supervise."

"Well now", said Gaius. "You can delegate your said subordinates to take over all of your duties (I don't expect they will miss you). I now appoint you in charge of finding suitable property for this priest and his followers who have been foisted upon us. You will search along the border until you find something resembling his requirements. I want this done as quickly as possible, for I believe these people are on their way as we speak and I don't want mealy-mouthed missionaries in my camp converting my fighting men. Got It?"

Clodus, whose knees were beginning to tremble, saluted and left. He was not a coward. Cowards do not become officers in the Roman Army. But he was new to this Legion. He was a tall thin man, quite unlike the usual stocky build of most soldiers and he stood out among them. He left the building and waited by the door to take in a breath of fresh air, when Sergaeus caught up with him. "Don't take it too hard Clodus, we have all felt the lash of his tongue at one time or another. Can I suggest that you first contact the Mission school in town. It may be that they will be only too pleased to help you welcome a fellow Christian, especially a famous one." Clodus was grateful for the advice and nodded thankfully.

When Sergaeus returned to the main office, Gaius was sitting by his desk with a flagon of wine and a glass of the golden liquid in front of him. He looked up at Sergaeus. "Have you ever seen such a jelly kneed daisy as Clodus? I thought he was going to burst into tears. He's almost as dim as this priest who's coming who thinks he can convert the Picts and the Scotti."

Next morning, Clodus rode to Dunbriton and found the school. A young lady teacher gave him directions to the home of the leader. He had to retrace part of his journey before he found the correct road. He rode up a hill and just over the summit - protected from the road by a row of poplars - was 'Hoel's Villa'. As his eyes feasted on the magnificent house, he thought, "There must be money in religion after all".

He approached cautiously, thinking as he went, 'I hope they don't set a dog on me; with my luck anything can happen. What have I got myself in to?' As he reached the gate, a servant appeared as though by magic and asked him what he wanted? "I would like to speak to the owner please."

"Wait here", said the servant who shuffled off, down a path and in through a side entrance. A few minutes later he returned and without a word opened the gate and let him in. "The mistress will see you in the garden. Please follow me."

Clodus tied his horse to a post inside the gate and followed the servant, who led him to a small secluded garden, designed to receive maximum sunshine and minimum draught. He was looking around admiring the flowers, when he heard a voice say, "Good morning - how can I be of help to you?". He turned around and saw one of the most beautiful women he had ever seen in his life. Her light golden hair was curled and piled on top of her head and her large soft blue eyes looked kindly and matched the colour of her gown. She invited him to sit on the wooden bench beside her. "I am Rhona. I understand you wish to see my husband. I am sorry to say he is not at home and I do not expect him until later this evening. May I know who you are and the nature of your business?"

Clodus became very embarrassed. "Madam, I do beg your pardon. I am afraid I have lived too long in exclusively male company, my social graces have been sadly neglected. My name is Clodus, Captain of the Sixth Legion. I have been asked by my Commander Gaius to seek your husband's advice on a matter regarding a Christian missionary, who will be arriving here very soon to open a mission and school near to the Highland border. Frankly madam, I don't quite know where to begin. It is something out of my range of knowledge. A friend suggested that your husband may be willing to give me some advice."

A maid arrived with refreshments, which were very welcome. As Rhona poured the glass of cool wine, she thought how young he was to have such responsibility. Yet, he was dignified and a little shy. "I am sure my husband will be very pleased to do all he can to assist you, however, I must warn you that neither my husband, or his brother are ordained priests of the church. True, they have been devoted Christians since they were children, but alas, they have been too busy working in the shipyard which they jointly own, until about two years ago, when they made up their minds to do something about it. Our son is now able to take over some of his father's work, which gives him more time to spend doing other more important things, especially teaching the children of the less well off and Harran's daughters are wonderful teachers of language, which is a great help to poor immigrants. It is the aim of my husband and his brother to guide people towards their faith and a better chance in life."

"Madam", said Clodus. "You have been most kind. I wonder if I may return tomorrow and inquire as to whether your husband can help me?"

"You may be sure, If he can, he will", said Rhona confidently.

Rhona walked with him to the gate. She asked him, "How do you like working with Gaius?".

"Very well" (he lied), "Though the great man was dismayed to find out that there was already a Christian mission here that he'd never heard of".

Rhona laughed. "If Gaius has not heard of us; we have most certainly heard of him and his dreadful reputation. So we had better be careful and not upset him."

Clodus laughed with her. "Yes Madam, he has a reputation for being severe with those who cross him, but I assure you he is a most civilised man; but one with heavy responsibilities. It is not easy to maintain discipline when in charge of so many men and the safety of some thousands of citizens."

"Yes I agree", said Rhona. "I suppose it takes a strong man."

They reached the gate. Clodus thanked her for the refreshments and her hospitality. "Until tomorrow Madam, I bid you good day."

Rhona looked after him and thought, 'I wonder if Gaius realises what a loyal and trusted young officer he has there?'.

Next day, Clodus rode back to the villa and was pleased to find Rhona's husband at home. She introduced him. "Captain Clodus, this is my husband Councillor Calim." The men saluted each other by showing the palm of their right hand.

"I think", said Calim, "I may be able to help you. I have a property in mind which may suit the needs of our fellow Christian. I will, however, have to consult my brother, who is part owner. We bought this property hoping to convert it into a fishing lodge, but alas we have never found the time".

Clodus was pleased. He felt that he was actually making progress.

"Did I mention to Madam that this priest is the younger half brother of Bishop Martin of Tours? Which explains why Commander Gaius has been asked to make arrangements to protect him at all times and why the positioning of the property is most important? If it is beyond the range of Gaius's command, we would not be able to afford him or his helpers total security."

"So", said Calim. "The Legate has a hand in this. That is most interesting. We must not let the Legate down." Clodus detected a smile on Rhona's face and got the distinct impression that she cared as little for the Legate as she did for Gaius, which was not much at all.

"My brother and I will meet Gaius and come to some arrangement regarding the property. Perhaps Captain, you would be good enough to make that appointment." Clodus was beginning to feel more important, for instead of dealing with raw recruits, he was now associating with the upper class and he liked it.

He made his way back to camp and reported to Gaius. He entered the office with his head held high and told him of meeting with Calim. "Why was he not there the first time you called; out trying to convert the locals was he?"

"No Sir", said Clodus. "He was at the shipyard which he owns. He is also a Councillor."

Gaius raised his head slowly. "Are you trying to tell me that this man who is going to come here to see me is the leader of the Christian mission? Well, well, well. And here was I thinking that anyone who was a Christian had to be soft in the head. Why though, if these Councillors are known to the Legate, did he not ask them to meet the Priest?"

"I think I can answer that", said Clodus. "The Councillors only retired within the last two years and the Legate would not know that they were Christians."

Gaius studied Clodus's face; perhaps the lad was not as stupid as he'd first thought. "Keep up the good work, Clodus," he said with a grin.

The appointment was set up for two days on and as the hour grew near, Gaius became more anxious. Sergaeus watched him strut up and down in front of his desk with his hands behind his back and his chin out in front. He tried to hide his amusement, for Gaius's posturing reminded him of an old cockerel marching to and fro in front of the chicken house.

Clodus waited outside headquarters for Calim and Harran to arrive. He had ordered two immaculately dressed guardsmen to stand either side of the double doors, ready to either help them from their carriage or take their horses, as he had not established their mode of travel.

Neither Calim or Harran were worried about the meeting with Gaius. They were going to help him, out of their Christian duty and Gaius had no choice but to accept their offer. When they arrived they were a little surprised at the elaborate welcome.

Clodus and Sergaeus escorted them into Gaius's office and he greeted them warmly - 'charm personified' - was how Clodus described him later.

"Welcome gentlemen. Thank you for coming. I trust my officer Captain Clodus has informed you of the situation regarding the arrival of the Christian missionary priest. Had I known of your excellent school earlier, we may have saved him a journey; but no matter, we will make the best of it. I thought as fellow Christians it was right that you were informed and consulted." Clodus and Sergaeus glanced at each other and rolled their eyes at Gaius taking the credit for their work.

Calim told him that it would not have made any difference, "Since we are only simple Christians who want to give the children of the town an education and perhaps a better chance in life". Gaius studied the two men who stood before him. They were dignified, richly dressed, intelligent and had arrived on two of the most magnificent horses. 'Simple' was not a word he would have chosen to describe anything about them.

"I trust that no suitable property has been found since I last spoke to the Captain?"

"No Sir", answered Clodus. "Not yet. We are, however, most interested in the property you spoke of. We have the added problem of not knowing how many helpers will be with the missionary."

Sergaeus added, "Nor do we know if they are men or women". Everyone turned to look at him. "Well, women make very good missionaries."

"He is right, of course", said Harran. "My own dear daughters are teachers at the school and, therefore, could be in that category." Harran was a little shorter than his brother and his hair was darker. Also, his face was rounder and more jolly than Calim's. Most of the time, he was happy to let Calim do the talking, but now he addressed Gaius. "As it happens Commander, this property we have in mind is an old farmhouse. There is a small house, a large barn, stables and several outer buildings suitable for fuel storage."

Gaius's eyes lit up. "But, where exactly is this place? Did Clodus not say that it had to be near the border? This Joseph - that is the priest's name - has orders to attempt to convert the tribesmen of the Highlands."

"The village is called 'Bonavon Tibernae'" said Calim "and lies about seven or eight miles north west of here." Gaius walked behind his desk and studied the hand drawn map of his area. He ran his finger in the direction given and Calim helped him find the right spot.

"Could not be better", he announced. "It is almost on the border. It only remains for my representative Clodus to visit and inspect it." He then looked around for Clodus. but he had stepped outside to check on his guardsmen.

The mention of Clodus's name again, reminded Calim to say, "Your young Officer Captain Clodus - my wife found him a most charming man. So polite and well spoken".

Gaius almost choked and Sergaeus, who was making notes, raised his eyes to witness Gaius's reaction, but Gaius recovered his composure. "Yes", he said. "Clodus is one of my finest officers. I selected him personally for this diplomatic work." Sergaeus marvelled at how lies slid over Gaius's tongue unhindered by conscience, for it was only a few days before that he had called him 'A jelly kneed daisy'. Sergaeus had worked for Gaius for several years and at first he had been terrified of him, but now he was used to his ways and discovered that he made a lot of noise and issued threats daily, but only in extreme circumstances did he ever carry them out. Sergaeus lowered his eyes and continued to work.

Calim continued. "If Captain Clodus wishes, I will ride with him to Bonavon tomorrow to inspect the property."

Gaius told him he was satisfied that it would be just right. "Frankly, Councillor Calim, it will have to do if we are to be ready in time. However, Clodus will go with you as planned. Then we can discuss further arrangements. You may know that we are responsible for security and will be building a small fort near the site and guardsmen will patrol the grounds. It is necessary to move as quickly as possible."

"If the farmhouse is suitable, we shall do everything to make it habitable as soon as we can. But should it happen that they arrive before we are ready, my wife and I will be happy to receive them at the villa until it is", said Calim.

Gaius was pleased, for it meant that he need not have them in his camp, or have to entertain them.

When Calim and Harren left, Sergaeus stood before Gaius. "If Sir, you do not mind me asking, when did you decide that we required to build a fort at Bonavon?"

Gaius looked at him with a rather sneaky expression on his face. "We cannot allow these civilians to steal the whole show; besides it might be interesting to watch what goes on there."

The next day, Clodus called at headquarters to check if there were further orders before he left for the villa. He found Sergaeus waiting for him, out of uniform, wearing the softened leather breaches and long coloured waistcoat reserved for off duty leisure. "I am coming with you", he announced.

Clodus was suspicious. "Why?", he asked. "Has Gaius ordered you to spy on me? I know he thinks me incapable."

Sergaeus laughed. "You've got it all wrong Clodus. It was me who asked - no begged - the old man to allow me to accompany you."

"Explain", said Clodus angrily.

Sergaeus took a deep breath. "It was Calim."

"Calim?", repeated Clodus. "What has he to do with you coming with us? I heard nothing of the kind."

Sergaeus continued. "I was in the office yesterday when Calim mentioned 'his wife'. I thought 'a wife'? What is a wife? Ah, yes I remember now, it's a woman. One of those soft and delicate creatures who fill their hair with ironmongery. Wear silk gowns and smell of flowers in a hot summer breeze. One of these lovely creatures God made from Adam's rib. Well, my dear Clodus, I realised that there was a great chunk of my life missing. For since I was appointed Gaius's slave, I have hardly thought of a woman, let alone seen one. Then, I remembered your trip into the country, so I set out to convince Gaius that a second opinion on that farm you are going to see was necessary and to my surprise, he agreed."

"Go along", he said "And make notes".

"So, here I am."

It was a more cheerful and confident Clodus who led Sergaeus the few miles from the Camp to Rhona and Calim's villa. On the way they passed several young women out walking and Sergaeus eyed each one admiringly. Clodus smiled at him. "My my, it has been a long time. You had better be careful Sergaeus, you are leering and may frighten them off. Your longing glances could be mistaken for lustful desire."

"Is there a difference?", asked Sergaeus.

They reached the villa and as usual a servant appeared quickly and opened the gate, having seemingly come from nowhere. He held their horses and told them that the Councillor was awaiting their arrival. Within seconds, Calim appeared and invited them into the house for drinks. Once inside Calim led them to a large room with a long table and almost enclosed by three couches.

It was a comfortable room, warm and inviting. Rhona entered carrying a tray of food. She was followed by a maid with a jug, which was placed on the table in front of them. "You must eat and drink, for it is not known when your next meal will be."

Clodus introduced Sergaeus to her as "Gaius's right hand man".

Calim then apologised. "My dear, I am so sorry. I forgot that you had not met Major Sergaeus before." Rhona smiled and encouraged the men to eat. Calim poured out the wine, given extra flavour with added fruit juice.

There was a tap at the door. Rhona called, "Come in" and two young ladies entered the room. They stayed near the door.

"Sorry Uncle Calim, we did not know you had visitors."

Rhona said, "Do come in and meet Major Sergaeus and Captain Clodus".

Clodus could not resist glancing at Sergaeus, for one of the young ladies was as he described as his ideal. Julia, the younger of Harran's daughters was beautiful. Her long light brown hair was curled in the latest fashion. She wore a dress of cream muslin. Her body almost too delicate to touch. Portia too, was beautiful, but older and wiser. Clodus recognised her as the teacher who had directed him to the villa on his first visit. She acknowledged him with a smile, then led Julia away. Calim informed his visitors that the two charming young ladies were the daughters of his brother Harran and teachers at the Mission school in town and they were pleased and excited that real missionaries were coming from Gaul.

Having eaten their fill, the three men set off for Bonavon Tibernae. It was an interesting and scenic route, but the journey was uneventful.

The farmhouse lay in a wide valley with a fairly steep hill on one side and a river not too far away on the other.

The farmhouse and other buildings were in good condition, all that was required was decoration and a clean up. Clodus breathed a sigh of relief, for it meant that he did not have to look any further. There was everything here to fit the priest's requirements. Calim told them that it had been bought for a fishing lodge, because of its closeness to the river and the excellent fish to be caught there. "There are fish in this river unseen anywhere else, a large white fish that tastes like salmon. But, alas we never got around to it. Too much work and not enough leisure."

When they were finished looking around and agreed that it was perfect for what the priest would need, they walked down to the river and stood watching the water flow past, as though in a hypnotic trance. "I have never seen anything like this in my life", remarked Clodus. "It is so very fast, anyone falling in here would not stand a chance, they would be swept out of sight before they could call for help."

"Well, my friend that is why it is called 'The Little Tiber'."

Clodus looked puzzled. "I'm sorry Clodus", said Sergaeus. "I quite forgot that most Roman soldiers have never been within a hundred miles of Rome. You see, when the army of Antonine the Great surveyed this country, they could see that this river had its source in the mountains that surround the Great Lake. It then winds its way through the valley in a north to south direction at tremendous speed, which renders it unnavigable and enters the Clyde at Dunbriton. Those who knew Rome laughed. It could be the Tiber in miniature", they said, "For the Tiber has its source in the Apennine Mountains, flows rapidly in a north to south direction and enters the sea south of Rome and that too is unnavigable - at least most of it is. The big difference is that the Tiber is about two hundred miles long - our little river is about five miles".

Clodus picked up a twig and threw it in. It was out of sight in the blink of an eye. "So, my friend, our river was given its name by some home-sick Roman surveyor and it stuck. What about the other part of its name?", he asked. "I know that Avon is our name for a river, but what about 'Bon'?"

Calim answered this time. "Do you see that hill behind us, the one with the flat top?"They all raised their heads to look. "That my friends is 'The Old Bonfire Hill'. In other parts of the country, it might be called, 'A Beacon Hill'. But, it's the same thing whatever they call it. They are sacred places where a fire was kept burning, for many reasons, but mostly to reassure the primitive people that the fire would keep evil away. Then, I suppose it had practical uses also. The whole name of the area is 'The Bonfire Hill by the Avon Tibernae' - shortened to Bon Avon Tibernae".

"A big name for a little village", remarked Clodus.

Calim smiled. "Now it's shortened even further to simply Bonavon, which is a pity, for I rather like the old name. It has a certain dignity."

The three men walked back to the farmhouse. Clodus breathed in, a deep satisfying breath of one who feels as though he's accomplished something.

On reaching the house, they saw that some children had gathered in the yard. "Is it true mister, that there is going to be a school here?"

Calim smiled. "You have heard correctly my boy and a famous priest is going to live here and teach you."

"Will he teach us to read and write?"

"Yes, my boy, he will and many other things too." The children looked pleased.

"When is he coming Sir?"

"We don't know yet, but I can tell you that it will be soon, for he is already on his way. I wonder", said Calim, "If you children would like to earn some money?". There was an enthusiastic response to the promise of payment. So, Calim took a key from a bundle and gave it to the eldest boy. "In that hut over there you will find some tools and brooms. Clean up the yard of weeds and stones and when I return in a few days, I will pay you handsomely."

"What is your name, young man, in order that I may find you again."

"My name is Fergus, Sir, but you need not worry, I will be here."

Sergaeus and Clodus were already mounted and waiting for Calim. As they rode away, Fergus flicked the key in the air and caught it again. "Come on, let's get busy and show him what we can do."

The return journey seemed longer and it was dusk before they arrived back at the villa. Calim invited them in, but they declined the offer, saying that they had to be back in time to make out their report. As Clodus and Sergaeus rode off, Sergaeus remarked, "I think the old man will be well pleased."

"He'd better be. I think we have done rather well."

"I wish", said Sergaeus, "that it was not so late. I would have loved to go into the villa. I was looking forward to seeing Julia again".

Clodus laughed at him. "The lovely Julia is a school teacher and probably has several young, good-living Christian men trailing after her."

Sergaeus replied, "Maybe a good-living Christian man is not what Julia wants. Could be she would prefer a handsome Army officer, even if he is slightly more mature."

Clodus gave him a sideways glance. "Sorry Sergaeus. I fear even if she did, her father would certainly not approve. You must be twenty-six. Little Julia is about seventeen."

"I know, I know", said Sergaeus. "But I can dream can't I, she is a little beauty is she not?"

Clodus was just a little annoyed. "You're as two-faced as Gaius. I saw you this morning when you met her. You acted so innocent. Little did she or her uncle know what you were thinking."

"What do you mean? I am innocent", said Sergaeus in a hurt tone. "Ever since I became Gaius's slave, I have not had time to be anything else."

CHAPTER IV

BLISS

Over the next few days, a small army of volunteers descended upon Bonavon Tibernae. Artisans from the shipyard and the Army and young men and women from the mission school, turned up and started work. Roofs were renewed, wood floors were put in the barn and the farmhouse was cleaned and decorated. Most of the fine decoration was done by Calpurnius, Calim and Rhona's son, while Fergus and his friends were kept busy fetching and carrying for the workers and enjoying every moment - especially getting paid. When Calim praised them for their hard work and gave them the promised payment, they were very pleased. Calim inquired if they knew of anyone who could cook? "If we don't find any one soon, we will starve."

The children laughed. Then, one young lad said, "My Mum is the best cook in all the world. She can make rabbit pie and stew".

"Sounds like she is the one we want. Would you be so kind as to ask her to come and see me, if she is interested."

Calim was amused by his eagerness to convince him. The boy ran off and returned soon, holding his mother's hand, almost pulling the reluctant woman along. She approached Calim shyly. He put her at ease. "Your son speaks highly of your cooking. Do you think you could cook for so many of us?"

She looked up at him. "Yes Sir, providing you like rabbit stew?"

Calim laughed at her honesty. "We are so busy here and so hungry, I don't think we will mind, for a while anyway. I am Councillor Calim, what might your name be?"

She looked up at him for the first time and said sweetly, "My name is Bliss. I am a widow. My husband died last year. I will be very glad of the work Sir and I will try my best to learn to cook other things for you".

"Come along then and I will show you the kitchen." He took her on a tour of the house, before ending up in the place where she would work.

"Thank you Sir, I will do my best."

The village of Bonavon had never witnessed such excitement. So many people, such coming and going and all the villagers helping cheerfully and willingly. When Bliss cooked her first great pot of stew and rang the bell to attract attention, everyone rushed to get their share, carrying various plates and bowls. Then, they made their way to the yard to sit wherever they could, to eat their meal. A wonderful community spirit quickly developed.

Clodus arrived to see the work in progress. He had spent the day on the hill above the farmhouse, where Gaius's men were busy digging the foundations for the Fort. Gaius had accepted responsibility for the coming missionaries' safety and he was not going to be 'outdone by mere civilians', as he so often said.

Clodus was well pleased at how things were going for him. He thanked God, any god who happened to be listening for Calim. "How would he ever have managed without the help of this kind and generous man?"

He found Calim in the house, thanking Bliss for the stew. It was delicious. Everyone enjoyed it so much. "I can see that the pot is empty", said Clodus. "I am starving! Is there anything left?"

"Afraid your too late Captain. There is some bread in the bowl if you are desperate." Bliss held out the bowl containing the last few pieces and Clodus took one and stuck it in his mouth.

"You know, Councillor Calim, this place has already altered beyond recognition. It is no longer a farmhouse. It is a mission school. I hope that this priest and his helpers realise just how much hard work has been done for them. He is a very lucky man."

Calim asked Clodus if there was any more news of the priest's arrival? "If we only knew how many helpers were coming with him, it would be so much easier to plan. Why, it has been suggested that some of them may even be women!"

Clodus swallowed his mouthful of bread. "I hope not. The Army has little idea of how to treat men, let alone women."

Calim smiled. "As bad as that is it? Don't let it worry you Captain. My wife and Harran's daughters will be only too pleased to help if you have any difficulties."

Calim left that problem in the air as something to be sorted out at a later date. "Come Captain and I will show you around." As they walked from one building to another, the smell of newly sawn wood and fresh paint was strong. Men, women and children working away happily. "There isn't much left to do now. Perhaps another few days, then it will be up to the women folk to put the finishing touches."

"I'm impressed", said Clodus. "It is wonderful to see the village come alive like this. Now I must go back up the hill and see how the Fort is progressing."

It was another few days before the signal came that the ship carrying the missionaries had entered the mouth of the Clyde and would be docking with the morning tide, at the Port of Dunbriton. Gaius sent a message to Calim and his brother Harran and informed them that he would be at the Dock in full military regalia to greet the missionary - as he was duty bound to do, seeing as it was the Legate's orders to provide security at all times. Although Gaius was grateful to Calim and Harran and was thankful for all they had done, he could not allow them to steal the whole show, so he selected four of his smartest guardsmen - and Clodus and Sergaeus - to be there in full military dress uniform.

CHAPTER V

FATHER JOSEPH

In one of the ship's tiny cabins, Joseph, a shy unassuming and gentle soul, was gathering his few personal belongings together. He was tired, for it had been a miserable journey. Sea water had got into the food store and as a result everything had tasted 'brackish'. The storm in the Channel had not helped either. They had all been very sick.

The latter part of the journey had not been too bad, but he was worried. Not so much for himself, or his adopted son and companion Paulus. It was his daughter Conchessa and her friend Alana. Conchessa was just seventeen, a beautiful young woman - but stubborn.

He had heard tales of the Picts in the north of Briton, or at least just over the border in the Highlands. Wild men who painted their faces and went about naked. This he had heard was a country that was cold, wet, unfriendly and downright dangerous.

He had not wanted to come here, but orders were orders. He had thought that his daughter and her friend would stay at home, but she would have none of it. "Father, you are not going anywhere without me. I would rather face danger with you, than stay at home worrying about all the things that could happen to you."

At that moment Conchessa entered the cabin. She was wrapped in a long dark red woollen cloak. Her face looked pale and delicate in contrast with the dark hood. She pushed the hood back but drew the cloak closer around her body. "It's bitter cold out there Father, better put on an extra garment. I have spoken to the Captain, it will still be a little while before we can disembark." She held his arm and snuggled up to him. "Father, do try not to worry about all of us. Why don't you do what you always do when you are anxious?" He looked down at her and patted her hand. She smiled. "Pray Father, then put your trust in God. Well, if you can't concentrate, lie on your bunk and rest until we are called. I will join Alana and leave you in peace."

Once outside the cabin, she sighed. She knew her father. His life had not been easy, but his faith and his great love of God had kept him sane in a world that was - at times - unbearably cruel and heartless, especially to the poor. The most important thing in his life was to bring as many souls as he could into the family of his Lord Jesus and the Church, knowing that it would give them a measure of comfort and security.

Joseph decided to take Conchessa's advice. She was right. He was worrying too much. So he sat on his bunk intending to pray, but he could not concentrate. Instead, his mind wandered over his life and the events that led up to this moment in time. It was seeing his daughter standing there, telling him what to do. She was the double of her mother Alicia, who had died shortly after her birth. 'What a terrible experience that had been.' He had been devastated and even now, after all these years, he missed her. Only the sympathy of some of his friends helped a little, but he was unable to live in the same house, with all of her clothes and possessions around. The memories were too painful. It was then he remembered his half-brother Martin, who was a respected Bishop. One day, when he could no longer bear the pain and the guilt, he wrapped his baby daughter in a shawl and made his way to Tours.

It was Martin who had convinced him that his beloved wife was now safe with God and that in time he would see her again. It was also Martin who suggested that he become a priest and knowing what comfort he had been given, he agreed.

He hired a housekeeper who brought with her, her own little daughter Alana, a delightful four-year-old, who immediately loved his baby. She sang to her. Rocked her cradle and seldom left her side. All the years of his study and preparation, his little family had been happy.

Then one day soon after his ordination, he was walking in the town, when he came upon two men beating a small boy with sticks. "STOP. Stop at once", he shouted. "What has this child done to warrant such treatment?"

"Don't waste your pity on this wretch. He's a thief", he was told.

"What did he steal? Something of great value?"

"He stole our bread", was the angry reply.

"Do not strike that boy again. I will pay you for your bread." He took some coins from his money pouch and paid the men, who went off, still grumbling to themselves. The boy lay on the ground curled up, his head and hands covered in blood. "Can you get up?", he asked. "Are you well enough?" What a stupid question he thought. It was obvious he was far from being well. "Where do you live my boy? Come I will take you home to your mother." He helped the boy to his feet, who groaned painfully and without uttering another word led him to a building in a poor quarter of town, then to a door under an outside stairway. The boy opened the door to reveal a small compartment with a pile of rags on the floor. Joseph was shocked. "This cupboard - this is where you sleep?" The boy nodded. Joseph's heart filled with pity. This will never do he thought. "You, my boy, will come with me." He took the boy home, much to the displeasure of the housekeeper who thought she would be expected to look after him, but he had assured her that the boy would work to earn his keep, when he was well enough to do so.

His duties were to clean the boots and shoes, brush the clothes, and light the stove fire. This had been his first encounter with Paulus, who had remained loyal and steadfast ever since. At first it had not been easy, for the boy had no education and knew no manners. He'd had to teach him everything and it was slow and at times he wondered if he had taken on too much. But, gradually he responded to the kindness and care given. Eventually, it had been the two little girls who finally brought him out of his shell. They used to make him play with them. He had to sit in a small chair to have his hair curled, or drink water from their tiny cups. Then, one day, Conchessa had fallen over and she cried bitterly. Paulus picked her up and ran into the house. "Pa, Pa. She is hurt", he cried. Those were the first words he had spoken. From then on he learned fast.

The years passed until Conchessa was about fourteen, Alana eighteen and Paulus was twenty. The housekeeper announced she was going to remarry. This was a terrible blow for Conchessa, who thought Alana would go with her mother and her new husband. But, as it turned out, the new husband did not want Alana, nor did Alana want to live with him - she was determined to stay with Conchessa. Both now considered themselves old enough to be independent. They took care of all the household duties while he, accompanied by Paulus, rode about the countryside searching for souls to save. They were a happy family for about three years, until one day he was called to the office to see his superiors. "Your work has not gone unnoticed", he was told. "Your dedication and compassion has brought many new souls into the Church. It has been decided that you are the best priest for the work we have in mind." He had wondered what was coming. Then the terrible blow. "We want you to go to the north west corner of Briton, right to the far corner of The Empire. If anyone can convert the heathen Picts, you can. It's a challenge," they said. What could he do? He felt as though he was being sacrificed. Terrible feelings of forboding crept over him. But, he was a Christian, a priest of the Holy Church. He had to show face. At least, pretend to be strong.

Now they had arrived in this God forsaken country. He shivered. Conchessa and Alana entered the cabin. "Did you rest, father?", they asked him.

"Yes, a little my dears."

Just then, Paulus knocked and entered, his face flushed with excitement. "We are almost there", he said "And there must be someone of importance aboard amongst the passengers. On the quay there are men in uniform and horses and carriages and crowds of people". Joseph thought for a moment. How strange, the Captain never mentioned anyone. I would have thought he would have done. Perhaps, whoever it is, was just as sick as us and did not want to be disturbed. We all spent a considerable time in our bunks. Perhaps, this person is not arriving, but going away and we have landed at an awkward time? Paulus said "I'm going on deck again to watch". He seemed fascinated with the docking procedure, but he soon returned. It is cold and wet up there. They shivered.

The four passengers stood in the small cabin. Four satchels lay at their feet. "What happens now?", asked Alana.

Paulus answered, "The Captain said he would come and get us when it was time to leave".

They were apprehensive. Joseph looked at the bunk he had slept in for the past few weeks, then said, "It was not much and not at all comfortable, but I wonder where we will lay our heads down this night?".

There was a sharp knock on the cabin door. The Captain stuck his head round. "Father Joseph. Your escort has arrived." He stood aside and Gaius appeared in the doorway. A giant of a man dressed in full military splendour.

He saluted. "Commander Gaius at your service sir. In accordance with arrangements. I am in charge of your security."

The expressions on the faces of the four passengers were of shock. They stared wide-eyed and open-mouthed at Gaius. Joseph managed with great self control to bow in acknowledgement and desperately trying to hide the bewilderment he felt inside. Gaius then stood to one side to allow Calim to enter.

"This", said Gaius, "Is Councillor Calim who will be you host for a few days".

Calim smiled reassuringly. "You will all be my guests until your own home is ready. But now, may I welcome you on behalf of all the Christian souls here in Dunbriton."

Joseph said "Thank you Sir", but his mind was buzzing. He thought 'Did I hear right?'. Did he say 'Christian Souls?'.

Gaius then said, "Is your party ready? Are there more of you?".

"Why no", said Joseph. "There are only the four of us."

"Then let us proceed", said Gaius in a booming voice, as though ordering a regiment of soldiers.

If the crowd of people waiting and watching on the quay expected to see a King or Emperor arrive, they were going to be disappointed. The first to walk down the gangway was Gaius, followed by Joseph and Paulus, who wore plain long blue cloaks. Then Conchessa and Alana began to descend, the crowd showing more interest in the two beautiful young women, with their long linen dresses under their woollen cloaks and their long, waist length brown hair, that fell forward as they walked cautiously down the gangway.

Suddenly, a shaft of sunlight broke through the morning mist illuminating the scene on the quay. Conchessa looked up. She saw the magnificent coaches. The guardsmen in their shiny plumed helmets and breastplates. The beautiful colours of the robes worn by the civilian dignitaries and the horses also wearing official decoration. Considering what they had been through and their expectations, this reception seemed unreal. They wondered if there had been some mistake and they had been mistaken for some other people.

Conchessa (although fascinated with the scene), realised they were waiting for her to move on and tried to hurry, but the gangway was wet after the rain and as she moved forward she slipped. She stumbled forward trying to grasp at the rail. There was a gasp from the crowd! However, a strong arm caught hold of her. She looked up to thank her rescuer and saw the handsome and concerned face of Calim's son Calpurnius. The onlookers who had gasped as she fell, now cheered.

Alana, who was following her friend and who had panicked when she saw her in danger, now stood transfixed as she watched Calpurnius place Conchessa's arm over his own and lead her to the waiting carriage. Then, Alana heard a voice beside her say, "Madam". It was Clodus. He took his lead from Calpurnius and placed Alana's arm over his own and escorted her to join her friend in Calim's stately carriage.

The crowd loved this spontaneous display of courtesy and chivalry and cheered, showing their appreciation. Clodus, having seen Alana safely into the carriage, turned to the crowd and bowed in a slightly exaggerated and theatrical way. The crowd loved it and cheered even louder.

Gaius, who was not given to tolerating civilians, but appreciating the diplomatic implications and looking awesome astride his great stallion, acknowledged the crowd by saluting them. Then, seeing everyone was ready, he gave the signal to move forward.

In the first carriage (which was the one belonging to the military), sat Calim, Joseph and Paulus. In the second carriage - which was Calim's own - was Harran, Conchessa and Alana. Gaius led the way, with Clodus and Sergaeus riding behind either side of the first carriage. The four guardsmen were escort to the second carriage. Once this little spectacle left the quay, Calpurnius turned in the opposite direction. He had some unfinished work to do at Bonavon.

The procession continued towards the villa, though Clodus had to join Gaius in front to show him the way. People out walking, stopped to look at the colourful procession.

They reached the villa and on the steps to welcome them were, Rhona, Harran's wife Elinor and daughters Portia and Julia. There were also servants ready to take the luggage, but there was very little - which surprised them.

Calim alighted first, to assist Joseph and Paulus and take them to the reception room, where the long table was laden with platters of delicious food, jugs of wine and fruit juices. Portia and Julia met Conchessa and Alana and asked them, "Would you like to eat, or prefer to be taken to your quarters to freshen up".

Alana answered, "We are both hungry and tired - perhaps a drink? - then we could eat later." Julia led them to join Joseph, who was already being encouraged to eat.

Rhona and Elinor invited Gaius and his men to join them. "We should return to camp", he said.

However, Rhona insisted. "Please come in and enjoy the food, there is plenty of it. You and your men have worked so hard and may I say how magnificent you all look. You must all be so hungry waiting at the quay all morning."

Gaius knew he was being flattered, but the smell of the food had reached his nostrils and the temptation was too much. "You are right, Madam. My men do deserve a break." So, he gave the order for the men to remove their helmets and breastplates and relax. But, he also warned them that they were still on duty. "Misbehave and you will be in trouble."

As soon as Conchessa and Alana had a morsel to eat and a drink of milk, Portia and Julia took them to their quarters, a large room with highly waxed furniture and two beds covered with pink bedcovers. These were the beds slept in by Portia and Julia when they visited their aunt and uncle.

Portia drew back a curtain to reveal a bath tub and a shelf containing a row of jars filled with perfumed oils. Portia saw their expressions. She smiled. "I will see that the tub is filled right away. Please make yourselves at home and if there is anything you want, don't hesitate to ask. There are several servants who will be happy to get you whatever you want."

"Thank you my lady", said Alana. "You are most kind."

Within a short time, a line of servants arrived carrying jugs of hot water and proceeded to fill the tub, three quarters full. The sound of the water was music to their ears, for during the long voyage they had dreamed of being clean again.

While Conchessa undressed, Alana ran her fingers along the line of oils, reading the labels. She selected one and poured a generous measure into the hot water, then she waved her fingers through it. A wonderful floral aroma filled the air.

33

She left Conchessa to soak away the dust of the old ship, while she unpacked their satchels. She shook their best dresses to get the creases out and hung them up beside their beds and put their best slippers on the floor. That task done, she became curious as to what was happening in the reception room and wondered if their handsome escorts were still there? She quietly left the room and went along the corridor until she came to the reception room door. She had no intention of entering, so she stood there with her back to the wall and peeped around it. She could see Father Joseph talking to Calim and Harran; Rhona and Elinor either side of Gaius laughing and Clodus and Sergaeus in deep conversation. At the sight of Clodus, her heart skipped a beat. Back in the bedroom, she found Conchessa out of the tub and brushing her hair.

"Are we expected to join the gathering?", asked Conchessa.

"No, I don't think so", said Alana. "There are only men there talking, except, of course, for our hostess."

"In that case, I am going to sleep for a while, that is if you think we won't be missed?" The bed looks very comfortable. Conchessa snuggled under the covers and quickly fell asleep.

Alana tested the water in the tub. It was still warm. She took the jar of oil from the shelf and poured another few drops into the water and got in. This was luxury indeed. When finished, she too brushed her hair, tied it with a ribbon, got into bed and slept soundly.

They were awakened by the smell of fresh food cooking and people talking as they walked up and down the corridor outside the door. They got up, put on their best dresses and slippers and made their way to the reception room.

Rhona and Elinor were encouraging their guests to eat and drink and it appeared as if the Commander did not need much encouragement. He was obviously enjoying himself very much. Sergaeus and Clodus were standing by the doorway at the main entrance to the porch, talking to Portia and Julia. Sergaeus could hardly contain his pleasure at being in the company of Julia and she was flirting with him quite outrageously. Sergaeus looked up and saw his boss being pleasant and enjoying himself. 'I don't believe it', he thought, 'The old man actually has a human side'. Rhona and Elinor were mothering him and he was loving every minute of it. Then, he heard Julia's voice say, "Your not listening". She gave him a playful punch on the shoulder - which he hardly felt - but he pretended it hurt.

"Yes, I did hear you. I heard every word" (he lied).

"Go on then", she said smugly, "Repeat what I just said". Julia looked at Portia and Clodus with a look that said "Watch him try to get out of this".

Segaeus looked Julia straight in the eyes and said, "You were saying what a strong handsome and intelligent man Sergaeus is and I would love him to kiss me".

Julia was shocked! "I did not say anything like that, did I Portia?" But, Portia and Clodus were laughing at her and she realised she was being teased.

It was at this moment Conchessa and Alana entered the room. Alana looked over to where the laughter was coming from and her heart filled with jealousy, an emotion foreign to her nature. For not only was Clodus enjoying the company of Portia, the two young ladies were wearing beautiful dresses, cut in the latest fashion. High waisted with the skirt falling in deep folds and made of the finest silk. The sisters had also been to their hairdresser and they both looked so beautiful. Suddenly, her best dress seemed drab and colourless. She smoothed out another imaginary crease with her hands and followed Conchessa, who was walking across the room towards her father. He looked up at them. "Ah, there you both are. Have you rested?"

"Yes, Father. We slept soundly."

"You must eat some of this delicious food", said Joseph.

At that moment, a servant arrived to take away empty plates and replace them with full ones of even more appetising dishes. Conchessa and Alana placed a napkin on their laps and ate.

From the direction of the porch came more laughter. Joseph looked up. "Is that not a truly wonderful sound, laughter from young people being happy?"

Alana cringed and felt even more ashamed of her jealousy.

Elinor spotted the new arrivals and came over. "My dears, you both look wonderful. Travel is such an exhausting business. You must try while you are here to rest as much as you can, for I hear you have such a lot of work ahead of you. A new mission and a school, for people who are probably fixed on their own religion."

"Yes", said Joseph. "It is not an easy thing to alter peoples's long held beliefs."

Elinor nodded. "Yes, Father Joseph, it has many difficulties. My husband Harran has spoken often of the frustrations." She excused herself. "I really must go and chase the servants up, we seem to be running out of refreshments."

Joseph then turned his attention to his daughter and Alana. "Is this not wonderful? I am so relieved for you two. I imagined you both having to suffer untold discomfort and misery. I cannot believe how lucky we are."

Rhona was again sitting by the Commander. She looked so refined. Tall and fair, her mop of blond hair secured with pins and decorated with flowers. Gaius, sitting beside her, appeared all the more coarse. Yet, they had obviously found some common ground.

Joseph began to tell his daughter and Alana of his conversations with Calim and Harran, which had taken place during the time they were asleep. "Do you know my dears, these good people have worked hard over the last few weeks, in order that we should have a home of our own, ready for our arrival."

Conchessa and Alana were astounded. "You mean father, we have a home for ourselves?"

"We have indeed daughter", said Joseph. "Our host, Councillor Calim insists that we wait here for another few days to recuperate from our voyage." He was about to add more, but Harran and Elinor approached them.

"Father Joseph", said Harran. "We are so pleased that you and your charming family arrived safely. I know we will meet again very soon, but for this evening we must go home and leave you to get some rest."

Elinor called upon her daughters. "Hurry my dears." Portia obeyed and still talking to Clodus, began to enter the reception room to join her mother. But, as Julia moved to follow them, Sergaeus gripped her arm and pulled her behind the door out of view of the others. He drew her close to him and kissed her passionately. Clodus looked around and seeing what was happening, whispered to Portia to "wait". She too glanced behind her and saw her sister being embraced.

Elinor called again. "Now come along my daughters."

Portia answered. "A moment please, mama. Julia has lost a shoe."

Sergaeus looked into Julia's eyes and whispered tenderly, "I think I love you Julia". Her eyes met his and she knew that he meant it. She backed away from him reluctantly, still looking into his eyes. Then turned away to join her sister and Clodus. She was shaken. It was one thing to flirt with the boys. It was something very different to be so close to an older man and feel the warmth of his body through your dress and his powerful arms holding you. Julia kept hearing his voice in her head, saying, "I think I love you Julia". Harran's coach arrived at the entrance and having said their goodbyes to everyone, they left.

Clodus then turned his attention to Joseph, Conchessa and Alana. "I am happy to see that the young ladies have rested, but you Father Joseph have been awake all day. I don't know from where you get your energy."

Sergaeus, having regained his composure, joined them. "Father Joseph. We are all happy and relieved that you have arrived safely." They were interrupted by a servant who told them that the guardsmen were ready and waiting to take the Commander back to Camp as arranged earlier. Everyone looked towards Gaius, who was sleeping on the couch and as there were several empty ale glasses in front of him, they suspected some difficulty waking him up.

Clodus told the servant to say "they would be out presently", but to make sure the coach was as near to the door as possible.

Clodus made excuses for his Commander, saying, "It has been a very unusual day for Commander Gaius. He seldom leaves the Camp and is always on duty. He has enjoyed the informality of civilian life for a day. It has helped take his mind away from his heavy responsibilities".

Then Clodus turned to Joseph. "I shall be visiting you at Bonavon often. I have the good fortune to be in charge of security there." Then glancing in Alana's direction, said "I do hope I can be of service and keep all of you safe".

"That is most reassuring", said Joseph

Sergaeus and Clodus looked at Gaius, wondering how they could wake him without causing him embarrassment. Calim and Rhona joined the group and seeing their predicament, conspired a plan.

Rhona returned to the couch and sat next to the Commander, as though she had not left her seat. Then Calim picked up a heavy tray and hurled it to the door furthest away. It landed with an enormous clatter. Gaius woke up to see Rhona sitting beside him. Rhona called to her husband. "What was that dreadful noise?"

"Nothing to worry about my dear", called Calim. "I think one of the servants dropped a tray."

Rhona stood up. "Do excuse me Commander. I must go and see what the trouble is." Gaius attempted to stand, but fell back on to his seat. 'Fortunately, everyone is looking in the opposite direction towards the noise', he thought. Clodus and Sergaeus were watching their boss from the corners of their eyes and came to his rescue. They told him that the guards had brought his horse to the door.

Gaius looked up at them with an expression close to contempt. "Will you two pansies haul my arse out of this couch?" They did as they were bid. Gaius stood up, but wobbled. He then asked them, "How the bloody hell am I going to stay on my horse?".

Sergaeus then whispered to Gaius, "May we suggest Sir, that you ride in the empty carriage?".

"Good idea. I will do that. You use your brain sometimes then. Makes a change."

The guardsmen were patiently waiting at the door and the carriage was brought forward. Sergaeus and Clodus stayed close to Gaius to give support, as with enormous willpower Gaius approached his host and hostess. He took Rhona's hand and pressed her fingers to his lips. "Thank you for your hospitality. You are most kind." Then turning to Joseph. "You Sir, are my responsibility. Any trouble, you let me know and I will sort it out. Good night to you."

The coachman opened the door and held it open, while Sergaeus and Clodus helped Gaius into his seat. He sat very upright by the window of the carriage, while Sergaeus and Clodus mounted their own steeds. The order was given to move forward. The coachman cracked his whip and as the horses and carriage moved off with a jolt, the Commander was thrown forward off his seat on to the floor. He lost his dignity, but was too drunk to care. Calim, Rhona, Joseph and Conchessa were standing on the steps to wave goodbye to their important guests and managed to keep a straight face when they saw Gaius disappear from view. However, when the military party was out of sight, Calim laughed, just a little at first, but then they all laughed, although Conchessa was worried in case Gaius had hurt himself.

Alana had not gone outside to wave with the family, but went in search of Paulus. He had not been seen since shortly after their arrival. Not that she thought anything amiss had happened to him, but she was curious. She went down the corridor until she met a servant and asked, "Where was the other guest?".

The servant smiled. "Master Paulus has slept soundly since he arrived. He ate a little first, then went to bed. I called in to see if he was well several times, but he has not stirred. Do you wish me to wake him, madam?"

"No. No thank you. I just wondered where he was."

"Don't worry madam, I will take good care of him. I expect the long journey has been very tiring for him."

Alana smiled at him. "Yes. I expect it has. Thank you."

She joined Conchessa and they both said goodnight to their hosts and returned to their room. Now only Calim, Rhona and Joseph were left. Joseph thanked them "for a wonderful reception. This day has been so full of excitement and surprises and so very special, I am loath to end it, but now my eyes refuse to stay open".

Calim walked Joseph to his room and said "Good night and God bless you Father Joseph".

Conchessa and Alana lay on their beds. "I wonder who he was?", said Conchessa.

"Who do you speak of?", asked Alana.

"The young man who walked me to the carriage this morning."

"I don't know", said Alana. "But I do know that he did not come back to the house with us." Conchessa was bitterly disappointed.

Next morning they got up early, curious to look around the garden and the house. The sun was shining inviting them to go outside and feel its warmth. They made their way along the passage to the reception room and were about to make for the outer door, when they heard someone call out. "Good morning ladies." They both turned to see who it was? Conchessa caught her breath when she saw Calpurnius. He was sitting at a small table. "Won't you join me for some breakfast?", he asked. "It's freshly baked bread and hot milk." They joined him and ate a little. "Did I startle you when I called out to you?"

"Yes, you did a little", said Alana, "For we did not expect to see you here".

"Why ever not?", he said, "This is my home".

"But, you were not here last evening", said Conchessa.

"Regrettably not. I had some work to do. Work I had to finish before you move into your new home. I worked until it was too dark to return home and I have only this hour returned from Bonavon. Allow me to show you the garden and tell you about your new home." Alana saw that they had eyes only for each other and conveniently remembered she had promised to help Joseph with some work and asked to be excused.

She stood in the doorway and watched her beloved Conchessa walk towards the garden, chatting away with this young man as though they were life long friends. She returned to her bedroom, only to find servants there cleaning. From there, she went to the reception room and was relieved to find Father Joseph and Paulus there. He smiled and looked pleased to see her. "I wondered where you were. We are waiting for Councillor Calim who is going to take us to see his mission school at Dunbriton. Where is Conchessa?"

"I don't think she will want to come with us", said Alana. "She is being entertained by Calpurnius, the Councillor's son and I doubt she will thank us for interrupting her walk."

Joseph went to the door and looked up the garden and saw his daughter and Calpurnius laughing as they strolled. "Humm … Yes my dear, you are right. Better leave them be."

"You must come with us, Alana", said Paulus. "We can't do anything here anyway. Whenever I try to do anything, a servant arrives and says 'Allow me, Sir'".

Joseph laughed at him. "Your not complaining, my son, I hope?"

"Far from it father, but it does make me feel helpless."

"Our hosts", said Joseph, "Want us to use these few days to rest and recover from our voyage before we begin our work".

Calim arrived with the coach at the front of the villa. "Are you all ready?" He looked around curiously. "Is your daughter not coming with us?"

"No Sir, not today. She is being entertained by your son. He is showing her the garden."

"Oh!", said Calim. "I was unaware he had arrived home. Well, we'd better be off."

Conchessa and Calpurnius sat on the garden seat. He told her about the work being done and the children who would be her pupils. How much everyone in

Bonavon was looking forward to the new school. She told him of her father's work and what their life had been like in the city of Tours and how they came to be sent here to Dunbriton. "I am so glad you are here", said Calpurnius.

She looked at him shyly and blushed. "I think I am going to like being here", she said. They continued their walk, content to be in each other's company. Both shared the strong feeling that they belonged together.

Calim and Harran had given much thought as to how they should present their Mission church. Money had not been a prime consideration, for of that there was ample. But, if they had made it too luxurious, with plush drapes or golden candlesticks, the well healed citizens of Dunbriton would perhaps, assume that it was a kind of club house for them and the poor would be excluded. Yet, if they made it too plain, the well off would not come. It had to be a place of welcome to all - for this Mission - dedicated to Christ Jesus - had to attract everyone who wanted to come.

The whole family had discussed this and were asked to put forward their ideas. Everyone chose Calpurnius's designs. His were simple and most attractive. Calpurnius was a keen student of art and philosophy. His teacher, Professor Theophilus (a Greek political refugee), was also a professor of astronomy and astrology. His influence upon the young Calpurnius's work was strong.

The temple was painted white. A dome in the centre of the ceiling was painted midnight blue, with a large gold star in the centre, representing the the Star of Bethlehem. A wide frieze around the four walls at ceiling level, was painted in pale blue and bore the symbols of the Zodiac. Potted plants and small trees showed up well against the white background and on the wall of the temple, facing the seating, was a large picture of Jesus blessing the children. Calpurnius had little knowledge of how Jesus looked, but he was told by Theophilus that there had been a description of Jesus, written by a man called Publicus, who stated that Jesus had hair the colour of new wine. Armed with that information, the picture was painted of a rear view of Jesus, with arms outstretched touching the childrens's heads in blessing

It was a large painting, very colourful and looked magnificent in its setting.

Pure white muslin drapes hung the length of the wall on either side of the painting, gathered and tied just above it. There was no alter as such, only a table in the centre of the temple, bearing a lamp and some flowers. The seats were of woven hazel wood and the floor was highly polished with beeswax and oil.

Calim, Joseph, Paulus and Alana, arrived at the Mission school and headed for the temple. Joseph had been warned that it might not be to his taste, but when he entered, he was pleasantly surprised. True, it was nothing like those he was familiar with in Gaul. He made it clear that he believed any dedication to the Lord would please him. "It really is most beautiful", he said, as he walked around, looking closely at the painting. "Tell me. This converted barn you speak of, is it decorated like this?", he inquired.

"No Father. Apart from the new floor, it has been left for you to choose the decor most suited to your taste. But, I may tell you that the carpenters and other workmen are at your disposal and will follow your instructions to the letter.

Whatever you choose, will be done."

"Had it been just like this, I would not have complained. I find this most enchanting", said Joseph.

"Why thank you Father Joseph", said Calim. "How kind of you to say so, though I must confess I am rather proud of my son's talent. We had nothing to guide us in temple decor and had to use our own imagination. We were delighted with the result, until we heard you were coming, then, we began to worry."

"You need not have worried on my account, Councillor. Quite frankly, I rather favour the simple design. Sometimes I feel that our temples are a little cluttered. I must say to all of you that we came here not expecting anything, Our welcome has been a thousand times better than anything we ever imagined You have honoured us and we are exceedingly grateful."

The following day, outside Gaius's office at Army headquarters, Clodus arrived to pick up the four guardsmen to escort Father Joseph and his family to Bonavon. He was early, so he went into the office to speak to Sergaeus. "You live very dangerously my friend. I could not believe my eyes when you grabbed that poor girl and kissed her, not five steps from her father and her mother!" Sergaeus looked up at him and smiled. Clodus shook his head. "What would you have done if she had screamed? You took one hell of a risk. Gaius would have been obliged to have you arrested."

Sergaeus spoke with an air of self confidence. "I knew she would not scream. She loves me and she knows I love her."

"Nevertheless", said Clodus, "It was a thoughtless thing to do and things could have gone wrong for all of us."

Sergaeus did not seem to care. "If I had been arrested and thrown to the lions, or whatever they do to prisoners up here, it would have been worth it. She is so delicious I could eat her. That beautiful face, those big eyes and that body covered in silk."

"Stop drooling", said Clodus. "We have work to do today. I want to see the faces of the missionaries when they feast their eyes on their house at Bonavon. It's a big day for the members of your Julia's family. We don't want to let them down. We have to inspect the outgoing guard and make sure that the new guard understand their duties."

Gaius arrived, saw that everything was in order, then said in a much softer tone than usual, "Remember me to the lady of the house, Madam Rhona". Then under his breath, he said, "A wonderful woman".

Back at the villa, there was great excitement. Their guests had loved their few days spent there. They had rested, but were now anxious to start work. They had heard so much about Bonavon and wanted to see it for themselves. Considering the small amount of luggage they had brought with them, there was now a mountain of it waiting to be loaded on to the carriage. Gifts from well-wishers and the family had mounted up; everything from furniture to ornaments and warm rugs. So, it was arranged that all the men would ride horseback and the ladies would travel in the carriage.

Clodus and Sergaeus arrived with the guards and soon they were on their way.

The carriage, loaded on top and partly inside, trundled along the cobbled streets of Dunbriton, escorted by ten riders. They did not hurry, but moved at a steady pace.

Once outside the town and into the countryside, Joseph, for no good reason he could think of, began to feel apprehensive. He was anxious to start work, but he began to realise that they would not have a kindly host to back them up. They would be on their own. There was his little church to decorate and furnish. And, would he, a foreigner be accepted by the local people? 'I'm being silly', he thought and worrying about nothing. Has God not provided for us very well so far? Why should I fear he would desert us now?"

He looked around the landscape. The high sloping hills. The wide valley, with the river running through it like a silver thread. There was in the far distance a flat topped mountain, like an extinct volcano.

Joseph was puzzled, for the whole scene was so familiar. 'It's impossible', he thought. 'I have never in my life been here before. Perhaps, I have travelled somewhere similar? In the distant past? No, that won't do, because I know what lies ahead of us before I see it. How can this be? The only other explanation is that I have been shown this place in a dream.' This explanation seemed reasonable and acceptable, so he did not say anything about it.

A little further on, Calim brought them to a halt. "I thought you might like to see what your new home looks like from here."

The ladies stepped outside the carriage, with a little help from Calim. The view was worth stopping for. They could see all over the valley and the orange tiled roof of the farm house, stood out amid the lush greenery. "I never imagined that this country would be so beautiful." Conchessa was visibly moved , though perhaps the presence of Calpurnius influenced her mood. "It is so very different to what I imagined it to be." She smiled at Calpurnius, who was still astride his horse, looking into the distance.

"I love this view", he said. "I never tire of it. I hope you will like it too." She said nothing, but thought, "I will love anything that you love".

The farmhouse was indeed welcoming. A few workmen were still there and the children were out in force to greet them, as was Bliss - the cook-cum-housekeeper. She, having aquainted herself with the big stone oven, was now able to produce excellent meals.

Calim introduced everyone to Joseph. "This is your new employer. I know you will look after him and his family, as you have all served me and mine." Calim told the carpenters. "You know we have left the barn untouched, except for the floor? That is because we expected Father Joseph to want to decorate his church as he so wishes. No doubt, he has his own ideas on how this should be done. I know you will all carry out his instructions." They then went on to inspect their new home.

Conchessa and Alana were shown around the house by Calpurnius. Each room was unique. His paintings of birds and flowers were superb, nothing was overbright or intrusive; delicate pastel colours being used throughout.

Bliss had proved her worth as cook-housekeeper, by preparing a large honey roast ham and turnips stuffed with rice, onions and herbs for the hungry travellers.

"My Father", said Calpurnius, "Has employed Bliss for half a year, but hopes that you will all find her too valuable to part with".

Then Calpurnius showed them the school room, which was his pride and joy. A large window made from small squares of glass (left over from the construction of the villa), allowed ample light and he had painted little animals on the plaster walls, as well as scenes of houses and children playing games. Conchessa and Alana had not said very much and Calpurnius began to wonder if they were disappointed? But, when the tour was over, Conchessa told him, "I will love being here, everything is so very beautiful".

As they walked back towards the house, they saw Clodus and his men about to leave. On seeing Alana, he came over. "I see by your smiles, you are pleased with your school."

"Yes Captain. We are very happy."

He then turned to Alana. "May I speak with you, madam?" Calpurnius nodded and led Conchessa away.

"What would you wish to speak to me about Captain? I am but a servant in this house."

Clodus smiled at her. "Are we not all servants? I am a servant of the Army. Father Joseph is servant of the Church."

Alana was shy and unused to attention. "Yes, that is so, but I thought Madam Portia was more pleasing to you."

Clodus thought for a moment and remembered the last time they met. "Ah! Yes, Portia. She is indeed a fine woman. One I would be proud to escort, if she were free, but alas, she has set her heart on another … the physician of the town, no less."

"I understand they are very close."

Alana felt foolish for allowing her jealousy to show. She looked away and changed the topic of conversation. "Shall I inform Father Joseph and the Councillor that you are ready to leave?"

"No. Not yet", said Clodus. "The men are not quite ready. I will wait for them to finish eating." He looked over to where his men had been - under the big tree by the gate - only to see that they had already gone. Sergaeus had seen him chatting with Alana and decided to take the new guard on to the fort himself. Clodus smiled and thought, "I will do him a favour one day". "Will you wait here with me until Major Sergaeus returns and we are ready to leave?"

Paulus was waiting by the carriage, after he and the coachman had unloaded the luggage. They had eaten, but were now thirsty, so he went in search of water. Guessing he would find some at the back of the house, he made his way there. The back door was open and Bliss was there clearing the kitchen. "Madam", he called. She turned around surprised to see him there. "May I have some water?"

She showed him a large stone pot and a ladle hanging nearby. "Are you one of the people who will be living here?", she asked him.

"Yes. I am the servant of the priest."

She smiled at him. "Then you are fortunate, indeed Sir. This is a good house. Everyone here has been so kind to me and my children. I trust you will be happy here too."

Conchessa and Calpurnius sat on the doorstep of the house watching the scene before them. Clodus and Alana talking; Paulus sharing his drink with the coachman and now Calim and Joseph came out of the church, still deep in conversation and quite unaware of the group of children following them around. Conchessa giggled at the sight of their fathers, for they were oblivious to their audience.

Suddenly, Calpurnius's mood changed and he became serious. "We have been together for two days now - two very special days. But, when I leave you in a little while, I don't know when I will be able to see you again. I have spent so much time here over the last few weeks, but now I must get back to my work and my studies. But, I promise I will try to see you as often as I can."

She answered him in a voice shaking with emotion. "I am so silly. I should have known you had other things to do in your life, but in the excitement of the day, I did not think. I took it for granted we would be together."

He took her hand in his and held it to his lips, then whispered, "One day we will. I promise".

Meanwhile, Calim and Joseph had wandered, over to the house. Calpurnius and Conchessa moved off the step to allow them entrance. The children remained in the yard, while Joseph and Calim went from room to room admiring Calpurnius's paintings. "Such talent in one so young is astounding," said Joseph. "I don't know Councillor, how I can ever thank you for all of this, but I must tell you how concerned I am."

Calim was puzzled. "Why Father? What is there that worries you so much?"

Joseph explained. "It's like this Councillor. My superiors have sent me here to convert the natives to Christianity and now I find that others have arrived on these shores long before me. When my superiors hear of this, they may recall me and send me elsewhere, where the need is greater."

Calim thought about this for a moment. "Tell me Father, who will inform your superiors?"

"Why, I must do so and Commander Gaius will be making his report to his Legation. He is duty is bound to tell everything, is he not? One way or another, the information will get back."

Calim studied Joseph's face. "Father Joseph", he said. "I have found in life that it is not a good thing to overburden people with too much information, especially if there is the possibility of misunderstanding. There is no need for you to inform anyone of anything which you feel would be detrimental to your family or the citizens of this village, who have waited anxiously for you to come and open this school for them. Think of the children!"

Joseph looked up at Calim. "Are you Sir, suggesting that I should lie by withholding the truth?"

Calim smiled. "Exactly."

Joseph's eyes widened in horror, but Calim continued unashamed. "We must, as responsible men, concern ourselves with what is right and fair for those souls under our care and if this means - shall we say - conveniently forgetting to tell absolutely everything. then so be it. I ask you Father Joseph, do you really think it would please God for you to uproot your family and take them all the way back to Gaul and to disappoint the children of Bonavon after all the trouble he has taken to get you here?"

"I must confess", said Joseph, "I had not quite thought of it in that way. But what of the Commander and his report?"

"No", replied Calim. "I have not forgotten him. YOU Father are a man of God. A priest of the Holy Church. I am a mere convert to the ways of Christ. The good Commander is a military man. A cunning strategist. He will have no qualms about withholding information, if it is in his best interests to do so. All we have to do is to suggest to him that he confine his report to the work that he and his men have done, like building the Fort and providing the troops to guard you, which he has done. That is the truth, is it not? Besides, Gaius will not want to admit that he himself had never heard of our mission in Dunbriton. That would appear lack on his part."

"Yes", said Joseph, "I understand. But we cannot dictate to the Commander what to put in his report".

"You are right Joseph, but I know someone who can."

"Oh!", said Joseph, "And who might that person be?"

Calim smiled. "Never you mind about that. I can assure you that this person is discrete."

Joseph was a little out of his depth with such intrigue. But, one thing was very clear, Calim and Rhona wanted him to stay. They wanted to learn of the Orthodox Church, as it was in Gaul.

Then there was his beloved daughter, who had bravely accompanied him, ready to face danger for his sake. Now, he could see she had fallen in love with Calpurnius. If he stubbornly decided to go all the way back to Gaul, she would never forgive him. He looked around the room where he stood. It was delightful. A lot of people had worked very hard on their behalf. And what of the Church? He had always dreamed of one of his own and he could decorate this one exactly as he chose. I'm a prize fool for even thinking of leaving.

Joseph gave little outward sign of his inner thoughts. But, it seemed as if Calim could read them. Calim smiled at him. "I do understand your conscience, but I believe that you are needed here. I feel strongly that there are deep spiritual reasons why God has sent you here."

Joseph - whose thoughts were often in a similar vein - said, "Yes, Councillor. I agree. Those are my feelings also. I have said nothing of this to anyone, but this place has felt familiar ever since we arrived, especially that hill where the Fort has been built. It is a very strong feeling".

Calim said, "You mean the old Bonfire Hill?".

"Yes, if that is its name."

Calim looked at Joseph with a steady gaze. "That Father Joseph, is an old religious site from many years back. I will tell you all about it one day".

Calpurnius called out, "Come on Father. Major Sergaeus has returned and we are ready to leave".

Calim and Joseph emerged into daylight. "It has been a wonderful day seeing you installed in this your new home and we hope you will be very happy here. Now we must all go and allow you to settle in. I expect you all have a lot to do."

"What about the remaining workers?", asked Joseph, as they walked towards the horses.

Calim told him, "The carpenters and the local men were all employed for six months. If you require them for longer, let me know". Joseph nodded and smiled, then waved goodbye. Joseph, Paulus, Conchessa and Alana were sad to see them leave, especially Conchessa, for she had been warned not to expect to see Calpurnius for a while.

The yard looked empty and much bigger with everyone gone. They could hear hammering from the Church as carpenters carried on with their work. Only the children sat on the wall under the big tree, watching them. Conchessa went over to them. "Do you all know that there will be a school here for you?"

"We do that, Miss".

"When will you open it?"

Conchessa looked at their eager faces. "Would tomorrow morning be too soon?" The faces beamed back at her. "Now, why don't you go and tell all your friends and come tomorrow when you hear me ring that bell." They ran away in a flurry of excitement. She called after them, "Don't forget to tell your friends".

Next morning, they were up early. Bliss was not due until later, so they ate some fruit and bread and drank only water. Alana heard a noise outside and looked out of the window to see who was there. "Quick, Father Joseph. Come quick." He and Conchessa rushed to look out and were surprised to see the yard full of children, of all ages, shapes and sizes.

"Where did they all come from?" There are only a few houses in the village.

"They must have come from further afield", replied Conchessa.

"Will they all fit into the school?", asked Alana.

"If they don't", said Joseph, "We will have to bring the little ones into the house". Surprisingly, they all fitted in well.

The very first lesson, on the first day at Bonavon was, the story of a baby born in the old town of Bethlehem long long ago.

CHAPTER VI

LIFE AT BON AVON

The following months were busy ones. Calpurnius kept his promise to visit Conchessa whenever he could, but that was not very often, for he had to catch up with work he had left undone in order to spend time decorating at Bonavon. 'The drawing office at the shipyard had been his usual place of work for the past two years and he enjoyed his work and the companionship of his fellow workers, but since returning, he could not settle in to it again.

The excitement of having a free hand to paint as he wished and the opportunity to express his artistic talent had unsettled him. His mind was not on designing ships.

When he did get away to go and visit Conchessa, she was usually overburdened with work, for even when the school was closed for the day, she was obliged to prepare lessons for the following day - or help with the household chores.

Calpurnius, having at times helped his cousins at the Dunbriton Mission, was able to help her, but it wasn't the same There was no time to sit and talk, or walk by the river. It was wonderful to see her, but it was different.

Paulus was very happy. He had elected to take care of the horses, the two he and Joseph had ridden from Dunbriton. Councillor Calim had told them to keep them here, as there was a fine stable and they would need them to get about.

He was proud to have a man's job now. He liked horses and there was a bothie above the stable that would have - in its day - housed several farm workers and he had it all to himself. He cleaned it out and put his few personal things in.

He still looked after Joseph, but often he found that Joseph had already cleaned his own shoes, or brushed his own cloak. It dawned on Paulus, that all those years he'd done these things for him, he'd been more trouble than help and that Joseph had given him these tasks merely to justify giving him a home. He loved Joseph like a real father and, indeed, he was the only one he had ever known. He was thoughtful and brave as well as kind.

When he had started as a boy to ride alongside him on his trips to find souls, they had to go into the roughest parts of the towns and villages. Very often they had to make a quick getaway and Paulus laughed to himself, as he remembered the woman who had poured a bowl of slops over their heads from an upstairs window. It had not been funny at the time. They had to discard their clothes!

Now, he was a man - an independent one - and it felt just wonderful. Recently, he had spoken to Joseph and told him how much he had appreciated him giving him a home. "I must have been a burden to you Father. You had to acquire a pony for me, so that I could travel with you. You had to feed and cloth me. You must have wished at times that you had never saved me."

Joseph was astounded. "My son. My dear boy, do not ever think it. I ask you. Who else in this world would have listened patiently to me rehearsing my sermons? Who would have been my sounding-board for all my ideas? Who else but you would have stayed by my side when danger was looming, yet never complained or criticised. I remember you my son by my side in the scorching sun and when it poured rain for days on end. Ever since the day we met, I have valued your companionship beyond price and will continue to do so. Never my son, think otherwise."

CHAPTER VII

YSU

The Mission very soon became the focal point of, not only the small village of Bonavon, but of the whole valley and for miles around. More people wanted to come and live nearby to be within the hub of activity.

As for Joseph, he was in heaven. His church was beginning to take shape and there was no shortage of people offering help.

On the few days when Calpurnius came, he could go out and about, though he had no need to search for souls for his Lord Jesus - they came looking for him. So, with a little time on his hands, he did something he'd wanted to do since the day he arrived - climb the Bonfire Hill, for it held a fascination for him which he could not explain. As he made his way up, he had the strange feeling that he had climbed this hill a thousand times before.

He reached the fort, Gaius had built for his protection and walked around it. "Yes, Yes", He said to himself, "This is an ideal spot to view the whole valley".

A strange feeling came over him, like pins and needles through his whole body. He looked around for somewhere to sit and saw a large stone. He made his way towards it and sat down with some relief. With his eyes closed, he saw pictures of people that were familiar, but wearing clothes of a another era way back in time.

He heard a noise and turned around to see an elderly man walk towards him. "I know you", said the man. You're the priest from the Mission down there."

Joseph smiled at him. "I am He", he said.

The man nodded. "I see you've found it then."

"Found what, Sir?", asked Joseph.

"Why, the site of the old Bonfire."

Joseph remembered Calim had mentioned it. "Would you care to enlighten me, Sir?"

"Well! It's a long time since we had a priest here. But, many years ago, this was a place of worship. The people believed that the smoke from the fire carried prayers to the gods. The priest would send prayers on behalf of those who asked, for a price, of course."

Joseph nodded and echoed, "Of course".

The old man went on. "The people put their request to the priest, who would write it out and then place it on the fire with a great deal of ceremony and everyone was happy. This practice went on for hundreds of years, until a new priest had other ideas. He demanded even greater gifts, He used threats to make the people pay up. Not a nice man at all! He demanded their most valuable possessions and told them if they did not hand them over, it would bring disaster to the village."

There was a man who lived in the village, his name was Ysu. He was wise and suspected the priest of being evil, but no one would listen, until the day a woman asked the priest to appeal to the gods to make her husband recover from an injury. She had few possessions. The priest told her that it was the law that she give her most treasured item, in order to attract the gods' attention. All she had was her baby. It was not exactly what the priest had in mind, but he was ever more conceited, when he realised just how much power he held over these poor people.

However, some of the onlookers ran to tell Ysu, "Come quickly, the priest is going to bum the baby".

Ysu dropped everything and ran as fast as he could, over the river by the wooden bridge and up the hill. He reached the top of the hill gasping for breath. He was furious. "Have all of you lost your senses? Enough of this foolishness. How could any of you believe that it would please God to kill a helpless child? A precious life that God himself gave you to nurture. God our Father knows that you are grateful for his mercy, but all that he wants in return is for you - all of you - to increase and prosper. And prosper you would, if you did not squander your treasures on this wretch," pointing accusingly at the priest.

By now, the priest was extremely frightened, lest the crowd turn on him. Ysu then spoke to the mother. "Take your child home and believe in your heart that your babe is God's gift to you. He does not want you to destroy it." Then he turned to the crowd. "Shame on you. Have you learned nothing in all the years of your lives?" And with that he turned and went back down the hill. Everyone followed him. They gathered outside his hut and begged him to be their leader and priest.

The other priest ran away and was never seen again. When some of the men went to his home to look for him, they found all the precious gifts that he should have burnt as offerings to the gods on behalf of the people. Ysu was their leader for many years and led them through great wisdom and truth.

The valley prospered under his guidance and they were happy.

When Ysu became old and knew he was about to die, he told his people, "If ever you are in danger, I will return to help you".

"Quite a story", said Joseph. "Tell me, have you told many people this?"

"No Sir. It's just one of those legends that persist through time. I have told you because I thought as a priest you would be interested. I must go now and leave you to enjoy the view." Joseph bid him good-day but remained sitting. He closed his eyes and prayed. Then opened them again and allowed them to wander over the whole valley again. 'His Valley'. He knew in his heart and in his mind, that he had lived before as Ysu. He had never been more sure of anything in his life before. But one thing puzzled him? If he had promised to return to help them when they were in danger, where was that danger? As far as he could see, everything was well. There was no disease. No hunger. No war. So what was going on?

Such things as Joseph believed were not taught him. They were instinctive. For some years before he had been a gardener. As he planted his tiny seedlings and watched them grow day-by-day into strange trees or beautifully coloured flowers, he marvelled at the miracles of life. Working alone, his mind allowing idle thoughts to filter through, very often he would ask questions and was surprised when answers came. He was thinking one day, of time and the life cycle of the various plants he was tending, when he began to receive answers; at least answers that satisfied his curiosity. It was as though an invisible person was whispering in his ear, "Not only do trees and flowers have their season", the voice said, "People also have theirs. Time neither marched nor rolled on, but was beyond mankind's understanding. Time is an illusion designed to allow heavenly beings to experience life on earth in many guises." He was given to understand that 'The light of heaven' constantly poured upon earth and each seed from its parent was slightly improved or changed in order to perfect itself. Joseph was given to believe that each human soul, when he or she could no longer learn from his life, or improve it in any way, would allow his body to die, in order to try again, to be reborn into a new life, with more scope for learning. One with more potential to further the soul's experience.

Now, sitting here, his whole being tingling and looking over 'His valley', he wondered again why the people flock to church. They seem happy and contented. He was puzzled. Then he remembered Calim and his pressures upon him to stay. Indeed, he had made it difficult for him to leave. Something was going on. Calim knew about it - but what?

CHAPTER VIII

THOUGHTS OF MARRIAGE

Time seemed to pass slowly for Calpurnius. Try as he might he could not concentrate on his work, his mind wandering back to Conchessa and the days he spent with her at Bonavon. Designing boats was the last thing on his mind. He just sat there with his chin on his hand, resting on his elbow. From time-to-time, he'd sigh and continue to look into space.

Rob - his manager and friend - could not help noticing his mood and came over to ask, "Was he ill?".

"No, I'm fine", said Calpurnius.

"Well, in that case," said Rob, "Do you mind if I give you a bit of advice?".

"Why, no Rob, of course not."

"Then get yourself out of here. Go and see your girl. You are no good to us mooning around here."

Calpurnius was embarrassed. He had not realised that the men were watching him. He blushed, then mumbled, "Thanks Rob. I'll do that".

He got up to leave. Then realised that his fellow workers were all laughing at him. One called out, "Why the hell don't you marry the girl and give us all peace".

Another said, "You're not the first young buck to fall in love with a woman".

Calpurnius was quite taken aback. It had not occurred to him that he was in love. Or, that he should get married. He thought Conchessa was much too young, but the more he thought about it, the more the idea appealed to him.

He went to the stable, collected his horse, but instead of going home, he walked along the quay leading his steed, thinking as he went, 'What would his father say? What would Father Joseph say? Oh dear. Maybe it's not such a good idea after all'. But the thought would not go away. By the time he reached the end of the quay, his mind was made up. The thought of spending his life with Conchessa was just too tempting. 'Yes,' he thought, 'That is what I want'. Having made up his mind, it felt as if a heavy burden had been lifted from his shoulders. 'Now, it only remains for me to ask her father.'

The quay was an interesting place. Sailors, anxious to get hold of local currency and not knowing when they would get their next pay, would have items brought from different parts of the world to sell at the market on the dock There were always crowds of people gathered there looking for a bargain or unusual gift.

As Calpurnius strolled along, holding his horse's reins and watching individuals barter, he warmed even more, not only to marriage, but to giving up his old lifestyle. Going out with Rob and the others, falconing, or horse racing. And those nights spent gambling. He could well do without them. It was then that a voice penetrated his thoughts. "Master. Master. Buy some silk for your lady," the voice said. Calpurnius looked at the man, little more than a boy really. He was holding up a length of bright violet coloured silk. On a trunk by his side, there were more lengths in a variety of colours. He tried, but could not visualise Conchessa in any of them.

"Sorry, but they are much too garish for my lady" (saying 'my lady' gave him a warm feeling).

"What do you mean, garish?", said the sailor.

Calpurnius tried to explain. "Too bright", he said. The sailor thought for a moment, then hurried up the gangway of his ship and returned holding a parcel, which he proceeded to open. He watched Calpurnius's face, clearly expecting him to be pleased, Out of the parcel fell a long piece of pale cream silk. Calpurnius simply could not refuse to buy it, or disappoint the young sailor. He tipped out his money pouch into the sailor's eager hand, tucked the parcel into his saddle bag and went home.

As he approached the villa, he saw a rider leave and make off in the opposite direction. His mother and father were in the garden and Calim called out to him, "How nice to have you home early. But, you have just missed Captain Clodus. He had delivered a message from Father Joseph. We are invited to Bonavon for dinner tomorrow".

"Did the Captain say if they were all well?"

"Yes. He said they were still busy, but better organised."

"Why are you home so early my son?", asked Calim.

"Would you believe it, Father? Rob threw me out. He accused me of moping about!"

"You, my boy - and were you?"

"I'm afraid so father. I had something on my mind."

Calim and Rhona became interested. "Something you can tell your mother about, I hope?" Calpurnius smiled at their blatant curiosity. So, he said, "I've made a decision. To ask Father Joseph for Conchessa's hand in marriage".

His parents stood silent while they took the news in. Then Calim put his arm around his son's shoulder and said, "Congratulations, my boy. What a good idea".

"You mean father, that you approve?"

"Why should I not approve? You are of age. You have your own means of support."

Rhona hugged him. "Besides, Conchessa is a sweet hard-working Christian girl. Of course we approve."

"Don't be too hasty with your congratulations. She may not accept me. She may only like me as a friend."

Calim looked concerned for his son, but Rhona laughed. "Of course, she will accept you. I know by the way she looks at you. I know that look. What is more, I bet she is the reason behind this dinner invitation from Joseph."

Calim studied his wife's face. "I would like to know, my dear, how you can be so certain?"

But Rhona simply said, "Women know such things".

"Honestly Rhona, one whiff of romance and your imagination runs riot. I expect the invitation means just what it says. Joseph wants us to see how they are progressing and to say thank you for our help."

"You men are so blind", said Rhona. "Conchessa loves you my son and will accept your proposal - I guarantee it."

Calim scoffed at her. "You were not so sure when I proposed to you. I never saw anyone more surprised. It was only weeks after we met. You were completely taken by surprise, if I remember correctly."

Rhona turned to her son, "You listen to your mother very carefully. Twenty years ago, not long after my mother died, my father wanted me to marry the son of a friend of his, a nice enough boy, mind you, but he was not for me. One evening, I had to take mother's place and escort him to a business meeting, followed by dinner. Sitting opposite us - with his two sons - was Hoel, the ship builder, a big bully of a man, who although already wealthy, made his sons work until they dropped. I nudged my father. He said, 'What is it my angel' and I said, 'Father, that's the one I want!'. He said, 'What's that! You want old Hoel's son? Then my girl, we'd better do something about it and make sure he catches you. Then he laughed".

"Now hold on", said Calim, "I have never heard such rubbish" and turning to his son said, "As it happens, I remember that evening very well and it was me who made the first move. I was talking to my brother Harran and father, when someone came over to talk to them and took them off. I looked up and saw you there looking shy and helpless. It was I who went over to you because you looked so lost".

Rhona was smiling, "And do you remember who it was who took your father and Harran away? Did you not think it strange that they did not ask you to join them?".

Realisation dawned on Calim. "Do you mean to tell me, it was a conspiracy?"

Calpurnius had stood looking from one parent to the other in amazement. Then Calim spoke to his son. "To think I have been married this twenty years to a scheming hussy!"

But, Rhona moved towards her husband and took his hand in hers. "No my dearest. You have been married this twenty years to a woman that has loved and adored you from the moment I first saw you."

The next morning Calpurnius told his parents that he wanted to go on ahead of them in order to speak to Father Joseph. He wanted to find out if he had any objections to a marriage before he asked Conchessa. He rode off, expecting to reach Bonavon long before this parents.

The ride from the east of Dunbriton to Bonavon was pleasant, but in spite of his mother's certainty, he was nervous, going over in his mind all the reasons why Joseph would be against the marriage. Maybe, even Conchessa herself was just happy to have him as a friend? He would have to move very carefully.

At the gate of the Mission, Paulus was waiting to welcome him and take his horse. "You are a welcome sight, Master Calpurnius. This place is not the same when you are not here."

Calpurnius was curious. "What makes you say so Paulus? Is there something wrong?"

"Nothing I can speak of, Sir. Not my business."

Calpurnius went into the house. In the kitchen Conchessa, Alana and Bliss were preparing dinner. He did his best not to focus too much attention on Conchessa, telling the others how wonderful the food was. Conchessa shyly looked up at him. "My Father is over at the church. I understand he wishes to speak with you. I will take you over."

"Don't bother Conchessa. I know the way." He left the house annoyed with himself. "Why did he not let her come with him, if she wanted to?"

He found Father Joseph in the small anti room. He looked up when Calpurnius entered. "Ah! There you are, my boy. Thank you for coming over to see me at such short notice. I hoped you would."

Joseph seemed ill at ease and shuffled his feet nervously. Then after a short hesitation, he looked up into Calpurnius's face. "I will come to the point right away. It's about Conchessa. You do know that she is very fond of you?"

"Yes", said Calpurnius. "I am aware of her feelings."

Joseph looked uncomfortable, then blurted out. "Is there another woman in your life?"

"No Sir. There is not", answered Calpurnius.

"Well, has your father selected a wife for you yet?"

"Not to my knowledge, Father Joseph." Calpurnius smiled at the priest who was becoming very embarrassed. "Before you say another word Sir, may I say something?"

"Why, of course, you may my boy."

Calpurnius then said, "I came here early today, ahead of my parents, to ask you to allow me to propose marriage to Conchessa. I wanted to consult you before I asked her".

Joseph closed this eyes as though in silent prayer for a moment. The look of sheer relief lit up his face. "Thanks be to God. Now I can tell you my son. Conchessa only lives for your visits. When you are not here, she does not eat and lacks concentration. She tries to hide her feelings, but we all know her so well. It is clear that she misses you."

"I miss her too", said Calpurnius. "So, yesterday I told my parents of my intentions and both mother and father gave me their blessing. They both wished me luck."

Then Calpurnius laughed. "Forgive me for laughing Father, but I have just recalled a conversation my father and I had with my mother last evening, which my father found amusing. Do you Sir, think there is any truth in this thing called *women's secret knowledge* - or intuition? That they are able to sense things more easily than men."

Now it was Joseph's turn to laugh. "My boy. I would not be a priest if I did not believe in the mysteries of life and women, even without their incredible intuition, are indeed a mystery to me."

Calpurnius returned to the house, having left Joseph to his prayers. Alana offered him some wine and cake. He drank the wine and complemented the ladies on the food prepared. Then he turned to Conchessa, "I hoped to have a walk by the river before my parents arrive. Would you like to come with me, Conchessa?". She blushed and Alana rushed to get her cloak and put it around her shoulders.

As they strolled along the riverbank, there was a strange silence, as though they were afraid to say the wrong thing. Calpurnius was now well aware from what Joseph said, that she would accept his proposal, but he did not want to appear to take her for granted. So, after a short time, he said, "This is a very special day for us Conchessa".

She stopped walking. "Why so this day?", she asked.

"Well. Our parents are meeting to discuss our marriage."

"How can this be?", she said. "No one has asked me."

"So!", he said, "No one has asked me either, but I think it is a wonderful idea - don't you? There is nothing in this world I want more, than to have you as my wife and I hope you will consent to have me as your husband". He took her hands in his and kissed her fingers. She put her arms around him and held him, then looked up into his face. "Do I take it that the answer is *yes*?", he asked.

"I was happy enough that you were coming today, but I did not expect this. You have taken me by surprise and the answer is, *yes*. I am sorry to be so foolish, but I love you so much, I find life difficult when you are not here."

They both wanted these precious moments to last and sat on a fallen log, holding on to each other, until they heard Alana ring the bell to call Joseph and Paulus for dinner.

"My parents must have arrived. We had better get back."

"I don't want to", she said. "I want this time to last a little longer."

He stood up. Took her hands in his and gently raised her to her feet. "I do too, but from now on we will have our whole lives together to look forward to. Come on. Let us go and break the news to the family. They are all waiting anxiously to hear your answer."

Conchessa was shocked. "You mean to tell me, they all know?"

"Yes. At least they will if mother is here. Keep her waiting for a while", said Calpurnius. "That will teach her to be patient."

They arrived back at the house. In the main room, Joseph, Rhona, Calim and Alana looked up at them eagerly, anticipating their announcement. Paulus and Bliss peeped round the kitchen door. Conchessa took her time removing her cloak, then walked slowly towards a hook to hang it up, then she walked back to stand beside Calpurnius.

Rhona could not bear it another moment. "Will you two stop teasing me! *Well?* When is it going to be?"

Everyone laughed. Then Calpurnius said, "Conchessa has consented to be my wife".

There was an outburst of congratulations. Calim hugged his son and patted this shoulder. Joseph held this daughter and whispered in her ear, "Is my little girl happy now?".

"Yes, papa. Very happy."

"Then, my dear one. So am I."

There was much celebrating. Eating and drinking. Rhona was excited. Already making plans. After all Calpurnius was the only son of one of the wealthiest families in Strathclyde. This would have to be something special.

Sitting in the kitchen, relaxing after they had celebrated with the family, Paulus and Bliss were sharing a piece of cake and helping themselves to another glass of wine. Paulus knew that he was welcome to be with the family, but he preferred the quiet company of Bliss. He helped her clear the dishes away and put the surplus food into the cool cupboard. Even though they sat alone with their feet up, they enjoyed the cheerful banter drifting in from the dining room.

Bliss, knowing Paulus's slight backwardness and his quiet nature, always made sure he had his share of the very best. So she poured another glass of wine. "Let's enjoy it. It's not every day a marriage is announced."

Alana was happy for her young mistress, for she knew only too well how she felt about Calpurnius and had been worried in case Calpurnius did not feel as strongly about her. After all, he had lived here all of his life and probably knew lots of girls. But now everything was well. She wished that her Captain Clodus was here to share with her this happy occasion.

Rhona approached Conchessa. "My dear, I could not be more happy. I always wanted a daughter and now I have got one - almost - and I could not wish for a better, or a more beautiful one. You know, Conchessa," said Rhona (in a confidential tone), "There are those who would tell you that I can be bossy and over bearing (she nodded towards her husband and son). But, my dear, do not believe a word of it. It is just that I like to get things done. I hate shilly shallying about. I know that you are a very busy and hard-working young lady. So, with your consent I would like to help you with your marriage arrangements. Would that upset you too much?" She looked askance at Conchessa, almost pleading, "Only to make suggestions, you understand".

"Thank you Madam Rhona", said Conchessa. "Thank you for being so thoughtful. I would appreciate all the help I can get. I doubt very much I will find time to arrange anything for myself. The children take up every moment and the country is still quite new to me."

Rhona was delighted; her face shone with pleasure. "Thank you Conchessa my dear. Yours will be the most wonderful wedding ever seen in Strathclyde. Our only son and his chosen bride deserve the very best and that you will have."

Calpurnius joined them and Rhona stood back and looked at them in admiration. Her eyes filled with tears and one trickled down her cheek. "You will make a wonderful bride and groom." She excused herself and withdrew to dry her eyes.

"Was mother asking you if she could assist with the arrangements?"

"Why yes. She kindly offered to help me."

Calpurnius laughed. "Ever since I told her that I was going to propose to you, she has been making plans. Believe me she has it all planned already."

Conchessa smiled. "I am very grateful to her, for I am quite helpless. We are indeed fortunate to have her. I would not know where to start. Is it not a pity that we cannot make our vows within the family - very quietly."

Calpurnius put his hand over hers and looked at her tenderly. "That, my love would be ideal. But, mother and father have a position in this town to uphold. So we, my love, will just have to do what we are bid from on high."

"I don't really mind, said Conchessa. "Just so long as they don't take too long about it."

Everyone agreed that the ceremony should take place in the Mission church at Dunbriton, as the one at Bonavon was not big enough to accommodate all of the family and guests. The lists - which grew daily - included church members, Council Decurians and their wives; Commander Gaius from the military camp and the guards from the fort and all of the children from both church schools. It was also decided that Father Joseph would perform the ceremony.

Portia and Elinor were the musicians of the family and they composed a little song for the children to sing.

Portia made several special trips to Bonavon to make sure that all of the children knew the words and would sing nice and loud - and in harmony. Conchessa was able to spend time with Rhona's dressmaker being measured, which was very strange to her, as she seldom owned more than two dresses at one time. Alana, also had to be measured, for she was to be, a handmaiden.

Rhona engaged her favourite dressmaker to fashion the cream silk Calpurnius had bought. The days leading up to the wedding were very tiring for Conchessa, but Rhona seemed to have endless energy and enthusiasm.

Conchessa longed for Calpurnius's visits, which were now more frequent. He could always give her support and reassurance. Her father too, rehearsed the ceremony several times, as much for his own benefit as hers.

The big day drew nearer and everyone and everything was ready. Seating was re-arranged, with an extra large seat being brought in especially for the Commander and placed where he could get a good view. Clodus and Sergaeus were to act as ushers and robes of blue with green facing were made for them.

Flowers were added to the green foliage to create colour. The whole effect was fresh and aromatic.

CHAPTER IX

THE WEDDING

The church began to fill with guests, the men in official robes and their ladies looking delightful in brightly coloured dresses. Commander Gaius was every bit as imposing and terrifying in his civilian robes as he was in his uniform.

Sergaeus and Clodus escorted each guest to their seat, in a most dignified manner. When all the guests were seated, they stood by the pillars at the door to wait for the bride and groom.

Joseph and Harran dressed in robes of peacock blue, waited nervously in the small office at the back of the church, going through the order of service - yet again.

Joseph was thoughtful. "Little did I think Councillor Harran, that the first marriage I would ever perform, would be for my own daughter."

Harran placed his hand on Joseph's shoulder. "They are two fine young people. Your daughter will be safe and happy with my nephew. He has always been a hard working and honest young man. A credit to his parents."

They could hear the children singing. Elinor and Portia had taught them well.

Two coaches arrived outside the Mission church at about the same time. In the first one, was Calpurnius and his father Calim; Rob (his friend) and his tutor Professor Theophilus. In the second carriage, was Conchessa, Rhona, Julia and Alana.

The plan was for the bride and groom to enter by the main door; separate and then follow the pacemakers (Calim and Rhona) down either side of the church; then come together before the alter - in perfect unison.

As there was no alter, a long polished table was placed under the picture of Jesus blessing the children; golden lamps placed on either end.

The men alighted from their carriage and waited - one on each step - followed by the ladies. Rhona stood on the step opposite Calim. Conchessa stepped from the carriage, beautiful in her pale cream silk gown, her long brown hair decorated with flowers. Then Alana, followed by Julia. For the first time in her life, Alana was proud of her appearance. Today, she could compete with anyone. Rhona had supervised every detail. Her dressmakers and hairdressers had done a superb job and Alana stepped from the carriage, hoping that Clodus would see her looking like a lady.

Clodus was anxious to see Alana, for he knew she was worried about not looking good enough beside Julia and Portia. When he saw her step out of the carriage behind Conchessa, he hardly recognised her. Although he expected to see her in a pretty dress, she looked wonderful! She was so slim and shapely and her hair shone. She glanced quickly at him and smiled, showing her perfect teeth. 'Why had he never noticed how big her eyes were?' It was all he could do to take his eyes off her.

Sergaeus had eyes only for Julia. His thoughts were on being able to be with her later at the reception, for how could he pretend not to be interested?

Rhona gave the bride and her handmaidens a final look over. Satisfied that they looked their best, she led them forward.

Portia had been waiting for the signal and seeing that everyone had arrived, she led the children in song. They were sitting on small cushions, the boys wearing white robes and the girls white dresses. All of them with blue belts or ties around their waists. Their voices sounded so beautiful and in harmony. Rhona led Conchessa and her handmaidens, slowly down one side of the temple, while Calim led Calpurnius and the witnesses down the other.

Just as the singing ended, the bride and groom came together before the alter and Harran and Joseph stepped forward.

Joseph looked at his daughter and thought, 'How like her mother she was. How he wished Alicia were here to see her'.

He then turned to Calpurnius. What a fine looking boy he was, although the only thing that mattered, was that he loved his daughter.

He was so deep in thought and Harran had to cough a little to attract his attention. Once Joseph started the ceremony, his voice rang out loud and clear throughout the church.

It was a well rehearsed ceremony, that went smoothly and as he pronounced them 'husband and wife', there were tears of joy amongst the more sentimental of family and guests.

Harran led the bride and groom to a private room to sign a certificate of marriage and at this point, Elinor and Portia were to sing. However, Harran returned quickly and suggested they allow him to speak. They readily agreed.

Harran whispered to Elinor to sing very quietly and the children to hum while he spoke. The effect of this overall sound was a perfect background to Harran's impromptu sermon.

"It is a great pleasure to see our temple full today. For a building, no matter how beautiful, is only a shelter from the storms of life.

"A building only becomes a 'Holy Place' when it is blessed by the presence of God's children.

"Our Lord Jesus did not preach his message from a building, but from a hillside. Or a boat anchored off shore, or by the road-side. Indeed anywhere where people were gathered.

"Jesus was not like other religious leaders, who speak down to their followers and dictate to them how they should live their lives; how they should dress or what they should eat. Jesus did not concern himself with such things.

"He talked of the quality of the 'human soul'; that we are all children of 'The Father'. He told them that anything he could do, they could do also. He said, he was 'The son of God'. Yet, we too, were God's Children.

"Many years ago, my brother Calim and I met a 'Holy Man', who told us that one of his ancestors was a follower of Jesus and witnessed many miracles performed by him. He told us that when Jesus was given a new coat, his old discarded one was claimed by his followers, each being given a small piece. Our holy man's ancestor, treasured his own fragment and had made for it a special camphor-wood box, lined with silk to keep it safe.

"To our astonishment, our Holy Man took from his satchel that very box. He opened it up, to reveal a small blue-grey square of linen. He allowed Calim and I to touch it. The feeling was magical. From that day on, my brother and I have been Christians. That tiny piece of cloth, treasured by one family for over three hundred years, still - it seemed - held the very essence of the wearer.

"Had it not been for that meeting thirty years ago, we would not be here this day, celebrating the marriage of my nephew Calpurnius to the very beautiful daughter of our own Father Joseph of Bonavon. We, all of us, are here this day because of that meeting that took place all those years ago."

"I have brought this event to your notice to make you aware of how important it is to do good; to love and honour God. For what you do this day, may well be remembered well into the future. I thank all of you for bringing the bright light of your souls into our church this day and making this occasion a truly spiritual one. May each one of you be blessed with good health and happiness. God bless you."

Calpurnius and Conchessa were waiting in the background and as soon as Harran's sermon was over, the choir resumed singing a little louder. Bride and groom, their handmaidens and escorts, walked down the centre isle. Out in the street, children waited with baskets of flower petals and threw them on the ground on the pathway towards the waiting carriages. No one seemed to notice that Calim, Harran and Joseph had already left, making their way back to the villa, ready to welcome the guests.

Whilst they waited for the bride and groom to arrive (or the first guests), they drank a toast to the successful outcome of all their hard work. Outside the temple, the guests were still watching the singing and dancing children. But, gradually they filtered away, the promise of a wonderful feast beckoning them towards the villa.

Elinor, Portia and Bliss gathered the children together and Paulus brought their special long wagon forward, which they all piled into. Bliss sat up front with him, while some of the parents sat at the back to make sure nobody fell off.

A magnificent banquet awaited them at the villa. Every baker in town had been kept busy baking small loaves of bread and cakes; household staff had roasted hams, stuffed eggs, smoked fish and stacked platters of delicious food - enough to satisfy and please the most fastidious guest.

Joseph, Harran and Calim stood on the steps of the villa, ready to welcome the guests and direct them into the garden. While they waited, Joseph, who was much moved by the occasion, remarked to Calim. "To think Councillor, less than one year ago, I was afraid to bring my daughter here. I had heard terrible stories of natives who painted their faces blue and were wild and dangerous. It was a revelation when you and the Commander met us at the ship."

Calim remembered that day too. He'd never seen four such terrified people. They stood motionless, with their mouths open, gaping up at Gaius. It took some effort to keep from laughing. Then he realised that they really had been very frightened and made moves to put them at their ease.

Calim smiled at the memory. "It was a wonderful day Joseph. We are all happy that you came and stayed."

"Yes", said Joseph. "It has all been a most wonderful experience."

The three men raised their glasses. "Let us drink to a future full of happiness and prosperity for our children".

Celebrations continued well into the evening. Calpurnius and Conchessa mingled with their guests, thanking them for coming to share in their happiness. Harran was busy trying to keep an eye on Julia. He suspected she was with Sergaeus and that worried him. Clodus and Alana found each other. She was free for the evening, no need to watch over, or protect her young mistress - there was another, whose resposibility this was now. Shortly, her mistress would be leaving to spend a few days at the home of Theophilus, who was about to leave again on his travels to distant shores. His servants were instructed to take care of the newlyweds.

The guests lingered, unwilling to let the celebrations end. But, eventually the children were taken home. Paulus brought the long wagon to the front of the villa and Bliss and some of the parents joined them for the long journey home to Bonavon. They sang until they fell asleep.

Then, the elderly church members left, followed by those who could still walk. Some guests were asleep where they had sat eating and drinking all evening.

There was one guest, who although quite sober, was obviously moved by Harran's sermon. He sought out Father Joseph and approached him. "Do you think you could spare me a moment?"

"Why, certainly my son. Come and sit here beside me. How can I help you?"

The man sat down and coughed a little uncomfortably. "You can tell me more about this fellow Jesus, Father."

Joseph smiled. "That will be my very great pleasure, *Commander*."

CHAPTER X

JOSEPH'S GUILT

The Mission school at Bonavon Tibernae was kept going with the help of Calim and Portia, while Calpurnius and Conchessa were away at the home of his tutor, Theophilius - a political refugee from Greece who made a living tutoring the children of the rich. Calpurnius was one of his favourite pupils, for he shared the professor's interest in astronomy and astrology.

The professor was now pleased that Calpurnius had decided to teach, saying, "My boy, you can do a grand job helping to build ships, but if you teach others to read, write and think, then you are much more valuable to many more people".

When Calpurnius and Conchessa returned, Calpurnius moved into the house and Joseph had to move into the small side room and office within his church. This suited him very well, for it was quiet and he could meditate at any time he chose without having to consider what the other members of the family were doing and Conchessa had made it most comfortable for him. He could, of course, meditate in the church, but when not in use it was quite cold and Joseph was sensitive to the cold.

It was during one of his meditations, that he began to feel guilty about not trying to convert the Highlanders. This country seemed to him civilised enough. He would have to give it some thought. Now that Calpurnius was here permanently he was going to have time on his hands and Calpurnius had proved an excellent teacher. He enjoyed relating stories of the ancient Greeks and Romans, myths and legends and Christian martyrs.

Calim was not completely happy about his son spending all his time teaching and insisted that he put his name forward to become a Councillor and take his place in local government. This meant that he had to spend at least two days a week in town. This pleased Rhona, who missed her son very much and looked forward to being able to spend some time with him when he would be obliged to come to town.

One evening, Joseph brought up the subject of his making inroads into the Highlands. Calpurnius was horrified. "Why Father? Why must you go? It is very dangerous country. There are wild animals, bogland, deep cold water. And the Picts would cut your throat for the fun of it! Cannot you be content with the excellent work you do here?"

"Since you arrived here, you have worked every day God sends. Teaching, decorating your church and visiting the sick. Please Father Joseph. Please reconsider. I have good reason for asking you, because I believe Conchessa is having our child." Joseph expressed his delight and agreed to postpone his travels for a while, or at least until the first few months were over and he was sure she was safe, as he understood the first months were most dangerous.

"I do not want to upset my daughter, but I do know that she will understand my need more than anyone. I was sent here not only to gain new converts for Jesus, but to break new ground among the heathen.

"All I have found so far, have been good souls, grateful for everything. Blessed souls who have taught me as much as I have taught them."

"Father Joseph. You are too modest by far. Don't be so hard on yourself. You are dearly loved by the people here, especially the children. Think of their misery if you were hurt."

Joseph put his hand on his son-in-law's shoulder. "Believe me, my dear boy. I do understand your deep concern. But, I would rather die doing my duty, than live into old age, perhaps, suffering illness or disease. There are times when we must take risks and I must salve my conscience."

Calpurnius sighed. "I can see you won't be happy until you go up there and see for yourself. Shall I come with you as a guide?"

"No no, my son, that would never do. My daughter could suffer losing her father, but never the father of her unborn child."

"Then I beg you to ask Gaius for a guard. He has made himself responsible for your care."

But Joseph shook his head. "No No, my boy. How could I approach people and ask them to believe in an invisible God who loves us, yet have so little faith as to need a guard. However, if Paulus volunteers his services, I will accept, for he is my right hand man and it will be easier to get a villager to do his work."

Paulus was not overjoyed about setting foot in the Highlands. He had grown into a nice comfortable and contented way of life and did not want to leave it.

But, he had always thought of himself as Joseph's servant and he did owe him his very existence. He would have to go. He sighed. He would miss his days chatting with Bliss; hearing her laughing at his jokes and funny stories - the fact that they were not always meant to be funny was neither here nor there.

He had always felt comfortable with Bliss. He liked helping her with her work. Peeling hard skinned turnips was a man's job. How would she manage without him? He felt protective towards her - for she too was a servant.

When Alana heard of Joseph's intentions, she was very distressed. She could not bear the thought of him going into danger unprotected. She had been warned to keep this a secret, lest Calim or others tried to talk him out of it. But, this was more than she could bear. So, she confided in Clodus and pleaded with him to keep secret any plan made to escort him or protect him and she explained Joseph's reasons.

Clodus thanked her for her faith in him. "Don't worry Alana. I will be discrete. We will work something out."

Clodus told Sergaeus and they both decided to see Gaius. "He will be angry", said Clodus, "But he would be even more angry if anything happened to Joseph. He would have to answer to the Legate and that would fall back on us."

Sergaeus took Clodus in to see Gaius. They both stood to attention before him. "It's Joseph the priest, Sir", said Clodus. "He is making plans to go soul hunting in the Highlands."

"He's What! Does that old fool not know that my superiors will have my head if anything happens to him?" Gaius paced up and down, then appeared to calm down. "I don't suppose we can talk him out of it?"

"No Sir", said Clodus. "He is very determined, even though his daughter is having a child. He feels guilty because he does not think he has fulfilled his instructions."

Gaius was thoughtful. "He doesn't need to go up to the Highlands to find heathens. There are plenty here in camp." This was meant as sarcasm, but it reminded Clodus that he had enlisted men from the Highlands some time ago.

"Sir. That's it. If these Highlanders are still in camp, they could follow Joseph."

"You mean to tell me that you enlisted the enemy in our Army?", said Gaius, with some irritation.

"Yes sir", said Clodus. "They were men from the east of the country and were more interested in being educated than fighting!"

"Well", said Gaius. "What do you intend to do about it?"

"I propose that we find out if the men are still with us and if so, we prepare them for a secret mission", said Clodus.

Gaius nodded his approval. "Right Clodus. You find these men and if they are here, find their old clothes. From there on, we will make plans."

The Highlanders were found and their old clothes. Sergaeus went to the stables to find the oldest horses, but was told, "We don't keep old horses. We eat them!".

"Then make young horses look old, four or five of them. We need them for a special assignment.

Four young soldiers were marched in front of Gaius. They looked smart and brave, but were inwardly very nervous. They could not think of anything they had done to warrant Gaius's attention. On being told of the secret mission, all of them breathed a sigh of relief.

"You will not speak of this to anyone", Gaius told them. "You will follow the missionaries at a distance, but do not let them out of your sight. Now, is that clear? You only intervene if they are in any danger."

"Yes Sir. We understand", answered the four.

"Do not shave or have your hair cut. You will each be given a pass to excuse you from this. Otherwise you could be arrested several times a day." The four laughed nervously, saluted and left.

Conchessa was five months pregnant and keeping fit and well, when Joseph decided it was time to go. Alana lost no time in passing the word to Clodus, who in turn passed the news to Gaius. And so the plan was set in motion.

On the day Joseph and Paulus packed their satchels, Calpurnius and Conchessa no longer tried to persuade them not to go. Joseph had made up his mind and would not rest until he was satisfied. So they wished him luck. "Be very careful father and come home soon. Remember, you do not have to convert the whole country all at once."

Joseph laughed. "No, my dear daughter. I will be content with just one soul."

Unknown to them, the night before they were due to leave, the four soldiers were transformed into wild looking Highlanders and moved into the fort on the hill. As morning broke, they were watching to see when the two riders would leave the Mission.

As Joseph and Paulus rode off, Calpurnius held Conchessa. He said, "We must have faith and believe that what he is doing is God's will."

Alana's eyes were on the hill above, for she alone among them knew that they would be followed, though she dare not tell them that she had betrayed a confidence.

Paulus and Joseph covered mile after mile up the west side of the great lake, after crossing the river at the drovers's bridge. They followed what seemed like a well used path, but saw no one, or any sign of life. Cottages were empty; obviously for some time. Eventually, they did come across some dwellings, but there were only women there and they did not understand one word of what Joseph said, not even when he asked for water.

On and on they went until they reached the summit of a hill. They paused and surveyed the land. "This is very strange, Paulus. I expected to see more people, yet we have seen no one for miles. Funny thing is, I feel we are being watched."

They ate some food and drank some wine, mixed with the last of the water they had brought with them, then wrapped themselves in thick blankets and settled down for the night under some bushes. It was an uncomfortable night, only snatching sleep a little at a time.

Next morning, they were awake and up early, ate a little more of their food and set off again. They rode along the ridge of a high mountain and far below, surrounded by lush scenery, was a deep blue lake. They scanned the scenery all around them. It was beautiful and Joseph thanked God for the joy of seeing such a sight. But, he was deeply disappointed, "I had thought by now Paulus, we would have met many more people."

Back at the Mission school, Calpurnius was comforting Conchessa. "Try my dearest not to worry so much. Your father is a survivor. He has gone into rough areas before."

"I know", she replied, "but I cannot envisage life without him".

Calim came to see his son. He was distraught to hear that Joseph was in danger. "I may have been able to help in some way. Why was I not told of this venture?"

"Father, you were not told, because Joseph thought you might try to dissuade him."

Calim thought about this for a moment. "Yes, he would have been right. I would have tried to talk him out of it; because I know how evil these Highlanders can be. They are a wild bunch. But, now I find you and Conchessa overworking and you, my son, have missed two Council meetings - very important ones. My boy, to be a Councillor carries a great responsibility. You must be consistent if you want to get on in life. These meetings are where we are kept up to date with what is going on in business and politics and in the country as a whole. It is also where we meet people who can help us. I have brought you documents to read, relating to the latest projects being discussed."

"Thank you father", said Calpurnius. "I do know the importance of our work in local government. I also know that if you and Uncle Harran were not there, votes would be taken by one or two that would enable them to fill their own money boxes to the detriment of the citizens of this town. But with her father gone, my place was with Conchessa."

Calim looked around. "Is there anything I can do whilst I am here?"

"No father. We have many volunteers. They are very good and can turn a hand to anything I ask them to do and they are grateful for any small payment they get. They say that they are pleased their children are being educated."

Calim mounted his horse ready to leave. "Take care my son and don't forget, your mother and I want to help you, so do not be afraid to ask."

"I won't", said Calpurnius, "Thank you father and give my love to mother - and I will read these documents carefully."

Joseph and Paulus travelled on and they actually met some ordinary people, but it was quite hopeless. No one understood them. "I have to admit Paulus, this trip has been a total waste of time and effort. We have been on the road for three days now and our food and drink are finished, well almost …", feeling the thin satchel hanging from his shoulder. Joseph shook his head, "We will have to get back before we starve to death".

Paulus shivered, "That's if the cold doesn't kill us first".

They reached the top of the mountain again on their return journey and had begun to descend. Joseph said, "I know that I said this trip was a waste of time, but that view of the lake I will never forget". Paulus agreed with him, though his mind was not on the view, but on getting home to Bliss and some good food. "It is strange", said Joseph, "But I still get the feeling we are being watched. We are not alone."

Just then there was a blood curdling yell and a gang of vicious looking bandits brandishing daggers and clubs appeared from out of the bushes.

They dragged Joseph from his horse and he hit the rough ground with a thud. One bandit held him by the shoulders, while another held a dagger to his throat, while making gestures with his right hand to give him his money or valuables. Paulus's horse had jumped about a bit in fright and he had fallen off. A club struck him across the back and as he yelled in pain, Joseph thought his end had come. Suddenly, there was the sound of galloping horses and a lot of whooping and shouting and the four soldiers, their appearance as frightening as the bandits, arrived on the scene.

Without a word, the newcomers grabbed the two attackers who were threatening Joseph and knocked them to the ground, then they chased the rest of the gang who were running off with the horses and brought them back. One of the newcomers then helped Joseph back onto his horse, as he was badly shaken and his back was very painful, while Paulus, who was unconscious, was attended by the other two.

They bathed his head with cool water on a rag and he began to moan. That was a relief for Joseph, who thought Paulus was dead. But, he slowly opened his eyes and looked around. When he saw the men in rough dress he began to struggle, but then he saw Joseph back on his horse. One of the men poured him a drink from a small bottle, which Paulus drank. It tasted foul, but once down, he felt his whole body warm up. The four soldiers then accompanied Joseph and Paulus down the mountainside, but when they came to the huts where the women were, they stopped and spoke to them in their own language. Joseph saw money changing hands and a meal - of sorts - was cooked for all of them. After that, they were taken into one of the huts and made to rest on a straw bed.

Paulus woke up groggy, but Joseph, although in great discomfort, watched everything that went on and he saw their rescuers talk and laugh with the women.

After a while, they were helped up and placed very carefully on to their horses, one of the men sitting behind Paulus to ensure that he did not fall off, his own horse tethered behind.

When they stopped to make camp, Paulus and Joseph were well wrapped up against the cold and placed nearest the fire to keep warm.

Joseph realised they were being taken home and with this in mind, he slept.

Next morning, they were given food. Paulus was beginning to recover and Joseph told him, "I remember passing this place. These men are taking us home and I tell you, Paulus my son, I have no wish ever to leave again".

"Nor I", said Paulus. "But Father, we had better thank God, for I never expected to see it again."

Joseph was apologetic. "My dear Paulus. I am so sorry my son. I had no right to put your life in danger. It was an ill prepared trip and the language was incomprehensible."

The four soldiers were listening to their conversation, but as instructed they did not speak, or give any indication that they understood a word of it.

Paulus remarked that it was a pity about the language difficulty. "You might have been able to convert these four Highlanders."

But Joseph replied. "My son. These men have put themselves in danger to rescue us. They have bathed our wounds; gave us food; made us rest and now they are taking us home. I have no need to try to convert these men to the ways of Christ. They know them already. They are good and kind, just like in the story of the Good Samaritan. There are some who call themselves Christians, yet do not live as such. These men would surely be recognised by our Lord himself as his own."

"Father Joseph, forgive me for asking", said Paulus, "but, if it matters not what a man or woman is called so long as they are good, why do we bother to try to convert them to Christianity?"

"A good qestion", said Joseph, "And one I will attempt to answer. You see my son. Every soul upon earth is a spiritual being seeking worldly experience. But, over time, many have taken on tasks that have been far too difficult. In their earthly struggles, they have forgotten their angelic beginnings and their heavenly life and sink deeper into material living, often spending a whole lifetime believing that money, fame, or notoriety are all they have to live for".

"Did you watch our friend here this morning, when he discovered that the camp fire was almost out? He went to great trouble to rekindle the flame. He blew on it. Fanned it with a branch of leaves. Then, the wonderful satisfaction he experienced when that tiny spark finally burst into flame. Well! That is how I feel about my work, Paulus. I know that there is that spark of God inside the soul of every man. I try to talk to it, persuade it, cajole it, almost anything to get that spark to burst into that magnificent spiritual flame that will carry that soul back to their home with their Father God. Only then am I happy. So, you see my son, it is a futile waste of labour to huff and puff into the already blazing heart of an established fire. You see my son, it matters not to me what a man chooses to call himself. God does not need to understand language. He sees only the light and colour of the soul. He is not fooled by fancy clothes, or eloquent words, but he can see the colours of the spiritual cloak and hear the voices of love and truth."

"I look into the eyes, my son and I can see that our friends here are good. Indeed, I get the feeling that they would like to speak to us, if they could."

The four soldiers, who had been ordered not to speak lest they give the plan away, did not flicker an eyelid at this conversation. But, neither did they move until it was over. Only then, did they decide it was time to move on.

They arrived at the Mission about dawn on the third day of their journey home. They had been gone six whole days. They entered the courtyard and Joseph and Paulus were helped from their horses. Then one of the men banged on the door very loud and then they fled, mounting their horses as they sped away.

Conchessa and Calpurnius arose from their bed and rushed to the door, followed by Alana. When they saw Joseph and Paulus, they were overjoyed and helped them in and looked them over to see if they were in good condition. Apart from their backs, which were very painful, they were fine. "All we need, my dear, is rest. We have been well taken care of", said Joseph.

Alana went and brought them some soup, which they welcomed. Joseph was puzzled about their rescuers? He knew that God worked in mysterious ways, but the appearance of these men was just too good to be true. "One day I will get to the bottom of it." They were both pleased to get into their own comfortable beds.

Conchessa was happy to have her father home. "Thank God", she whispered as she hugged him.

"Now I hope father, you won't want to go there again. Not for a very long time."

The four soldiers headed for the fort on the hill, where they removed their rough leggings and sheep skin waistcoats. They shaved off their beards and put on their uniforms and by midday they were back in camp, shortly afterwards reporting to Gaius.

"So! The old man and the servant got a beating. Well, maybe that will teach them a lesson. You men did a fine job and it will be noted on your reports. But, you say he saw few people?"

"Yes Sir. Only the wives and children of the hunters. Fortunately for us, they had all gone on a hunting trip. The women cooked us a meal."

"Such a pity, the old fellow did not get at least one convert. Then we could be sure he would not want to go on a return visit."

"Not after the beating they took, Sir. I should not think so. But, as for converts, he may have got one or two at least.

Gaius gave them a strange questioning look.

Then one said, "Well Sir. They are very brave men - of the kind we admire".

"Yes", said Gaius. "I know exactly what you mean."

Some time later, Bliss arrived for work, bringing her children to school. She went to the house and was met by Alana, who told her the good news of Father Joseph and Paulus's return. "Where are they?", she asked. "Where is Paulus?"

"They are both very tired and suffered back injuries. They are resting."

Bliss was working in the kitchen, wondering if she should take Paulus a drink and thinking, "He really should have someone to look after him". She decided to prepare him some bread and milk and was about to get the milk from the cool cupboard when she heard his voice behind her. She turned around quickly and could not hide her happiness. She hurried towards him and hugged him. "Thank God you are home. I have been so worried." Paulus was very surprised, for as much as they were fond of each other, they had never touched, respecting each others privacy. But, now Bliss had hugged him, in a way no other woman had and he liked it. When she began to move away to continue her work, she realised she had crossed a barrier and invaded his privacy and she was embarrassed. Paulus was surprised at her show of emotion, but it had given him a warm and loving feeling. They stood looking at each other for several moments, then he said, "I hope I don't have to go away again and get beaten up in order to get another hug".

She blushed and in a voice still trembling with emotion said, "No. You don't have to do either. You can have one anytime you like".

"Then, can I have another one now, please?", he said, holding out his arms.

She went over to him and they embraced, holding each other and she kissed his cheek. They did not part until they heard Alana's footsteps.

Alana entered the kitchen. She was surprised to see Paulus there. "I did not expect to see you out of bed, Paulus. You must be feeling much better?"

"Yes", said Paulus, looking at Bliss. "I do feel much better."

CHAPTER XI

JULIA

Julia had been meeting Sergaeus in secret and had become pregnant. But, at the mention of marriage, Sergaeus appeared to lose interest and made excuses not to see her. Although there was never any doubt that his love for her was strong, it seemed as if his sense of responsibility was weak.

Julia was devastated, unable or unwilling to tell her family, who had warned her against him. She knew they would blame her and call her foolish.

So, when her cousin Calpurnius arrived at the villa on one of his Council days, Julia was also visiting. She asked him to meet her in the garden. "Whatever is the matter with you, Julia, are you ill?", for she looked so pale and distressed.

She told him her troubles. Calpurnius was angry. "How could he do this to you? But, I don't understand Julia, for I could swear he loves you."

Julia turned her face away from him to hide her tears and replied, "Not enough apparently".

"I don't know what I can do about it", said Calpurnius, "But, I will think of something. Should you not tell your Mother and Father?".

"I will tell Portia, though there is nothing anyone can do. However, if you could find out why he is behaving so, it might make it easier to bear."

When Calpurnius reached home late that afternoon, he told Conchessa about young Julia. She was sympathetic, bearing in mind her own condition. Alana - who missed little of what went on in the household - wasted no time in telling Clodus. "He's done *what*!", yelled Clodus. "I will get to the bottom of this." He was furious, for he felt responsible for bringing them together.

Clodus rode to the camp and on the way his anger did not diminish, but grew. He went straight to headquarters and barged unannounced into Sergaeus's office. He bent his tall frame over Sergaeus's desk, until they were almost nose to nose and snarled menacingly, "What the hell are you playing at? Treating Julia like a harlot! I will tell you once and once only. If you do not get off your backside and make it right with her, I will personally see to it that Gaius takes a whip to your back".

Clodus took a deep breath, then said more calmly. "If there is one thing I hate in this life, it's a so-called man, who cannot lift his thoughts above his belt."Then with a look of thunder, he stomped out of the office, leaving Sergaeus sitting back in his chair stunned. Clodus was the only friend he had and now he had turned on him.

He heard a noise and looked up. In the connecting doorway stood Gaius. Sergaeus closed his eyes and thought, "My God I am finished". He felt as though his legs had turned to jelly and every bit of strength had been sucked out of him. His mouth dried up. Gaius stared at him and without a word indicated with his finger for Sergaeus to go into his office. Sergaeus did not know how he managed to walk the short distance. He tried to stand to attention, but he feared his legs would give way.

Gaius paced the floor in front of him, eyeing him up and down, like a hungry lion wondering which limb of his victim to devour first. Then he appeared to calm down a little. He went to his cabinet and took from it a small flagon of liquor, poured one glass of it, then walked towards Sergaeus. "Here, sit down and drink this." Sergaeus took a large gulp of the liquid and gasped as it burnt his throat. He closed his eyes and shook his head. Gaius turned his face away lest Sergaeus see that he was softening.

"So, Major. You have got yourself into trouble?"

"Yes Sir", said Sergaeus, "And what do you intend to do about it?", inquired Gaius.

"I don't know, Sir. There is nothing I can do. I have no money to support a wife like Julia."

Gaius stood up. "So, that's what its all about - money. I might have known. Do you really want this woman, or is this an excuse for you to avoid your responsibilities?"

Sergaeus looked Gaius in the eye. "I want Julia, Sir. But, I doubt her father will allow it, even if I did have money."

Gaius went unusually and uncharacteristically calm.

"When I was your age, I found myself in your position, not once, but several times. I had no intention of marrying anyone. The Army was my life. I held high rank for my age. And frankly I was an arrogant bastard. No woman was going to trap me into marriage. Why, I must have several sons or daughters in Gaul - I hardly bothered to inquire."

"Then one day, many years later, three young recruits were marched in front of me on a serious charge of 'assaulting and robbing a civilian'. The normal punishment for such a crime, would have been ten lashes; a week in solitary confinement and loss of pay. When I looked up at the young soldiers, I could hardly believe my eyes. For one of them was exactly as I looked at his age. I made an excuse to look at his records and saw his mother's name and where the father's name should have been, it said, 'Father unknown'. This boy was *my son*. For the first time in my life I was deeply ashamed."

"What kind of man was I to desert my children, or the women who loved me?"

"I sentenced the young men to three strokes and disregarded the rest of the punishment."

"Soon I will retire. Leave the Army for good and when I do, there is not one soul who will give a fig whether I live or die; no home to go to; no wife to meet me. Nothing or no one. And do you know, Major? I deserve no better; for these things are built up over the years, by love and trust and I gave none. Now fate has dealt me another punishment, to pay me back for my years of neglect. For now, I find that I love a woman of great beauty, intelligence and wit and I cannot have her, for she is another man's wife." Gaius sighed, "We pay a heavy price for our learning".

"Now, to get back to you, young Sergaeus. I am going to discharge you from the Army."

Sergaeus was shocked and was about to plead for his job, "For how was he to live without it?". Gaius continued. "I am going to discharge you on grounds of compassion. That way I will be able to pay you gratuities - sufficient to provide you with a house of your own. I will also add the equivalent amount as a marriage gift. Now, you have no excuse for not asking your young lady to marry you." Sergaeus was staring at Gaius in disbelief.

"Now go to your quarters. Clean yourself up. Wear civilian robes, for that is what you are from this moment on. Then go to your young lady and beg for her forgiveness. Explain to her the reasons for your behaviour and hope she loves you enough to forgive you."

Sergaeus stood before his Commander staring, unable to adjust to this new situation. "Sir. You would do this for me. Why?"

"Because, Major. I will not be responsible for another fatherless child; even if it is not mine."

Sergaeus saluted his Commander for the last time and was about to leave, when Gaius called after him. "This conversation has been in secret. I trust it will remain so. Remember, I have a reputation to maintain."

Sergaeus, whose mind was still reeling, said, "Yes Sir. Just as you wish".

Gaius now alone in his office, sat at his desk to make some notes. He scribbled, 'Promotion for Daisy', then after thinking for a second, crossed this out and wrote 'Promotion for Clodus'. Looking up, he shook his head, thinking, 'I never knew he had the guts. He certainly told Sergaeus what he thought of him'. He continued writing, 'Find myself another adjutant', then the thought crossed his mind, 'That won't be easy - every time I enter the Officers' mess hall, it empties. If they know I am looking for a new adjutant, all the officers will take their men on a very long route march. The camp will be deserted'.

"Oh! To be popular", he uttered.

Sergaeus did as he was bid. He bathed, shaved and smelling clean and looking his best, he rode to the home of Harran and Elinor.

On the way, his mind went over the events of the day. One moment he was a poor junior officer with a load of worries. Then Clodus arrived and verbally abused him. Then, that horrifying moment when he realised Gaius was watching and knew what an idiot he had been. Now, he was a civilian with more money behind him than he had earned in five years. But, he still had to face Julia and her father.

When Julia's maid told her, "Sergaeus is at the door", in her heart she wanted to rush into his arms, but, she had been deeply wounded by his behaviour, so in her head, she wanted revenge.

'Why won't you see him?", pleaded Portia?

Julia sobbed, "I never want to see him again", she whispered through her tears. And to her maid, she said, 'Tell him I am not at home".

Before the maid could relay the message, Harran arrived home and met Sergaeus on the steps. He was not overjoyed to see him, but asked politely, "Does Julia know you are here?".

Just then the maid opened the door. On seeing Harran, she did not know what to say and was silent. "Wait here", said Harran, "While I inquire as to where my daughter is".

He found Elinor comforting Julia and Portia in a state of distress. "Julia are you aware that your young man is waiting on the doorstep to see you?"

Julia looked up at him. "Yes father, but I don't want to see him like this".

Harran saw the pain on his daughter's tear-stained face. It hurt him to see her like this - her eyes red and swollen. He knew also that his wife and Portia were suffering too. Elinor spoke to her husband. "Sergaeus has hurt her badly."

But, as much as Harran felt pity for his youngest daughter, he had glimpsed the same anguish in the eyes of Sergaeus. "Come Julia, come to me." He held her and wiped her tears away. "As much as I love you my daughter, I must remind you that in this house we are Christians. We do not believe in 'an-eye-for-an-eye'. We believe that everyone should have a fair hearing and you will never know what Sergaeus has to say in his defence, unless you speak to him. It is not a good thing that you asked an innocent maid to tell lies on your behalf. If you really never want to see Sergaeus again, then you must tell him yourself."

Julia sniffed and with that, Harran put his arm around his daughter and led her to the outer door. He opened the door and gently pushed her through.

Sergaeus was waiting a few steps away and watched her, but she would not let her eyes meet his. She walked down the steps, passing him and stood at the bottom with her back towards him. He moved closer. "Julia. Please forgive me. I've been a heartless fool. A stupid insensitive brute. I love you more now than ever and I want to marry you."

There was no response from Julia. She had been badly hurt and regardless of her father's advice, she wanted Sergaeus to suffer. Then he began to explain. "When you told me about the baby and indicated we should marry, I panicked. Not because I did not want to. I did, more than anything else in the world. But I had no money. How could I support you? And what would your father say when he discovered that I had taken his youngest daughter? If you're heart has been broken, it is no more than mine. I had to face the thought of losing you."

Julia began to soften and asked him, "If you could not support me several weeks ago, what has happened to alter your circumstances?".

"I have left the Army and accepted my gratuities", said Sergaeus. "They are quite considerable and sufficient for us to set up home. Perhaps, not as good as you are accustomed, but comfortable".

Now she turned to look at him. He saw her face and how she must have suffered. He went to her, put his arms around her and held her close and pressed her head on his shoulder. "My dearest Julia, I promise before God, I will never ever hurt you again." She raised her arms and put them around him.

Elinor and Portia were watching discretely from the window, Elinor giving her husband a commentary on the actions of the lovers. Harran was annoyed. "Honestly Elinor, I expected better from you. Spying on your daughter like that!".

"I know it's not right, my dear, but I wanted to see if they would make up, then I could prepare myself for what lies ahead, for I really cannot bear to see her so upset".

Harran understood. "Nor can I, my dear. We will know soon enough."

Portia called to them, "Julia is bringing Sergaeus in Mama".

"That is what I expected", said Harran, "I want to speak to that young man".

He went to the door to meet them. He told Julia to join her mother and sister and he invited Sergaeus into his private office.

"Sit down Sergaeus." Then after a pause said, "You have caused my daughter and her mother a great deal of heartache. I hope you do not intend to make a habit of such behaviour".

Sergaeus counted himself lucky that Harran was a civil man. "No Sir", said Sergaeus, "I can assure you it won't ever happen again. May I Sir, explain what happened? It might help you to understand."

"I was born in Londinium, the youngest child of a very large family. We were very poor. When the slavers came in search of fair children to sell in Italy, my parents sold me. I was about four years old. I was bought by a wealthy merchant and his wife, who were childless. For some years I was treated well and only ate the very best of food. Then two things happened. My yellow hair turned brown and the mistress had a child of her own and she very quickly lost any feelings she had for me. But, then the master began to take an interest in me. That was when I ran away and joined a gang of destitute children. We had to steal food to live. Sir, I have seen such poverty and cruelty you could not imagine in your worst nightmares."

"One day, I wandered near the military barracks and watched the soldiers on parade. They looked so smart - so clean and well fed - and I could see that some were no taller than myself. So, I stole clothes from a wash line and sandals from another doorstep and went to enlist. I was surprised when I was accepted, because I guessed that I was far too young and even though my education was limited."

"Councillor Harran. I have worked hard to educate myself. I have joined classes in any subject available in my pursuit of promotion in order to better myself. After about two years, I was sent to Gaul, when I heard that a certain high ranking officer was on the lookout for a clerk. Even though I was warned that this man was difficult and would make my life a misery, because it meant promotion, I went for it. It was not easy. The Commander was then a very hard taskmaster. But, I managed to get promoted to his personal clerk and when we were both posted to north Briton, I was promoted to Major. Since then Sir, it has been work and more work."

"That Sir, is how I came to be here. Believe me, I am not a womaniser, indeed I am quite the opposite. I have worked so hard in order to raise myself from poverty, that I have seldom thought of women, or considered myself worthy of their attention. I have heard Clodus say that I am too old for Julia - that could be true - for I do not know how old I am. During my years on the streets of Rome, I lost count. At a guess, I would say I am about twenty two, but I could be wrong."

"Sir. I love Julia more than I ever imagined it was possible to love anyone. When I first saw her, I thought she was the most beautiful woman on earth and just to be near her was magical. When she returned my love, it was as though I had finally discovered heaven. Then, she told me she was having my child! This Sir, was a part of my education I had neglected. I awoke from my dream and remembered the poverty. How could I care for her? I had nothing to offer her. Only this morning, my Commander offered me my gratuities if I left the Army and I accepted. All I can offer your daughter is a modest home, but a husband who loves her and will work hard to bring the child up in a happy home."

Harran had sat quietly and listened carefully while Sergaeus spoke. He understood and sympathised. His opinion of Sergaeus altered. He could now see in this young man what his daughter saw. So he put his hand on Sergaeus's shoulder. "Welcome to our family," he said, "I am sure we will get along fine".

They went into the main room, where Elinor, Portia and Julia waited. They looked anxiously at Harran's face, for they thought he may have expressed disapproval. However, it was obvious that they had become friends and the look between Sergaeus and Julia indicated their complete happiness. Elinor put her hand on Julia's back and pushed her towards Sergaeus, a gesture that said, "You now belong to him". Julia walked over to him and stood by his side. He held her hand.

The family talked for some time, discussing plans for their forthcoming marriage, settling for a quiet family affair in the private chapel at the villa.

Father Joseph would be asked if he would perform the ceremony; Portia would be 'maid of honour' and Sergaeus hoped that Clodus would have forgiven him and consent to stand by him.

A date would be set, the moment these arrangements could be made.

CHAPTER XII

THE BIRTH OF MAUN

Two more months passed. Conchessa was worried about her baby. She had spent a restless night and next day paced the floor and complained of backache. Bliss, having had three children of her own, told Alana that the baby was on the way and they had better put their plans into action.

Conchessa was anxious, knowing that her baby was coming early - two months too early. By afternoon, there was no doubt whatsoever, for all the signs of impending birth had taken place.

Word was sent to Rhona to come and bring Markus, her physician, but even if they responded immediately, it would still take them a long time to get to Bonavon. Calpurnius rubbed Conchessa's back, which gave her some relief, but she whispered to him, "I love you dearly, but please go to the church and comfort my father. I know he is desperately worried because of what happened to my mother and please, my darling, don't you worry about me, I am in good hands. Very soon your mother will come with Markus".

Calpurnius was reluctant to leave but, could understand Conchessa's worry. "Just as you wish my love, but keep us informed and if you want me, I will come running." She smiled at him, managing to conceal her growing pain.

Calpurnius went over to the church and found Joseph on his knees by the alter. Calpurnius took a seat and waited for him to finish his devotions.

"There you are, my son. I take it your presence is no longer appreciated over there?"

Calpurnius smiled at him. "It is a worrying time. I hope my mother and Markus arrive soon. It has been a long time since Conchessa began her labour."

Joseph turned his face away, lest Calpurnius see how worried he was. He decided to change the topic of conversation.

"When you came in, my son, I was asking God to help my daughter through her labour. I was also asking a blessing on the strangers who undoubtedly saved the life of Paulus and myself. It was so strange. One moment we were standing on a mountain top, looking down into a beautiful lake of deepest blue, surrounded by lush green vegetation and thanking God for allowing us to see it."

"We had only just set off again, when those bandits attacked us. They were yelling and threatening us with daggers. It was dreadful, especially when I saw my dear Paulus hit with a club. I really thought they had killed him. Another of them held a dagger to my throat. I thought my end had come. Then out of the blue rode these men, who saved our lives and brought us home."

"I keep asking, my son, who were they? How did they know where we lived?" Joseph shook his head. "I am mystified."

Calpurnius had thought about this too and said, "Father is it not possible that the guards got to hear of your trip and decided to protect you. They may have followed you?".

Joseph was doubtful. "I hardly think so. There was no doubt they were of a Highland race - in dress and language."

Both men were pacing as they spoke, for at the back of their minds was Conchessa. They were both only too well aware that her mother had died giving birth.

Just then the door of the church opened and Alana burst in. She was flushed with excitement. "We have a son - Conchessa has given birth to a beautiful little boy."

Both men asked anxiously, "and Conchessa, Is she well?".

Alana beamed. "She is well and happy, but very tired. When we are ready, I will call you to come and see him." Then she hurried away.

Joseph went to a small cabinet and retrieved two glasses and a flagon of wine. "While we are waiting, let us drink to the new baby and his mother." There was obvious relief in his voice.

They left the church and walked the short distance to the house in anticipation of Alana's call, when they heard the sound of a coach and horses - Rhona and Markus had arrived. "No need to hurry, mother, Conchessa has just delivered a son."

Markus hurried into the house, in order to see for himself if the baby had had a safe passage into the world. Just then they heard a cry, like the tinkling of a small bell. Calpurnius heard it first. "Listen - will you all listen? That is my son calling!"

Joseph said, "And my grandson!".

"And mine", said Rhona.

There was great pride in their voices. The three went into the house and waited in the dining room, until Markus came to speak to them. He spoke to Calpurnius first, "Your wife and son are well, though the baby is very small. He is lively and I do not foresee any problems. I may add that the two women taking care of them, have done a wonderful job. It always helps when an experienced mother is present to encourage and reassure the new mother that everything is going to plan".

"They are ready for you now", called Alana, from the bedroom door.

Calpurnius went quickly to Conchessa's side. He held her hand and kissed it. "I am so proud of you. You have been so brave and your father is very relieved." Calpurnius really wanted to take her in his arms, but he knew how shy his wife was in front of people, even her family. But, as they looked into each others eyes, words were not really necessary.

Rhona went to the crib to see her grandson and Joseph joined her. He could hardly hide his pride as the gazed at the tiny baby and the fact that the physician had examined him and found him perfect, was a blessing. If only my own dear Alicia had had such care, things may have been different. He hoped Alicia was somewhere nearby looking on, for this last few hours had evoked terrible memories in his mind, but now it was over and he had a grandson. He corrected that statement, we have a grandson.

Alana joined them. "Isn't he just beautiful? We were so lucky to have Bliss here. She knew exactly what to do and it reassured Conchessa that everything was going well. I would have panicked without her."

Rhona turned to her. "My dear, I am sure you both did the right things - Markus is very pleased." Joseph joined them. "My daughter is most fortunate to have such devoted friends to help her at this special time." He bent down to kiss Conchessa. He could see how tired she was. "Goodnight my dear. I am going to give thanks. If anyone wants me, I will be in the church."

While Markus left in the carriage - with instructions to give Calim the good news and to remind him to come tomorrow and bring the gifts for their grandson. Rhona put on an apron and started work, saying, "You young ladies who have worked long hours without rest, go now and get some sleep or you won't be fit for tomorrow. I will stay here for tonight". Alana and Bliss were grateful, for it had been a hectic evening.

Calpurnius was sitting beside his wife still, but Rhona told him, "Go in the other room and sleep on the couch. Conchessa needs to sleep". He felt like a little boy again, being sent to bed by his mother. Conchessa saw the expression on his face and laughed.

When Rhona and Conchessa were left alone with the baby, Rhona brought him to her. "Start to feed him right away. These tiny babies need to be fed often. Just because he lies quiet now, don't let him fool you. He will wake up and yell in the night, just as you have gone to sleep."

Having made sure that the baby had a little food, she made Conchessa comfortable. She took the baby in her arms and sat in the old rocking chair and very gently patted her grandson's back. She whispered to him, "Let your mama and papa sleep my precious, tonight you belong to Grandma …!".

Next day, Calim arrived bringing the gifts for their grandson, although the tiny gowns he brought were not tiny enough - neither Elinor, Portia, or Julia having any idea of just how small the new baby would be. Conchessa thanked him. "Do tell them how delighted I am. They will fit well by the time he is ready to wear gowns. At the moment a small piece of linen is enough."

While Rhona got ready to leave, Conchessa got up, bathed and dressed. She was quite determined to care for her baby herself, as much as she was able. She was not one to take advantage of others.

"Where is the little fellow?", asked Calim, as Rhona led him towards the crib, "And what do I call you little man?". He looked up when no one answered, Calpurnius, Conchessa, Alana and Rhona standing around with blank expressions. "He has no name yet, father", said Calpurnius.

Calim was surprised. "Is it not the custom to have selected a name before the babe is born?"

"Yes, it is", said Conchessa. "We have considered several, but he is so small, none of them seem to fit."

"Oh! I see", said Calim (who did not really see at all).

"He has come two months early, father", said Calpurnius. "We were not ready."

"I take it then that you have not chosen one yet?", said Calim.

Conchessa asked him if he had a name in mind he would like to suggest?

Calpurnius interjected. "Please don't let father choose the name, look at the one he selected for me!"

"What do you mean", said Calim indignantly. "Calpurnius was the name of a brave soldier Harran and I greatly admired. A young officer who arrived to rescue us in the war. He wore the plumed helmet of an officer of much higher rank. We discovered that was because every officer above him had been killed and the heavy responsibility fell on him. He was brave and kind and saved our sanity, for our father was greatly distressed at the loss of our mother."

"I am sorry, father", said Calpurnius. "I did not mean to be offensive. It is just that I am a teacher of small children and none of them can say Calpurnius. If you have a name in mind please say so."

Calim hesitated, then said, "As it happens, the name I have in mind is a very short one".

Everyone waited anxiously to hear what Calim had in mind, but he was in no hurry to tell them. Instead, he looked down into the crib and touched the tiny baby's cheek. Then he looked up and said, "It is Maun".

Calpurnius could hardly believe his ears. "Maun?", he repeated, "I have never heard that before".

Calim went on, "Do you all remember your uncle Harran's talk at your marriage ceremony? The Holy Man Harran spoke about who taught us of Jesus. His name was Maun. He told us that all the members of his family for many generations were named Maun. It comes from *Ill Maundat,* which means 'The Command' - the last command of our Lord Jesus to his disciples - which was 'Love ye one another'. Old Maun's parents had told him, 'Not only was the name a constant reminder to him, but when strangers asked him what his name meant, it gave him an opportunity to tell them of the love of Jesus".

There was silence within the room for a moment. Then Conchessa said, "Unless there are any objections, Maun it is?".

Julia and Sergaeus were married within a month of Sergaeus's acceptance into the family, Joseph performing the ceremony in the private chapel within the villa. Their baby, a little girl they named Helen, was born a few months later.

Clodus and Sergaeus renewed their friendship and Harran employed Sergaeus as his land agent and rent collector. Not the best of jobs, but then Sergaeus was used to people being difficult - he'd had years of experience!

The wedding was Maun's first outing and he behaved perfectly and did not cry.

Marriage seemed to be in the air, Conchessa noticing the growing love between Alana and Clodus. They both had one thing in common, a very strong sense of duty. Alana to Conchessa whom she had cared for all of her life. Now, there was little Maun. She thought she would be unfaithful and could not bear to think of life without them, or for them to manage without her. And regarding Clodus, his military duties came first. The Army was his life. His work as security guard officer was very important, for it meant he could see Alana almost every day.

Conchessa was well aware of the situation between them. She spoke to Alana and asked her, "When are you and Clodus going to marry?".

Alana was shocked. "Why we have never even discussed such a thing!"

Conchessa smiled at her. "Then, don't you think it is about time you did and do something about making a life for yourselves? All of your life you have taken care of me and father. Now you share in the caring for Maun - when you are not teaching the little ones. You would make an excellent mother."

Alana protested. "What about you and Father?"

Conchessa shook her head. "Do you really think that father and I would be happy knowing we were depriving you of your right to happiness and a life of your own?"

Alana thought about it. "I am sorry Conchessa, I did not think."

"Then my dearest friend you had better start", said Conchessa, "Before you end up an old maid and Clodus a crusty old bachelor".

That afternoon, Alana walked along the river bank until she came to the road that led up to the fort, knowing it was almost time for Clodus to arrive with the change of guard. She wanted to speak to him in private and not at the house.

After a short time she heard the horses. Then the group of five riders came into view.

Clodus was surprised to see Alana by the side of the road. He told the guards to go on ahead and he would catch up. He stopped, dismounted and approached her. At first he was curious, then worried. "What is the matter? Has anything happened?"

Alana bit her lip, for now as she stood before him, she felt foolish. She said quietly, "It's nothing really. It's just that", she hesitated feeling awkward. "It is just that Conchessa has told me that it is time I made a life for myself."

Clodus was confused for a moment. "You mean that you have been asked to leave the household?"

Alana wished she had not came. "Oh! No no. Nothing like that. It has been suggested that … I find myself a husband!" She blushed - but Clodus got the message.

So he said, playfully, "And have you someone in mind?".

"Yes", she said, "I have. He is a young, handsome guards officer, but I don't know if he will have me?".

"Is that so?", said Clodus. "And do I know this lucky fellow?"

"Yes", said Alana. "You know him well. He looks very much like you; same face, same tall skinny body."

Then Clodus said, "So, if this young, handsome officer - who looks like me - asked you to marry him - would you? I mean, do you love him?".

"Oh! Yes", said Alana, looking down shyly. "I love him very much. I have since the day I arrived in this country and he offered me his arm."

"Then", said Clodus, "I will have to ask you before he does. I cannot have another man take my woman. Can I?". He wrapped her cloak around her shoulders in a protective manner. "You go back to the house; it is getting cold and I will come and see you as soon as I am finished here."

She moved away to leave, but he called her name. She turned around. "Remind me to thank Conchessa."

She smiled at him, her heart beating faster. "Yes, I will", she said and rushed home. She had not felt so happy in a long time.

On arriving home, she told Conchessa where she had been and that Clodus was coming to see her soon. "There now, I told you so. Clodus is an honourable man and will make a wonderful husband."

Shortly afterwards, when Maun was tucked up in his crib, Clodus arrived. "We both thank you Madam Conchessa and at the first opportunity we will speak to your father and I for my part will speak to my Commander, a task I shall put behind me as quickly as possible. Though, I must confess he seems a fraction more mellow of late."

Conchessa went to see if Maun was still asleep. Left alone, Clodus took Alana in his arms. "I ask you. What kind of people are we? So intent on our duties, we neglect each other and need a friend to remind us that time is passing us by. Never again! From now on, you are my duty and my love, you will always come first."

Alana had to get up on her toes to kiss him. "And you will come first for me also."

Clodus, being of a more serious nature, was not given to boast, but he was not a poor man, the only son of a landowner and his wife from Eboracum. His parents died within a year of one another and the estate was his. Eventually, the estate proved too much of a burden for the young Clodus and he sold it to an older cousin and joined the Army in the hope of travel, companionship and adventure. But, he had only travelled from the east coast of Briton to the north west coast and his most exciting adventure was being put in charge of the guard at Bonavon and meeting Alana and her family.

He decided he would have a house built in the village, not too far away from her beloved Conchessa and Father Joseph, for he knew she would be unhappy if she were to move away.

His money was in a vault at headquarters and since his recent promotion, his income would be substantial. 'Yes', he thought, 'We will do very nicely'.

The system worked well. The eldest child of Bliss was a daughter of about fourteen. She quickly took over some of Alana's duties and with her mother's guidance, worked well, leaving more time for Alana to prepare for her forthcoming marriage. But, Clodus was told that permission to marry was not given to junior officers - he wondered where he got the idea that Major was senior enough rank - and he kept putting off asking Gaius for permission and even contemplated marrying in secret. When on returning to camp the very next day, there was an urgent message waiting for him to report to Gaius, Clodus uttered a curse he'd never used before. "Damn and blast the man! Has he ears everywhere?" He rode with haste to Gaius's office, all the time planning his excuses, then dismounted and tethered his horse to the rail outside. Once inside, he expected to find Gaius's new Adjutant and was astonished to find another very senior officer waiting for him. "I have an appointment with …", his voice trailed off as he realised something was seriously wrong. He looked around the office, the atmosphere was strained.

"You are Clodus?", asked the officer.

"Yes Sir. The Commander sent for me."

The officer then led Clodus into Gaius's office. Sitting at the desk was another officer very similar in appearance to Gaius.

"I have to tell you, Major, that your Commander has been taken seriously ill. We believe it is his heart."

'When did this happen?", asked Clodus.

"Three days ago", was the reply.

"That is not possible", said Clodus, "I saw him take the parade yesterday".

"No, you did not Major. You saw me impersonate him. With his uniform and horse and the excuse that the was suffering from a sore throat, I was able to get away with it. I used to impersonate him in the mess hall for fun. I never imagined I would have to do it for real!"

"The thing is, Major, it is very important that the Commander's illness is kept secret until a replacement can be brought here; for it is his name that keeps the peace in Dunbriton. This whole district is disciplined because of him. If it were suspected that he were not in charge, there are elements amongst the population who would take advantage of the situation to stir up trouble."

Clodus was still full of questions he wanted to ask. Such as, "Where is he? Why does he want to see me? What can I do?".

"We must not waste any more time, Major. We must go to him at once."

Gaius's double donned the Commander's helmet and cloak, then the three of them mounted their horses and rode off to Gaius's quarters, located in a small wooded area about half-a-mile away, but within the camp boundaries.

When Clodus was taken to the bedroom, he hardly recognised his Commander. It looked like him, but his power had gone. Gaius looked up at him, but did not speak until the others had left the room. "Come here and sit down". His breathing was laboured. "I want you to bring Father Joseph as quickly as you can. I have not much time left. Tell no one. If you bring him, it won't raise questions. I know I can trust you, Clodus. You are a good soldier and a fine officer. Now go - hurry please."

Clodus remembered what he had called Gaius earlier and felt guilty. He got up and hurried as fast as he could to Bonavon. Joseph was lecturing a class on his second most favourite subject, 'plants' when Clodus arrived and Alana, thinking he had came to see her, hurried towards him. "My dearest," he said, "I have come with an urgent message for the Father. Please fetch him". Alana, sensing his anxiety, quickly did as she was bid.

Father Joseph emerged looking worried, "What is it my son?".

"Don't ask. Just come", said Clodus.

Paulus brought Joseph's horse and his own to the yard. "Take my horse, Clodus", he said. "Yours is exhausted". He then helped Joseph to mount, the two then speeding off, leaving Alana and Paulus trying to peer through the cloud of dust raised by the horses' hoofs.

Clodus led Joseph to the house. They were allowed in by Gaius's servant, who took them to the bedroom, where the medical officer was bending over Gaius. He stood up as they entered and whispered to them, "He is waiting for you". Clodus told Joseph he would wait outside to escort him back to Bonavon, then he and the medical officer left the room leaving Joseph with Gaius.

When Joseph saw Gaius, slightly propped up in bed, he guessed why he had been sent for and he sat on the chair beside him. Gaius's breathing was laboured and speaking was difficult. "Father Joseph. Is that you?"

"Yes, my son. I came as quickly as I could."

"I want you to give me the blessings of your Jesus", said Gaius, "The rites of the Holy Church, if that is possible".

"Yes, my son. That shall be done".

"If you wish to confess to any sin, it is better if you release them. I have vowed never to reveal confessions made by anyone, for it is a sacred trust between me and our Father God."

Joseph listened carefully while Gaius confessed his sins, without indicating any grain of surprise or condemnation. Then, Gaius whispered that there was a list of names under his pillow. "Father. Write to your Bishop. Ask that the Church seek out these people and ask them to forgive me. There is also permission to open my vault at headquarters. All that I have, has to be divided between them."

Joseph took the list and put it safely in the money pouch attached to his belt. He had noted that all of the names were female, but made no comment.

"You are, my son, a man of the world. A man with huge responsibilities. You are also new to the Christian faith. Because of your unique position, I want to say something that I would not say to any other soul. I know that you have a conscience and seek forgiveness. And I could tell you that I forgive you and that our Father in heaven forgives you, for I believe that to be true. However, I believe also that a man must forgive himself and I tell you that life here upon earth is not so straightforward. I believe, my son that we are all part of a far greater plan, of which most of us remain ignorant. I want to remind you that the protection you have given me and my family has been invaluable and I have not forgotten your plan to escort me to the Highlands, which saved my life and that of my dear son. Your reputation has kept this whole area at peace, undoubtedly saving many lives and allowing many more to live in peace."

"For all the years you have been here, all who know you, are well aware that your reputation was contrived to keep order and no-one has been hurt who did not deserve to be. It has been a heavy burden you have carried."

"So, I say to you. Do not think harshly of yourself. You are most worthy of absolute forgiveness."

Gaius smiled. Joseph thought he wanted to say something and placed his ear nearer to his mouth, but there no sound. The medical officer came in and went to him. "He has gone", he announced. He saw the smile on Gaius's face. "I don't know what you told him, Sir, but whatever it was, he died happy."

There was some discussion as to how they could dispose of the body? The most senior officers wanted a grand military funeral, but thought they dare not risk it at the present time. "We don't want unruly elements raising riots."

Joseph suggested a simple Christian burial. "After all, Gaius had just received the rites of the Holy Church. For some time now, he has been interested in anything to do with Our Lord and I feel that he might well have chosen that, given more time. He could be moved at sundown to the church at Dunbriton and from there to the Christian burial ground near Alcluid, after a service among his civilian friends." The officers were amazed to learn that he had civilian friends and were pleased to hand over the responsibility to Joseph.

Within days, a very dignified procession left the church at Dunbriton.

Amongst the mourners were Joseph, who believed that he owed him his life; Sergaeus who was deeply saddened, remembering that without this great man's generosity, he would not have his Julia and his baby Helen or his beautiful home. Clodus felt guilt for accusing him of trying to prevent his marriage, when indeed, the poor man was on his deathbed. Calim, Harran and Calpurnius, as Councillors, recognised his value as a peace keeper. Paulus too was there, both to aid Joseph by carrying the lamp, but also in appreciation of his help. The six men carried the body on a special funeral cart to his burial place, where later, they placed a large carved stone, which said simply 'Antonius a Christian soul'.

Clodus and Alana decided to delay their marriage until a new Commander was installed - it seemed the right thing to do. The Legate was due for a visit and there would be questions to answer. Clodus wanted to be there to answer them and to ask one of his own.

Two months later he turned up, a plump man with a hearty laugh and an appetite to match. He beamed at Clodus, but his prying questions indicated a keen intellectual mind. He was no fool and as Clodus suspected, he wanted to know everything that had happened. He was delighted that Joseph had been protected, though a little surprised at how much Gaius had contributed to his distant cousin's safety and well-being.

He visited Bonavon and was pleased with what he saw there and he told Joseph, "I will report everything to your brother, the good Bishop." He looked around again smiling. "So, my friends, Calim and Harran had a hand in this. I will personally thank them for their hard work and generosity of spirit."

That Gaius was buried in a Christian grave came as a bit of a surprise, but then travelling around and meeting all sorts of people and situations, as he, the Ambassador did, he accepted it without too much comment. He assured everyone concerned that they had done the right thing, "After all", he said, "Gaius has no family in Gaul to receive the body".

"Before I leave, I will advise that the officer next in line for promotion should take Gaius's place, for it will take too long to send one from another camp."

Clodus asked him about the marriage laws for officers. The Legate laughed. "These old laws are well and truly out of date. Anyone within a year or two of leaving the Army can now marry, providing they want to stay put. It was decided some time ago that a man needs to prepare for civilian life." Then added, "About time, too. Men need their women. And the Army needs men. Unless the men marry and have sons, we could well run out of recruits". He laughed again as he glanced at the two ladies who had accompanied him. Clodus was pleased and could hardy wait to tell Alana.

At the end of a hectic day, he hurried back to Bonavon with the news. He picked Alana up and swung her around and kissed her. "At last, we can marry just as soon as Father Joseph can spare the time." Such happiness was a rare event for Alana and Clodus and their joy was shared by the rest of the family.

With their house almost ready to move into, they hurried to finish it, although as they married within the month, there was still quite a lot of work to do. "But what did that matter?" They were together.

Life for the inhabitants of Bonavon was exciting. There was always something going on; new houses being built; another classroom for the school and happy children running around. Joseph was busy, for every young couple wanted to be married in the little church and have their babies baptised at the font.

Clodus and Alana had their first son, whom they named Arnus.

CHAPTER XIII

PAULUS AND BLISS

Maun was growing fast, though still small for his age, but very lively and full of energy. Conchessa had to take him with her to the classroom when she was teaching the little ones and he was very good, sitting with the other children pretending to do lessons.

Paulus and Bliss were still very friendly, helping each other with the chores.

Bliss was busy in the kitchen one day, when her eldest son entered. He wanted to go fishing with his friends, who had all bought new nets from a local fisherman, who made them. Bliss told him she had no money left to buy such things. "There are more important things we need - like clothes to cover our backs! Think yourself lucky we are all well fed", she told him.

"All my friends have nets. I never get anything new. If I had a father, he would see that I got one, and would not be left out."

Bliss replied, "If your father had heard you speak to me in that way, more likely he would thrash you".

The boy stormed out banging the door behind him, straight into the path of Paulus who was coming to see what all the shouting was about. He grabbed the youth by his long hair and marched him back into the kitchen. Bliss was drying her eyes. "Now, say sorry to your mother."

"I'm sorry, mama", said her son. Another tug on his hair and he bent down and kissed her cheek.

Still holding on to his hair, Paulus took him outside. He was very angry. "We are men. We are supposed to take care of women. They are not as strong as us. It is a cowardly thing to take advantage of our strength and bully the very people who take care of us and cook and clean for us. Now go and never in your life let me hear you speak to your mother like that again." Only then did Paulus let go of him.

He went back into the kitchen where Bliss was working, but who still had tears in her eyes. "Don't worry about the lad. They are a bit stroppy at his age. He will grow out of it. If I were not a servant, I would take the place of his father gladly, if you wanted me to."

Bliss, still drying her eyes, stopped and looked around at him, "Do you really mean that Paulus?".

"Yes. I do. I would take good care of you."

"My dear Paulus", said Bliss, "That must be the strangest proposal of marriage ever and I would love to have you as my husband".

"Can I have a hug?", said Paulus. Bliss dried her hands on her apron and they held each other. "I will speak to my father and ask him to wed us."

Bliss stroked his face and kissed him. "I would like that very much."

Paulus wasted no time. He went in search of Joseph and found him about to enter his classroom. "Can I have a word, Father?"

"Certainly", said Joseph, "What can I do for you?".

"Father. I have been with you for a good many years now. What would you say if I asked you to allow me to marry?"

Joseph tried to appear surprised, but he and everyone in the household knew of the growing affection between Paulus and Bliss.

"Am I right in thinking that the bride would be my housekeeper - Bliss?"

"Yes Father. She has taken care of me ever since we returned from the Highlands injured."

Joseph winced at the memory. "Of course I will perform the service. It will give me the greatest of pleasure. Just tell me when you and Bliss are ready and congratulations my boy. I am so happy for both of you."

"Father. I am puzzled?"

"Oh!", said Joseph. "Why Paulus?"

"Well Father. If I marry Bliss, to whom do I give my first consideration?"

Joseph understood. Paulus was finding it difficult to divide his loyalties. He had been in service for so long and had always considered himself a servant, regardless of how often Joseph had told him he was like his son - indeed he had long since thought of him as his son. "My dear boy. Once you take a wife, she is your main responsibility. When my daughter married, she became the responsibility of Calpurnius. But, I never thought for one moment that she loved me the less. Nor did I love her less. Nor did it enter my head that things would change between us. I love her as I always have and she loves her father."

"I pray my son, that it will be the same with you and Bliss. When something wonderful, like a marriage happens in a family, it is a joy for all of us to share. We will all wish for your happiness. There is a home here for you for as long as you wish it. But, should it be that you want to alter your life and live elsewhere, then you are free to do so."

Paulus looked relieved. "Father. I was thinking of moving into Bliss's cottage. She needs me to keep her boys in hand. They are beginning to grow up and are now hard work." Joseph felt great pride in Paulus, for here he was displaying a great love of family life, when he'd had such a cruel start to his own life.

"My son", said Joseph. "I am so proud of you. I would consider it an honour if you would still take care of the horses once you are married. I have come to depend on your skill and judgement and if Bliss wishes to remain as housekeeper, I will be very happy."

"We have no desire to leave father, for we need our work. It is our way of life and although we have no part in the teaching of the children, it is wonderful to see them growing up from little urchins into educated, clever and confident young people."

"Why, thank you, Paulus for that compliment. It also pleases me to see them make progress."

Paulus was delighted that his remarks had pleased Joseph. "I will go now and tell Bliss. She will be relieved."

Joseph watched him hurry away towards the house and thought to himself, 'It has been a pleasure to see you develop into a responsible and hardworking man, my beloved son'.

CHAPTER XIV

THE DANCING BEAR

Conchessa, Calpurnius and Maun now had the house to themselves, save Bliss and her daughter who did the cooking and household chores. Joseph decided to move back in, as the small room at the church, although cosy, was lonely. Also, Maun was now running around, getting into mischief, but sleeping all night through. Now three years old, he was asking questions and seemed quick to learn. However, it was obvious that he was over sensitive and easily hurt by any suggestion of unpleasantness.

One day as the children were leaving school, a man arrived in the village with a bear. He banged on a drum and shouted, "Come and see the dancing bear!" and all the children rushed to look at the strange creature. Two little girls called to Conchessa. "Madam. May we take Mauny to see the dancing bear?"

"Yes", agreed Conchessa, "But watch him. Hold his hand".

"Yes, madam." Maun went with them cheerfully enough, but when he saw the bear with a ring on his nose attached to a chain, he began to cry, "I don't like it. He is not a happy bear".

The man got angry. "Take that child away. He is frightening my bear."

The little girls sadly took Maun back to Conchessa, "Madam Conchessa, Maun did not like the bear. He said it was not happy". Maun was sobbing. Conchessa had to explain that the bear was the man's way of earning money to feed both of them. But Maun would not be consoled.

When Calpurnius got home and Conchessa told him of the bear incident, at first he laughed, but then said, "In this world so full of sadness and death, I fear that our son is heading for a life of great pain".

CHAPTER XV

THE FARM

Two years passed, years that saw massive improvements in the standard of living in the village, the people becoming more self-assured, assertive and inventive. There were, however, one or two black spots, where it seemed as though enlightenment had not penetrated.

One of these was a farm, where several slaves were kept hard at work.

Joseph had approached the farmer's wife two years before and talked her into sending her eldest son to school, but for several days now he had not turned up. Joseph asked the other children if they had seen Eric? One boy answered with some relish. "Sir, we saw him working in the fields, as his father had beaten the slaves and they all ran away." Joseph was upset, for Eric was a bright pupil. So, he made up his mind to go up to the farm and try to persuade his parents to send him back to school.

Joseph rode the short distance to the farm and was not pleased with what he saw there. Slaves, dirty and frightened, peeped around doors at him timidly and a man's voice could be heard raised in anger.

Joseph knocked on the farmhouse door, which was opened by the farmer's wife, who looked very nervous. Joseph asked her if Eric was well, as they had missed him at school? Before she could reply, the farmer pushed her aside. "What do you want?" Joseph knew at once what the trouble was, for the farmer's breath smelled of alcohol. The smell from his breath and his clothes made Joseph stand back. "Eric is not going back to school. I need him here where he should be. I can't afford idle hands. Now get off my property before I throw you off."

Calpurnius had been away on Council business overnight and arrived home late the following afternoon. Joseph wasted no time in telling him about the previous nights events and Calpurnius decided to try and use his official status to see if he could change the farmer's mind.

Seeing Maun standing by the doorway waiting to greet him, he asked Paulus to lift the child up on to the horse. "Come on my boy, we will go for a ride to see the animals" and with that they rode off, Calpurnius holding firmly on to his excited son.

Once there, Calpurnius saw with his own eyes what Joseph had described. Clearly, desperate measures were required to solve a desperate situation.

The farmer came out of the house ready for a fight, but when he saw Calpurnius, he controlled his temper. Calpurnius smiled diplomatically, "Good evening, Sir. I wonder if I could look around your property? I am considering buying a farm and I hear your landlord is eager to sell. Oh! I am sorry Sir - allow me to introduce myself".

"No need", said the farmer abruptly. "I know who you are. And the farm is not for sale." Calpurnius dismounted and lifted Maun down. "May we look around?".

"I am sorry", said the farmer, "We are behind with our work due to some trouble with our workers".

Calpurnius appeared not to hear him and went on, "I am not surprised that you know nothing of the sale of this farm. I understand it is a recent decision to sell. I was looking for a smaller one, but this one is so much more conveniently situated, although I would not require so many slaves".

At that moment, the farmer's wife appeared, her youngest son 'Cedi' hanging on to her apron.

"Can I offer you a drink, Sir?"

"That would be much appreciated, for I came here directly from my office. Thank you kindly, Madam." The farmer was much relieved, for now he could avoid showing Calpurnius around his neglected buildings.

Once inside, Maun and Cedi sat on the mat playing with a small wooden horse. "You were saying Sir, that you would not require so many slaves. What would you do with them? This has been their only home. They have no other."

Calpurnius saw that the farmer seemed genuinely concerned. "I expect", said Calpurnius, "I would keep the men on the land and the women I would make responsible for the care of the small animals. The children I would send to school to prepare them for their freedom".

The farmer's wife, who was sitting quietly watching her son and Maun playing, raised her head and allowed a feint smile to cross her lips. "So, is that what this is all about?" She glanced at her husband, but he was so concerned about his farm, he had not noticed, as Calpurnius was so convincing, talking now about rotating crops and odd bits of farming jargon he'd picked up at his Council meetings.

When they left, it was as friends. The farmer, his wife and young Cedi waved them off.

The farmer was impressed. "That young fellow will be a far better landlord. He has some good ideas on how to run a farm. And he is right. We do not earn enough to feed so many mouths."

Back at the Mission, Joseph was delighted to hear that Eric would be returning to school next day and maybe, his younger brother as well.

"However did you manage it? He would not listen to me."

Calpurnius smiled a sly smile. "It is going to cost me, father. I told him I was about to buy his farm and become his new landlord."

Joseph was surprised. "I was unaware you had any such intentions."

Calpurnius replied. "I didn't, but, now I will have to see what I can do about it."

Next morning, Calpurnius was saddling his horse ready to go to town, when an old farm cart pulled up in the yard, the farmer's wife holding the reins. Beside her was Eric and in the back on a pile of straw, were four little children - Cedi and three of the slaves's children, two boys and one girl. On seeing Calpurnius, she approached him. "I must thank you, Sir. I am so glad you are going to be our new landlord."

"I am not yet so", said Calpurnius, "But, I can see that I will have to act quickly".

The farmer's wife looked at him pleadingly. "You know, Sir. My husband is not a

96

bad man. He was ill for a time and tried to do too much too soon. As a result, we all suffered. After you left last evening, he spoke of the difference it would make to have an understanding landlord who would take an interest in the workings of the farm. How it made good sense not to have so many mouths to feed and to prepare the slaves for their independence. He is a different man this morning. It's as if all his worries were lifted from his shoulders."

With help and advice from his father, Calim and his uncle Harran, Calpurnius bought the farm from the absent landlord and all of the children continued their education.

Maun and Cedi became best friends.

CHAPTER XVI

THE GOLDEN PONY

Over the next few years, it became clear that Maun was behind with his lessons. The other children of equal age raced ahead. He was bright and intelligent, but the written word proved difficult for Maun to comprehend. Conchessa reluctantly mentioned her worries to Calpurnius and Joseph. Both said he was still too young and he would most likely catch up with the others later on. Her father suggested she praise Maun more for the lessons he enjoyed and did well at.

But, as time passed Maun's attempts at reading and writing only improved slightly and he became aware that Cedi and the others were way ahead of him in their lessons. He began to feel inferior.

Maun was going on eight, when a terrible thing happened to two of his friends. Sisters - Emma and Carina - caught fever and died. Maun was devastated at their loss. He yelled at his mother through his tears, "You told me that God loved little children. Why has he taken my friends?".

Conchessa tried to console him by saying, "Sometimes, God calls his children home if he has another task for them to do". But, it was no good. He was inconsolable. No explanations were satisfactory. He was mourning the loss of his friends whose absence left a great gap in his life that no other could fill.

Several weeks went by and Maun attempted to get over his loss, but could be heard at night sobbing and he spent long periods in his room in silence.

One evening, Calpurnius arrived home and brought with him a golden pony - a truly beautiful animal. He spoke to Paulus confidentially, "Walk the pony around outside Maun's window and make sure he hears you. I know that a pony cannot make up for the loss of friends, but perhaps a new friend might help to take his mind from morbid thoughts".

Paulus understood. First he brushed the pony, saying as he did so, "You have a wonderful golden coat. First a brush, then I will take you for a walk". Eventually, Paulus's voice and the clip-clop on the cobbles of the pony's hooves penetrated Maun's gloom. He opened his small bedroom window and stuck his head out. On seeing the pony, his eyes opened wide.

"Paulus", he called, "Who does the pony belong to? Has father got a visitor?".

"To your first question, Master Maun, your father has not got a visitor and to your second question, I do not know to whom it belongs."

"You got that the wrong way round Paulus. You answered my second question first!"

Paulus smiled to himself and thought, "He might be slow to read, but he's sharp".

"Can I come and see him?", asked Maun.

"I expect it will be alright", said Paulus, "There's no one here".

Calpurnius was eating his supper and Conchessa pouring his wine, when Maun sped past them in a great hurry towards the door. "I think he's taken the bait", said Calpurnius.

"You can be sure he has", replied Conchessa, smiling, "Let us go and watch through the window in the kitchen."

Maun joined Paulus and the pony. He stood looking up at it. "He is very beautiful, Paulus. Do you think he would let me have a ride on his back?"

Paulus looked around him. "Well, young Mauny, there's no one here. I think we could risk a trot around the yard." He helped Maun up. "Now hold on tight and I will walk him around"; he did so, not once but several times. "I think that's enough now Mauny. We had better stop in case the owner comes back."

Calpurnius and Conchessa, watching from the window, realised that the ride was over. As Maun ran back towards the house, they hurried back to the dining room, as Maun came running in breathless, "Papa, do you know there is a pony in the yard?".

"Yes, my son I do. I brought him home."

"Who does he belong to Papa?"

"He does not belong to anyone at the moment. I have to sell him for a friend who's fallen on hard times."

"I have had a ride on his back Papa - Paulus let me", Maun said excitedly.

"That was very brave of you, my dear", said Conchessa, smiling at her son. "I did not know you could ride. Would you like to show us?" Maun took his mother's hand and rushed her outside, Calpurnius following. Paulus winked at Calpurnius, as if to say 'It worked', then he obliged by leading them around again.

"Well, well", said Calpurnius (in an attempt to sound surprised). "Now that I know you can ride, maybe I won't sell him after all. Maybe, I will keep him for you Mauny."

Maun was beside himself with excitement. "You mean I can have him?"

"On one condition, my son. That you learn to look after him properly and do not expect Paulus to do it for you."

"I will Papa. I promise."

Once alone, Conchessa remarked how it pleased her to see a smile on her son's face again. "Yes", said Calpurnius, "Hopefully he will be so busy taking care of the pony, he won't have time to brood".

That evening, father and son went riding. Through the village and along the road, then home again by way of the river bank. Maun was very proud riding beside his father and happy that at last he was good at something - and his father could be proud of him.

In their bedroom, next to Maun's, Conchessa again said, "How wonderful it was to see their son happy again".

Calpurnius laughed, "Seeing Mauny ride today, reminded me of my own first pony. I thought I was so grown up. One day I rode into town, my head held high. When I heard Portia and Julia call, 'Yoohoo, Calpurnius, Yoohoo'. I was annoyed, for they were not my most favourite people at that time. They had been in town collecting new dresses. I stopped and asked - most ungraciously - 'What do you want?'. 'Don't be like that cousin, we are family after all', said Portia. 'More's the pity', said I (under my breath). 'Anyway', said Portia, 'The dressmaker said to tell Aunt Rhona that her dress has been repaired and she will call at the villa tomorrow to deliver it. Will you tell your mother?'. 'I suppose so', I said, not that I intended to discuss anything so unmanly as dresses with anyone. They carried on chatting and giggling, until I insisted I had to go. I had not gone far, when I noticed that everyone who passed smiled at me, some even laughed. I thought, 'How friendly everyone is today'. It was not until I got home and dismounted, that I discovered a pink flower and a ribbon tied to my saddle. Then I knew what had amused Julia so much".

"That was not a very nice thing to do", said Conchessa, "And I thought your cousins were kind and helpful girls".

Calpurnius repeated, "Kind and helpful? Not to me! As far as I was concerned, they were to avoided at all cost. There was the time, when they convinced me that a very pretty girl liked me and wanted to meet me. I should not have trusted them, but I hoped it might be true, so I agreed to meet her. The girl who came to meet me, was the biggest, and strongest girl I had ever seen. She came rushing towards me. 'You came. You came. Julia said you would.' She hugged me so tight I thought my bones would break. I had an awful time trying to get rid of her".

Conchessa looked up at her husband's face and simply said, "Oh!".

Calpurnius remembered how possessive his wife was and it crossed his mind that he should not have mentioned being attracted to another girl, even though it happened several years ago. Feeling annoyed at his own lack of tact, he left the room, but stood on the other side of the door, cursing himself for being an insensitive fool. Then he heard Conchessa giggle, then she laughed louder. He opened the door and looked in. Conchessa was sitting on the bed, arms folded over her stomach, bent over laughing, tears running down her face, She looked up at him and made an effort to control her giggles. "So, Miss Conchessa, this is what you do when my back is turned, you laugh at your poor husband's misfortunes."

"My love", said Conchessa, "It's just that I never thought of you as being the object of your cousins' pranks. How they must have enjoyed seeing you with their large friend".

"Yes", said Calpurnius, "The joke was supposed to be on me but, when their friend discovered she had been used as a joke, she was none too happy. Uncle Harran gave them a lecture and they lost several months dress money. So, in the end, I had the last laugh".

Maun, who was tucked up in bed next door, heard his parents laughing. He snuggled down under his covers and thought about his golden pony asleep in his stable and his very special mother and father next door. "I am lucky", he thought.

And for the next few years, they were all happy.

As the years passed, Calpurnius attempted to interest Maun in local government service. He talked to him of the need to take an interest in political matters, but his efforts were in vain, Maun was not interested. Instead, he spent all of his spare time at the farm with Cedi and Eric. Calpurnius had always hoped that his son would follow in his footsteps. Now he was certain that it would not happen and he found it difficult to hide his disappointment.

There were no slaves at the farm now. The old ones had died. The women stayed to help Cedi's mother with the house and the care of the small animals, but after the day's work, they went to their own homes in the village.

And all the children went to school.

The slave children who joined school at the same time as Cedi, now all worked as bakers, shoemakers, carpenters and some were studying to become teachers. They were free to do as they pleased.

Maun loved the animals and if one fell sick he and Cedi would sit with it.

On one such occasion, he forgot the time. Fooled by the light of the summer evenings so far north, he and Cedi were discussing a sick sheep and trying to decide on the best treatment, when Calpurnius and Joseph arrived.

They were worried and angry. "We thought you would be here. Don't you realise how late it is?"

"Your mother is frantic with worry."

Surprised and hurt, Maun stood up. "I am sorry, I was not aware of the hour, but why should mother be so worried when she knows where I am?"

"Come along", said Joseph, "You have missed your meal and you must be starving".

"Your mother has a right to be worried, for since the fort was closed and the guards left, there are more strangers and robbers arriving in the district. You must be more careful."

Maun got on his pony and the three rode home in silence. But, anger rose in his heart. He felt he was old enough at fourteen to be trusted and treated like a man. So, when they arrived home, he let go his pent-up feelings and yelled at his father, "When I am at home, all I hear is praise for pupils who do well. The only people you care about are those who read or write well. I am no good at anything, except caring for the animals. They like me for what I am. The cows don't care if I can read, nor do the sheep if I can write. Why don't you leave me be?". He then ran to his room and shut the door noisily.

Calpurnius and Conchessa realised how it must have been for Maun and felt ashamed that in praising others, they had isolated their own son.

Joseph approached his daughter and Calpurnius and simply patted her shoulder. "Don't worry my dear. I will go and speak to him."

He knocked on Maun's bedroom door. "It's me, Mauny. Your grandfather. Can I come in?"

"The door is open", called Maun, "Come in, if you want to".

"My boy, we were so worried that you could have fallen from your pony, or been set upon. Ever since the fort was disbanded and the guards withdrawn, our area has become more dangerous and whether you believe it or not, we all love you very much."

"Do they really, grandfather? It does not seem like that to me at times."

Joseph looked around Maun's room, then asked, "Have you a spare seat in here? It is late and I am tired".

"I am sorry, grandfather. I did not think. Come here and sit beside me."

Joseph sat on the edge of Maun's bed and spoke softly. "You do not really feel jealous of the children who do well at school, my boy - do you?"

"I don't suppose so, grandfather. It's just that father and mother always lavish praise on others and I can do nothing right. When did you last hear them praise me? Believe me, grandfather. I have tried to make them proud of me, but they never seem to notice and now tonight I have been made to look foolish in front of Cedi."

"My dear boy", said Joseph, "Your mother and father's only sin is in taking you for granted. They believe that you love them, no matter what, as they love you. They lavish praise on the other children because these little ones receive so little and it is so important. You know Mauny, life for so many, is very short and it is important never to grudge anyone their achievements, for that may be all they will ever get from their lives - the only good thing to happen to them". Maun remembered his friends who died so tragically with fever and understood what his grandfather was trying to tell him.

"I want to tell you something else that I have never told anyone before - not even your mother."

"What is it grandfather?", asked Maun, as he moved closer to listen.

"When I was a boy, all I ever heard from my father was how wonderful my elder brother was - how proud he was of him. Believe me Maun, I was tired of hearing it, for you see my boy, I was just like you - *my* reading and writing were just as bad as yours, which is why I took to growing things. The plants and trees never expected me to do anything, but feed and water them. I am afraid Mauny, you take after me - we are two of a kind."

"But grandfather", protested Maun, "You had to be clever to become a priest".

Joseph shook his head. "No, my boy. That came to me later in life, when I did not worry so much about being a poor scholar. Martin helped me some and he would always say, 'Little brother, have faith, take one day at a time, for Our Lord is patient'. So, that is what I did. I put my faith in God and took a day at a time. By trusting in God that he would help me, I found the strength to go on."

Maun saw his grandfather in a new light. "Have you always believed in God, grandfather? Was there never a time when you doubted?"

Joseph eyed his grandson. "Why, of course, there were times when things happened. Times like when your grandmother Alicia died, without even having the joy of holding her baby. That Mauny, was my hell on earth. That was when I called out loud to my God for help. And do you know what he did? He sent me all the way to the city of Tours to my brother. The brother I had been jealous of was God's answer to my prayer. Now, I never doubt and neither should you."

Maun smiled. "I hope, grandfather, I grow up just like you."

"Then", said Joseph, "You can start now. For I never go to sleep until I have settled my quarrels".

Come on. Let us say good-night and God bless to your mother and father".

CHAPTER XVII

THE FISH POND

Some months later, a Councillor who had just returned from a journey abroad, told Calpurnius of a strange thing he had seen - a fish breeding pond!

"You simply make a large pool near a river and allow pipes to channel the river water in and out of it. Put in some fish and special food and they will breed."

It worked too well. There were far too many fish. So many in fact, that they could not give them away. What fish the people required, they preferred to catch the traditional way. So, the pond was made redundant. A victim of its own success.

The pond, a big oblong hole lined with mortar and small pebbles, lay unused until the scorching hot months of high summer, when the children discovered the disused pool, full of wonderful cool water.

It became a gathering place for the children after school. They splashed and shouted. Maun discovered he had a talent for clowning. He would walk along the edge of the pool, pretend to trip over his own foot and fall in with a great splash; or run at great speed from a long way off and keep running in mid-air, until he fell in. The children loved it and would shout, "Do it again, Mauny".

Later in the evenings, it was time for the older children to meet their friends there; boys and girls of Maun's age would learn to swim; Cedi, Arnus, Anna and many more, splashed about making more noise than the little ones.

Conchessa and Calpurnius watched them from an upstairs window and remarked on their son's talents. "If only he was half as good a scholar as he is a clown". There was sadness in Calpurnius's voice, for he always had ambition for his son to follow him into government service. Now, he did not know where Maun's future lay? It was a puzzle to him how Maun could be so bright, yet have such poor writing skills. "Don't worry so much Calpurnius", said Conchessa, "As you say, he is bright and intelligent and will find his own way". Maun was sensitive to his father's concerns and knew of his disappointment at his lack of interest in his political world and in his poor reading and writing ability. He had tried hard to improve them and had some success, but still not good enough to please Calpurnius. 'I'm a dunce,' he thought, but then he remembered his grandfather and the secret talk they had had and he cheered up.

The happy evenings by the swimming pool allowed Maun to forget his problems, at least for a little while.

One evening, Calpurnius watched them from an upstairs window. Maun, Cedi, Sophia and Anna were chasing each other and screaming. Having great fun. Returning to Conchessa downstairs, he remarked that he would have to cut away some of the trees and bushes in order to get a better view of the pool and make sure that the children were safe. Conchessa laughed. "My dear. I don't know about being able to see them - they can be heard miles away!"

They were talking of the day's work and preparing new lessons, when Calpurnius suddenly looked up. "What is it?", asked Conchessa.

"I cannot hear them. It is much too quiet." He leapt from his chair and fled out of the house and down towards the pool, Conchessa at his heels. On reaching it, there was no sign of anyone. They called out frantically, "Don't play games, Mauny. Come out from wherever you are". But, there was no reply.

Joseph and Paulus came in answer to Calpurnius's shouting. They walked the length of the river bank, but found nothing. "Maybe they have gone to the farm, or to Anna's house?"

But, they all knew in their hearts that something was desperately wrong. Their worst fears were confirmed when Paulus emerged from the bushes carrying a club covered in blood. His face was deathly white. "There are signs of a struggle and marks on the bank where grappling hooks have been fixed."

Calpurnius was stunned. He could not take in the dreadful news.

Conchessa clung to her father, crying, 'Tell me it isn't true?" and Joseph had to lead her back to the house - she was clearly in a state of shock.

Calpurnius was running up and down the river bank demented, still calling his son's name in the vain hope he would turn up safe. But, Maun was gone. So were Sophia, Anna and Cedi - taken by persons unknown.

For weeks, all the family, Calim, Harran, Clodus, Sergaeus and many of their friends rode along the banks of the Clyde, looking for strange boats. They found nothing. As the weeks turned to months, all hope of finding their sons and daughters alive faded.

The village was silent. Gloom and mourning touched everyone. The school closed, though Joseph kept the church open for the villagers to pay their respects. Many came to say how sorry they were and offered help. However, there were others who were surprised that such a thing could happen to Christians. "I thought your God protected you from evil", they said.

Conchessa and Calpurnius were inconsolable. Devastated, no deed or word could lift their spirits. Joseph tried to remind them of their duties, but they simply raised their heads slowly and looked at him, as though he was a complete stranger. Their whole beings were consumed in such terrible grief and guilt, for they blamed themselves for not being vigilant enough.

The silence of the village indicated the horror of what had happened. Children were not allowed out to play, in case the kidnappers returned.

Joseph went to his alter to pray, as he had done every day since Maun was taken, but his beloved church did not offer him solace, for there were too many memories there. He kept thinking of how he and Calpurnius waited there on the night Maun was born. So, in desperation he grabbed his long warm cloak from the hook and left.

He climbed the Old Bonfire Hill, until he came to the site of the Sacred Bonfire, beside the now deserted fort that Gaius had built for his protection.

He sat on the stone for a while, trying to compose himself.

Then he stood up and looked up to Heaven, tears streaming down his face. With his arms held out, palms upward, he called out loud:

"Blessed Father in Heaven.
You know that I love you and trust you with my life, but my heart is breaking and my faith sorely tried.
From this Bonfire Hill, I plead with your angels to find my grandson and his friends and bring them home.
Almighty God, make me strong, for I cannot crumble before my daughter.
She needs my strength and my faith and I need your strength.
I need yourhelp."

Having spoken these words, Joseph sat again on the large stone. He felt empty and alone. After a while, there came upon him a feeling of stillness where no sound was heard, but a haze fell around him. It was as though he had been granted a few moments of peace. Then he felt a kiss on his lips, then another on his forehead. He opened his eyes and in the haze he saw the beautiful face of Alicia, his long dead wife, only she was not dead, but very much alive. He whispered her name softly, "Alicia, my love. You have come to comfort me".

She smiled. "I have never left you, or our little girl. I have always been close."

"I have a message for you. Our grandson will come home."

"When?", asked Joseph. "What can I tell his mother?", but his question remained unanswered, as though Alicia knew nothing of time.

Then, just before her vision faded, she said, as though in triumph, "With the snowdrops".

As soon as the vision and the feeling of stillness and timelessness left him, Joseph felt a cool air and a returning sense of reality. He stood up and looked over the ancient valley. He remembered the very first time he came here and listened to the story of Ysu. He wondered then why he had been called back here. Now he knew. The workings of God were mysterious indeed.

He made his way down to the house with a lightened heart, for he had seen Alicia and her message that Maun would be home in the spring, renewed his strength and his faith. That was what he had asked for and that was exactly what he was given.

PART III

SLAVERY

CHAPTER XVIII

SLAVERY

Maun lay in the bottom of a rowing boat unconscious, his head in a pool of blood. Water swished about mingling with the blood, carrying a little of it away from time to time. Anna and Sophia were terrified. They were at the other end of the boat sitting close together, their hands tied, in front of them. They were crying and calling out, "Take us home. We want to go home". The six men rowing were muttering to themselves and showing signs of irritability. Cedi sat on the seat nearest Maun, his hands and feet were tied with strips of rag, but unlike the girls, his hands were behind his back. He was now fully conscious and looked around, taking stock of their situation. He looked out of the boat to see where they were and realised that they were being rowed to a ship anchored not very far off. He struggled with the ties and feeling the rotten material give way, he quickly freed his hands. His captors were facing Anna and Sophia and he moved himself to the edge of the seat, pulled himself up, then slithered snake-like over the side. The men stopped rowing when they heard the splash. Two of them rushed to look over the side, but there was no sign of Cedi, as he had hid under the boat. Waiting there until it moved off again, he swam to the nearest land, in the hope that he could raise the alarm. However, he quickly discovered that the land was an island and that it was deserted.

Their captors were cursing now more than ever. They were not happy about the young girls, who were screaming, for now that Cedi had gone and Maun was still unconscious, they felt even more vulnerable and in terrible danger.

The next thing Maun remembered was being dragged off the ship and thrown on to a cart, then a very long journey along a rough track.

He had never felt so bad; pain consumed his whole body and he was unbelievably cold. Eventually, they stopped at a farmhouse and again, he was dragged from the cart and taken inside. A woman placed some food in front of him, but he was too sick and frightened to eat. He was then taken away from the house and forced to walk up a slope where cattle were grazing. He saw an animal shelter with straw on the floor and one of the men indicated for him to go in. When he did not move fast enough, he was pushed in and the door closed behind him, Maun then crawled into the straw and sank into unconsciousness again.

He was awakened at dawn by the farmer, who led him outside and indicated that he had to watch the cattle to prevent them from straying. Then he was left alone dressed only in his swimming tunic and shorts. He had no idea where he was, or how far he was from home. He found a stream nearby, an outpouring from a natural spring a little further up the hill. He forced himself to first douche his face with the cool water, then cup his hands and drink. He felt only mildly better and he realised that his mouth was bruised and swollen and the wound on his head was still throbbing; his hair soaked in clotted blood.

He wandered around exploring his surroundings. There was not much to see, only the farmhouse down in the slope about quarter of a mile away. 'If only I were not so hungry and cold', he thought as he went back to the hut, crawled into the straw and shivered. 'Where was he?', he wondered. 'Not in Gaul. They spoke Latin there. Maybe, he was in the Highlands? There was no way of knowing'. Tiredness eventually overcame him and he sank into a restless sleep.

Next day was the same. He got out of the hut, drank some water and douched his face, then went for a walk amongst the grazing cows. The woman appeared again, bringing him a piece of meat and some bread and he searched her face, hoping to see a hint of sympathy or pity in her eyes. There was none and he thought that, 'She was as miserable as the stale bread she brought'. Nonetheless, Maun ate the bread, but was immediately sick again.

The third day was the same, only this time the bread stayed down and he hoped it would make him feel better. Again, the woman left without a word.

Most of the time he spent curled up in the straw, just trying to keep warm. The pain in his head and other wounds in his mouth made it difficult for him to think clearly. But, if Maun was sick and utterly miserable, he had worse to come - much worse! Next day, the farmer came and took him down to the house. There was another man there. He spoke in Latin, "Your new master and mistress have been good to you. They have allowed you to rest after your journey. They expect you to repay them with hard work from now on". Then he explained Maun's duties to him: hard work from dawn till dusk; everything from milking the cows to cleaning out the stables. There would be no slacking.

He was to take the place of the farmer's two sons, who had been called to serve in the Army of King Drufus. "You do understand that you are now a slave and have to bear the mark of one". It was then that the farmer emerged from the stables with a branding iron. Maun caught a glimpse of it and tried to get away, but the stranger and the woman held him. He did not have the strength to fight. Maun screamed as the hot iron burned into his arm. There was the horrible smell of burning flesh and Maun's body shuddered. He then blacked out. When he woke up, he was lying in the hut next to the animal shelter on cold straw. A handcart was nearby and he guessed they had brought him up on that and dumped him in the hut.

All he could think of was his burning arm. He struggled up and went to the stream. Too weak to do anything else, he lay down and held his arm under the cold running water, which gave him a little comfort. As he lay there, he suddenly remembered his grandfather and the stories he had told of Christ's suffering.

He began to weep. "My Lord Jesus. Now I am suffering as you did. Have some pity. I am ashamed that for so long I had forgotten you. If you can, help me to survive so that I can see my mother again and all my loving family."

From that moment on, Maun made up his mind that he would live. No one had the right to take his life. He went about his work automatically. With his every breath he prayed, 'Thank you Lord for that breath. Thank you Lord for allowing me to walk and to move. Thank you Lord for my life and for the food I eat'. He never stopped giving thanks. Always his mind was on Jesus or his grandfather, as he remembered his words, "Now I never doubt and neither should you". These words stayed with him. There were some things in his favour; his experience of caring for and his great love of animals. The farmer noticed this and as a reward gave him a little more food, also he could drink as much milk as he wanted. Things began to look up for him, although he was still miserable and home-sick. But, as the warm days of summer turned to autumn, followed by a bitter cold winter, Maun became ill. For several weeks he had been sleeping in the stables, gaining warmth from the horses. A bundle of rags had been thrown out and he found amongst them a warmer shirt and the rags he tied around his feet. But, they were not enough to save him from the cold and ward off the damp of the winter. He gasped for breath and his lungs felt as though they would burst from his body.

Maun was made to watch as the farmer killed a pig and then drink some of the still warm blood. The farmer then instructed Maun to do the same, but he found it so revolting, that he vowed he would never eat pig flesh again. The farmer laughed at him and went into the house, no doubt to sit by his peat fire. Maun did not return to the stable. With what seemed to him his last breath, he went to the animal shelter and sank into the straw, the frostbite on his toes, making him writhe in agony. His lungs were burning. Then a strange feeling of peacefulness came over him and his pain began to subside. Warmth filled his body. "So, this is what it is like to die," he prayed, "Thank you Father for releasing me".

When morning came, the farmer and his wife came to see why Maun had not turned up for work. They looked into the hut and saw the pathetic little body curled up in the straw. The farmer uttered in his own language, "He's a goner. Didn't have any stamina".

"What are you going to do with the body?", asked his wife.

He shook his head. "Can't bury him, the grounds too hard. Leave him and let the wolves have him."

"What a waste of good money he was", said the woman.

"Oh! I don't know", replied her husband, "He did well with the animals". They walked away leaving the rotting door swinging open in the cold winter wind.

CHAPTER XIX

MEETING THE MASTER

Maun was close to death when he heard someone call his name, "Maun. Maun. Wake up". He grudgingly half opened his eyes. His vision was hazy, but he could just make out two bare feet and the hem of a garment He looked up and saw a man bending over him. He noticed his kind face and gentle manner. "Give me your hand and I will help you up. Don't worry, It won't hurt this time."

Maun was helped to his feet, but was puzzled. "Where am I?", he asked.

The man was walking away. He turned round. "Come", he said, "We will stop soon. I want to show you something".

They entered a room, but a very strange one. The walls were not solid but appeared to be translucent.

The man sat down on a bench and invited Maun to sit beside him. "Now to answer your question. You are now in a state of being between one world and another. From here we can view people on earth." The man pointed to one of the walls. "Look over there, Maun." The wall cleared to show Maun's home, the Mission school at Bonavon. The picture then showed Conchessa waving goodbye to the little children after school. She then went to her bedroom, her expression changing to that of deep sadness. She knelt by her bed and prayed. "Sweet Jesus, take care of my beloved son."

Maun then watched as the picture changed and he saw his father ride home from his Council meeting and stop at the trough to let his horse drink. It was his favourite view that usually gave him a great deal of pleasure. But, not this day. Calpurnius, looking older and so tired prayed, "God Almighty. I ask you bring my son home - my life is empty without him".

Maun saw that both his mother and father had colours around them and asked, "What were they?".

"They are the colours of their thoughts. The light of the soul." The man in the robe, now told Maun to look at the other wall. As the picture came into view, Maun caught his breath as he recognised his grandfather, but not as he had ever seen him in life. All around his body was bright swirling light and around his head a golden halo, like the sun illuminating his bedroom. Maun looked up at the face of the man, who smiled back at him. "Your grandfather is a very special soul. He has faith in 'The Father'. He asked for you to be sent home and believed. He now awaits you. Call on him."

Maun called out, "Grandfather". Joseph did not respond.

"Go closer Maun, right up close."

Maun moved towards the light and called again. This time Joseph heard. He looked up from his prayers and smiled broadly as he recognised his grandson and his companion as clearly as life. "Tell him you are on your way home," instructed

115

the man.

"I don't know how grandfather, but I am coming home. Tell mama and papa that I love them." Then, as the picture faded, they heard Joseph say, "'Thank God".

"Now for some instructions, for we have to help you reach home and it is a long way. So pay attention Maun." The screen lit up to show a wide landscape. Maun looked and recognised the farmhouse and the surrounding land. He saw a ship in a distant harbour. "That ship will take you over the sea to your own country. You will encounter many difficulties on the way. However, we will be watching over you", said the man.

"Sir", said Maun, "You said 'we' will watch over you, but I see only you".

The man in the robe put his hand on Maun's shoulder, turned him around and pointed. What he saw was almost unbelievable. There were two beautiful angels, neither male or female, pouring streams of light into his dead body as it lay in the shelter.

"What are they doing to my body?", he asked.

"They are restoring it. Replenishing it with the life force. Making it well again."

Maun was horrified. "You don't want me to go back into my body again? Oh, No! Please, I could not bear that pain again."

The man was quick to reassure him. "Do not concern yourself. I promise you there will not be any pain. We have made sure of that. You have asked to see your family again and your prayers are being answered. Besides, we have need of it. You have work to do, very special work and you will be helped. Now, you must look below and observe the journey from the shelter to the ship. The distance is great, but the angels will stay with you all the way."

At this point, the man held Maun's face between his hands and spoke with great tenderness, "Go now my son, back into the world and take with you the Love, Light and Truth of Heaven. Never be afraid, for the Angels of the Lord are with you".

CHAPTER XX

THE ROAD HOME

The next thing Maun knew, was hearing the door of the shelter banging in the cold winter breeze His body was cold, but not unbearably so. He moved cautiously, turning his head to look at the door. Then he arose from the straw bed and walked. He looked outside; there was a thin layer of snow on the ground. Then the enormity of his experience hit him. The most wonderful, tremendous, feeling of elation and happiness overwhelmed his whole being. *'I am going home!'* Then he heard a voice in his head say, 'What are you waiting for?'. He ran from the shelter, further up the slope, through a fence and just kept on running. The rags that had bound his feet loosened and so he removed them. Now barefoot, he continued his journey, instinctively following the way he was shown in the visions. Maun covered mile after mile, day after day. Eventually, he climbed a hill and at the summit he looked over and saw the harbour and sure enough, there was the ship - as promised.

Maun's heart was pounding and he moved as quickly as he could until he reached the ship.

There were several sailors on deck working and two were on the quay, bartering over the price of a very large dog. One of the sailors on deck spotted Maun and nudged the other to look at the strange sight, for Maun did look odd. Practically naked, a mop of matted hair that no longer looked fair and seemingly oblivious to the bitter cold.

The men on the quay, bartering with the trader, were Captain Bruner and his next-in-command, who was simply known as 'Chief', both old friends and shipmates having sailed on the same ship for many years.

They had a customer in Gaul who was willing to pay a high price for a giant hunting dog from Hibernia. However, the Captain was reluctant to take aboard his ship several dogs. He could not tolerate the barking, or the smell of them, "Heaven knows, the men were bad enough". He wanted only the one pregnant bitch. That way, he would pay for one dog only and deliver several, although he knew he was taking a risk, not knowing if the father of the puppies would be of the same breed!

Eventually the bartering ended, the Captain agreeing to pay an extra keg of wine. They shook hands and Chief shouted to the men on deck, "Tell Evan to bring two casks".

Evan was the biggest and strongest man in the crew. He walked down the gangway with one cask on his shoulder and another under his arm and lowered them on to the trader's donkey cart. The trader then handed the dog lead to Evan and the three men walked toward the gangway with the unhappy hound.

Evan spotted Maun, who had now moved nearer to the gangway. He drew the Captain's attention to him. "What do you want, lad?", asked the Captain.

"Sir", said Maun, "I want you to take me home".

Captain Bruner was surprised to hear Maun speak with a high-bred Latin accent. "Where is your home, young man?" asked Bruner.

"My home is at Bonavon, near the town of Dunbriton."

Chief was about to ask him how he came to be so far from home, but then noticed the snake-like brand on his arm - the mark of a slave! "Sir. I was taken from my home by bandits. Now I must find my way home. My mother is crying for me."

Evan had to hide his face. He was an emotional man, with a family of his own and he and the Captain exchanged glances. "You can come aboard, if you have the money for your fare", Chief told him.

Maun was crestfallen. "Sir. I have no money."

"In that case", said the Captain hesitantly, "You will have to work your passage".

"I will work, Sir. I will work hard", pleaded Maun.

"Right then. You can take charge of the hound", said the Captain. Evan handed over the hound to Maun and he proudly walked on board.

Evan became distressed every time he saw Maun's malnourished body and painful sores, now in the process of healing. It was obvious he had suffered terrible deprevation. The Captain called Evan aside. "The lad is in charge of the dog. I put you in charge of both of them. See that they are well fed and made comfortable." Then he said in a louder voice, "See that the hound has sheepskins to sleep on" and, in case his crew should think him soft, he added, "She is a valuable dog. We must take care of our investment!".

"When did you last eat, boy?", Evan inquired.

Maun had to think. "Maybe two or three days ago, I cannot remember".

"Then we had better visit the galley and see what our cook can spare - for you and the hound." They left the galley with a bowl of meat scraps, some water and some bread and cheese for Maun.

Evan watched as Maun tried to swallow the food, but it was as if his body had forgotten how to eat. Evan went back to the galley and returned with some warm milk. "Here you are lad. Try and get that down you. You should be able to swallow it more easily."

Maun accepted the milk gratefully. "Thank you very much, Sir."

Evan laughed heartily. "I'm not 'Sir'. I'm a sailor. Just like you are now." They laughed. "Call me Evan. That's my name. What do folks call you?".

"My name is Maun, but my friends call me Mauny" and with that, Evan smiled and shook him by the hand.

Below deck, there was a large cage which was normally used for transporting animals. However, Evan decided that for this hound, the cage wasn't necessary, as the bitch was large and docile and seemed content in their company. Evan then removed her muzzle, saying, "I don't like them things, they are not natural". He then gently ran his large fingers over the dog's head and scratched her neck. He placed the bowl of scraps in front her and when this was finished in record time, he then poured some water into the same bowl.

One of the other crew members came over. "I've brought this for you. I seem to have grown out of it." He handed over a rather good grey shirt.

Maun thanked him, stripped off the ragged one he was wearing and put it on. "It's a bit big for you lad", said Evan, "But hopefully, you will begin to put on a bit of weight now". Evan then went to look for some sheepskins. He had seen Maun stripped to the waist and he had never in his life seen anyone so thin. He thought of his own sons. When he last saw them, Adam, his eldest was nearly as big as himself, yet from what he could gather, Maun was the same age. "If I ever get hold of these slavers, I will cheerfully wring their cowardly necks. How could they treat a young boy like that?"

Evan made his way back on deck, loaded with a great pile of skins and spread them near the ring post on which the dog's lead was fixed, then he placed around her some protective bales. The hound did a few turns around until she found a position to her liking, then flopped. Watching the dog make itself comfortable, Maun thought how much he would have appreciated these skins at the farm.

"You take over now, Maun", said Evan, "For we are about to cast off and I am needed below. You watch her carefully in case she gets worried when the ship moves off". However, he was gone only a few moments before he returned, carrying some leggings and boots. "Try them on lad. They are not grand, but at least they will keep you warm. It gets bitter cold at sea. I couldn't find you a coat, but maybe this will do for now" as he handed Maun a thick woollen blanket, "Put that around you".

Maun wrapped it around his shoulders, it felt warm and comforting. "Thank you, Evan. You are very kind."

"Never mind all that", said Evan, slightly embarrassed, "I've got sons of my own. I would like to think people would look after them if they got into trouble. Now, I had better hurry".

The ship was carrying a full cargo, so there was very little space below decks for another bed roll. Captain Brunar scratched his chin, "The only space on board is in my office, under my map table. That will have to do until room can be found below, I can't have the boy sleeping on deck".

All the crew, except the Captain and Maun, went below to row the ship out to sea until the wind could fill the sails.

After they had been at sea for a while, the crew returned on deck and Maun looked around for Evan, but there was no sign of him. Chief saw him and came over, "Looking for Evan?".

Maun nodded. "I have not seen him since we sailed."

Chief did not appear very happy. "I think he is with the medical orderly. Seems he cut himself on a rusty nail some days ago and the wound is beginning to bother him. I expect he will arrive soon."

The orderly examining Evan's hand was worried. "I don't like the look of it. All I can do is bandage it up and hope it does not get worse before we reach the Lorne. The sooner you see a real doctor the better."

"Is there such a thing as a doctor in that lonely place?"

"We had better hope there is", said the orderly. Evan was very worried. He had seen men with similar wounds during his years at sea and he had heard that when a limb changed colour and puffed up, it was very dangerous. The men he'd seen, had all died terrible deaths.

"You won't be able to work", said the orderly. "I will go and speak to the Captain."

Evan joined Maun on deck. He was sitting on a bale, talking to the dog, his woollen blanket around his head and clutching it under his chin.

Evan had decided to say nothing about the wound, unless he was asked. He did not want everyone feeling sorry for him and so they tied some rags into a tight ball and played with the hound. "How is your hand Evan? Chief told me you went to see the doctor."

"I wish he were a doctor, Maun. He's just an orderly. He is very good on most things that bother sailors, but there are some things that only a doctor can fix."

The Captain arrived and told Evan that he could rest the following day. "It will be quiet anyway and you can stay here and help look after the hound." He looked at Evan's hand, the skin was taut and underneath looked purple and yellow. "Let us hope there is a physician at the Lorne", said the Captain.

Evan was a strong man, but secretly he was filled with terror. He did not want to die at sea. He longed to see his wife and sons again and now he feared that would never be.

He said to Maun, "In a while, you will hear the cook call the crew to supper, If you take the dog with you, he will most likely have something for her. I don't think I will eat tonight. It's been a long day".

Maun took the hound and went to the galley, where they had to crush in to the limited space and suffer some good humoured remarks about the dog's smell.

"Hurry up and feed the animal and get him out of here. He's putting me off my supper", said one of the crew.

Maun replied, "She's a lady dog and needs her food".

"Yes", said another, "It looks like she's eating for ten!". Nonetheless, each man gave her a morsel from his plate.

"Where is Evan?", someone asked.

"He said he was not hungry and has gone to rest for a while", said Maun.

"He must feel bad", said one of the men, "It's not like Evan to miss a meal".

Chief came to see Maun. "Do you know where you have to sleep tonight?"

"Yes Sir", said Maun, "The Captain told me".

"Then, when you have finished your meal, go there and get some sleep. That is the Captain's orders."

Later on, Captain Bruner entered his small cabin - which also doubled as his office and chart room. Although he had to make do with a narrow bunk that barely gave him room to turn over, it was much better than his men had to put up with. Below decks, it was dark and stuffy and there was not enough room to even stand upright. Also, the crew had to make do with their bed rolls all jammed up together. Some of the men chose to stay on deck and find a comfortable slot between the bales of linen.

Although exhausted, the Captain smiled as he spotted Maun and the dog, curled up on some sheep skins under his table and covered with a blanket.

He lay on his bunk worrying about Evan, 'What would he do without him? He was not only an essential member of the crew, but a close friend. He knew his family well and dreaded the thought of having to break the news of his death to Margaretta'.

It was very late and he was just dropping off to sleep when Chief entered the tiny cabin, after first quietly tapping on the door. "I'm sorry to disturb you, Sir", he whispered, "But, you asked me to keep you informed about Evan. I'm afraid it's not good news. He's burning up with fever and mumbling. We are doing all we can to cool him down".

"I will come now", said the Captain.

Chief told him, "No Sir. There is nothing you can do for him that is not being done already. Better you get some rest and I'll keep you informed if there is any change". He left closing the door behind him.

The Captain was tired and soon sank into a deep sleep. So deep that he did not hear the hound whimper or the door of his cabin open and close.

Maun had no idea what made him wake up, but he did and heard the brief conversation between the Captain and Chief. Now he understood why Evan had been acting strangely. He knew instinctively what he had to do. He felt different, stronger and more alive than he had done for a very long time. The compulsion to do for Evan what the angels had done for him was irresistible.

Once outside the cabin he felt the chill wind. The moon lit up the ship and he saw several members of the crew standing around Evan, who was resting on some bales beside the ring-post, where he and the hound had spent the best part of the day. He moved towards them, handed the hound to Chief, then went to stand by Evan's head. He put his hands on Evan's brow for a time, then stood beside him, holding the injured hand between his own. He did not feel pity for Evan, he was only conscious of the power flowing through his hands, knowing that he had to wait until it subsided naturally and he was impressed to stop.

Eventually the energy faded. Without a word spoken, Maun took the hound and slipped quietly back to the cabin, curling up with the dog on the sheepskins and going back to sleep.

The men standing around Evan were amazed at what had taken place, for - even if they had wanted to - they had been powerless to intervene. At once, they noticed that Evan had stopped moaning. "Is he dead?", asked a crew member.

Chief put his ear to Evans's chest, "No, he is breathing. He is sleeping. Fetch something warm to cover him up. Then take it in turns to watch over him".

No one had expected Evan to live until the morning and already feeling a deep sense of loss, some of the more soft-hearted were openly crying.

Morning came and with a knock on the Captain's cabin door, Chief entered. Captain Bruner sat up with a start, "Have I overslept?".

"No, Sir", said Chief, "It is your usual time".

"How is Evan?", he asked in the sombre voice of one who expected bad news.

"He is still sleeping, Sir. And his fever seems to have passed."

"I don't believe it", said the Captain, "He was too far gone. How is it possible?".

"It is true, Sir. I have just been to see him and he is snoring like a pig."

The Captain beamed, "This I've got to see for myself". He put on his coat and hood and followed Chief on to the deck. Members of the crew were standing watching Evan and moved aside to let the Captain through.

Evan snorted, then woke up. He looked around him at the concerned faces of the crew, "What's up?", he asked.

"It's you! That's what's up. We all expected to be feeding you to the fish this morning."

Evan's memory slowly returned. He drew his hand out from under the cover and held it up for everyone to see. There was hardly a trace of swelling, only a little redness remained. The men gasped, "It's a miracle". Evan moved his fingers. They were still a little bit stiff, but there was no pain or discomfort.

"It's the boy", said the youngest crew member, "It's the boy. He came here last night. It was after he touched Evan that he went to sleep".

The Captain looked around at his men, 'Were all of you here? Did all of you witness this miracle?".

The men all nodded, "We were there, Sir. That boy is a magician".

The Captain laughed, "If he is, then we are all right. He is on our side. But, I think Evan healed himself. He is a strong man and it would take a lot more than a swollen hand to get him down. The rest he had was probably all he needed to make a recovery". Satisfied with his own explanation, he ordered the crew back to work and instructed Evan to rest until he felt ready to resume his duties.

But, the men had been there. They saw and believed their own eyes. They had witnessed Evan rocking with pain, burning with fever and then sinking into delirium. They had done what they could; everything the orderly had advised, but to no avail. They had been forced to stand by, feeling totally helpless. Then, the lad appeared with the dog. He knew exactly what he was doing. "Trouble with them officers," said one member of the crew, "They have all their natural instincts educated out of them".

The men went about their duties, pleased about Evan's miraculous recovery and a with new respect for Maun, but also slightly irritated by their Captain's down-to-earth explanation.

The Captain and Chief went to the cabin to study their navigation charts. There were so many islands in these waters, steering a ship was not easy.

Maun and the hound were still asleep.

"What do you really think, Captain?", asked Chief, "Do you think Evan healed himself?".

"I don't know what to believe", answered the Captain, "It's a mystery - but you know how superstitious sailors are. There's something unnerving about being on watch during the night, with only the sound of the ship cutting through the waves. It's possible to hear voices and allow your imagination to run riot. So, I try to keep a cool head".

Chief said, "Normally I would agree with you, Sir. But I was there. There was an atmosphere that was unworldly. I can understand the mens' attitude".

"Yes", said the Captain, "I also can. But it's my job to keep discipline and a sense of reality aboard this ship".

The day for Maun began very pleasantly. The cook made him a special breakfast and Evan - who was excused duties until he was stronger - kept him company. First, they walked the dog around the ship, everyone they passed exchanging cheerful greetings, then they sat on the bales and chatted, For Maun, this was very pleasant, it had been a long time since he'd relaxed with a friend and just talked, for in captivity, there was no one to talk to except the animals. It was then that they noticed the hound was becoming restless. "I don't like it," said Evan, "She is behaving as though she is going to drop her pups".

"Your right, Evan," said Maun, "I have seen the animals at the farm act like this when they were about to have their young. I think we had better report her condition to the Captain or Chief".

"This is not good," said Evan, "She is not due for several weeks, unless that trader was lying to us. The Captain won't be pleased. We could lose her and her litter. She is valuable cargo - as he keeps reminding us".

The Captain and Chief were discussing procedures ready for when the ship docked, when the Captain suddenly looked skyward, "Better warn the men to tie everything down. There's a storm brewing".

"I can't see any signs of it", said Chief.

"Oh! Yes," said the Captain, "It's the stillness, as though everything is sleeping. Take my word for it. I can smell a storm".

Chief laughed, "You had not better not let the crew hear you talk like that - smell a storm indeed!".

The Captain remained serious, "I tell you, Chief, my intuition has saved this ship many a time, as well you know. Tell the men to clear the decks and batten everything down and find a place below for the boy and our hound. My cabin can get a bit rough and wet during a storm".

Evan found the Captain in his cabin, "I see we have orders to make everything secure. Does this mean that your second sight is at work again?".

"Yes, it does Evan."

"That's a pity, Sir, for I have come to tell you that the hound is restless. Both Mauny and I think she will drop her pups soon."

"All I can say is that I hope the trader was lying about how far on she was, otherwise the pups will be far too small to survive and we could lose the bitch as well. Get the orderly to have a look at her - you never know, he might have some ideas. Before you go Evan, how do you feel now?"

Evan smiled, "Sir. I feel wonderful, as though Mauny's God has given me a second chance".

"I was very worried about you, Evan. I'm glad you are back with us, for I feared we had lost you. Is the lad giving you any trouble?"

Evan shook his head, "No, Sir. Mauny is a fine well-bred lad. He's been telling me about his home and his parents and how he is longing to see them again. But, there is a strangeness about him. I often find him talking to himself".

Captain Bruner laughed, "Talks to himself, does he? That is not strange, Evan, I do it all the time, only I call it eccentricity - or getting old".

"That's as may be", said Evan, "But, Mauny answers himself as well. He also has conversations with the dog".

The Captain laughed even louder, "Don't worry about it, Evan. I am sure he is harmless".

"I have been thinking", said Evan, "About how he is going to get home from the Lorne, to the Clyde. The Highlands are difficult country to move around in; rivers to cross, mountains to climb, peaty bogs and bandits all over the place. If only we could talk him into staying with the ship until our return journey, we could detour to Dunbriton. I will put it to him again, Sir, but I think that when we reach the Lorne and the ship docks, the lad will start running for home. I doubt he's got the patience to stay aboard for another few months".

"Well, Evan. Do what you can. Chief has gone to make a safe place for him below deck until the storm passes. Make sure he gets there and ties himself secure."

"Right Sir. I will take care of him."

Back on deck, Maun was stroking the dog, doing his best to keep her calm. He had noticed that the crew had become very active and he wondered what was going on? Evan arrived and asked him if he had been told of the approaching storm. "What storm?", asked Maun, looking up at the clear blue sky.

Evan looked up too and understood Maun's doubts, but said, "It might look clear now lad, but sailors know a thing or two about the weather, that is why the crew are all so busy lowering the rigging. One little tear on a sail and if the strong wind caught it, it could be torn to shreds. Also, anything left lying around loose, could do a lot of damage".

"I wondered why everyone was rushing around", said Maun.

Evan bent down and patted the dog, "She might be very upset by the storm when it comes. The Captain thinks she could loose her pups if they come too soon".

"Oh! No!", said Maun, "She must not - I will take care of her".

"The Captain wants you and the dog down below. The Chief is sorting out a place for both of you. There are hooks against the side of the ship. Be sure and attach yourself to one, otherwise you will get tossed about."

The cook was ordered to feed the crew early, to enable him to secure his pots and pans and douche the fire and although it was some time before the storm clouds gathered, when they did it was with a vengeance. The rain started, hitting the deck like thousands of pebbles. The gale-force winds rocked the ship, making the timbers groan and crack as it was bounced over the high waves at top speed.

Maun was tucked up in a corner of the sleeping quarters and attached to a hook on the inside of the hull by a short length of rope, along with the rest of the crew.

It was a terrifying experience for all of them, but Maun remembered that in his meeting with the man (who he was now becoming to believe was the Lord himself), he had been told that he and the ship would arrive safely at its destination. He took comfort from that and decided not to worry.

The hound was frightened, whining and whimpering and Maun did his best to comfort her, by constantly stroking and talking to her and praying for her puppies.

Eventually the weather calmed and the crew called back on duty.

It was at this moment, that the hound gave birth to her first pup. It was alive and well and no sooner than she licked some life into the tiny body, than the second one was born.

Maun was delighted. When he was at home helping Cedi on the farm, he had seen lots of animals give birth. So, when the last two of the pups were born and appeared lifeless, Maun was able to rub their tiny bodies with a cloth, then hold them between his hands and let the life and light from his body pour into them. In all, six puppies were born, all healthy, squeaking for food and in Maun's eyes 'beautiful'.

"You are a very clever, mama. You have such wonderful babies."

Just then Chief appeared, calling out as he moved towards them, "You can come back on deck now Mauny. The men have all eaten and cook is looking for you".

"I cannot come yet, Chief, I have to look after the puppies."

"What?", said Chief, "You mean they are born?".

"All of them."

"Are they all alive?"

"Yes", said Maun, "All six of them".

"The Captain will be pleased", enthused Chief with a broad grin, "Wait till I tell him. I will get Evan to bring the dog and her family on deck and make her comfortable, then everyone can have a look at them".

Evan (with a bit of help), brought the hound and her pups on deck and settled them in a large wooden crate, with part of one side removed, to ensure that the dog could get out, but not the little ones. Every member of the crew came to have a look and admire them and the Captain (as predicted), was overwhelmed as he had been sure they would all be born dead. As he watched them wriggle and squeak, his pleasure was obvious, "Look how she gathers them to her. She is a wonderful mother".

One of the crew reminded his Captain about his earlier remark about 'not having smelly dogs on his ship'. "This is different", said the Captain, "These little ones are ours, born on our ship. They are going to be with us for a while, we had better get to like them".

Another member of the crew, mindful of another remark made by the Captain said (under his breath), "They are valuable cargo?".

"I heard that," said the Captain, "Yes. They are valuable cargo and don't let any one of you forget it, they are your wages".

Chief was equally pleased that everything had turned out so well. The storm had been horrendous, yet they had suffered no damage to the ship and they had a litter of beautiful pups.

A little later, the Captain and Chief returned to the cabin to study their navigation charts. Frustrated in their efforts to decide exactly where they were, the Captain said, "We may not have suffered damage, but, we have certainly been blown off course". He turned to look at Chief, then said, "Since Mauny came on board, Evan's life has been saved and we have six dogs to sell, as well as the mother. I think we should get the boy up here. Maybe, with his good luck, he could tell us where we are?".

"I don't think its all luck", said Chief, "There is something special about him".

Maun ate his meal in the galley. It was great to be up on deck in the fresh air again. It had been unbearably stuffy below and the unpleasant aroma of unwashed bodies was not one Maun was familiar with. Still, he was not really complaining. The memories of his captivity were still with him; the cold damp straw, the lack of food and the terrible loneliness. He loved being on this ship. Everyone was so kind and helpful and appreciated the things he had done, even though he knew beyond a doubt that Evan's healing - and the safe birth of the pups - were not entirely due to him, but to the angel companions that were with him. In his mind always, was the thought of seeing his family again. He visualised the look on his mother's face and the relief on his father's. But, most of all, 'I will be home, where I belong'.

The cook gave him a bowl of scraps for the dog and a dish of water and he was happily making his way towards the crate, when he heard Chief call his name, "Maun, when you have fed her, we want you along here". Maun wondered what they wanted, so hurried. He put the food down and said, "Sorry, madam dog, I am wanted by our Captain. I will be back to see you just as soon as I can".

The Captain and Chief were scanning the horizon. "We thought, as you Maun have the youngest eyes, you would like to help us find out where we are. The storm has thrown us off course. We are looking for islands. Each one is marked by either a pile of rocks, or trees set in a different way. These waters Maun, have been sailed for thousands of years by lots of different people from far off countries and each one has marked the islands so that they could easily be identified. We want you to use your young eyes to tell us what you see". Maun nodded and took his place by the side of the Captain, his blanket wrapped tightly around him, the wind and sea spray blowing in his face.

"Your parents will be pleased to see you safe and sound. I expect they have been worried."

"Yes. They have been very worried - and my grandfather - but he is different, for he now knows that I am on my way home."

The Captain looked at Maun curiously, "How can that be lad? How can your grandfather possibly know?".

"I spoke to him and told him", replied Maun. Captain Bruner thought that Maun's unpleasant experiences of the past months had turned his mind. Then the Captain heard him say, "It was like a dream and I saw him".

"Oh! A dream", said the Captain (as if that explained everything).

"I saw my mother and father as well."

The Captain thought he had better change the subject, so he asked Maun, "Have you made up your mind as to whether you are going to stay with the ship until the return journey, or are you still determined to walk?".

"How far is it to Dunbriton from the Lorne, Sir?"

"Well lad, I don't rightly know. You see, it's not just the distance, its the kind of country it is. We are given to believe that it is full of wild animals, lots of lakes and rivers to cross and worst of all - bandits. So, you see, it's not straight forward. At a guess, judging by the distance we sail, it could be seventy miles or more."

"Seventy miles", repeated Maun, "I could walk that in about four or five days".

The Captain could see that he had made up his mind. Evan was right, as soon as the ship docked he would start running. Yet, he felt that he could not let him go as he was, dressed in rags, with filthy hair and looking half starved. They had done what they could to feed him up, but it was going to take a lot longer than a few days to fatten him. "What does your father do for a living lad?", asked the Captain.

Maun looked up at him, "My father is a Councillor and a teacher at the Mission school. My mother also is a teacher - she teaches the little children. My grandfather is a priest of the Holy Church".

The Captain was impressed, "You must be a fine educated young man, then".

Maun shook his head, "No Sir. Not me. I am a grave disappointment to everyone. The only thing I am good at is helping on the farm".

"Now my lad," said the Captain, "I don't believe that. You are the very best healer I have ever met and we have your good friend Evan to prove it. And, what about the hound and her pups? No one on this ship had expected them to be born alive. Everyone, I believe, has a special gift. Mine is being able to sail a ship across the sea. Evan's is his strength. And your special gift is being able to heal people who are sick. That young Mauny, is the finest gift of all".

The Captain thought what he had said would cheer Maun up, but Maun looked even more sad. "Trouble is Sir. I could not heal before I was taken." He was about to tell the Captain where his gift had come from, but there in front of him, a small island came into view. His hand shot out from under his blanket, "Look Sir! Land ahead!".

The Captain strained his eyes, 'Where lad?".

Maun pointed triumphantly, "There Sir. I see it".

"Now lad, tell me if you can see anything on it."

"You mean, like a clump of bushes and a pile of rocks."

"That's exactly what I mean", said Captain Bruner.

The crew were alerted and the ship was soon back on course. Maun returned to his duties as dog watcher and Evan, who was working nearby said, "I've been keeping an eye on her for you and cook has fed her - now she is sleeping".

Maun studied the hound and her family, who seemed to grow bigger every time he looked at them, "Isn't she a wonderful mother, Evan? See how she protects her little ones with her paw". "You are going to miss her, Mauny", said Evan, "And she is going to miss you".

A bell rang. Evan told Maun that it was to call the crew to a meeting with the Captain, "We always have one just before we enter port. We are given instructions on what has to be unloaded and things like that and if the men had obeyed orders during the voyage, they might get a jar of grog".

"I don't expect I am included. I will wait here and watch the puppies", said Maun.

Most of the crew crushed into the tiny mess room, where as expected, jars of grog were passed around. They listened as the Captain spoke, "The port we are entering tomorrow is a small one that serves several villages - communities who have settled here from different countries over a very long time. The town itself has a few hundred people who cater for the traders who wait for the ships to arrive. After the ships have unloaded, the traders load up their wagons with the goods and leave the following morning, having spent the evening in one of the

127

three ale houses on the quay. So be warned. I will not tolerate any fighting. I need a healthy crew and we have to trade with them. Keep a clear head".

One of the crew called out, "What about the boy? Should he not be here, for his share of grog".

"Yes he should, but, I want to speak to you about him. I do know that I made him an official member of the crew and by right he should be here, but grog is not what the lad needs".

"Maun has told me how he was taken from his home and sold into slavery. He has also told me that his family are Christians, who have a school and that they are teachers. His grandfather is a priest. Now, it would look bad on us, if we sent him home looking the way he does, dressed in rags. He has a long way to go without shoes and a warm coat. Here is my suggestion. We all contribute something towards a new cloak to keep him warm on his journey and, if we have any money left, a pair of boots. We should be able to buy them at Lorne. If I remember this place correctly, they have a tailor and a boot maker."

"He is a brave lad. Taken from his home, beaten, starved and treated most cruelly, yet he has never to my knowledge complained. So, give what you can and if you have no money, perhaps you have some small thing to sell. Your contributions will be gratefully accepted."

The crew members reached into their money belts and threw coins into a one of the empty grog jars. "Thank you men. This I am sure will go a long way to getting the lad the things he needs."

"Sir", said one of the men, "Do they have a bath house at the Lorne?". Everyone laughed.

"Yes, they do", said Chief, "Even though it is a bit primitive, it will serve our purpose. Before you ask men, they also have a bath attendant who is quite good with hair cutting shears. We must make sure Maun has that mop of hair cut".

The men finished off the grog and gradually left to go back to work, but Evan lingered behind. Captain Bruner raised his eyes from counting the contributions and looked at him, "Is something wrong, Evan?".

"Sir", said Evan, "I know you are short handed, but I want to go with Maun. I cannot bear the thought of him out there in wild country alone. You said yourself how the hills are full of bandits. After what he had been through, he deserves to go home safely and what is more Captain, I believe that I would have died, but for his intervention".

"I agree", said the Captain, "I've been worried too and wondering what we could do to ensure his safety on the road. If the hound had not been needed to feed her pups, I would have suggested he take her with him for protection and company, but alas, the pups are too small to be separated from her".

"He has a long and dangerous road ahead of him and he is going to need all the help he can get. If only he were not so frail." The captain sighed, "So, my old friend, you have decided to leave us. Well, I can't say I am pleased to see you go - I'm not. I will miss you. We've been together a long time. Yet, my friend, I will be happier knowing you are with him and protecting him from further hardship. That knowledge will allow me to sleep easier in my bed". The Captain smiled, "Go and tell him the good news - I know he will be pleased".

The ship sailed up the estuary and the small harbour came into view. Maun watched from the deck, excitement building up inside him. He thought, "In just a few hours I will be on my way home".

The crew were busy and Maun decided to take the hound for a walk around the ship. Evan caught up with him below decks and called out to him, "Come up here, Mauny".

"Sorry", said Maun, "It's the only place she can exercise without getting in everyone's way. I will come up now Evan".

Once on deck, Evan broke the news to him, "When you leave the ship Mauny, you will have company. I am coming with you".

Maun was indeed pleased, "That is the best news I could have been given, but what about your work? Does not the Captain depend on you?".

"Don't you fret about that lad, the Captain is in full agreement. He said, 'He would sleep better in his bed, knowing that you were not alone on your journey".

"Are we leaving as soon as the ship reaches port?", Maun asked eagerly.

"I'm afraid not, my boy. I have to help with the unloading, then we are going to buy you some clothes."

"Clothes", repeated Maun, "I have no money!".

"Yes you have", said Evan, "You have four days wages to come, enough to buy you some decent clothes to go home in. You don't want your mother to see you in these old rags, do you?".

"You are right, Evan. I doubt she would recognise me."

Evan put his arm around Maun, "That's settled then" and hugged him, "You are returning home - a gentleman".

Maun was touched by everyone's kindness, "I don't know how to thank you. Words don't seem enough".

"You don't have to say anything lad. We just want you return to your home and see the joy on your mother's face. We sailors know all about leaving home and the sweetness of seeing our wives faces when we arrive home."

Although Maun was indeed very happy that Evan was coming with him, he was just a little frustrated, for he had planned to move as quickly as he could. He wondered just how many miles he would have covered in the time spent buying clothes? Then, he thought how hurt Evan would be if he knew what he was thinking? 'I really must try to be more patient', he told himself.

The ship was rowed into the harbour and almost at once, the hard work of unloading began. Sacks of rice and nuts; amphoras of lamp oil; casks of French and Spanish wine.

Leaving Chief in charge, the Captain, Evan and Maun left the ship and made for the bath house which was situated in a wooden hut behind an ale house. Inside, were two large wooden tubs and after the Captain had spoken to the attendant and paid him, several men, carrying leather buckets of steaming water began to fill one of the tubs.

The Captain, said, "Now, young Mauny, in you get and soak the grime from your skin - and make sure you put your head under the water!". This was a luxury Maun had almost forgotten. It felt wonderful! He was given a brush to scrub himself and he used it until his skin turned red, however, he avoided the ugly scars and bruises. For the first time, Evan, who had waited with him while the Captain went to seek out the tailor, was again able to see the full extent of the terrible suffering and neglect Maun had endured. Even though the scars were in the process of healing, there was no mistaking the damage that severe malnutrition and neglect had caused.

When Captain Bruner returned with an armful of clothes for Maun to try on, he was reluctant to leave the tub - continuing to dip his head under the hot water and popping up again. Eventually the Captain, with a grin said, "Right lad. Out you come! We have lots of work to do".

Maun's hair was impossible to comb and the attendant had to bring the shears and start to cut away the tangles and knots. When he finished, there was not a lot of hair left, but the attendant had done a good job and he looked very smart. Then, Captain Bruner held up each item of clothing he had brought for Maun to try on: A pair of long linen pants, a woollen undershirt, a robe of green and brown with long sleeves, a leather waistcoat and a long cloak with a hood. Excitedly, Maun dried himself on a rough cloth and started to put on the clothes. Evan said, "You look good Maun. What a difference clothes make".

Captain Bruner agreed, "You look a treat! Now, all we need is some good boots, for you have a lot of walking to do".

Maun looked down at the pile of rags he'd discarded and the locks of hair which covered the floor, "You are right, Evan. My mother would have been shocked to see me like that. I did not realise how bad I felt, but now I feel almost human again".

The Captain was beaming with pleasure and nodded, indicating pride in his achievement, "Now lad, let us go and get you those boots".

As the three of them left the bath house and went back onto the quay, they saw several men building a circle of bricks. "What are they doing ?", asked Maun.

Evan answered, "They are building a fire, to roast beef. It is the custom here to have a feast when a ship comes in". He laughed, "Not only a feast, young Mauny, but a celebration, with music and dancing. Everyone in the town and the crew join in. It is to celebrate the safe arrival of their goods and for our part, a safe voyage".

"A pity we won't be here to join in", said Maun.

"Oh! But we will", said Evan, "I'm afraid we cannot leave until the morning". Maun could not help, but show his disappointment.

Captain Bruner explained, "When the traders fill their wagons, they spend the night at the ale house. Then, in the morning, they leave for their various destinations. If you can get to travel with the one who is going in your direction, it will save you time and energy. Now, you may be able to run like the wind and survive without food, but Evan would not be able to for long. So, it is better if you have a good rest, enjoy the festivities of tonight and leave in the morning - fresh. Tonight I will speak to the traders and find one who is going your way. I know that you are impatient Mauny, I would be if in your position. But, believe me, it is better if you both leave well prepared for the journey".

Evan tried to cheer Maun up, "You look and smell so different, the hound will think you are a stranger after her pups and bite you", the joke raising no more than a weak smile.

The three returned to the ship, after purchasing a pair of boots for Maun, who having resigned himself to the situation, stood by the rail of the ship watching the preparations on the quay. He could see that the ship's cook was there with some of the crew, as well as some men from the ale house. He saw that they had built a fire and had already placed an enormous side of beef on a spit. Soon the delicious smell of roasting meat filled the air and wafted up towards him. Further along the quay, others were still unloading and he had to admit that he was beginning to enjoy the excitement.

As members of the crew passed by and saw Maun in his new clothes, they called out to him in friendly banter, "Ready for the road then? … Are you sure you want Evan to guide you? … You're bound to get lost! … Good luck, young un".

Maun, although grateful and happy, still felt a little disappointed. He kept wondering just how far along the road he could have got by now? Instead, here he was still in dock. He thought, 'I think, my Lord must be trying to teach me patience', then added, 'He's having a hard time, but Lord, I promise I will try'.

When darkness fell, it was still quite early. Chief had handed over to the Captain and was making his way to his quarters, when he saw Maun and came over to him. "What a difference clothes make. You look grand! Don't feel too bad about not getting away earlier, but you know how early it gets dark so far north in winter. You would not have got very far. Believe me, our Captain has your best interests at heart, both for you and his old friend. You would have lost your way very early on in this strange and mountainous country. After the celebrations tonight, you will sleep well and be ready to start your journey tomorrow bright and early."

The fire on the quay was red hot and the beef was almost ready to eat, it smelled good and for the first time in months, Maun was looking forward to enjoying a man-sized meal.

The cook started to slice the meat up, then called out loud, "Come on. Come and get it!". All at once, the quay was full of people, lining up and holding out their plates. Evan came along and in his usual cheerful and friendly manner said, "What are you waiting for lad? Let's go and get ourselves some good food and take a look at all those treats that the women have made for us".

Later, sitting on a wooden case, their plates piled high. Evan looked at Maun's plate and said, "You're never going to eat all that, are you?".

Maun smiled, "Maybe not, but I'm going to try".

First they cut their meat into pieces, then ate it from the point of their sharp knives. The other delicacies they ate with their fingers. Then the music started to play. Two of the men began to play flutes, then the women took each other's hands and giggling with excitement, began to dance around in a circle. The men also formed a circle and danced around them in the opposite direction.

Gradually, the music grew louder and faster and then the drumming started. Men with sticks drummed on the rail of the ship; on the pots and pans and any other hard surface available. The dancers stamping their feet in time with the music, were spinning around at speed and the women began to squeal and shout as some found it more difficult to keep up. The men enjoyed this part and were laughing.

Finally, the music stopped and the exhausted and breathless dancers turned around to face the person nearest to them and taking their hands, flopped down on the sacks, Evan explaining to Maun that this was a "choose your partner for the evening dance". The ale provided by the tavern owners and the wine provided by the Captain continued to flow fast and furious and when the music began again, this time, it was at a more gentle pace, the couples swaying back and forth in time to the music. It was not frenzied and exciting as the previous dance - just the opposite. The women put their arms around the mens' necks; the men holding the ladies around their waists. Some of them hardly moved at all.

Maun and Evan were enjoying the evening, watching the dancers and the other men standing around laughing, joking and drinking.

Evan watched Maun's face and saw him smile, the happy smile of boy with no worries, "Are you glad you waited lad? This is the fun part of being a sailor - there are not many!". Then, in a more serious mood said, "Don't think I don't know how disappointed you are. If I were you I would have wanted to run like the wind as soon as the ship docked. That is the impatience of youth. But, my boy, we must be sensible. I have found that we often move a lot faster when we think things out first".

Cook came over, "Any of you want more meat? Come on Maun, I'm sure you have room for another" and he tipped a slice onto Maun's plate, adding, "Don't give that to the hound - she has already eaten an enormous pile of scraps".

Evan and Maun shared the food while they watched the dancers, who were still hanging on to each other, swaying to the music.

Evan asked Maun, "Would you like to dance with a pretty girl?".

"Me dance? No, thank you. I am quite happy watching. What about you Evan, you're not dancing either?"

"My dancing days are over, Maun. I have a good wife and two sons. I've done my courting."

The fire was allowed to die and the couples who had been dancing drifted away in the direction of the ale house. And, so the evening ended.

The night watch told Maun that they would take care of the hound to enable him to sleep in peace. So, he went to the cabin, wrapped himself in his blanket, but he lay awake thinking, 'Tomorrow, I will be on my way home - at last'.

At first light, he got up and full of excitement, dressed and packed his few belongings in his satchel. He spoke to the crew member on watch, then took the hound for a walk around the quay. He was not alone, traders were already loading their wagons ready to leave and the quay was a hive of activity

Captain Bruner did not arrive back in his cabin during the evening. He and Chief had been busy bartering, attempting to get the best deal on the goods they had carried. It was a difficult job trying to balance the worth of what was being bought and sold. "How many boxes of cooking ware for a quantity of hides or furs?" Or, "How many casks of wine for enough fresh food to feed the crew till the next port of call?". Eventually, deals were struck and the Captain - exhausted - had collapsed into his bunk, half way through the night.

Maun brought the hound back on board and she settled down with her pups. It was a sad moment for him and he knelt beside her and spoke softly, "My dear friend, if it had not been for you, I would not have got my passage on this ship. I owe you a lot. Today, I leave you. I am going home to see my family, but I will never ever forget you - or your little ones. This is a good ship and I know that Chief will take good care of you".

He sat on one of the bales, a strange feeling came over him. He had been impatient to begin his journey home, but now it was almost time to go, a mood of calm reflection had taken over. Seven months ago now, he had become a prisoner and made a terrible journey by boat. He did not remember much about it, except the pain. He was not the only one on that ship being taken. He vaguely remembered opening his eyes and seeing many more faces looking at him. Then those horrible months - painful and degrading. Never would he forget the agony of slavery.

But, then my Lord, 'Did I really experience death and life in Heaven?'. His heart leapt at the memory. That light. That wonderful light that filled his soul with pure love. Tears filled his eyes as he relived that glorious experience.

He pulled himself back together again. For, now he was across the sea. Not quite in his own country, but only about seventy miles from home.

It was almost time to go and he heard Evan's voice say, "Might have guessed you would be up and ready. Come on then, lets go to the galley. Cook has left us some food for the journey".

Cook had indeed done them proud. On his workbench were two large chunks of bread, several hard boiled eggs, some dried dates and figs and a large piece of cheese. Cook turned up as they were packing the food away, "You don't think I would let you go without some breakfast?". There was a large pot of gruel on the stove and he poured out two bowls, "It is not much, but it will help to keep out the cold", he said as he cut some more slices of bread, on which he put some meat, left over from the night before.

They thanked the cook for everything. Evan told him, "It is thanks to you that Maun is on his way to good health. You made him eat. That roast last night was delicious. Do you know he ate *two* slices?".

"Only one and a half", Maun corrected him. He held his stomach, "That was the most food I have ever eaten all at once".

The mood on board was quiet, almost sombre, unlike the happy, noisy, celebrations of the night before. For the crew were losing a shipmate - an old, trusted and hard working one - and a new young friend, who had shown them a miracle of healing and demonstrated a rare brand of forgiveness for the people who had ill-treated him.

A heavily loaded wagon came to a halt in front of the ship. A very loud and cheerful voice called out, " Ahoy there, Captain".

Captain Bruner appeared from the cabin minus one boot and hopped towards the rail. He waved back at the man. He saw Evan and Maun waiting, "Can't say I'm happy to see you both go, but I am pleased you will be together. Take good care of each other". Then he touched Evan's arm, "I will make sure Margaretta gets your wages and explain to her where you are - so don't worry".

"Come on and meet the man who will take you the first few miles of your journey. He will give you a good start and make up for the delay."

CHAPTER XXI

BARNEY AND JASPER

On the quay, they were introduced to Barney - the trader who they were going to travel with - a plump man with a round pale face, rosy cheeks and bright blue twinkling eyes. As he was on his way home after some weeks absence, he also had treated himself to a wash and shave at the bath house. In turn, Barney introduced them to 'Jasper', his heavy horse, who was black, with some white feathering around his feet.

The trader, with a grand flourish, invited them to "Climb on board and we'll be off". Evan found himself sitting up front with Barney, with Maun in the back of the wagon, wondering how he was going to fit in amongst all the boxes and sacks? He decided that once they got started, he would move things around but, for now, he wanted to take his last look at the ship and all his new friends. Chief was standing beside the hound, as if to reassure Maun that he would look after her, while cook and other members of the crew, stood along the rail watching in silence.

As Captain Bruner stood back from the wagon, Barney cracked his whip in mid-air, Jasper moved forward with a jerk, throwing Maun back on to a sack, although he soon sat up again and waved goodbye - as did Evan. Only then did some of the crew call out ... "Good Luck" ... "Take Care", although, most were too upset to say anything.

Maun, facing the ship, noticed for the first time that there was a name on the bow, just below the rail - *S.V.S. Sudius* - 'I must remember to ask Evan what that means', he thought. The waving and shouting continued until Barney and the wagon turned off the quay and out of sight.

If Evan was sad at leaving his ship and shipmates, he did not show it. He and Barney were natural friends, both larger-than-life characters and with similar looks and attitude. They took to each other on sight, like old friends who had met up again after a short absence.

Maun began to move things around in the back of the wagon in an attempt to make himself more comfortable. He piled one sack on top of another, put his bed roll down on the floor of the wagon and leaned against the sacks.

Evan turned around, "You alright in the back, lad?".

"I am now", replied Maun. If there was the slightest hint of sarcasm in his answer, Evan did not notice, engrossed as he was in his conversation with Barney.

There was a chill in the early spring air and Maun began to feel it on the back of his bare neck, now exposed since having his hair cut, so he wrapped his blanket around his head and snuggled down.

Evan and Barney were chatting away in Latin, a language Barney had learned while hanging around the docks. It was essential for the trader's business, most of the ships arriving in the Lorne being from the Empire and he spoke the language fluently and with expression.

The wagon trundled on along a well-used and often bumpy road and Maun lay back, watching the clouds being swept across the sky, at times leaving patches of blue, allowing shafts of sunlight through to illuminate the countryside. He watched hares dancing with their young; the occasional wild boar and a deer, away in the distance.

They had travelled for some time, when Barney suddenly brought Jasper to a halt. He leapt from the wagon and brought out from underneath, a basin. Next, he produced from under his seat, a flagon of water, poured some into the basin and gave it to Jasper, saying, "It's time for some refreshment". Back on his wagon and reaching under his seat again, he brought out a flagon of something for themselves. He handed the flagon to Evan, saying, "Have a swig of this, Sir. It will keep the cold out".

Evan took a large mouthful and gasped with pleasure as it passed his throat, "My! That's grand stuff".

Maun had looked up to see why they had stopped. Barney thrust the flagon at him, saying "Here you are lad, this will warm you up" and as he was still feeling the nip in the air, without thinking, took a large gulp of the contents.

He suddenly shot up, eyes bulging, cheeks pouched, red faced, the liquid spraying out of his mouth - all over Jasper! He gasped, coughed and spluttered and fanning his mouth with his hands, managed to croak, "Water! Water!".

Evan and Barney sat wide eyed and open mouthed until Barney jumped down, grabbed Jasper's basin and what was left of his water and gave it to Maun, who scooped handfuls into his mouth and splashed his face with more.

Evan and Barney laughed fit to burst. Then, when they had controlled themselves a little, Barney said with exaggerated understatement, "Do I take it, young Sir, that this was your very first taste of real grog?".

Maun, who was still coughing and spluttering and holding his throat, reached for his satchel to find something to eat that might take away the offensive taste. He settled for a piece of bread and a lump of cheese. He tried to settle down again. "How can you drink that awful stuff", he asked Evan.

"Well, my boy, It's not so much the taste, its the way it makes you feel once its down."

"Well", said Maun, "I liked the way I felt before I drank it!".

"Fair enough", said Barney and winking at Evan said, "That leaves more for us then".

Maun ate his bread and cheese, then followed that with some very hard dried dates, which he had to chew on. He tried to settle down again, laying back on the sacks of grain and attempted to forget the previous incident.

His mind wandered over the last six months of his life and he began to realise just how much he had changed. His suffering had made him older and wiser and his experience of death had taken away his fear of it. His knowledge of truth; that the soul is indestructible, gave him a sense of purpose. Knowing that prayers are both heard and answered, strengthened his faith in God, 'No more will I envy or resent others, who are more handsome, or smarter. I know that my God in Heaven loves me, for who I am, as I am' and with that comforting thought, he slept.

Evan asked Barney about the bandits on the road south. "I've seldom travelled in that direction", answered Barney. "I have heard a tale or two though. I can only speak from experience and so far I've never been bothered by them. That's because they don't steal from their own kind! But, there are a few around and if the tales I've heard are true, then you had better look out. They will have the lad's new clothes off his back for a start. Better if he covers them over with an old coat. If we met some now, they would take what food we have and anything on the wagon they fancied, but they would not kill us. Jasper would also be quite safe. They have no need for an old horse like Jasper, as they like to move fast and make a lot of noise."

"Wherever there are young men thrown out of the family nest; with no trade or learning, a weak father, or without a good woman to love them or take them in hand, you will find these gangs roaming the countryside. It's best not to antagonise them, or try to outsmart them. Better still, keep your eyes open and your ears to the ground and avoid them at all cost."

"Thanks for the advice", said Evan. He turned to ask Maun if he'd heard what Barney had told him, but saw that he was sound asleep.

"I wish I could sleep like the lad here."

Barney glanced back. "You sure he's not dead? Maybe, the grog has killed him."

Evan laughed. "Dead! The way he jumped about. I don't think so." Both men chuckled.

"Never seen anything like that in my life before", said Barney.

The wagon rolled on - mile after mile. Then sounds and signs of habitation appeared. The path became wider, a dog barked and the smell of smoke from burning wood filled their nostrils. "We are almost home", said Barney and he produced a bell from under his seat. "Hold your ears lads. This makes a wicked noise. I ring it to let the folks know that 'Old Barney' is back with their goods." Maun was awake now, but not altogether prepared for the din that followed. Barney rang the bell for some time, making their ears tingle.

They entered a small village of about a seven or eight houses, spread equally on both sides of a wide stream, which had stepping stones placed at equal stride lengths across it. Women were there filling pots and jars with the crystal clear water, while bare-footed children played on the moss covered stones. Men were busy sawing wood and chickens pecked amongst the straw, placed on the road to soak up puddles.

The houses were strange. Built of reddish coloured stones, the roofs were made of half logs and covered with a black substance. The windows were small with shutters.

It was a tidy village and the people looked neat and clean. A small group of men and women were gathered outside one of the houses and Barney said, "That's my place and these people are my customers". With a "Whaw, Jasper, Whaw", he drew the wagon to a halt, then jumped down. The door of his house opened and a woman stood there. She looked reasonably pleased to see Barney.

There was just the trace of a smile at the corner of her lips. She looked strong and efficient - muscular rather then fat. Her dress was basically simple. Made from one long length of material, with a hole for her head to go through, only the neck and hem of the garment required any sewing. She also wore an apron that covered a good part of it. Her long brown hair was tied back, not in any particular style or fashion, just practically restrained.

Barney smiled at her and introduced Evan and Maun. "These are my friends. They are on their way south." He spoke their own language. She nodded politely. Barney said something else to her. She then turned and went back inside the house. "My wife is going to prepare a meal for you before you continue your journey. I am just going to serve my customers, who, no doubt, have waited patiently for 'Old Barney' to bring their goods."

Evan and Maun watched as Barney handed out a new axe head to a delighted man; a sack of grain for the baker; cooking pots for another. Everything anyone could want was being distributed, including new boots, salt, nuts, honey - even clay animals for the children. Barney's wagon was almost empty, only one amphora of lamp oil left. Barney looked around as though expecting another customer, but no one else came. "Well", he said, "That's business finished for the day. Lets go inside and see what my wife has prepared for us."

The room they entered was opulent, considering the house and its setting. Brightly coloured rugs from the east covered the seats, while a delicately carved table held an ornate oil lamp and it was clear that Barney had acquired some fascinating and exotic things over the years from his journeys to and from the port.

Barney then led them through this room and into another behind, this room being very different. A plain stone floor; a wooden table, with stools either side and a stone-built fireplace cum cooking stove. This was the room where they lived, worked and where the children played.

Two boys of about seven and eight looked up from their game of fives. "Have you finished your work, father?", one of them said.

"I have", said Barney and the boys went to their father, expectantly.

His daughter, a very pretty girl of about fifteen, said, "Papa, stop teasing the boys. You know that you always bring them a gift".

Barney reached into his bag and produced several clay animals, some of which were very strange. "What kind of creature is this father?", said one, holding up a camel, "I don't believe there are any such creatures as these".

"I am assured", said Barney, "On the highest authority, that such a creature lives in a country where there is nothing but sand". The boys looked at him disbelievingly.

Evan was about to confirm that he had actually seen such an animal, when there was a knock at the door and a young man entered. He looked grave. "Barney", he said, "Can you come? Father is dying".

Barney was shocked. "I will come right away. What happened to him?", he inquired. The young man explained that his father had gone to the woods to chop down a tree. Making away from the falling tree, he tripped and fell and the tree trapped him in the mud. "He could not free himself and had lain there for a long time - until I went to look for him - by which time he was unconscious."

Barney turned to Evan and said, "Fen is my best friend. I wondered why he did not come to collect his oil".

Maun had been sitting on one of the stools, watching the children play. But, when he heard that someone was in danger of death, he stood up. "He is not yet beyond help, we will come with you, Barney. We may be able to help". Barney and Evan left the house and headed for the stream, followed by Maun, Barney's wife and Fen's son. They hurried across the stream, leaping from stone to stone, the weight of the two heavy men causing the flat stones to loosen in the bed of the stream. Consequently, when Maun, who was following, jumped on them, they began to wobble and he had to try and keep his balance by thrashing his arms about and shouting. Evan, turning around, saw him in danger and hurried back, giving Maun his hand and yanking him on to the bank. Barney's wife followed, skirts held high above her knees.

Other neighbours, seeing everyone running, joined in the race to see what was happening. They all reached Fen's house, Barney calling out to Fen's wife - Shona - to open the door. A very tired-looking and tearful woman appeared, "I'm afraid Barney, you are too late". She made a strained effort to smile at him.

"Can we see him?", asked Barney and entered the house before she could reply. He rushed directly to Fen's bedside and stood there, waiting for the others to catch him up.

Fen lay under a cover on his bed. He was cold, grey and only just breathing. Everyone who entered, stood in silence, not quite knowing what to do, or why they were there.

Maun went to him and placed his hands on the side of his face and neck. Then he looked up at Evan. "He is so cold. Can we have more covers?" He moved his hands on to Fen's heart. Now Maun's hands began to warm up, until they were very hot. He invited Barney and Evan to hold Fen's hands and rub them.

With more warm covers and the heat from those around him, Fen began to stir slightly. "Could someone please build up the fire?", asked Maun, "We must have more heat". Evan and Barney were given a stool to sit on and they remained either side of Fen, each holding one of his hands. Suddenly, Fen's heart began to beat stronger. Maun asked, "Is there any soup available?". Barney's wife rushed back to her home to bring hot liquid from her own stew pot and by the time she returned, Fen had recovered sufficiently to eat a little.

Fen's son was astounded to see his father partly sitting up and being fed. He went to his father's side, knelt beside him and wept. Barney made way for him and comforted him by putting his arm around him and saying, "He's all right now. Keep him warm and fed. Let him rest until he is strong enough".

As Maun gave him the last spoonful of soup, Fen opened his eyes and slowly looked around at all the faces. In a weak voice, he asked, "What has happened?".

Shona hurried to his side and hugged him. Then, she said to Barney, "I am so pleased you came home when you did".

Barney was about to say that it was his young friend who was responsible, but he saw Maun shake his head, as though to say, 'Don't trouble her with details'. So, Barney said, "We will leave you now. My friends here are ready for their supper".

Evan, Maun and Barney slipped out of the house unnoticed, leaving Shona and her son sitting by Fen's bed. Barney's wife said, 'I will wait a while in case I am needed".

"Yes, that would be best", said Barney, touching her shoulder with affection, "But don't stay too long".

Back at his house, Barney ladled the remaining stew into six bowls, leaving enough in the pot for his wife, then slicing a loaf of bread that he had brought from the baker at Lorne that morning. He passed it around to eat with the stew- it tasted good. He said, "My wife is a wonderful woman and not a bad cook, except that she has not mastered the art of removing the pot from the stove before the food burns! We are all so used to it now, we think, if the food is not burnt, then it isn't ready!".

Evan laughed, "I would rather it was overdone than raw, I always say", he hoped he sounded convincing?

There was a silence for a few moments, then Barney said, "I still find it difficult to believe what we all witnessed at Fen's house. If you two had not been here, my old friend would have been no longer. He would surely have died. No doubt about it. If there is a true God, then he sent you both here this day".

"Not really", said Maun. "He was not injured. The soft mud saved him. It was the extreme cold that made him so ill."

Maun wished they would stop talking about 'The Healing' and concentrate on their journey, but he was too polite to say anything.

Evan was getting along with Barney so well, that it seemed to Maun that he would be happy to stay. Then Maun felt a strange feeling as though eyes were upon him. He raised his eyes and saw that Barney's young daughter had been watching him. As their eyes met, she looked away shyly. He was embarrassed and felt his face and neck flush. She was a very pretty girl, her round face and pale skin resembling her father's. She had the same blue twinkling eyes and reddish crinkly hair. He watched her in admiration, until she became aware of his gaze. He looked away and groaned silently as he realised Evan was smiling at him - and no doubt had seen his embarrassing moments. He guessed that Evan would remember it and tease him about it at every opportunity.

He whispered to Evan, "Is it nearly time to go?".

Barney overheard him, "I am sorry, my young friend, but it would be foolish to move on now. It is later than you think. We spent quite a long time at Fen's house and it is nearly dark outside. You would not get far before having to camp down for the night and believe you me, there are few places to find shelter on that road, until you reach Baccarra. You might as well stay here for the night and make a fresh start tomorrow morning".

Maun was again bitterly disappointed. Here they were, nearly two whole days since the ship docked and they were only five or six miles away. At this speed, it would be take months to get home, not days. Yet common sense prevailed; he knew they could not travel in the dark and he had felt as though he was being guided into doing what God intended him to do, which was, 'To heal the sick'. The strange thing was, that when he healed others, he too was being made stronger.

He was unaware of how he looked, but he felt immensely stronger. He also knew that his usually nervous nature was changing. For, with his new found way of life, came more self-assurance. He was still only a boy of sixteen, but his experiences of the last months had aged him considerably.

Barney told them they could put their bedrolls on the floor of the room they were in. It was warm, and the stove was kept burning all night. The children went to their beds in the loft and when Barney's wife arrived home tired, she went into the front room, while Barney and Evan had another drink of grog and sat chatting for some time.

Maun had slept, but woke up early. Evan was snoring and the room was stuffy, so he decided to go outside for some fresh air and to relieve himself. Afterwards, instead of going back inside, he went to the front of the house to the stream, where he washed his hands and face.

He sat on a rock watching dawn break, remaining there for a while enjoying the sound of the water trickling over the stones and listening to the birds singing. He had always loved early mornings and for him this was by far the best time of the day.

He heard a noise behind him and turned around to see Mora - Barney's daughter - walking towards him. She smiled, "I am sorry I appeared so foolish last night. I wanted to talk to you. To ask you questions, but the grown-ups didn't give us the chance".

Maun was pleasantly surprised. "You speak Latin?"

"Yes. My father taught me. He said that all the men from the ships from whatever country understand it and it would be useful one day. He also promised to take me with him to the Lorne one day soon."

"I wanted to ask you", said Mora, "Is there anything else you do, besides heal? I mean, do you see or hear people, other people cannot?".

Maun thought for a moment. "I suppose I do. Yes. Why do you ask? Have You?"

Mora was looking at him intensely. "Yes, all the time. Papa thinks I talk to myself, but I don't. I have friends no one else sees and they tell me things. One of them told me that a special person was coming to our house. At the time I could not understand, because no strangers ever come here, but as soon as I saw you, I knew it was you they spoke of." She spoke softly, as she looked into his eyes. "My friend told me that you were special. That God had chosen you to be his hands on earth."

Maun was warmed by her words and her simplicity and said, "You have very special friends and for them to be so close to you, means that you too have been blessed. Thank you for telling me your secrets, Mora".

He repeated her name, "Mora. that's a pretty name. I like it".

She smiled. "Father named me after a ship. That's what comes of him spending so much time by the sea."

He laughed, "You know, my friend Evan, well he has been telling me of the virtues of patience. 'Take things easy', he said, 'don't rush through life. If you hurry you will miss so much', and he is right. Last night, I was desperate to be on my way home, but was convinced by your father to stay over, as it would be the right thing to do. Now I am so glad I did. If I had insisted on leaving I would have missed this meeting with you. I have so enjoyed your company and will in future remember to make haste slowly".

Mora smiled, "So will I". She looked thoughtful. "I will say goodbye now, for I may not get the chance later." They touched hands and he watched as she disappeared around the back of the house, sitting for several more moments in silent prayer before following her in.

Maun found Barney preparing breakfast, while Evan was leaving to wash in the trough by the back door, although he had gone outside earlier, but seeing Maun and Mora talking, had decided not to interrupt them. 'What could they be saying to each other?', he had wondered.

As Maun entered the house, Evan joked, "Ah! there you are lad. I thought you had gone without me".

"No you didn't", said Maun. "You know Evan, I could not manage without you."

Barney looked over and smiled at him. "Here you are lad. You have the first lot" and he placed before Maun a large platter of fried bread and eggs. Maun thanked him and ate as much as he could. Evan returned from his ablutions ravenous and on finding an even larger breakfast waiting for him, sat down with Maun and quickly set about devouring the lot.

Soon they were ready to leave and they watched as Barney's wife wrapped some freshly baked buns in a piece of cloth in case they got hungry on the way. It was still very early and they thought they might slip away unnoticed. but several of the villagers came out to see them off. Fen's eldest son approached them and with Barney translating said, "I must tell you, that while you were healing my father, I was in the wood digging his grave. When I arrived home and found him alive, it was wonderful". Evan thanked him for getting up so early to tell them. He was so proud of Maun and he turned and patted him on the shoulder.

CHAPTER XXII

THE ROAD TO BACCARA

Evan eventually tore himself away from Barney. They were on their way at last, a full day's walking ahead of them. "I liked Barney", said Evan after a while.

"Yes", said Maun, "I did notice that you and he had a lot in common. Especially the same liking for that unpleasant tasting ale".

Evan gave him a sideways glance, but decided to ignore his comment and continued, "He was telling me about the town we are heading for. He said that the people there are different".

"Different", exclaimed Maun, "In what way different?".

"Well, it seems they look odd - kind of unusual. Not like others you might meet in these parts. Their skin is olive coloured. Their eyes are dark brown and their hair is thick and straight and they build their homes different."

"Are they dangerous?", asked Maun.

"No. According to Barney, they are very kind and helpful but, they are wary of strangers. Barney said that he had been to most towns in the area and only the people of Baccara look like this."

"Well", said Maun, "As long as they are not dangerous, we will be fine".

They were striding on at a fair pace, when Maun said, "In my village we all look different. Some people have dark hair, some have fair hair and we all have either blue or brown eyes. My grandfather Calim is fair and his brother has much darker hair. At least Uncle Harran did have dark hair, until it turned grey. My grandmother Rhona has very fair hair".

Evan stopped walking. "Mauny look at me." Maun obeyed and turned to face him. Evan looked him up and down, then peered into his eyes, "You've got kind of grey green eyes and yellow hair. Not a bad looking lad at that". Just as Maun was feeling puffed up and rather pleased, Evan added, "In a funny kind of way". Maun raised his eyes to heaven in exasperation, then Evan said, "Look at my eyes and tell me what colour they are?".

Maun studied Evan's eyes. "They are brown with little bits of green in them."

"Oh!", said Evan, "Exactly like my father's were. Anyway, I don't think people bother much about looks. Character and good nature are more important. If looks mattered, my Margaretta would not have married me".

They followed Barney's instructions, keeping to well trodden paths, with the sun to the right of them and they covered many miles in silence, Evan realising Maun's need to make up for lost time.

They came to a narrow valley, which looked as though it should have had water running through, but it was dry, the road lay between the sloped hills. About half way along the length of the valley, Maun suddenly stopped, saying, "Listen Evan?", followed by "Quick hide!".

They scrambled up the hill on all fours, as quickly as they could and lay flat behind some rocks. Keeping perfectly still they waited and within moments, the sound of galloping hooves grew ever louder. Then they came into view, men on horseback, whooping and yelling as they passed, then fading into the distance, their passage leaving behind them only churned-up mud. There must have been nearly fifty of them.

Maun's heart was pounding, when he heard Evan ask, "Have they gone?".

"Yes", he replied, "Thank goodness! Did you see the cart they had? It was full of valuables. Looks like they have just raided someone's home".

"No. I did not see anything Maun. I was afraid to look. That, my boy was too close for comfort. We will have to be more vigilant. They sounded bloodthirsty - I hope they do not decide to come back this way?"

"I agree", Maun said, "The sooner we reach Baccara - the better".

"I'm starving after all that excitement", said Evan, "Have we anything left to eat? If I don't have something soon …?" and he patted his stomach.

"All we have left are the buns Barney's wife gave us", said Maun. "I left them to last, hoping we would reach Baccara before we had to eat them."

"I will have one now", said Evan, "I'm desperate!". Maun reached into his satchel and took out two of the buns and handed Evan one, both were decidely overcooked, being a deep shade of black.

"Good grief!", said Evan, "Now I know why Barney spends so much time eating out at the ale house on the quay". Maun ate one of the buns without comment, remembering that a very short time ago, he would have been grateful for Barney's wife's cooking - and for her kind and thoughtful nature.

"I liked Barney's wife", said Maun. "She did not say much, but she was always on hand to help. With her husband away so much, she had lots of work to do."

At this remark, Evan became quiet, for he was aware of his own situation. Being away at sea for months at a time, Margaretta had to bring up their sons by herself. Admittedly, she did have her widowed mother to help her, but it wasn't the same as having a husband around. He firmly believed that a father should be around to influence the upbringing of his children and to be a pattern for them to set themselves on.

It was at this very moment that Evan made a vow to himself, 'Once he had seen Maun home safely, he would go home and spend the rest of his life with his wife and sons', although he realised this would be difficult, for he had no talent or trade, other than the sea.

He remembered the night he lay on the deck of the ship dying. Then Maun came and saved his life, although he did not actually remember everything. He had been told by those present, who had been thrilled by the healing.

He looked across at Maun, now striding out eagerly and thought, 'That slip of a boy has given me another chance at life and I'm sure as hell not going to waste it'. He felt gratitude well up inside him - he owed that lad his life.

Maun sensed Evan's eyes upon him and he looked at him and smiled. Evan returned his smile and with that, they both strode on, keeping up a fairly fast pace, but taking just enough time to glance at and appreciate the grandeur of the scenery; each bend on their path, or summit of a hill revealing even more splendid views.

There were signs and smells of wild animals, but so far nothing to cause alarm. The weather was clear, the sky bright, but it was cold and they shivered a bit as the wind blew against them. They quickened their step to keep warm and when a stone shelter appeared, they reluctantly took refuge for a while. The cold had sapped their energy - if not their enthusiasm - and they rested until they got their breath back.

Evan said, "We really must keep moving, lad. It's important we reach Baccara before dusk as it begins to get dark early so far north."They had followed Barney's instructions to the letter in order to avoid crossing water and so were confident they were on the right track.

They eventually came to the edge of a lake and they saw two men working on a rowing boat. They appeared to fit the description given by Barney of the people of Baccara; olive skin and straight brown hair with a hint of red in it. They were also tall and slim. They wore simple loose shirts belted at the waist and dark trousers tucked into calf length leather boots. Two padded jackets lay on the seat of the boat.

"Good day to you", said Evan. "Could either of you direct us to the town of Baccara?" The men answered in Latin, with a strong foreign accent that was difficult to follow, but sufficient to inform them that Baccara was roughly two miles along the road.

They covered the two miles in record time and found themselves in the centre of the town. They had passed some fishermens' cottages on the side of the lake, but the town was a surprise. A wide street with imposing buildings on either side and market stalls occupying the ground floors of most of the buildings. It was a busy place. A group of children were being led along by their school teacher and groups of men stood about talking and Maun sensed that they were angry about something.

Evan went to one of the stalls and asked the owner if there was an inn in the town where they could have a bed for the night, the man politely directing them to a house on the corner of the street.

As they approached the inn, Maun again remarked that the atmosphere of the place was angry, though he could not be more specific. Evan thought that the people seemed fine, just a bit reserved and wary of strangers. "I'm not so sure", said Maun. "I've never seen men gathered in the street talking like that. Something is not right."

"Well", said Evan, "Whatever it is, it has nothing to do with us. Let us try this inn and hope they can provide a good meal. All that walking has made me hungry".

The inn was a fine building, with pillars on either side of the doors. Evan knocked and it was opened by a tall, elegant and very pretty lady, although plainly dressed. She spoke in the same accent as the boatmen and upon inviting them to enter, they were surprised to hear her say, "Please remove your boots". As they sat on the step and kicked their boots off, they noticed that Maun's feet were covered in blisters. "Why did you not say something, lad. We could have stopped for a while. You must have been in pain?"

"I did not want to waste time," replied Maun.

The lady came to see why they were taking so long to come in and when she saw Maun's red and blistered feet, she cried sympathetically, "Oh! You poor boy. While you are waiting for your food, I will bathe them for you". Evan raised an eyebrow in surprise.

Maun smiled at him and whispered, "Jealous?".

"Not at all", said Evan. "I'm glad you are receiving attention. I'm only sorry you did not get it sooner."

The lady re-appeared, this time carrying a bowl of tepid water, a drying cloth and a jar of balm. She led Maun to a seat and placed the bowl of water in front of him. Then saying, "The water will soothe them", she tenderly placed Maun's feet in the bowl and bathed them, Maun wincing as his feet touched the water. However, he tried not to show how much it hurt.

She then turned to Evan, "My husband - the landlord - is also cook. We have only a few passing guests, therefore we do not keep a lot of food in stock. But, we do always have a good supply of fresh fish, which I can recommend".

Evan selected baked salmon with herbs and butter for both of them. Sitting beside Maun, he rubbed his hands together in anticipation and said, "I like it here already".

The lady returned, carrying an old pair of sandals and measured one for length against Maun's boot. "These will do - for a while", then she removed his feet from the bowl and dried them. The balm was soothing and Maun relaxed, while Evan, watching from a large cosy chair, allowed the smell of cooking to gently waft up his nostrils.

"Madam", said Maun, "May I ask you a question?".

She looked up at him. "Yes Sir. You may ask me anything. What would you like to know?"

Maun and Evan exchanged glances. "Well. When we arrived here in town, we noticed men outside in the street, talking. They seemed very worried and angry. Has something unpleasant happened?"

Her expression altered. She hesitated, then said, "Yes Sir. It has. Something has happened". Evan and Maun looked at each other, wondering what it could be that would cause so much concern.

She took the bowl of water away, leaving Maun's feet on the cloth. A man came in to the room. He was the landlord and the lady's husband. "Your meal is almost ready. I will bring it for you presently. My wife has told me that you are curious to know why the town's people are upset. Tis better if you eat your meal in peace. When you are ready, I will come and talk to you. It would upset my wife too much to talk about it. Please do not worry. There is nothing to be done - nothing anyone can do."

Evan and Maun enjoyed their salmon and although they did not speak of it during the meal, they wondered what the awful thing was that had happened to this small, polite and friendly community.

The landlord then entered with a tray of glasses and a jug of a special brew of wine. There were three glasses and Evan guessed that the story of what troubled these people was going to take a little time to tell.

Having poured the wine, the landlord sat down beside them. "We are a peace loving people. Our elders forbid violence of any kind, which makes our town, a haven or refuge for some and for others, an easy target to rob."

"For many years now, we have been attacked by bandits. Gangs of them ride in, take whatever they want and ride out again, laughing and whooping at our stupidity. Over the years, they have taken our horses, our cattle and anything else that takes their fancy. However, they do not touch our women, nor do they hurt us."

"Our young men are sick and tired of it. They want to retaliate and the time is well overdue. They are beginning to plot revenge and to defy our elders, who have always taught us that evil brings more evil and we should resist the temptation to strike back. But, the young men have fire in their bellies and we fear they may be planning some kind of trap. I do not blame the young men of the town, for I feel that they have reached the limit of their endurance."

"Today, the bandits rode in very quietly and very slowly. They stopped in front of the hospital and gently laid on the doorstep one of their men, who we understand was thrown from his horse and seriously injured. Then, they had the nerve to order our doctors to save his life! If they did not oblige, our town would be torched. Then they filled their cart with our property and raced off, shouting threats as they went."

Evan and Maun, who had listened very carefully, realised that the men on horseback who had given them such a fright, were the same ones that raided the town.

Evan asked, "Was it reasonable to expect that the doctors at the hospital can heal this bandit?". Shaking his head, the landlord said, "Our doctors are excellent and they help keep the people of the town fit and well, hardly suffering a days illness in a year. They also grow their own herbs and make their own medicines. They are indeed very skilled, but this bandit is no longer young. He has led a long, hard and violent life. I have heard that he is in so much pain, that he has called out for death to relieve him. Although the doctors are keeping him heavily sedated, he no longer wishes to live. This makes it very difficult and I think we are in a grave situation".

"Sir", said Maun. "Is it not possible that these threats made by the bandits to burn the town, are empty threats? For surely, to destroy it would deprive them of future rich pickings. It would not be wise to do so."

The landlord nodded, "You are right, my friend. However, wisdom is not known among people such as these. They act only on evil instinct".

"Then", said Evan, "I think Mauny my boy, we must pay the hospital a visit".

The landlord and his lady looked puzzled. Evan explained, "My young friend here is something of a healer. Perhaps, his talents can help? Would you Madam, point us in the direction of your hospital".

"I will do so presently, but first the boy must have his feet covered."

Maun smiled at her and put on the sandals she had brought. "Thank you, Madam. I am most grateful for your kindness."

They hurried along the road towards the large building at the end of the road which they had been directed to. Unlike the inn, the large doors were open and the inner doors were unlocked. They were met by a young man, who on seeing Maun's blistered feet, assumed he was a patient and ushered them into a treatment room. He indicated for Maun to sit on a chair and to remove his sandals. Maun was about to tell the young man his blistered feet were not the reason for their visit, but Evan held his finger to his lips, indicating for him to remain silent. So, Maun's feet received another treatment, while Evan questioned the doctor about the sick bandit.

The landlord was correct, they were keeping him sedated. "Would it be possible to see this man?", asked Evan.

The young doctor was suspicious. "Why would *you* want to see this man. Is he a friend of yours?"

"Oh! No", said Evan, "But we might be able to help him".

"Help him? After how they have treated us over the years? I know what I would like to do to him - if my profession and our Elders did not forbid it."

"I understand your sentiments", said Evan, "But, from what I hear, that attitude will not save this town".

"You are right, of course", said the doctor, "I will take you to him".

In a room by himself, the bandit lay, obviously in great pain. The sedative was wearing off and he was regaining consciousness. The doctor, in spite of his harsh words, looked sympathetic saying, "It must be in my blood, for I cannot bear to watch anyone in pain, regardless of who they are". His patient groaned. "I will ask for more sedative for him." As the doctor turned to leave, Evan asked him to wait, for he could see that Maun was already working.

First he held the patient's hand and silently prayed, "My Lord. I ask that this man be healed of his wounds and that the people of this town, who have kept faith in your eternal presence, be helped".

He then moved his hands to the man's heart and from there, slowly over his shoulders and arms. The power flowing from him was intense. The patient, whose face, which only a short time before had expressed agony, was now relaxed. He was awake and searching Maun's face. "Who are you? Why are you bothering with such as I?".

Maun smiled at him and replied, "It is my work".

Other members of the hospital staff heard what was taking place and came to watch. They were amazed to see the patient was at peace and not screaming, as he had been previously. However, one of them asked, "Why have you healed this evil man, when there are innocent people here, who are in need?".

Maun addressed him. "I was informed that this man was suffering. If you care to tell me of any one else who is in need, I will gladly see them."

Of the few other patients, only one required desperate help and Maun was taken urgently to another room, where a small child sat crying in a cot, rocking back and forth in pain, her tiny hands clasped around her head. Her mother - clearly deeply distressed - sat close by her sick child.

One of the medical staff said, "We have tried everything we know to cure this little one and although we have had some success, the pain keeps returning".

Maun then knelt by the bedside of the little girl and placed his hand on the side of her head. She immediately stopped rocking and sobbing, leaned forward and took Maun's other hand and held it to her other ear. She smiled at him.

Maun, still holding her, moved her head carefully on to her pillow, then took her hand and placed her tiny thumb in her mouth. She had fallen fast asleep.

The child's mother was so very happy. "How were you able to heal her, when our own doctors could not?"

Maun told her, "Your doctors heal the body. It is my work to heal the soul".

There was a buzz of excitement, as the news of the two healings were passed around the hospital. The chief physician also heard and asked for Maun to come to his office.

He welcomed Evan and Maun. "Please sit down". He paced the room once or twice before he spoke. "I wonder if you know the true value of your work here?"

"You are the answer to our prayers. We at this hospital and the Elders of our town have been praying for a miracle. For we have found ourselves in an almost impossible situation."

"You see, that man you have healed today, is not just any bandit. He is their Commander! It is from him they take their orders. Without him they are lost."

"Since he was placed on our doorstep, I have wrestled with my conscience, for I would dearly have liked to allow him to die. It even crossed my mind to hasten his end for what he has done to our people."

"What I wanted to ask you was this. Why has God chosen that evil man to be healed and why have we - a peace loving and gentle race - been made to suffer the indignities he forced upon us?"

Maun replied in his usual quiet and slightly nervous way. "Sir. I cannot answer for God, but I can tell you that your trials are over. The bandit is not only healed of his broken bones, but of his mental afflictions also. When he is completely recovered, you will see a different man. He will believe that he has been instructed by God to guide his men along a more peaceful path, one of right and fair thinking. You will not only live in peace, but will have gained loyal friends."

The chief physician breathed a deep sigh of relief, "I really do hope so. For we have been sorely tried, our manhood questioned regarding our ability to protect our property and the constant worry for our wives and children. All of it has been a nightmare. Our only weapon available, has been our prayers. Our Elders too have suffered, even more, for they have found it difficult to keep both faith and discipline, knowing what their people were being asked to tolerate".

"When they hear what has happened this day, they will be overjoyed, for they have insisted throughout that God would take care of us."

"Which leads me to my next question." Looking Maun straight in the face, he said, "Who are you to have such power? You are but a boy".

Maun answered, "I am Maun - my name means 'The Command' - the last command of our Lord Jesus to his disciples. That we should love one another, even our enemies".

"My friend", said the physician, "Our Elders have taught us to live by that very code, insisting that in order for our souls to reach the highest spiritual state. we must be free of all anger. That love is God, as God is love".

Maun then asked him why they had such a large hospital for such a small town?

The physician, who had been so moved by Maun's reply to his question, was surprised that he had now asked such a mundane one. He replied by saying, "You already know that the bandits stole our cattle and horses, we had, therefore, to get our sustenance from the lake - we practically live on fish! We also trade with the people of the other settlements along its banks. They supply us with some meat and milk. We provide them with honey and vegetables. We are also on call when they need medical help. We deliver their babies and give them advice - healing the sick is what we do best".

Maun recalled how eager their hostess at the inn had been to tend his feet. So, he nodded and smiled saying, "Thank you Sir. Now we must go".

Evan was relieved and hurried Maun out of the door, "Come on lad. All that work you do makes me hungry".

They reached the inn and having knocked on the door, they sat on the doorstep to remove their footwear. Evan said, "Its fine for the local people, all this taking off and on of shoes. They wear those funny little slippers, so they don't have to bend down to take them off".

Maun smiled as he watched Evan struggle with his boots and he said, "The fishermen wore boots!".

Evan glared at him. "Trust you to notice that", he mumbled under his breath.

Their hostess opened the door and held it open for them to enter. As they passed through the doorway, she caught sight of Maun's feet and she could not believe her eyes, for the feet she had so carefully bathed - covered in raw blisters - were now completely healed. "I know my balm is good, but not that good," she told her husband.

Maun looked down at his feet and said, "Good, that means we can set off on our way soon".

"Not before I've had a good meal", said Evan, "And not at this time of day. That is, of course, if our hosts here can accommodate us for the night?".

Their hostess seemed pleased, "Yes. We have rooms. You are both most welcome", she said with a smile, "Besides, it has just started raining and it is not advisable to go walking on the hills in such weather".

As they sat eating the landlord's freshly cooked fish and vegetables, they could hear the rain pouring down and noisily battering on the wooden shutters. As he drank some more ale, Evan said, "If we have to stay over anywhere, I'm glad it is here. We will have a good sleep and leave early in the morning".

"I think I need a good rest," said Maun, "I'm a bit tired".

"Why does that not surprise me", said Evan.

The landlady then came to remove their dishes and hearing Maun's comment, she said, "If you are ready Master Maun, I will show you to your room".

He was taken to a small room upstairs and was pleased that he had been given a room to himself. For as much as he enjoyed his friend's company, after Evan had eaten and drank his fill, he would go to bed and snore like a pig!

The landlady had told him she would bring him some milk a little later.

Maun lay on his bed, listening to the rain and thinking of the day's events. Everyone had been in awe of his power to heal and he felt humble knowing that all credit must go to those who were guiding him.

He began to pray and give thanks for his great gift to heal: 'The memory of the day when he was taken to that in-between world and seeing his parents and his grandfather in his Spiritual robes. My God, if only I had known these things before. Why was my grandfather so different? I always imagined that my father was the more superior'.

His impatience to get home returned.

Just then there was a knock on the door. Maun got up and opened it and their hostess entered carrying a lamp which sent a flickering glow around his small room. "I am sorry, I forgot to give you a lamp." She shivered, "It is quite cold in here. You know, you don't have to stay in your room Master Maun. There is a good fire in the hearth downstairs and it is cosy. Your friend has gone to sleep. I heard him as I passed".

"Thank you Madam, I will come down presently."

When she had gone, he looked around the room. Next to his bed there was a jug of water on a small table and the bed looked very comfortable, being filled with wool scraps, rather than the usual straw or horse hair. He took his over-gown from the hook behind the door, put it on and went downstairs. The landlady was there and she said, "Come and make yourself comfortable and I will bring your milk in here".

"You are very kind, Madam", said Maun as he sat on one of the biggest chairs, curling his feet under him.

As he sat looking into the flames, he wondered if his friend Cedi had been as fortunate as he? And the girls - he had a vague memory of them screaming. He prayed again, asking that they be well treated wherever they were.

The landlady returned with his jar of milk - with a spoonful of honey added - and gave it to him. "May I join you for a while?", she asked.

He smiled, "Yes Madam, I would welcome your company". She did not sit on one of the big chairs opposite, but brought a stool and placed it beside him. "Is the constant rain bad for business?", he asked her, remembering how the children never came to school in rainy weather, because if their clothes got wet, they took forever to dry again.

"No Sir. We try not to let the rain stop us do anything. We are encouraged to welcome the rain, for without it life would be even more difficult."

"We are taught from the beginning of our lives, that many hundreds of years ago, our ancestors lived in a very hot country. Every year they prayed for rain and usually some came. However, one year none came. The earth dried up. The well ran dry and the people also began to dry up. Their bodies shrivelled, their lips cracked open and they died. The few that were left began a journey to find water. Everywhere they went, it was the same story. But, eventually they reached the sea. However, that was not much help, as it was salt water, but at least it was cooler. Then the Elders decided that they would keep travelling until they found a land where the well never ran dry."

"They continued to pray and one day a ship arrived. The Captain was sympathetic and he told them that there was such a land, but many miles away. The Elders begged to be taken there and finally the captain agreed."

"When they arrived and saw this beautiful country, they were thrilled to know that they would never be thirsty again. But it was not easy. There were people already here and they protested at their presence, So, they had to work very hard in order to be accepted and that came about because our ancestors treated their injuries. They gained the trust of the local people, so were left in peace."

"It is a long story Sir, but one that explains our presence here and why we never complain about the rain. Our Elders call it 'The water of life'."

"I am terribly ignorant", said Maun, "I don't think it ever occurred to me that there could be such a country, as one without water. This must have seemed like Heaven to your ancestors?".

"It did, Master Maun and ever since then, we all give thanks for the rain. It is possible to shelter from the rain, but you cannot escape from the scorching heat of the desert."

Maun was feeling very content. Here he was sitting tucked up in a comfortable chair; in front of a roaring log fire, a jar of sweet warm milk and to top it all, a handsome woman relating a very interesting history of her people.

They heard someone coming downstairs and go out to the washroom. "That sounds like my friend, Evan," said Maun, "I expect his snoring has woken him up".

"Yes", agreed the landlady, "I'm afraid it does. And if you don't mind me saying so; it often wakes up everyone else within earshot". They both laughed.

The door opened and Evan came in. "So, this is where you are lad. Could you not sleep?"

"No, Madam thought my room was not warm enough, so invited me down to warm myself by the fire."

Evan rubbed his hands together, "And a grand fire it is at that".

Madam went to get Evan a drink, but she was hardly out of the door, when she returned, looking quite nervous. "Master Evan. Master Maun. Our Elders have come to see you. Can I show them in?"

They looked at each other, then said, "Most certainly". Maun stood up and waited to welcome them. Two very dignified gentlemen, their dark red cloaks flowing behind them, entered the room. They bowed their heads. Evan and Maun bowed back.

They introduced themselves as Reuban and Hammish. "We have heard what took place at the hospital today. We had to come and see you."

"For many years now, we have worked hard to keep our faith in our rules of 'non violence', knowing that violence invites more violence, just as evil begets more evil. Our people are few enough, we could have been wiped out in one battle and gone to Hades for our trouble."

"Young Man", said Reuban, in a voice of deep sincerity, "Without your timely arrival in this town and your miraculous skill, it is altogether possible that very soon, we would have no town left. That, young Sir, would have been tragic. Now, thanks to you, we may have the joy of surviving for many more generations".

"We have kept meticulous records of our peoples history; their travels and other settlements, to give them the security of knowing who they are. And for their special guidance in life, we feel that it is important for each soul to know from whence he came, that he or she may uphold the highest and best of our racial traditions."

Maun was slightly puzzled. "I am indeed sorry Sir, but I do not understand what you say. I have never heard anyone speak of racial traditions. In my home, there are many people in the Roman Army from many different countries. Some are very white. Some are very brown. The only race of which my grandfather speaks, is 'The human race' and the love and dignity that should be given to each and every person. He teaches that we are all God's children."

Reuban raised his eyebrows, then spoke with as much dignity as he could muster. "You are still very young and have not learned of the cruelty of racial wars - and pray God you never will. It is evil beyond all credulity to see one man kill another because of the colour of his skin, the language he speaks, or for the way in which he chooses to serve his God."

Maun felt chastened and decided that he was not qualified to offer further argument. Instead he said, "No doubt Sir, I have time to learn of such things".

Reuban thought it was time to change the subject and turned to Hammish who was holding two scrolls and indicated for him to spread one of them on the table. "I understand you are travelling south and we thought that this map may be useful to you. It shows the contours of the mountains around here for several miles. The main pathways are also clear, as are the lakes and rivers."

Evan was fascinated as Reuban pointed out the route that lay before them. "I have never seen such detailed drawings" and he pointed out to Maun where they had to travel in order to reach his home. The map and the writing on the map meant nothing to Maun, although he tried to look interested and said, "It appears to be a long way". Reuban rolled up the scroll and Hammish brought the other one forward and spread it before them.

Evan looked closely at the second map as Reuban pointed out coastlines. "These are magnificent drawings. I have sailed these waters for the past twenty years and how much more interesting it would have been if we'd had a map like this. How on earth did we manage?" Reuban's pride and dignity was now restored. "Our peoples have sailed for, not twenty years, more like twenty hundred years. They made records of all their travels."

Maun could not understand the marks or writings on the map and simply said, "They are most interesting". But, Evan was truly excited by them.

Hammish came forward and rolled up the precious map, saying, "I will have a rough copy of the map made showing you the road you have to take on your way south. We could not, of course, part with the original".

"We are grateful that you took the trouble to show us these treasures", said Evan.

Hammish added, "They were not created within a short time, but built up over many years".

At that point, Evan thought the Elders were preparing to leave, but instead,

Reuban turned to Maun. "There is a young man at the hospital. He watched you perform your healing of the bandit. He has been anxious to travel and gain experience of the world and he has requested we ask you to allow him to accompany you on your journey - you will find him a great asset."

"He is a young man of high intelligence and has many other skills to his credit. If you accept him, I am sure he will be a help to you." Evan looked at Maun, but did not voice the question.

Maun answered him - a nod was sufficient. "We will welcome this young man. Indeed, we need all the help we can get."

"That is settled then", said Reuban. "We shall inform him that he may call on you to make arrangements." With that the Elders left.

"I found them heavy going", said Evan.

"They were a bit", Maun replied, "But, you found their maps of great interest".

"I did. They were wonderful. Drawn as though you were a bird looking down upon the world. We have maps of a kind, but drawn looking to the land from the sea."

The rain poured unceasing, saturating the earth and creating deep puddles. Maun was becoming used to these delays and disappointments and it was obvious that to leave now would be folly. They would be sliding and slithering in the mud and their clothes would get soaked. "I'm sorry lad", said Evan, "I know how anxious you are to get home, but it is not possible until the weather changes".

Maun smiled and shrugged his shoulders, indicating his resignation to the inevitable. "Never mind, Evan. It could be a lot worse. At least we have comfortable beds, a wonderful cook and a lovely lady hostess."

"Your right lad. It could be a lot worse. Let's make the best of it."

Next morning, they were tucking in to an enormous breakfast, when their hostess arrived saying, "Master Maun. You have a visitor". She bent over and whispered, "It is a student from the hospital".

"We are expecting him", said Evan. "Will you ask him to join us, or if he would prefer it, wait for us in the other room. We are almost finished."

Their hostess left to deliver the message, but returned almost at once with a young man in tow. They saw that he was good looking - in a serious kind of way. He wore a simple grey gown, the uniform provided by the hospital and his long thick straight hair was tied at the back with what looked like a thin black snake.

He bowed before them. Maun offered him a seat at their table, but he declined, saying "The Elders have explained that I wish to travel with you?".

"Yes", Evan replied, "Yes they did. We shall be leaving just as soon as the weather breaks. We will be very pleased to have your company - and your guidance. We understand that you have some knowledge of the journey and that will be a great help to us".

The young man said, "I do know that we may have to wait several days until the rain drains away and the wind dries the earth. Meanwhile, I would like you both to spend some of the time we have to wait at the hospital. There is someone there who wishes to speak to you".

Maun said, "Not one of the Elders?".

Their visitor laughed, "No, not Reuban".

"Thank goodness", said Maun, "I fear he does not think well of me?".

"No. It is not either of our Elders. But, you are mistaken - they spoke well of you and were surprised at how young you are. It is the bandit you healed. He keeps asking for you."

"We will call at the hospital this morning, just as soon as there is a break in the rain", said Maun.

The young man made to leave, then stopped and turned. "I almost forgot. My name is Hanno. I thank you both so much for allowing me to accompany you on your journey." He bowed his head and took two steps backward, as was the custom of his people. Maun and Evan stood up and bowed back. Once he was out of the door, they continued eating. "Seems like a nice young fellow", said Evan, "We will all get along just fine".

Hurrying between the showers and dodging the puddles, Evan and Maun made their way to the hospital. They were amazed at the reception they received, everyone greeting them enthusiastically. It seemed that the doctors and students were immensely impressed with the work Maun had done the day before and wanted him to tell them how he did it. Every time he was asked he would say, "I don't know how. I just put my hands on the patient where I think he feels most pain - and pray".

They reached the room where the sick bandit was and saw that he was sitting beside his bed, apparently making a rapid recovery from his wounds. The patient then asked to speak to Maun in private and Maun wondered how he could communicate, as neither spoke each other's language. However, after some persuading the bandit to allow an interpreter to be present, Hanno came forward to fill this role.

With Hanno translating the man said, "I thank you for giving me back my life; for taking away my pain. But, from now on it will be a life without causing pain to others, for you my dear friend have reminded me of a life I once knew, with love and compassion, not hate, aggression and fear".

"My friend. From the very hour of my recovery, I have dedicated my life, whether it be long or short, to helping my brothers."

Maun was pleased and happy to hear that this once violent man, had now found peace in his heart. He was, however, just a little embarrassed and self-conscious. He had always thought of himself as inferior to those who were more educated, intellectual types. His spiritual awakening had changed his life. He knew that God loved him and he was more confident. But, he found that those who were healed, *thanked him,* while he would have preferred them to turn to God. He had no desire to take upon himself gratitude or glory that really belonged to God. He still thought of himself as the boy, who longed to see his mother and father again and to question his grandfather on many mysteries that were close to his heart.

Maun spent most of the day talking to the physician and answering questions about his captivity and the place he visited when he died.

"How do you know it was not just a vivid dream? ... Did this room or place have a floor to stand on? ... What language did this Jesus speak?"

155

Maun did his best to answer all the questions honestly. However, it was not easy to explain the unexplainable, even to a people who lived by a strong moral and spiritual code, but appeared never to have experienced any angelic intervention or mystical insight or experience.

They walked back to the inn between showers at the same time searching the sky for a gap in the clouds that would herald a change in the weather. But, instead only low grey clouds announcing further showers.

Once inside the inn, Maun said, "I know these people are taught to appreciate the rain, but really this is too much of a good thing".

Evan laughed at him, "Getting impatient again are we? Though, it is a fact that I don't think I saw as much water all the time I was at sea!".

Morning light came. The sun shone through sparse clouds and a fresh wind swept over the land, drying up the puddles fast. Maun opened the shutters of his small window, looked out and uttered a short prayer of thanks, before rushing into Evan's room to wake him up. Evan taking a look for himself, agreed, "Yes lad. It looks good. Today is the day - but not before breakfast!".

"Do you think Hanno will be ready?"

"Don't worry lad. We'll send him a message before we eat." A note was sent to Hanno, who soon turned up all packed and ready.

Their hostess, who rather belatedly, told Maun her name was Mera, refused payment for their board saying, "But for you, we would not have our inn or even our lives. We thank you for coming when you did".

There was a crowd of people waiting to say goodbye and Maun was surprised to see Hammish amongst them.

Evan, Maun and Hanno followed a well trodden path out of the town, making their way through some beautiful countryside. The rain had cleared the air making everything look fresh and when they reached the top of a hill, they could see for miles in all directions and they instinctively took deep breaths of the clean air. Hanno, however, had bad news. He pointed in the direction he intended to take them. "Look over there", he said pointing into the far distance. "There are fires, all around the lake. That can only mean one thing - bandits! Unfortunately, their leader in the hospital will not have been able to speak to them yet and even now, they could be planning their revenge. We had better take another route. It will be longer but much safer."

They covered mile after mile without incident, stopping only briefly to eat or drink. Mostly the journey was enjoyable and once, in the distance, they spotted a herd of deer. Evan was fascinated to see a stag with what he called, 'A tree growing out of his head'. Hanno said, "These animals are eaten by the native people. They taste very good and it is most likely it is this meat our friends - the bandits - are cooking on their fires".

"Speaking of food", said Evan, "I am beginning to feel hungry. Have we anything left to eat?". "No", said Maun, "We have eaten everything".

"Then keep a look-out for a duck, or a rabbit. We could light a fire and cook it for our supper."

Several miles further on, they spotted a herd of wild pigs, at the edge of a wood.

"Quick", said Evan, "Let's catch that small one" and before Maun or Hanno could unload their back packs, Evan had run after the pig, making several attempts to grab the beast, which was always too quick for him.

Hanno joined in the chase, but Maun stood, mouth open, but speechless as the tiny pig darted back and forward. At one point Evan made a grab for it and landed his full length, catching the unfortunate animal by a back leg. Evan was triumphant. but the pig squealed so loud, that the herd who were waiting in amongst trees nearby, began to grunt angrily.

"Quick", said Evan, "Give me a knife", but neither Hanno or Maun had one. Evan looked at them both in disgust and still breathing heavily from his effort, placed the pig on the ground and watched in despair as his dinner scampered back to the safety of the herd.

"Did it not occur to you two to prepare for such an event? How do you expect to eat tonight?" Then he turned on Maun. "As for you, young Maun. You seem to be able to work miracles of healing. Perhaps, you can work another kind of miracle and produce some food, before we all starve to death."

Maun prayed silently, asking for food. "I'm sorry for laughing, Evan, but it was funny. I did not really want to eat that little pig anyway", he had a mental picture of the farmer offering him the pig's blood.

"You would if you were hungry enough", said Evan. Maun did not reply.

Within the hour they came to a stream, part of which was dammed naturally creating a deep pond. One glance and Maun knew that his prayer had been answered. It was full of fat fish, just waiting to be plucked out of the water. Hanno produced his flint and fire-making kit and within a short time, a fire was burning and soon they were baking fish on the end of sticks held over the flames. "You see Evan, *I* have come prepared", said Hanno.

With his stomach filled, Evan was in a much more jovial mood. "All we need now is a safe place to sleep for the night." They were, however, in no mood to hurry on. Sitting by the brook eating, was a very pleasant interlude, although they thought it was strange that they had not come across a friendly home, a cave or even a hut. Then Evan said, "Well, young Maun, Your prayer asking for food worked, for I doubt very much if that pond is always so full of fish. We could just as likely have found it empty".

"And as for you Hanno. How long does it usually take you to light a fire?"

"I have to confess", said Hanno, "That it usually takes a bit more effort".

"Well, I think you two had better pray for somewhere to sleep tonight." Evan looked at his two young companions with some pride. "Anyway, I don't think we will be hungry again - not on this journey anyway" and he stamped the fire out with his boot, then covering the embers with earth.

They moved on, covering many more miles and becoming tired, for the route was not a straightforward one. Unlike the straight roads of the Roman legions, these rough roads were over mountains and down dales. As the light began to fade, they were grateful to spot a shelter down in a hollow among some trees. "Looks like an old shepherd's hut. There should be a farm not too far away", said Hanno. However, as they were too tired to travel any further, they unrolled their beds on the floor, jammed the door shut and settled down for the night.

At first light, they were up and on their way again. They had covered about a mile and a half, when Maun suddenly stopped. "Listen! What can you hear?" The others stopped. Maun was concerned, "It sounds like an animal in distress",

"Yes. I can hear it too", said Hanno. "We must find out what is wrong - those sounds are unnatural."

As they hurried to where the sounds appeared to be coming from, in the distance, they spotted a farm and ran the last half mile. Now they could make out the noise of a dog whining and cows bellowing - all clearly in distress. As they got closer, they could also hear a voice calling, "Help! Help!". A quick search of the farm buildings and Maun called to the others after he found a man lying on the stone floor of a storage barn, one of his legs twisted in an unnatural position. A broken ladder lay nearby. Looking up as they entered, the man cried out in a weak voice, "I can't move".

Hanno took charge. He knew exactly what to do. They moved the injured man very carefully into the house. There were two beds in the room and another two in the room next door. They wondered where the other people were, but were too busy to ask. "I have seen this kind of injury before", said Hanno. "We must try to put the bone back in place, or he won't be able to walk again" and he sent Maun to look for some pieces of wood to make splints, while he told the man what he and Evan intended to do and why.

Maun quickly found some suitable splints and returned to the house with them, then went to find the dog that they had heard barking. It was weak from lack of food and water and Maun gave him some meat he found in an adjacent cool room. After being untied, the dog drank from a nearby puddle, before wandering off in search of his master.

The man screamed, the most piercing sound he had ever heard! Maun immediately rushed into the house and saw Evan holding the man, gripping him under the arms, while Hanno tried to move the broken leg into position. "Quick Maun. Put the splint on and tie it tight." Fortunately, the man had passed out and no longer felt the pain.

Hanno went to his bag and took from it a small bottle of liquid medicine, which when opened gave off a pungent smell. "What is that?", asked Evan.

"It's a mixture of garlic and herbs - it helps recovery from accidents."

The immediate crisis now passed, they left the injured man to come round and Maun said that he was worried about the distressed cries of the animals, "The cows need milking and there ia a bull that should be out in the enclosure" - he hesitated.

Evan said indignantly, "If there are cows to be milked, you two can do that. Milking cows is no job for a sailor - I will cook dinner. That is, if I can find anything to cook?".

Hanno joined Maun to help with the milking. There were only four cows, but it took longer than they expected. Maun said, "Now for the bull. I don't like the look of him. He is snorting and bellowing, we'd better take him some food and water, maybe that will cool his temper".

"We can then see to him later", said Hanno.

They took the fresh milk into the house and placed it on a bench. "Well, *we* have done the milking. How's supper coming along?", said Maun as he observed Evan having 'forty winks' on one of the beds.

"The patient seems calm enough", said Maun.

"Yes, he is", replied Hanno, "And so is our cook by he look of him". They laughed.

"I'm a bit worried about our patient, Maun. I gave him some mixture to relax him, but I'm afraid he will need something much stronger and more effective than a brew of 'mandrake and henbane', to kill his pain. These will make him drowsy, but are not powerful enough to give him rest."

Maun said, "I will sit with him when he wakes up. Meanwhile, we had better do something about the bull".

In spite of the food and water, the bull was still in a bit of a temper. 'He's the most ferocious bull I've ever seen', Maun thought. 'But, why am I so worried? I know that I am going to arrive home safely.' So he took courage from that knowledge, inhaled a deep breath, then strode boldly into the bull's pen and trembling, untied the rope that held the huge animal. Surprisingly, the bull ignored Maun and took off, out of the pen, through the gate of the shed and made for the enclosure. Maun ran after the bull and opening the gate of the enclosure, let him in. Still shaking, he turned round looking for Hanno and saw him hiding behind the door. "You are brave, Maun", he said, "I was so afraid for you". When they went back inside the house, Evan had found a pot and was mixing eggs and milk in a bowl, with much more energy that was really necessary and singing at the top of his voice.

Their patient was still asleep and Maun sat beside him, taking his hand and clasping between his own. He felt the power begin to flow though him. His hands got very hot, so he moved his chair to the bottom of the bed and placed them on the patient's leg. He sat there until, Evan called out, "Supper is ready. Come and get it".

Later, the farmer regained consciousness, but was clearly confused. He watched Evan through half-shut eyes and wondered who this big man was, cooking at his stove.

His leg was throbbing. Yet, he dare not speak.

Maun and Hanno went towards him. Hanno smiled, "Ah! You are awake now, Sir".

"Who are you people?", the patient asked.

Hanno told him, "We are travellers, making our way south. We heard the cries of the animals and came to investigate and found you. It looked like you had fallen from a ladder?".

The farmer nodded as his memory returned. "Oh! Yes, the ladder! I fell."

"Your leg is broken, Sir. It will mend though, given time. For the present, you should rest. Eat as much as you can to get your strength back."

They were not at all surprised that their patient showed signs of a speedy recovery. He sat eating and drinking cheerfully, thanking them for what they had done for the animals, as well as for himself.

"My sons rode off to market yesterday. When I went to get the salt from the shelf,

I remember hearing the ladder cracking and nothing else until I heard your voices calling to each other. I thought my sons had returned and called out. Then nothing else - until now."

"Ah!", said Evan, "You have sons. That explains the number of beds".

However, Maun was more interested in where the farmer's sons had gone to market. "It sounds like a fair sized town. Not too far away?"

"It's called Craiga," the farmer told them. "It's not all that big, but very busy. We send all of our surplus food to be sold there. My boys go regularly. It is their time off. They are gone for three days, sell what they can to the inn. Next day they sell the surplus at the market and the next day they shop for what we need here. They spend the evenings at the inn with their young ladies, then they come home. All the happier for being away. It does get harder for me though. There is a lot of work to do. Too much for one man."

"They are good boys, never any trouble, but we all suffered when my wife died." They sat around the fire talking. The farmer told them that his wife had died three years before. They had found it difficult to manage without her, for they had not appreciated just how much she had done for them - they had to learn fast. Night after night our youngest boy cried for his mother, then one day he stopped crying and told us that he was going to do all the work his mother had done. "After that we came out of our darkness."

Evan asked, "Is there was anything else we can do before we settle down for the night?".

"I think, my friends, you have done enough. The boys are due back the day after tomorrow. They will get a shock to see me like this."

On realising they would be held back another day or more, Maun was disappointed. At the same time ashamed of his selfishness, for he knew it was their duty to take care of their patient until his sons returned home. 'But, his home beckoned!'

They all slept soundly till early morning, until Maun heard the patient groan and got up to attend to him. The farmer pointed outside and Maun guessed that he wanted to relieve himself, Hanno also realising what was happening and got up to help. They let their patient put his arms around their shoulders and with their help, he made his way slowly, hopping on his good leg, outside the building.

When they got him back to bed and made him comfortable, the farmer told them his name was Mardo, then using Hanno as a translator, he asked Maun, "Who are you?".

"My name is Maun."

"He does not mean that", said Hanno, "He wants to know *what* are you?"

"Tell him", said Maun, "That I am a traveller - on my way home".

Hanno translated, but Mardo shook his head from side to side in disagreement. Hanno then had a long conversation with him, then repeating to Maun what the farmer had said. "Mardo says that when you are near him, he feels different, stronger and full of life. He says that you have a special gift."

"Yes, Sir. I am much blessed", said Maun, "But, then so are you. For I can tell you, that but for the bandits blocking our route, we would not have found you. God was on your side."

Mardo laughed cynically, " My friend. If God was on my side, he wouldn't have taken my wife from us, or allowed me to break my leg in the first place".

"Sir", said Maun, "I look at life as a child going to school. He must learn that if he runs hastily, he will fall over and hurt himself. And when a student doesn't study, he won't keep up with the other students or pass his exams. We must learn from our mistakes. If we do not learn, we may have to go back to the beginning and start all over again. It was not God who took your wife away. It is more truthful to say that God blessed you with a good wife, who gave you two wonderful sons to help you, but when her work was finished, she returned to her heavenly home to wait for you. You had to learn to be independent. Your youngest son showed you the way. Do not Sir, grudge your wife's peace. I tell you Sir, she is watching over you and knows of your love for her and your triumph over her loss".

Mardo looked into Maun's face and said, "For one so young, you have an old and wise head on your shoulders". Hanno agreed, then translated for him.

The day was spent tending the animals, sweeping out the stable and cowshed and the multitude of other mundane jobs which must be done on a farm. In the meantime, Evan prepared the food, making sure everyone had enough to eat.

Maun, once over his disappointment at having to wait another day, threw himself into the work and enjoyed it, thinking only of the happy times he spent helping Cedi. He was also reminded of that other farm where he had been a slave. Although only a very short time ago, it was sliding further away in his memory. It seemed as though it was in the distant past. He knew that it was all part of his own healing process.

He often wondered about Cedi, 'Was he dead or alive? And what of the girls Anna and Sophia?'. He hardly dared think what could have happened to them

They finished their work in good time, Evan called them in for supper. They washed their hands and helped themselves to a bowl of thick soup, although Evan handed the patient his, for he was now able to feed himself and to hop around the room unaided.

"This is good, Evan", said Maun and they were all enjoying their meal, when they heard the unmistakable sound of a wagon and horses approaching, then draw to a halt outside. "That's my boys back", Mardo announced and Evan went to the door to let them in.

Mistaking him for an intruder, the brothers quickly became very angry. "What the hell are you doing in our house? ... Where is our father?"

Evan held up his hands to indicate that he was unarmed. Then Mardo called out, "Its all right Dan. I'm in here and I'm well". On hearing their father's voice they entered, but still looked around at the strangers suspiciously.

Mardo reassured them, "If it were not for these men, you would have found me dead and the farm and animals in a sorry state. We owe these men a debt of gratitude".

The brothers said how sorry they were for mistaking them for robbers, but their first impression had been that robbers had broken in, killed their father and taken over the farm. "We can now see how wrong we were and what a grand job you have done for us. We are indeed very grateful".

Hanno said, "Think no more of it. Now that you are home, we can continue on our journey south, however, the hour is late and we do not want to travel in the dark. We would be grateful if we could stay another night and set off in the morning".

"That would be a pleasure", said Mardo, "We have little enough company". The evening was spent discussing Craiga, the small market town where the brothers went to sell their wares and the next stop on their journey.

Maun's only sign of further disappointment, was to close his eyes for a moment's reflection. He was aware that the things that were happening to him, were for his training. He was learning patience, tolerance and compassion for strangers, although it appeared to him that he was being sent on this journey, to show him just how much the people of the world needed to learn of their creation, something it seemed, everyone had forgotten. It was easy for him to love. He only had to recall the look in the eyes of Jesus, to feel the abundance of love and compassion for those in trouble, well up inside him. To be able to share this feeling with others, was becoming as natural as breathing. Yet, still the yearning to be with his family was strong.

He remembered that when he had died and had been taken to that heavenly place - where he had seen his mother and his father - how unhappy they were. 'How they must love me', he thought. 'Before I was captured, I was such a selfish boy who took them for granted. He longed to be able to tell them how much he loved them and make up for their unhappiness.'

He heard Evan and Hanno talking and forced his attention back to reality.

Hanno was teaching the younger boy how to care for his father after they had gone. "Leave the splint on for a while and only allow him to put his foot on the ground a little at a time", despite Mardo protesting that he was feeling stronger by the hour and felt sure he could walk unaided. The elder of the two brothers Dan, was telling Evan about Craiga, the small market town where they had been to sell their surplus food. "There is a fine tavern there. They serve the best food. We should know, it is our own. But, our stay there was spoiled by a gang of violent trouble makers. Seems they laze about all day, using foul language and laugh and sneer at good people going about their work. They were probably thrown out of another town."

Dan added, "And about to be thrown out of Craiga as well - if there was anyone brave enough".

Maun was sitting near Mardo and noticed how his eyes lit up as he looked at his sons. He was obviously very proud of them. Maun thought, 'I hope my father will look at me, just like that, when I get home. Instead of that hurt and disappointed expression I seen so often'.

CHAPTER XXIII

CRAIGA

Next morning, they were up early, hoping to cover some miles and reach Craiga long before noon. A very cheerful Dan and Duncan, his younger brother, prepared oatmeal, bread and butter, with honey for breakfast.

"It won't take you very long to reach Craiga. There are well marked roads, no steep hills and the weather looks like it will stay dry. We travel that road so often, our tracks will take you straight there," said Duncan.

"You will like this town. It is quite lively and there are some very nice young women there", said Dan, winking at his younger brother. Duncan blushed.

Their father on hearing this last remark, said, "Young women there may be, but none stupid enough to marry you and come here to live. We could do with a woman around the house".

"Now, now, father", said Dan, "There is plenty of time for that. We are too young to settle down just yet a while".

It was a happy trio that waved good bye to their hosts and headed for Craiga and Duncan was right, it was a good straight-forward road and they made good time. Hanno suggested that they could have a bite to eat here, then make for the next village. Maun was all for that.

Finding the inn, a very plump lady told them that the meal was roasted pig with chopped turnips. "Good", said Evan, "We'll have some of that". Hanno ordered the meal and told the lady they were friends of Dan and Duncan, who had recommended her cooking. That pleased her.

They took a seat in a corner by the window and waited until she brought them some ale. The cool winter sunshine was streaming through the shutters and the door and they thought, 'Dan was right: this is a pleasant town'. Just then, their peace was shattered. In burst four youths of the nastiest kind. No respect for man nor beast. They made for a table recently vacated and swiped the dishes onto the floor. They landed with a mighty clatter. The other customers got up and quickly left, or moved into another room.

Evan, Hanno and Maun were trying to ignore their vulgar language and insults and determined not to be intimidated. Then a young lad of about twelve years old arrived on the scene with a broom and a bucket to clear up the mess. He walked awkwardly, as though one leg was shorter than the other. As he bent down to pick up the larger broken pieces of pottery, one of the gang put his dirty boot on the boy's neck and pinned him to the floor. The rest of the gang thought this was hilarious and the youth holding the young lad down sneeringly said, "Say, Please let me up".

The boy did as he was bid, saying "Please, let me up", but, his pleas were ignored. Maun, who had his back to them, turned to see what was going on and he could feel the anger rising in him, an emotion unfamiliar to his nature. He stood up. Evan and Hanno tried to stop him getting involved, "Sit down Maun, you will get hurt".

But Maun walked over and stood before the bully. He spoke softly, "Allow the boy to rise", he said. Evan had his elbow on the table, his hand covering his eyes. Hanno watched nervously, bracing himself to defend Maun. But, to his amazement, Maun bent down and lifted the boot aside and helped the boy to his feet.

The gang watched mesmerised. All they could see was a blazing light around Maun's head. A magnificent halo that hypnotised them. They could do nothing but stare. Hanno nudged Evan to watch and he reluctantly opened his fingers and looked through them. Maun said to the boy, "Show me your foot" and the boy raised his gown a little to reveal a limb so twisted, that he was forced to walk on the outside edge of his foot.

"Come and sit here", said Maun and he led the boy to a low stool. Maun sat crossed legged on the floor opposite him and taking the twisted foot in his hands, he held it. He could feel the bone yielding to his touch as the power flowed through his hands.

Some of the other customers, who had vanished when the youths arrived, now filtered back to see why everything had gone quiet. They stood around watching fascinated at what was taking place.

When Maun removed his hands, to reveal a straight limb and a perfect foot, there were gasps of disbelief and wonder from the onlookers.

The boy began to cry. Not tears of hurt, but of joy! Maun smiled at him and stroked his hair gently. "Do not be afraid of anyone. You are a child of the Lord God who loves you." Then he turned to the audience and spoke only just loud enough for them to hear him.

"What you have seen this day, is not my work, but the work of our Father in Heaven. It is his wish that you learn of his divine presence. He wants you to know that he loves you as every good father loves his children", Hanno translated quickly.

Maun then turned away, leaving a stunned audience and went towards his friends, who were just as dumbfounded as everyone else.

Although they had seen Maun perform incredible healings on several occasions, this was different. In the past, there was always room for some doubt. The sceptic could argue that those who were healed would have got better anyway - in time. But, not now! The townspeople knew that the boy had been deformed from babyhood and they had seen with their own eyes that he had been made whole.

And what of the bullies, hell-bent on causing as much mischief as they could? They sat staring, at first into space, then at Maun.

Evan became worried. "I think we should get out of here fast."

"Why", Hanno asked, "We have not had our meal yet?".

"Never mind the meal. I've got an uneasy feeling someone is going to shout out 'Magician'. We could be in trouble."

Evan picked up Maun's cloak and put it around his shoulders, saying, "Come on lad", while Hanno picked up the backpacks. They left the tavern, hurrying as fast as they could, but without actually running. Evan asked Maun, "Are you feeling all right?".

"Of course I am. What is the matter?"

"Never mind, lad. It's just that it's still daylight and we can cover a good few miles before dark." Maun did not argue against that. The more miles they covered, the better he liked it. But, he was curious as to why Evan had foregone his meal?

Hanno glanced back over his shoulder and saw that the crowd from the tavern were now ominously standing outside and staring after them. They hastened their steps.

After a while they came to a fallen tree trunk and thought it a good place for a rest. Maun had been quiet since their hasty departure from Craiga and he wandered away to be by himself. Evan remarked to Hanno, "Maun seems despondent and downhearted. I thought that the nearer we got to his home, the more cheerful he would be. I wonder what troubles him?".

Hanno laughed, "Don't you know, Evan? I thought you would have guessed".

"What are you on about, Hanno? Guessed what?".

"Our Maun is becoming a man. Have you not seen him fiddling with that one 'whisker' on his chin? Or how he speaks quietly, so that his deepening voice is not so obvious."

Evan replied, "What an old fool I am. Of course, I should have realised. Well! Well! Our little Maun is a man. I wonder what kind of life he will have? I hope he will not be exploited by someone who sees an opportunity to make some easy money".

Hanno agreed, "Do you think he is aware of what ails him? I think Evan, you should have a talk with him and explain".

"Me?", said Evan. "I think it should be you, Hanno. You are nearer to his age. You have just passed that stage yourself."

"No", said Hanno, "You are a father figure. You should talk to him. When he comes back, I will go for a walk and you can speak to him".

"Very well", said Evan. "I will do it, but I still think it should be your job".

When Maun returned from his wandering, he sat down beside Evan and shortly after, Hanno casually strolled off, leaving Evan to explain the facts of nature to Maun.

"All right lad?", said Evan, he cleared his throat.

"I'm fine", said Maun giving Evan a sideways glance, "Why do you ask?".

"I've been thinking, lad. Your mother and father are going to be surprised when you get home. You left them a boy and now you are going to return a man."

Maun smiled, "Yes, they will be surprised", but his expression returned to one of moodiness.

"You know, lad. When you were captured and taken into slavery, you became very ill - that must have been some beating they gave you! Then, you were starved. These things would upset your development, for you were just at an age when your body was changing. You would be too pre-occupied with your suffering to develop. But, when you escaped and got aboard that 'old sweat rag' of a ship of ours, you were fed well and in good company. Well, lad. You are making up for lost time now and becoming a man very quickly. I'm surprised you're not aware of the changes?"

"When I was your age, I did feel peculiar and no mistake. I remember finding my first whisker - I was teased unmercifully by my friends."

Glancing sideways, Evan saw Maun lift his hand to his chin and he thought 'He's surely going to have to admit how he feels now?'. But, no! Maun simply said, "Thanks Evan. You are a good friend to me. What would I have done on this trip without you?".

Hanno studied the copy of the map he had made belonging to the Elders, which he consulted from time to time. He felt instinctively that they were on the right road, there being only one small village to pass before they reached Maun's home. He hoped that when they reached this village, that there would be a place for them to have a meal and sleep the night - they had missed the plentiful food at Craiga and felt very hungry.

Looking over Hanno's shoulder as he studied the map, Evan and Maun looked at where he was pointing. "Look here. This is the road we are on now - I think? All being well, we should reach this spot here in a short time" and Hanno pointed to some marks on the paper. To Evan and Maun, the marks were a complete mystery and Hanno looking at the blank expressions on his companions' faces said, "Perhaps, I should have taken more care in copying, but never mind, I know what is there - trust me".

They walked on for some time, eventually coming upon the signs and smells of habitation. The smell of wood burning; childrens' voices; a dog barking, then some houses came into view. They quickened their steps. Suddenly, Hanno said, "I don't want to alarm you, but since we left Craiga, we have been followed".

Instinctively, Evan turned to look behind them, "I don't see anyone", he said, "Are you sure Hanno?".

"Yes I'm certain. I've caught sight of them several times."

'What could they want of us?", asked Maun.

"Well", said Evan, "I suspect its those troublemakers from the tavern. They are probably just curious to find out where we are going. For, if they are following us with any evil intent, they could have caught up with us ages ago".

"I expect you are right, Evan. But, we will hurry on, just in case", said Hanno, "Best not to take chances".

When they entered the village, they were astounded at the size of the community, for according to the map, there were only a few houses and one or two work places. "That map must have been drawn some time ago", said Evan.

"You are right, Evan. There are many more houses now than are marked here."

They walked through the main street, which had a grassed area and a large dew pond, where ducks paddled contentedly and children were running around, playing games, screaming and laughing.

Maun remarked on the various styles of the houses - there was even several just like those at Bonavon. Hanno spoke to the children, "Do you know anyone in these houses who can give us lodgings for the night?".

At Hanno's accent, the children held their hands over their mouths and giggled and shrugged their shoulders, as children do when they are shy or embarrassed. Then, one little boy pointed to a house. "In there mister. They take in travellers sometimes."

As Evan knocked on the door, Maun smiled at the children, who had followed them. A woman opened the door, but before she spoke to them, she shooed the children away. "Now Sirs. Can I help you? I'm sorry about the children being so nosey, but we don't get many strangers around here."

"We understand that you take in travellers and we would be grateful for a bed for the night and a meal - if that's possible?" Hanno asked her. "We are travelling south and intended to go on, but it is dusk already and we are tired and hungry."

She stood aside and let them pass into the room. "We do have spare rooms, but only two and I will have to consult with my husband. He will be back presently. We have a daughter who lives across the way, my husband is over there at this moment. Can I offer you some water or other refreshment? We have some ale". Evan took up the offer of some ale immediately, but Maun and Hanno just asked for water.

"You are welcome to stay, but please don't be offended if we appear less than hospitable. Our daughter who lives in the cottage across the way, is having a baby and she needs our help. Porteous - that's my husband - is over there now, making up the stove to keep the house warm. When he returns, I will have to leave to be with her. Porteous will cook supper."

Hanno replied for all three, "Then we must doubly thank you for taking us in. You are most kind to do so under the circumstances. Many others would have turned us away".

She looked up to face him, "That is not our way Sir. Besides, there is no other place for miles around. I could hardly leave you out in the cold".

They sat in the main room of the small house and remarked on its cleanliness and neatness. It reminded Maun of something he once heard his father say "... More often than not, people who are born near harvest time, are very neat and clean and are most particular".

Evan frowned at Maun, "Your father said that? I wonder how he worked that out".

Hanno smiled at Evan's scepticism, "We are taught in our faith to believe that there are universal and spiritual laws which govern the universe. Most of them are hidden from mankind, until such times as an individual becomes curious enough to ask and having the level of wisdom to do so, is given the answer through their higher mind".

Maun nodded his agreement. Evan looked from one to the other of his companions. "I don't know about you two. You speak of things that I never in my life heard before."

This philosophical discussion was brought to a halt by the entrance of Porteous. "Good-day to you. Ilsa, my wife told me you were here. I don't expect she has had time to show you where your beds are. We have two spare rooms. One is large with two beds and the other small with one bed. You may choose between yourselves. They are all comfortable enough."

As Porteous led them along the passage, he explained that they had three children - two boys and a girl. He said, "One of our boys died. The other one left to join the Army. Our daughter lives across the way with her husband".

Evan decided on the small room with one bed, Hanno and Maun sharing the other room. He said - rather sheepishly - "They tell me I snore a little". Maun and Hanno did not contradict him, but both glanced at him, making him feel guilty. "All right. All right. I admit it. I snore quite a lot."

Porteous said, "That's settled then" and he led them back to the main room. He then announced that it was, "Rabbit stew for dinner. Is that suitable for everyone? I prepared it this morning for all the family, including our daughter and her husband. But, I doubt very much if either of them have an appetite at this time. They are very worried".

"Why are they so worried?", asked Evan, "Is there anything we can do to help?".

"Well", said Porteous, "I should not be troubling you gentlemen with our personal worries, but since you are here and as things may not work out, you most likely will hear all about it, so I might as well tell you".

"Our daughter has wanted a child for a long time. Twice before she has given birth and both times the baby died. This time we are praying that the baby will live. If it does not, I fear for our daughter's future."

"That is why my wife and I are spending so much time over there. Attempting to keep them calm and cheerful and free of worries."

"Tell me", said Porteous, "Where are you heading for?".

Evan was taken aback by the sudden change of subject, "We are escorting our young friend here to his home at Bonavon".

Porteous rubbed his chin and looked puzzled, "Can't say I've heard of it".

Maun was disappointed, "It is near the town of Dunbriton. Have you heard of that?".

"Oh! Yes, I have. That is not too far away - maybe twenty miles or so."

Maun should have been pleased with that piece of news, but he had an uneasy feeling in the pit of his stomach. He felt that some unforeseen event was about to delay them, yet again.

The meal was served, Porteous having prepared it early in the morning and allowed it to simmer on the stove for a few hours. It was tasty and tender and most enjoyable.

However, it quickly became obvious that he was not entirely at ease. His wife had not returned and he felt that no news, was bad news.

It was at this moment that Ilsa rushed in, red eyed and sobbing. "You will have to come. I cannot bear it alone. The baby is dead." She was greatly distressed and did not seem to care that strangers were present.

Porteous took his wife in his arms. They both looked devastated.

Maun stood up and said, "Madam, where is the baby?".

She looked at him and almost without a thought, she said, "I left it in the crib we prepared". "Please", said Maun, "Will you take me to it".

When Ilsa hesitated, Maun said, "Madam, please hurry!".

Although Porteous's wife was surprised at Maun's authoritative tone, she obeyed him and led the way to the small cottage opposite. As they approached, they could hear the mournful wailing of the distraught mother and on hearing these sounds, Ilsa slumped into her husband's arms again, forcing Porteous to say, "Come Ilsa, be brave", as he helped her along.

They stood by the crib, Hanno bending down and gently lifting the tiny bundle and handing it to Maun. He uncovered its tiny face, then cradling the baby in his right arm, he placed his left hand on its chest. Words filled his mind, 'Breathe your breath of life into her mouth'.

Maun obeyed instinctively. He bent his head as he lifted the baby's mouth to his own mouth and breathing deeply, he then slowly released the breath into the baby's mouth. He did this three times. Everyone present watched him, holding their breath as though the slightest sound would break the spell.

Suddenly, the baby coughed, a faint, just audible little cough, but enough to release the tension that had filled the room. The mother screamed, "My baby is alive!".

Maun held it until the power in his hands began to subside. The baby cried and Maun went to the mother and gave the crying infant to her. "She is most beautiful", he said.

The baby's father was speechless. He went to Maun and simply touched his shoulder. Ilsa was completely overcome. Her tears of grief, were now tears of happiness. She stood before Maun, took his hands and said, "These hands are magical, wonderful magical hands and you have breath that brings the dead back to life. Never in my life have I seen anyone like you".

Porteous saw that Maun was a little embarrassed, so he suggested they return to his house and have some refreshment.

Pouring large glasses of wine, Porteous said, "Let us drink to the health of the new baby", then turning to Maun, he said, "There is something I can do for you. I have a friend who owes me a favour. He owns a horse and wagon. I will borrow it and tomorrow morning. I will take you home, right to your door".

Maun was delighted. At last, at long last. The uneasy feeling in the pit of his stomach had gone. Now he knew that it was right. Tomorrow he would be with his family. Porteous asked him, "Is there anything you would like?"

Maun replied, "If I am to see my mother again after so long away, I would like very much to bathe".

"You are in luck, my friend", said Porteous, "There is a great tub of hot water in the wash room. I had it ready in case my daughter needed it. You are more than welcome to it. While you bathe, I will call on my friend and arrange to borrow his wagon".

Maun enjoyed the hot bath. To him, it was not just the pleasure of washing away the dirt, grime and sweat of the road, as was the case at Lorne. At that time, he had almost resented the waste of time, because it had delayed his journey. No. This was a symbolic cleansing away of the happenings of his months in slavery. The snakelike scar on his arm stood out bright red against his white skin and he shuddered at the memory of the smell of his burning flesh, the pain that filled him and his longing for death to rescue him.

There was also another smell he wanted to forget - that of the foul, vermin and insect infested straw on which he had been obliged to sleep. These parts of his memory he desired to throw out with the bath water.

However, in deep contrast, was the absolute peacefulness of death. That warm, sinking feeling that was free of pain. Then, to his amazement, the awakening to the reality that life is eternal and the exquisite beauty. The light. The feeling of timelessness and the sweet scent of the company of angels.

Maun wondered why more people on earth were not aware of this, 'for surely I am not the only person to have experienced dying and lived?'.

He dried himself on the rough cloth provided and after dressing, he returned to the main room, where a smiling Porteous informed him that the horse and wagon for tomorrow had been arranged. "We will leave at first light in the morning. I will wake everyone up, so don't worry about oversleeping."

"Won't your wife need you, Sir?", asked Maun.

"Need me?", said Porteous with a laugh, "I doubt she will notice I have gone! Since that new babe was born, she has hardly raised her eyes from its face".

Maun relaxed, until Evan said, "Lad. I've been thinking. What do you intend to do with your life at home?".

"What do you mean, Evan? I will live with my parents and hope never to leave again."

Evan looked at him with a certain amount of sympathy, "I'm afraid lad, that your dream of a peaceful life, is maybe just that, a 'dream'. People will not cease being sick or getting themselves injured, just because you are at home".

"Hanno and I have witnessed, that with each healing, your power has altered and strengthened. We believe that it will keep on doing just that. You, my young friend are going to need people around you who will understand what is taking place."

"Yes Evan, I know. I have thought about it, but my greatest desire for the moment is just to be with my family for a few days. To be with them and experience my life as it was, without having to think of work."

"I hope I don't sound selfish, for I am sure that if I am required to heal, I will be directed at the right time to the right place. So, please don't say anything to anyone until it is necessary. Do you both agree?"

"If that is what will make you happy lad, then Hanno and I will do as you ask."

"Yes, I agree with that", said Hanno, "No mention of healings until you say so".

Maun smiled, "Thank you both - I knew you would understand".

Evan decided he would go to bed and have an early night, seeing as he had an early start in the morning. Hanno was making notes.

When Porteous returned, he looked happy and very proud. He said, "It feels wonderful being a grandfather. I told my wife I would be taking you to Dunbriton tomorrow and she was pleased that we could actually do something useful for you".

Maun asked Porteous if he had built the house they lived in? "I ask Sir, because although much smaller than Calim my grandfather's villa, this house is the same shape - just like a Roman villa."

Porteous smiled, "That, my dear young friend, is because I am a Roman. I copied this house from one I saw many years ago in Italy".

"I liked the house as soon as I saw it", said Maun "And I wondered why I was so attracted to it".

Porteous went on to tell them, how many years before he had been in the Roman Army. "We were on a survey of the land west of Alavna, when we came across this village, the inhabitants of which were in quite a state. Things had all gone wrong at once and the leader of our Cohort decided that we could not leave them. So, we set about putting things right. We drained the dead fish from the pond, gathered up all the rubbish to be burned, then our Medical Officer treated the villagers for their poisoned stomachs. They were very grateful and our reputation soared, where previously it had been poor. I met Ilsa here. We kept in touch and I tried to see her as often as I could. As soon as I left the Army, I asked her to be my wife. We have lived here ever since."

By the time Maun went to bed, Hanno was asleep and at peace. Maun thought, 'I will never be able to sleep tonight - I am much too excited'. So, he did what his grandfather Joseph told him he did on such occasions - he prayed.

'I thank you Father for the gift that gave this family a beautiful daughter and for your help in guiding us home. My Lord, I know that you work through me in order to answer the prayers of those who ask your help, no matter who they are.' Then Maun heard the voice of his angel in his ear.

"My son. Mankind have taken with them to earth, grief or burdens which they feel strong enough to conquer. Life is a journey in which experience is gained and progress made. But, on earth, nothing is easy and very often they falter. It is necessary, therefore, to send help. You have done well. But, remember, you too have burdens. There are none on earth perfect, though all souls have the light of Heaven within them. Some know and believe. Others are blind. My son, open their eyes that they may see the light of the Christ."

Maun slept for some hours, but when he heard someone move around in the corridor, he was wide awake. A dim light flickered and shone through the crack in his door. He hoped that it was Porteous up and getting ready and not Evan looking for the closet, as he did sometimes after drinking too much ale. He checked himself, 'I must not criticise Evan. Where would I have been without his help? I must not forget the sacrifices he has made for me. By now he could have been home with his wife. Only yesterday, he and Hanno were ready to defend me against the trouble makers at the tavern'.

The door of the bedroom opened and Porteous poked his head round, "Are you awake, Master Maun? It's time to rise and get ready".

"I'm awake, Sir", said Maun.

CHAPTER XXIV

HOME AT LAST

The three travellers waited outside Porteous's small villa, their backpacks at their feet, when a horse and wagon appeared, Porteous and his friend sitting up in front. "Sorry I cannot come with you, Porteous", said his friend, "You will be careful with the wagon. Try not to go over too many bumps on the road".

"I'll be very careful", promised Porteous. "My friends here will see to that."

Ilsa came out of her daughter's house, "Please be careful. You know it has been a long time since you were in charge of a horse. You've never been at ease with them".

Porteous reassured her, "I will be no more than three days, my dear".

The travellers put their luggage in the back of the cart, Porteous's friend having laid lots of straw on the floor to make it more comfortable for them. With Evan sitting up front with Portious, they waved goodbye to Ilsa and her son-in-law and Portious's friend.

Maun could hardly believe it. He would actually be home in a few hours. He tried to contain his excitement - it was not easy. Porteous cracked his whip above the horse's head and it took the strain, slowly beginning to move the heavy cart over the rough ground.

As the wheels started to roll, Evan began to sing one of his favourite sea songs and they all joined in, continuing to sing as they waved goodbye.

Maun and Hanno lay back in the straw, but found it uncomfortable, so they unrolled their bedrolls and lay on them. "This", said Hanno, "Is the only way to travel!".

Several miles along the road, Porteous stopped the wagon. "Anyone else able to handle this wagon? I'm a bit tired. Maybe I've had more than my share of excitement this last few days."

Evan volunteered, "I'll have a go", he said with his usual buoyancy.

Hanno, who was about to volunteer himself, said "You can't drive Evan - you're a sailor!".

"So!" said Evan, "There's nothing to it, the horse does all the hard work. As it happens, I have taken charge of a wagon before. Admittedly, it was a long time ago, but I expect I will manage".

Porteous and Evan changed places and they set off again. Sure enough, it only took a short time for Evan to get the hang of it.

When Maun looked around, he saw a long trackway way ahead of them, but then he heard Hanno say, "Don't look back, those men from Craiga are still following us. I spotted them in the distance behind us. They must be worn out trying to catch us up. Though it is possible they only want to spy on us. Yesterday when we were walking, they could have caught up with us anytime they wanted".

"As long as they wish us no harm, I don't suppose we need to bother about them", said Maun.

The wagon trundled on and on over slightly bumpy roads, until eventually they stopped for some food. After their stop, Maun walked by the side of the horse for a while, before climbing into the back of the wagon, among the straw and bedrolls.

He was about to settle down again, when suddenly something caught his eye. He called on Evan to stop the wagon. Evan did so immediately and turned around, "What is it lad?".

But, Maun was staring into the distance. "I am home. I would recognise those dark and brooding hills, however long I had been away. Look, there is my father's farm." Then he caught sight of some people working in a field. One was leading a horse, the other was guiding the plough, while another walked behind, scattering seeds from a bag that was hanging around his neck.

Recognising one of the men, Maun put his hands around his mouth and yelled at the top of his voice, "Ce-di! Ce-di!". The men in the field stopped and then the man walking behind the plough, dropping the seed bag, cupped his hands to his mouth and yelled back, "Maun-y! Maun-y!".

As the two friends ran towards each other, everyone's eyes were on Maun. He had almost reached his friend who was running towards him, in the process leaping a ditch and calling out all the time. Finally they met, hugging each other and patting each other on the back.

"Mauny, I was sure you were dead. I lied to your mother saying you were well. She was so ill, I could not tell her what I thought. I must come with you. I want to see her face when she sees you." The two friends made their way back to the cart and Cedi was introduced to Maun's friends.

As they made their way along the very last mile of the way home, Maun tried his best to control himself. He wanted to run, shouting all the way, "It's me. Maun. I've come home". But, he didn't. He waited and walked with all of his friends, smiling, in a shy, but dignified way. "My home is about a mile along the road. Forgive me while I make myself presentable." Stopping briefly, he shook the straw from his robe and then ran his fingers through his hair. He asked Evan, "Do I look all right to meet my mother?".

Evan was emotional and answered, "Lad. You look a treat for any mother's eyes".

Cedi said, "You look so well, I can hardly believe it's you. Come on, let's hurry. I can hardly wait".

As they hurried on the last few yards of the journey, men working by the side of the road and women out with their babies, called out, "Look. It's young Mauny home", then followed, asking questions, "Where have you been, Mauny? How did you escape, Mauny?". He could not speak.

Meanwhile, Conchessa was telling a story to a class of infants. They had been interested and attentive, but Conchessa became aware of their restlessness. "What is the matter, children?"

"Madam Conchessa. There are people shouting." Then, she heard them. They were saying something about Maun. 'Could it be?' She hurried to the door followed by the children, just in time to see the crowd turn into the yard.

They were all beaming at her. Every face was familiar to her. She had taught all of them. She scanned the faces, searching for her son. Expecting to see him as she remembered him, but there was no boy with a mop of fair curls, nor could she hear his voice. Her heart was pounding.

Then, the crowd, some with tears streaming down their faces, separated, clearing a pathway. Then she saw him. "Mauny?" Could this young man be her son? She hardly recognised him. The young man who stood before her, was taller, older and so dignified, dressed in that tailored robe and fine leather boots. The crowd went silent. Everyone anticipating the absolute joy of the moment. They held their breath. Maun smiled and quickly moved towards her. She held her arms out to him. Then, he whispered into her ear, "Mama. How I've longed for this moment".

As they embraced, the crowd began to cheer and call out, "Welcome home, Maun. Welcome home".

By now, the rest of the family appeared on the scene; Alana and Bliss from the house; Father Joseph from the church.

Alana took control of the situation. She asked the older children to make sure the little ones reached home safely, then said, "Thank you. Thank you all for welcoming Maun home so warmly. But, I am sure at this moment he just wants to be with his family. Will you tell all of your friends and family the good news and we will have a celebration for him soon".

Most of the crowd left, running away to spread the good news. Then, she spotted Cedi, Evan, Porteous and Hanno, standing by the gate beside the horse and wagon. Cedi stepped forward, "Miss Alana. These people here are Maun's friends. They brought him home".

She said, "You must come in, all of you".

Paulus took charge of the horse and wagon and was about to lead it towards the stable, when Joseph intercepted him. "Don't bother about that now, Paulus. Take our fastest horse and race as fast as you can to Dunbriton and fetch Calpurnius. He is at the Council Chambers."

Cedi helped Joseph lead the horse and wagon to the stable, while Alana led Evan, Hanno and Porteous into the house. Bliss was ahead of her and had already began to prepare refreshments. "I am so excited", she told Alana, "I had to do something useful to keep me from crying".

Conchessa and Maun were still in the school room. She was holding on to him as though she thought he might vanish. "My son", she said, "I thought I would never see you again".

Joseph entered the schoolroom where they stood and smiled knowingly at his grandson. "I knew you would come home, Maun - I knew."

Maun looked into his grandfather's eyes. "Of course you knew, grandfather. I told you so."

"Yes, my boy", said Joseph, "You most certainly did. I saw you and your companion. We must talk about it soon. Meanwhile, Alana and our dear Bliss are entertaining your friends at the house. I think we had better join them".

Suddenly Maun felt guilty. "Where is my father? I have been home some time now and I have not asked for him."

Joseph smiled and shook his head, "Don't worry my boy. Paulus is already on his way to Dunbriton to tell him of your return. He will, I know, get home as fast as he can. Now let us go and join your friends".

Paulus saddled the fastest horse and rode off. At the same time, news of Maun's return spread around the village and reached the ears of Clodus, who was sawing wood in his grounds. He immediately saddled his horse and set off for the Mission school, realising that his wife Alana would be anxious.

He met Paulus riding towards him. Both riders stopped. "Is it true, Paulus? Is the boy home?"

"Yes, he is. I am going to fetch Calpurnius."

Clodus thought it wise to go with him and he turned his horse around. "I am coming with you. It is safer for us to ride together."

CHAPTER XXV

THE COUNCIL CHAMBER

The Council Chamber was the most imposing building in Dunbriton. Marble pillars supported a magnificent staircase and in one of the upstairs rooms, an important debate was in progress. The most senior Councillors, dressed in their formal robes of office, were seated in a circle, on their individually named and comfortable chairs.

Calim stood. "Councillors. This important meeting has been called to discuss a subject that has been put off time and time again" ... Calim took a breath ... "But, Gentlemen it has to be faced.

Every year the Army cuts back. Men are withdrawn because of difficulties in Gaul and wars elsewhere in the Empire, while more and more strangers arrive here to settle and take advantage of our peaceful and prosperous town."

"While most of these immigrants are peaceful and law abiding people, who only desire a chance to work and support their families, our agents inform us that there are hoards of unsettled tribesmen gathering in Hibernia and in the north biding their time until we are defenceless. I believe we are in grave danger. Even in the south of our country, Saxons are waiting to invade, ready to fill the vacuum left by our Army."

"I therefore propose that we begin to train an Army of our own - a 'British Army'! The knowledge of such an Army would keep these would be invaders in their own country."

There was grumbling amongst the councillors.

Councillor Magnus stood. "I appreciate what Councillor Calim has to say, but it is my opinion that he is being a little premature. We have been assured that the Army will be here for at least another twenty years. Think of the cost of an Army of our own? The people would not agree to the extra taxes. Therefore, I vote against your proposal, as I believe you exaggerate the seriousness of the problem. And the cost of such a venture would be prohibitive."

Councillor Petronus stood to reply. He got as far as saying, "I agree with Councillor Calim ...", when the sound of footsteps running noisily up the marble stairs, followed by loud knocking on the door, distracted them. Calim was ready to rebuke the intruders, but when the door was opened by the clerk, he saw Clodus and Paulus standing in the open doorway, gasping for breath.

"Forgive our intrusion. but we are to inform Councillor Calpurnius his son has arrived home." Calim reached out to support his son, who appeared to slump forward. However, he quickly composed himself, saying "Mauny Is home?".

"Yes", said Paulus "And he is well".

Calim gave his son a nudge, "Go home my boy. I will go and tell your mother".

Calpurnius turned to the Council members. "Forgive me. I must hurry home."

Each one of the Councillors stood and applauded as Calpurnius left. "Thank God", they said, for they were well aware of the suffering Calpurnius and Calim had endured.

Calim closed the meeting with as much composure as he could muster. Then he left to hurry home to the villa to tell Rhona. He could hardly wait to relieve her of her anguish.

At Bonavon, there was an atmosphere of light-hearted joy. Evan recounted some of their adventures, without mentioning any of the healings, as he had been asked. He told the family of their narrow escape from a band of vicious bandits at Baccarra. Hanno followed by embarrassing Evan with the tale of the baby pig which outsmarted him, "Though my worst moment was when Maun and I went to rescue the bull. I hid behind the door of the shed, while Maun went to untie him. I expected Maun to be chased by the bull. but to my surprise, the bull ran from the shed, snorting, being chased by Maun. I can tell you, my heart was pounding".

"And mine", said Maun.

Alana, Bliss and her daughter Rae, served what food they had, being unprepared for such a large gathering of hungry men. But, they were happy and did not complain. They simply set too and baked more bread.

Joseph, sensing that Calpurnius would be arriving home soon, invited Evan, Hanno and Porteous to look around the garden, the church and the new classroom which had recently been built to accommodate more pupils.

Conchessa, now alone with Maun, held his hand. She told him how she prayed daily for him to come home. "Now my dearest, my prayers have been answered. Yet, I dare not believe it, in case I wake up and find I am dreaming. Just look at you in your fine cloak and new boots." She then touched his hair. "But my son. You cannot fool your mother. For as much as you look wonderful, you have aged before your time, which tells me of great suffering."

He looked her in the eye. "Mama, I tell you the truth. If I have suffered, I have been doubly compensated by good and loyal friends and so much kindness and so Mama, if I seem a little older than my years, believe me, I would not change anything. I am happy this way - as I am. My only regret is that you and father and grandfather had to worry so much. I fear your suffering was more than mine."

Alana and Bliss came into the room to pick up the used bowls and plates. They stood beaming, not quite knowing what to say. Alana told him, "It is wonderful to have you home, Mauny. This place was not the same without you", then her eyes filled with tears and she hurried back into the kitchen. Bliss could not speak and so she cuddled him, before following Alana.

The sound of approaching horses announced the arrival of Calpurnius. Entering the room where his wife and son stood, he looked Maun up and down from head to toe, as though he could not believe it was really him. Then he clasped him in his arms and cried, tears he had held back since the day his son was taken. Conchessa put her arms around both of them and they clung to each other.

The sound of more horsemen signalled the arrival of Clodus and Paulus, exhausted after trying to keep apace with Calpurnius. Making their way to the kitchens to see their wives, they found them looking through the kitchen door, watching the reunion of the little family group. Both were red eyed. But, when they saw their husbands bent over, gasping for breath, their tears turned to laughter. "Just look at you both. Anyone might think you had been working hard", said Alana.

"Or getting old", said Bliss.

"Your right", gasped Paulus, "I am too old for this caper".

Bliss put her arms around him, saying "My poor old man. Old as you are, I am very proud of you".

Alana and Clodus were watching the family reunion through the partially opened door. "Thank God it is over. Now we can all begin to live again," whispered Alana.

"Yes", said Clodus "And perhaps we can speak of our own children without that dreadful feeling of guilt".

However, as Alana pointed out, "All the time Maun was gone, Conchessa continued to teach the children of the village".

Clodus put his hand on her shoulder, "Yes. I know she did. She was very brave. They were all very brave".

Calpurnius sensed their presence. "Clodus, Paulus. Please come in. I want to thank you both for coming to give me the news. I appreciate all your hard work."

Paulus replied, "Master Calpurnius, to do so was our great pleasure. Just to see the look upon your face when you heard the news was a joy not to be missed".

Then they turned to Maun, "We all missed you very much and we are so pleased you are home with your parents".

"We must go now and leave you to rest. You must all be exhausted."

No sooner had Clodus and Paulus left, than Joseph returned from showing Evan, Hanno and Porteous around the Mission school, garden and church. He also announced that he had shown them where they could sleep for the night, "Evan and Portious have chosen Paulus's old quarters above the stables and Hanno will sleep in my little room within the church. He has asked for vellum to write of your adventures - quite a scholar, your friend Hanno!".

"Yes he is", said Maun, "He also knows a lot about herbs and medicine".

Joseph wanted to speak with his grandson, but he had to chose his time carefully, as at the moment Conchessa would not allow Maun out of her sight, lest he vanish again and for now Maun was content to allow his parents to get used to having him around again.

The sound of another rider was heard arriving and Calpurnius went to the window saying, "I wonder if it is father?", but then he smiled and turning to Maun, said, "It's your Uncle Sergaeus. I thought he might come as soon as he heard. He's always been fond of you, my son".

Sergaeus was welcomed by Calpurnius, but he made straight for Maun and hugged him, "It's great to have you home".

"Thank you for coming, Uncle Sergaeus", said Maun.

"I had to come", said Sergaeus. "Wild horses could not hold me." He was the only other member of the family to have experienced slavery and knew the terrible loneliness of a child dragged away from family and deprived of love, no matter how poor the family might be. Sergaeus knew it would be worse for Maun who, because of his rich background, the contrast would have been the greater and more difficult to bear. He was therefore, all the more pleased to see him home.

He told them, how Calim had hurried to Harran's home as soon as he left the Council chamber, eager to tell everyone the good news. "He and your mother will be here in the morning - you may be sure it will be early. I couldn't wait, Julia and your cousins want to know everything … 'Please go papa. We want to know if it is true?' they said. … So, here I am. Who can resist the pleas of four women!"

"Thank you", Uncle Sergaeus, "I am so happy to see you. I thought of you often".

"Your grandmother and grandfather Calim will, I know, have difficulty sleeping this night," Sergaeus told him.

They spent the evening eating and talking. Eventually Maun went to his bedroom; strange how small it seemed, but the bed was comfortable and he was so very tired. He could not remember when he last slept the night through. He snuggled down under his familiar covers and before he could say his prayers, he was fast asleep.

Next morning, everyone was up and about, everyone that is except Maun. When Conchessa entered his room to remind him that his grandparents were coming, he did not stir and she did not try to wake him. Calpurnius met her at the door. "Not awake yet?", he inquired.

She shook her head. "Not yet, my dear. I think it is best to let him be until your parents arrive. I am sure that this is the first time since he was taken, that he has felt safe and secure enough to let himself relax."

Calpurnius nodded. "You are right, my love. It makes sense. They went into the main room where Sergaeus was finishing off his breakfast. "Is Maun awake, yet?"

"Not yet", said Conchessa. Sergaeus looked disappointed, but said, "I understand. I just wanted to talk to him a bit more. Julia and his cousins will want to know everything. However, I cannot wait any longer. I have some work to do today. Thank you both for allowing me to stay overnight. My old mare is not up to trotting both ways in one day".

"I will go and see Maun before I go. I won't wake him, I just want to convince myself that I am not dreaming."

"I know the feeling", said Calpurnius.

Sergaeus emerged from Maun's room and shrugged his shoulders, "He is still dead to the world. I will be off now. I am satisfied to have seen him. Has he told you where he has been?".

Calpurnius shook his head, "No, nothing - I don't think I want to know". Sergaeus understood.

Conchessa and Calpurnius escorted him to the yard, where Paulus, Joseph and Porteous were talking. Paulus went to get Sergaeus's horse and brought it forward. "When Maun has had time to rest, I will come again and bring Julia and the girls", said Sergaeus. as he mounted his horse.

As they watched him ride off, Paulus remarked, "I wonder why such a rich man as Sergaeus rides such an old horse, when he could have the best?".

Calpurnius replied, "Sergaeus is a very loyal man. That mare is like an old friend to him and he values his friends".

Joseph and Porteous were talking and Porteous remarked, "I was surprised to discover how fast we travelled from my home to here … I had it in my mind that we were going all the way to Dunbriton. When your grandson recognised his home and his friend, I could hardly believe it. It means that I can reach home in just a few hours - most certainly before dark".

Joseph said, " It was so kind of you to leave your home to bring my grandson and his friends here. I don't quite know how to thank you".

"Thank me?", exclaimed Porteous. "No Sir. It is I who should be thanking you for what your grandson has done for my family."

Joseph raised an eyebrow? Porteous remembered he had not to mention the baby, or any of the healings he had been told about, But, he could not help telling Joseph about the events of the past few days.

"Sir", said Porteous, "You have a remarkable grandson. I was asked not to say anything to his family, because the boy himself wants to spend some peaceful days with them".

Joseph was puzzled, "What Sir, were you not supposed to speak of?". Porteous confided everything about Maun saving his granddaughter's life, Joseph listening intently.

"I thank you Porteous for telling me. It has made certain things very clear. I wondered why so many people had arrived with him. Tell me, Porteous", said Joseph, "Are the other two gentlemen indebted in any way?".

"Well Sir", replied Porteous, "I don't know about the young one. But, I was talking to the older man - Evan - and he told me that the boy saved his life. I am sorry to have broken a confidence but, how could I leave and not tell his family of his wonderful ability to heal?".

Joseph could see that Porteous was worried about blurting out Maun's secret. "Please think no more of it. The secret is safe with me. I will not reveal one word until the others feel ready to talk."

"I believe our housekeeper is making some breakfast. After we have eaten, would you like to walk with me to the top of the hill? There is a wonderful view of the great lake and the snow-capped mountain in the distance."

"Yes, I would", said Porteous, "I would like that very much".

Maun's first night spent at home in his own comfortable bed, was the nearest thing to heaven on earth he had experienced. So, when morning came he was reluctant to stir. The long trek, the healing work and lack of sleep had taken its toll.

Suddenly, something touched his face. It felt wet and furry. He opened one eye and smiled, for sitting on his pillow was a tabby kitten. "Where did you come from, little one?" The kitten raised its tiny paw and hit him on the nose. 'I think she wants me up. Could be she wants to move into my warm bed?' It was then he remembered that his grandparents were coming this morning. The thought of seeing them again sent a warm glow through him. They had never chastised him for being a poor scholar. They had always loved him for being their only grandson.

At that moment his bedroom door opened slowly. Conchessa peeped round it. She laughed when she saw the kitten beside him. "I came to remind you …".

Maun interrupted her, "Don't tell me Mama. I know grandmother and grandfather Calim are coming today. I will get up in a moment".

"Where did the kitten come from?", Maun asked her.

"Your father found her on his way home, one evening. She was injured and hungry. He wrapped her in his cloak and brought her home. With good food and care, she soon recovered. Now she thinks she owns the household." They both laughed.

Conchessa sat on the edge of Maun's bed, then picked up the kitten and placed it on her lap. "It is so good to have you home. So many times I dreamt you were here and when I woke up, the disappointment was unbearable. But, today you are here and it is wonderful." She bent over him and kissed his forehead. The kitten darted from her lap and ran around the room, ears back, tail hooked - she looked so funny, quite unaware of the human drama around her.

"Mama, while I was away, all I could think of was you, father and grandfather Joseph. I never realised how much I valued my family and friends, nor had I ever realised that we had enemies."

Conchessa, picking up the kitten again said, "Uncle Sergaeus must have let her in, when he came in to say goodbye. He waited all night, sleeping on the couch. He said that his old mare could not trot both ways in one day. I think he wanted to be near you".

"He came in while I was asleep, did he?"

"Yes, he is very fond of you, Maun. He always wanted a son. But, God in his wisdom gave him three daughters - all three exactly like your Aunt Julia." They laughed again.

She smiled at him and left holding the kitten, but it had not escaped his notice that as soon as he mentioned enemies, his mother had become nervous and immediately changed the subject. Maun sensed that she was afraid. Afraid to know what had happened to him. Afraid for the future.

Maun resisted the temptation to snuggle down again between the warm covers. He forced himself to get up, open his small bedroom window and look out at the familiar view of the stables. His grandfather Joseph was there talking to Portious. He thought how old he looked, yet when he had seen him from that heavenly place, how different he appeared. So vital and lively - with all those lights and colours swirling around him.

As he washed his face and cleaned his teeth with some hard salt on a piece of cloth wrapped around his finger, he thought, 'There is great power within my grandfather that cannot be seen upon earth. How blind we are. If only people knew how they were watched over and how they are seen by others from above'.

Bliss called him to come and eat and he had just taken one bite of his egg and bread, when Calim and Rhona's carriage arrived.

Rhona, now almost fifty three, was still very beautiful, but today, she was looking a little tired around the eyes They were greeted warmly by the family, although unlike the excitement of the day before - when everyone was happy and noisy - the atmosphere today was quiet, peaceful and thoughtful. His parents hugged him, Calim then putting his arms around Calpurnius's shoulder. He spoke softly to him, "Thank God it is all over. Are you well now my boy?".

"Yes, father - just about. But, my poor Conchessa is afraid to allow him out of her sight."

"That is to be expected. It will take time", said Calim sympathetically.

Maun's hearing was sharp. He overheard these conversations and felt so sorry, almost guilty, for what his mother and father had suffered.

Calim and Rhona joined them for luncheon. The talk was kept cheerful with Calim's stories of his brother's difficulties, having now six females in his family to cope with! ... "Granted, Julia has Sergaeus and Portia is happily married to Doctor Markus. But, Harran, their father, still considers them his little girls and keeps them well dressed in the latest fashion, even though he never stops bemoaning the expense!".

Calim then addressed Maun, "Your Uncle Harran and your cousins are doing superb work at our school. We have to open new classrooms regularly and employ more teachers, as so many young men and women desire to be educated in all kinds of subjects. Latin mostly, although mathematics and science are popular. We are also gaining a reputation for excellent work".

When the meal was over, Calim and Rhona left, making Calpurnius promise to bring Maun to visit them more often.

Joseph and Porteous returned from their climb in time to say goodbye to them and Portious decided that it was time for him to leave also. However, Joseph insisted he ate first.

Conchessa made him up two packages; one containing food for the journey, the other baby covers and clothes that had belonged to Maun.

Evan and Hanno were on their way back from their walk along the riverbank. They were happy for Maun, but now wondered what they were going to do now that their work was completed? "I suppose", said Evan, "We should move on. You on your eastern adventures and me to my wife and sons in Gaul, although I'm afraid if we show undue haste, we might offend".

"Well", said Hanno. "Let us agree to leave in two days time. That will give us time to make plans".

They arrived back as Paulus brought Porteous's borrowed horse and wagon forward from the stable. "Where have you been Porteous? We were looking for you to walk along the river with us", inquired Hanno.

Porteous replied, "I was up early and did not wish to disturb anyone. I've been climbing the hill with Father Joseph". They thanked Porteous for his hospitality once more and asked him to give Madam Portious and their family their kindest thoughts and good wishes for the new baby's future.

Maun and Conchessa came to add their good wishes and Calpurnius - leading his horse - said, "I will ride with you as far as the farm, Porteous. I have some business with Eric and Cedi".

Just as Calpurnius turned on to the road leading to the farm, he saw four young men coming along the road towards them. They appeared strange and rather timid. He waved to Porteous, then thought no more of it.

Evan and Hanno had been for a walk along the river bank. On their return, they met Joseph who asked them if they would like to join him in his quarters for some refreshment? "There is a matter I would like to discuss with both of you."

Joseph poured three large glasses of wine and as they sat around his small table, Evan and Hanno were curious about what Joseph would want to discuss with them. On Joseph's part, he did not quite know how to begin. He coughed a little and in his usual shy manner, said, "It's like this. Porteous has told me how my grandson saved his granddaughter's life. He did not intend to, it just happened. When I pressed him for more information, he said that you Evan, would be able to tell me more. Is this so?".

Evan was embarrassed, "I am sorry, Sir. We should have been more open with you. But, it is Maun himself, who simply wants to be at home with his parents a short time, before he has to start work".

"It is true that Maun saved my life on board ship. Since then, there has been many more healings, the last one being Portious's granddaughter."

"I beg you to tell me everything you know in this regard", said Joseph "For while he was in captivity, I saw visions of him. I know something happened to change him."

Evan and Hanno looked at each other, then Evan told Joseph of everything that had happened on their journey through the Highlands. "Sir", said Evan, "We promised Maun we would say nothing".

Joseph reassured them, "Until Maun himself tells me of these things, I will not reveal one word to anyone. But, one thing I know is, our Lord will not allow his servant to be idle for long. We will have to make plans".

The following day, Conchessa felt secure enough to let her son out of her sight and she said, "School begins again tomorrow and we must get word to all of the children". She asked Maun if he would like to walk around the village and call at their homes and inform the parents? "The children have missed three day's lessons."

"Yes, I know Mama", said Maun. Conchessa watched him out of sight.

Maun was happy walking through the village, talking to everyone he met and calling at the childrens' homes. Some of the children were playing in groups, this saving him the trouble of calling at a few homes and he mentally crossed off the names on his mother's list. Only one was missing - young Victor - and he lived near the top of the hill by the stream that flowed down into the river.

'Now, why couldn't Victor be playing with the other children and save me this climb?', he thought as he struggled up the hill. When he reached the tiny cottage, he knocked on the door. There was no reply and he called out, "Victor, are you in there?". No one answered. He turned to leave, then he heard a sound from inside - like a sob. He called out again, "Victor, are you there?". He pushed on the flimsy door and it opened.

Victor's mother was lying on the floor, Victor kneeling by her side crying.

"What has happened here?", asked Maun. The little boy told him that his mother had fallen down some steps. She had managed to get back into the house, but once inside she fell on the floor and had not moved since. Maun immediately saw that Victor's mother was conscious, but in severe pain. "Why did you not go for help Victor?", asked Maun, one look at the woman's eyes telling him she was afraid someone might try to move her.

"Come Victor. I will show you how to help your mother and make her better." Maun took the boy's hand and bade him kneel one side of his mother. Maun knelt opposite. "Now, without touching her, copy exactly what I do." Victor nodded.

Maun began to heal. The power was stronger than ever and he became aware of the presence of angels. Because of her fear of being touched, Maun simply held his hands above the woman's body and the boy followed his every move.

Gradually the pain faded and she was able to move a little. She said, "I do believe I feel a little better". That she was actually speaking, was progress indeed. Later, she was able to tell Maun that her name was Laney and that her husband had died not long after Victor had been born.

Victor could feel the power in his hands and asked what it was. "That", said Maun, "Is the very power that allows us to live and move in our bodies. We - you and I - have given your mother some of our energy and that has given her strength to get better". Victor was very proud.

Laney told Maun, "I am very independent and I don't like to bother my neighbours. They have enough troubles of their own". She began to breath easier, so Maun asked her if she could try to get up. She nodded. Maun and Victor helped her up and on to her bed. She took a deep breath of relief, a heavy sigh, that expressed peace.

"Have you two eaten today?", Maun asked.

"No, I don't think so", replied Laney, "I haven't thought about it".

"I will go and fetch something for you and Victor. You rest quietly until I come back and don't worry - I won't tell anyone."

Maun hurried home and asked Bliss to make him up a basket of food. She did not ask him any questions, but just gave him some bread and cheese and a jar of milk. Quickly thanking her, he hurried back through the village and up the hill.

Before he gave them the food, he told Victor to wash his hands and face, then he took a basin of water to the bedside and helped Laney to wash also.

"Now, I have to go home, but before I go, will you promise not to repeat anything that has happened here this day." Laney promised.

Maun then said to Victor, "And what say you?".

"I also promise Maun", said Victor.

Maun left the cottage and made his way downhill, satisfied that he had done what he could and that Laney would continue to get better. The joy of knowing that his power to heal was stronger than ever, was mixed with sorrow, for he was well aware of what this healing would do to change his family life. He would surely be fooling himself if he thought it could ever be the same again.

He stopped on a quiet stretch of the road, by a large oak tree and leaned against the thick trunk. Emotion seemed to well up inside him and he wept. He now knew that he was no longer a boy. He was a man with responsibilities. To his parents. To the sick. But, most of all to God.

All the time he was with Victor and Laney, he was unaware that his grandfather, Evan and Hanno were making plans for his future.

"When the time is right, I will take him to Tours, where my half-brother is

Bishop. He will help him prepare for the priesthood."

Evan was worried, 'Suppose Maun does not want to be a priest', he thought, 'Joseph was taking too much for granted'.

But, Joseph seemed determined. "Forgive me, Evan", he said, "I know that you are thinking, that, perhaps, Maun would prefer to marry and live a normal life? That would be a terrible waste, for he has been given this wonderful gift to heal the sick. God will expect it to be used. If Maun does not know that already, he very soon will".

"But," said Evan, "It's no good making plans for the near future. His parents would not hear of it".

"You are right", said Joseph, "It would be extremely cruel to take him away from them now, perhaps, in a few months time? Or, if they should witness for themselves his work, I reckon they would not stand in his way".

The following day, the children of the village returned to school, Victor was not among them. Maun wanted to spend some time with his friends, and he hadn't yet had that talk with his grandfather. But Victor had not turned up for school and Maun feared that his mother was not well.

Hanno came looking for him, "Where have you been Mauny? I've been looking for you".

Whereupon Maun confided in him of the latest healing, "Although I'm a little worried, it may not have been successful, as the lady's son has not turned up for school. I am going up there now to find out if they are well".

"I will come with you in case you need help and wait nearby", said Hanno.

Maun found Laney up and walking about, a little slowly and carefully, but walking. "I am fine Maun, really. I am being careful where I put my feet down. I don't want anything like that to happen to me again."

"What would happen to Victor if I were not able to look after him? I don't know what would have become of us if you had not turned up when you did."

"It was nothing, Laney", said Maun bowing his head, "You were just badly bruised. It would have got better in time".

"That's as maybe, Master Maun, but we could have starved! As it was, we were cold and hungry and I pray no one else ever has to endure the pain I felt. Therefore, I must thank you. I owe you a debt of gratitude."

"Then, Madam Laney", said Maun, "I ask you not to discuss what happened here with anyone. I know I asked you before, but I would be grateful if you held to your promise of silence. I have good reason for asking".

"Very well, Maun. If that is your wish."

Maun then turned to Victor. "If your Mother is well enough tomorrow, you must go to school and not miss your lessons."

"He will be there tomorrow", said Laney, "But, he had to run errands today".

Hanno and Maun set off for home and on the way Hanno told him that Porteous had let slip about his granddaughter and that Evan had been persuaded to tell Joseph of all the other healings. "It was not Evan's fault, Maun. Your grandfather is very astute. He guessed there were others."

Maun was quiet. "It is all right Hanno, I had made up my mind not to pretend

186

any more, as it was a fanciful dream that I knew could not last. I will simply have to learn to place my life in God's hands and trust him."

"Yes, my friend", said Hanno, "That is the answer"

"I just wanted a short time with my parents, but I think God has other ideas", said Maun with some regret.

Hanno could see how distressed Maun was and decided to cheer him up, saying "Come on, then. I'll race you back to the Mission".

Two days later, Calpurnius was returning from Dunbriton and stopped at the watering trough as he always did. He could now enjoy this interlude again and while his horse drank, he could admire the view of the snow-capped mountain. While his son was in captivity in a strange land, he had been unable to enjoy this simple pleasure. Now his beloved son was home. He took a deep, pleasurable breath and was about to mount his horse again, when he heard a woman's voice. He turned quickly and saw Laney standing there. "I know you. You are young Victor's mother. I have met you at the school."

"Yes Sir. We have met. I wish to speak with you regarding your son."

Calpurnius stopped smiling, "Has he done something wrong?".

"Oh! No Sir. Quite the opposite." Laney told him about her fall and how Maun had healed her and even washed her hands and face. "I have broken my word in telling you this, Sir. But, he was so very kind and gentle. He did not want anyone to know. I wanted you to know that you have a very special son. Even my Victor who could be a bad boy, has altered because of what Maun did. I trust Sir, you will not tell him that I told you?

"Your secret is safe with me, Laney and I thank you for confiding in me."

In the evening, family and friends sat around the dining room in comfortable seats, eating and drinking and very relaxed. The ladies brought trays of food, while the men of the family poured drinks.

Calpurnius glanced around the room; Maun and Evan were talking, Conchessa was sitting close by watching him, lovingly, then Joseph arrived, having finished his work. "Sorry I am late, my daughter. I seem to have more and more work to do." As he sat on a chair behind Maun, Calpurnius noticed the strong resemblance in their looks and he thought, 'How could I have been so blind all those years. I never noticed. It is not only their looks that are similar. It seems my son is turning towards the Church'.

Calpurnius was seeing his son in a new light. Not as the dim-wit, who despite extra tuition, had a hard time spelling his own name, but something of a 'Holy Man'. He looked around the room at the men who arrived with Maun and he thought, 'They had given up their own way of life to escort him home. Why?'.

If Laney was to be believed, he was a sensitive healer.

Then Calpurnius studied his wife, Conchessa. 'Did she know something, or was she as much in the dark as himself?'.

Then there was Joseph. 'The old man knew something from the start. It seemed as if he knew Maun would come home. He said as much many times. My dear Conchessa and I were too heart broken and in too much mental pain to listen. Well, I am a patient man. I can wait, but not for long.'

Apart from telling Calpurnius, Laney had kept her promise. Victor also had not told a soul, until another two weeks had passed and he was on his way to school. He was just passing a neighbour who was out chopping firewood, when, suddenly the man dropped his axe and clutching his chest, staggered towards his doorway, before falling to the ground.

His wife, having heard him groan, came rushing out, but on seeing him she did not know what to do. She started to drag him into the house, but he was too heavy. She began to cry hysterically. Victor went over to her, "Maun will help you. I will go and get him" and remembering his mother's plight added "Don't move him", however, the woman was too frightened to do anything.

Maun was talking to Hanno and planning to walk up to Cedi's farm. Evan was earning his keep by helping Paulus and Conchessa was welcoming the children into their schoolroom, when Victor came running towards them. "Maun, Maun. You must come quickly. Our neighbour has fallen and he is ill. You must come." Conchessa was curious and wondered why Victor should call on her son. She was even more puzzled as to why Maun responded right away, without question.

Maun and Hanno hurried towards the house. It was not difficult to find it, because a crowd had gathered. Hanno soon asked them to stand back and while Maun knelt beside the man, he placed one hand over the man's heart, feeling his forehead with the other. The patient was obviously in a bad way and not helped by the state of his wife, who was wailing as though he were already dead. Hanno spoke to her, "Madam, please be calm. Maun will do what he can and your husband will recover". He smiled reassuringly and she became calm.

Maun was aware of the great power that flowed through his hands. He could almost see it. He raised his head to look at the man's face to see if his colour was changing and saw that his eyes were wide open and that he was staring at him. "I think he is now well enough to be moved inside", said Maun and with the help of an onlooker, they carried the patient into the house and placed him carefully on the bed.

"Now Sir, you must rest. No more chopping for a while."

To Maun's astonishment, the woman began to shout, "He must work … I cannot chop wood … I have enough to do looking after the children".

Hanno, who was expecting a show of gratitude, was astounded! Of all the ungrateful people he had met, she must be the worst. But, Maun was calm. "Madam. Your husband will *have* to rest and recover his strength. As for your little ones, are they not of age to go to school? If so, you will be able to help your husband. You look a very strong and healthy lady, who, I am sure would manage your husband's work until he recovers."

The woman was shocked. "*Me! Do mens' work!* I am a woman. All I know is how to sew and clean."

Maun became a little more stern. "Madam. You have a choice. You can help your husband, by doing his work. Or you can let him die. Then you will not have a choice. For you will have no husband!"

She began to sob. Maun felt pity for her. He spoke softly, "Madam. I can see from the cleanliness of your home, that you are an excellent housekeeper. You take pride in your beautiful home and that is good. But, there is more to life than housework. People must come first. If you tend your husband and allow him to rest. He will recover and you will soon be able to be a lady again".

The man lay on the bed looking from Maun to his wife - and back again. He was amazed that this boy was telling his wife to help him, something he had longed to tell her for years, but did not have the courage. His admiration for Maun spiralled upward.

He knew Maun. He had watched him when he was a small boy go riding on that beautiful golden pony with his father. He had been very jealous. When the news came that Maun had been taken by slavers, he had not been overly concerned. Horrible things happen to people all the time, 'So, why should he be sorry?'. But now, here was this spoiled little rich boy, all grown up and telling his wife what to do. He felt both shame and gratitude. He managed to say, "I thank you Maun and I will make this up to you one day".

CHAPTER XXVI

THE FOUR STRANGERS

The next few days were quiet and restful. Cedi came to visit and brought Anna and Sophie. They related the story of what happened to them after Cedi went overboard. They had screamed and wailed so much, that they had been taken to a farmer on one of the islands who was sympathetic to the cause of the slavers and sold. However, when the farmer's wife saw how young the girls were, she was not at all pleased. At the first opportunity, she took them to a relative, who rowed them back to the mainland and released them.

Cedi had not been so lucky. He told them, "I hid under the boat after going over the side and then swam underwater for as long as I could. On reaching land, I was exhausted and freezing cold. What little clothes I had on were wet and even in the summer sunshine, they took time to dry. I had to eat berries and anything I could find to keep myself alive, until eventually I realised that I was back on the mainland and had simply walked along a peninsula."

"From then on it got easier and with the help of a friendly fish merchant - who was only too pleased to have my company - I was safe", he told them, "But, I did stink! I eventually arrived home two weeks after Anna and Sophie".

There was a silent pause as they waited for Maun to tell them his story. But Maun said nothing and Cedi guessed that Maun had no wish to relive his story. He changed the subject.

"What do you think happened the day after you returned, Maun? Four strangers came to the farm and asked for work. We did not need four of them, but as they were brothers and not bothered too much about wages, Eric took them on."

Hanno asked him, "Were they Highlanders?".

"Yes, they were", said Cedi, "And they are very good workers. They have to sleep in the old slave quarters. Why are you so interested?".

Hanno told him, "I think they may be the same four who followed us all the way home from Craiga. We thought at first they were about to rob us - they had ample opportunity".

Cedi was curious, "I wonder why they followed you? Seems a strange thing to do, unless, of course, they felt safer in numbers while travelling". Nothing else was said on the matter.

As fate would have it, it was Calpurnius who broached the subject of Maun's future with Joseph. "I know that he is not capable of bookwork, nor does he enjoy studying. It is clear he follows your inclination toward the spiritual life."

It was then that Joseph reluctantly confessed to the healing work Maun had already done. "I know all about that, Joseph", said Calpurnius. "I was wondering though, why was I kept in the dark?"

Joseph was embarrassed. "I am sorry my son. It was the boy himself. All he

191

wanted was some time spent with his mother and yourself. Bless the boy, but I think he felt there was some little bit of his childhood he had to complete. That is the only reason, you and my daughter were not told."

"So! Father Joseph. We need not have worried about him. It seems as if God has taken a hand in this. Who then are we to interfere? However, if all my son wants is some time in the company of his parents, then so be it."

The next few days passed peacefully. Evan was enjoying working in the garden and did not mind shovelling horse manure into a cart to wheel to the vegetable plot and Paulus liked having him around, especially when he burst into song.

Hanno spent most of his time in Joseph's little spare room inside the church making notes. Joseph had asked him to make them even more detailed, as he hoped one day to use them to persuade the Church hierarchy - and his older brother Martin - of his grandson's gift of healing. Joseph was convinced that what he was planning for Maun was for the best, however he was nervous about broaching the subject with his daughter. She would not thank him for taking her son away again, so thank God Calpurnius now knew, as Joseph was counting on him talking to Conchessa.

Another few days passed happily and peacefully. All the family now knew of the healings. Conchessa, however, had mixed feelings. She was pleased to have her son home and her happiness that her son had been chosen to serve God was all a Christian mother could ask for her son, but why did she feel so uneasy? She looked earnestly into her father's face. "You would tell me father if there was anything wrong - wouldn't you?"

"My dear daughter. I know nothing you do not know yourself. I only found out about this latest healing when Calpurnius told me. However, perhaps, this is as good a time as any to put to you my thoughts concerning Maun's future." He waited for his daughter's reaction.

Calpurnius nodded, "Please go on, father. I am sure we would both like to hear what you have in mind".

Joseph then told them that he had asked Evan to stay on for a while and act as Maun's bodyguard and Hanno to be his scribe. "Because, one day ..." (Joseph stopped talking to search the faces of his daughter and her husband to see how they were responding, before he dealt the final blow) "... One day I would like to take Maun to Tours to see my brother, Bishop Martin. His great influence could help him become a priest of the Holy Church. I believe that your son, my grandson, has been given a rare and wonderful gift. The miracles of healing he has performed should be recognised, by the Church in Rome."

On hearing this, Conchessa gripped her husband's arm - and he held her. "Oh! No father", she pleaded. "Please don't take him away again. We have only just had him returned to us."

Joseph was quick to re-assure her, "My daughter. I will do nothing until Maun decides for himself what he wants".

"There has been no conspiracy to deceive anyone. Only Maun's wish to be with you both, as it was before he was taken. He was trying to recapture pleasant memories of being at home, as it was. Evan has told me of how Maun could only speak of the moment he would arrive home."

"At this time, he does not want these precious moments with you to end. But, sooner on later, God will call him to a life of service and we will all have to let him go with our blessings. Far better if we make plans for his protection and for his future."

The news of the second healing spread quickly throughout the district and soon people began turning up on their doorstep begging to be healed. At first only one or two, but soon their numbers grew daily until the church was overcrowded with the sick and the lame; children on stretchers, men and women on crutches. Eventually, one of the outbuildings had to be converted into a surgery, Evan and Paulus doing what they could to keep order, as the sick called out for attention.

People were found curled up on the stable floor, in tool sheds, anywhere they could find shelter, while waiting their turn.

Joseph held services in church and as long as Maun came and blessed them, the sick went away happy. But others were very sick and Maun was especially sorry for the children. Some he knew would only receive temporary benefit, unless they could have better care and good food.

The whole family rallied round to help; grandparents, Calim and Rhona, Portia and Markus, Julia and her daughters. All took their turn.

Everyone was kept busy from morn till night until they were exhausted.

The parents of the school children already healed joined the band of helpers, but the more people who arrived, the more crowded the Mission became. Calpurnius held his wife's face and looked into her tired eyes, "My dearest. How long can this go on? It will kill our son".

It was a busy time for Cedi at the farm. He was puzzled over the four new workers who had arrived the day after his friend Maun. Hanno had said they were the same men who had followed them from Craiga. 'Why?', he asked himself, 'They were quiet, thoughtful and hard working and knew everything about farming there was to know'.

Then, news reached Cedi that Maun had healed Victor's mother and he wondered how he had accomplished this? Perhaps, he had acquired a recipe for a new medication and was there a connection between these two incidents? He made up his mind that when next he spoke to one of the Brothers, he would ask outright what their interest was in his friend Maun?

The opportunity presented itself a day or two later when the one named Amyott came into the cowshed to borrow a rake.

Cedi asked him - partly in his own language - "Have you met my friend, Maun?".

Amyott having his back to Cedi, turned round. "Who is Maun? I know no-one of that name."

Cedi elaborated. "He is the one you and your brothers followed from Craiga."

At this, Amyott's eyes widened. He repeated Maun's name. "Maun! You know him well?"

"I do indeed know him", said Cedi, "We grew up together. His father once owned this farm".

To Cedi's astonishment, Amyott hurried away and as Cedi watched from the cowshed door, he saw him drop his rake and run to his brothers. He gathered them around him and they had an impromptu conference. Then, all four of them walked towards him, Amyott the spokesman saying, "Will you take us to your friend, Maun?".

"Yes", said Cedi, "I will, but not today. We are much too busy. Tomorrow evening - would that be all right?". As they nodded their acceptance, it seemed to Cedi that they were nervous. He could not imagine anyone being nervous of Maun - he would not hurt a fly!

Could it have something to do with healing? Had Maun healed one of them as he had done for young Victor's mother? Now, Cedi was as anxious to go and see Maun as they were.

He could hardly wait until the next evening. Nor could the brothers. They hurried through their work, making sure everything was finished, before presenting themselves in front of Cedi. They still wore their old clothes, but had made some effort to smarten themselves up.

Cedi said they could walk the short distance, for once off the farm, the Mission school was only about a mile and a half away, hardly worth the trouble of saddling the horse.

As they reached the Mission school, Cedi could hardly believe his eyes, The sight of so many sick people, made him catch his breath. He said to the brothers, "Wait here. I will go inside and find my friend. I know he will see you, if I ask him".

Calpurnius saw Cedi approach and opened the door for him. "How good to see you, Cedi. Have you come to help? We need more water from the river."

Cedi replied, "I will gladly help, but that is not why I am here".

"No?", queried Calpurnius, "Then how can we help you?".

"I have brought some young men who are anxious to see Maun - four very healthy young men", he added quickly, when he saw the look on Calpurnius's face.

"I have not seen my son today, Cedi. We are so busy. It is time Maun had a rest. I will go and fetch him."

At the temporary surgery, Hanno was writing down the name of each new patient and the nature of his or her illness, then they were taken to see Maun by Julia or Helen. Calpurnius interrupted them, "Maun, Cedi is here to see you on an important matter".

"Father, I am much too busy", said Maun without looking up.

"My son. You may not need rest, but we do. We are all very tired. I insist you come and eat and rest for a while. These people have been sick for long enough. Another hour or two won't hurt them. I insist."

Julia said, "Yes Maun ... *Please* ... Your father is right. We all need to eat and rest".

Maun helped the patient to his feet, then nodded, "Very well, I am rather hungry". Helen smiled and led the patient away. Calpurnius put his arm around Maun and led him to the back of the house and in through the kitchen, so as not to be seen by the crowd.

Cedi was waiting and when he saw Maun, he tried to hide his dismay. "Why was I not told of this? I could have helped in some way."

However, he continued, "While you eat Maun, there are some people who are anxious to meet you - may I bring them in?" Maun nodded and as he ate his bowl of rice, eggs and vegetables, he saw Cedi bring in the four men. Maun was not entirely surprised, for he was aware they had followed him, but he was very surprised at what they had to say.

Amyott introduced himself as the eldest of the brothers, the other three being Gillis, Arren and Greg. Amyott told those present of how they had been brought up on their father's farm. He had been a very cruel and hard man to live with and thought nothing of beating his sons, just for the fun of it. Amyott said, "When our mother died recently, after years of abuse, our father became even more cruel and we decided to leave. All we had ever known was bullying and hardship and we did not know how to behave. When we walked into town and people ran away, we thought it was because of our strength, that was, until the day we went into the inn at Craiga."

"We were enjoying our new found power, when most of the customers ran away, leaving their meals uneaten in fear. We laughed. A crippled boy was sent to clean up our mess (Amyott bowed his head in shame). Then you came and removed my boot from the boy's neck - and healed him. What we saw were rays of light streaming from your head. We each heard a voice say, "Be kind - like my servant. He heals the infirm. You can do likewise. Follow him".

"So, here we are, for on that day, we were reborn."

Maun smiled at them. "Then, you have found the right place to start work. You may all come with me now." Before leaving, Maun said, "Thank you, Cedi". Then he led the young brothers to take over from Hanno, Julia and Helen. While they were shown what was required of them, Maun went to the church to see his grandfather and give the blessing to those who waited patiently.

"I take it", said Cedi, "That my workers will not be returning to the farm with me?".

"No. I don't think so", said Calpurnius.

Cedi looked around at the crowd of sick people and the strained faces on the members of Maun's family and asked, "What has happened to my friend?". There was sadness and regret in his voice.

It was Conchessa who answered him. "It seems that while Maun was in captivity, he almost died. When he recovered, he found he had this gift to heal".

Cedi repeated, "A Gift? Some might call it that - but I doubt if I am of the same mind". Conchessa understood his sentiments and she said, "You have been a good friend to Maun. I know he has always been proud of that".

Cedi nodded. "I know. If he ever needs me, I will come, meanwhile, I must get back to the farm. I now have an extra four mens' work to do!"

Conchessa smiled and thanked him. As he walked away, Calpurnius and Conchessa watched him pass the crowd, stopping to wave at Rhona and Alana who were giving water and sweet honey cakes to the children.

CHAPTER XXVII

A CHANGE OF HEART

As spring turned to summer, the sick, the lame - and the curious - still arrived and two long huts had to be built on some spare ground to house the growing numbers who came to work, for when Calim and Harran spread the word at the Mission in Dunbriton, many young men and women asked if they could go to Bonavon to help. With the conviction that these intelligent students would relieve the pressure on his grandson, Calim paid for the huts to be built and planned for others to be constructed if required. Each of the huts housed eight people and were very modern, having their own wash room, a locker and hook to hang their cloak. As part of their duties, they had to keep their hut clean and take it in turns to fill the water butt.

The trouble was, as the numbers increased, the more food was required and Alana and Bliss organised the women of the village with the baking of loaves of bread, which were available for a small charge. However, this quickly became impractical and to provide the supply of bread required, a proper bakehouse was built with two large ovens and very reluctantly, it was decided to ask for payment for the bread from those who could afford it.

Calpurnius and Conchessa were not happy. Their beautiful house and grounds were overrun by strangers and the children of the village were becoming distracted from their education. They could also see that, as a family they were no longer required and they began to feel that they were becoming just another pair of hands in the ever growing industry that was building up around their son.

Something had to be done and a family meeting took place at the villa. All of the family were there with the exception of Maun himself, who if not actually healing, was teaching others how to.

Joseph put forward his thoughts on the matter in hand. "Frankly, we cannot continue as we are. Yes, there are many who have come to help - expecting no wages - but, all have to be fed and housed and if the ladies will permit my indelicate remark, they all have to use the lavatories - which in itself causes problems!"

"The sick are travelling from further and further afield and if we are to remain humane in our care of them, they cannot be asked to run along home immediately after treatment. Some have to stay over for several days. They also want to come to church to give thanks. Others want to stay permanently, just to be near Maun."

"We need more permanent houses for the helpers. Even more importantly, we need to separate the sick people from the school children."

Calpurnius stood up. "Father Joseph, may I suggest that your plan - the one that Conchessa and I rejected when we first heard it - should now be seriously considered. We have given it a lot of thought and concluded that if Maun is willing,

You Father Joseph, should take him to Gaul." Calpurnius fought hard to control his emotions, "Take him to your brother Martin, before he dies of hard work". He sat down and Conchessa comforted him.

Joseph studied the faces around the table, "Are you all agreed on this?".

Calim, Rhona, Harran, Calpurnius and Conchessa nodded, Calim speaking for all of them, "Yes, Father Joseph, we believe it is best for Maun".

"Indeed, it is", said Calpurnius, "It is time for change. Our next move is to consult Maun and persuade him that we have his best interests at heart".

In the end, Calpurnius was elected as the most appropriate to approach Maun and explain the family's concerns.

That very evening, after work, Calpurnius spoke to Maun, "My son, have you considered entering the priesthood - like your grandfather Joseph? You have been chosen to do God's work and it is possible that you would fare better with the power of the Holy Church behind you".

Maun raised his eyes to look at his father and realised, not for the first time, just how tired and worried he was. He was well aware of how difficult it was for his family; their peaceful way of life was no more and part of their beautiful home was being used as a shelter for the sick. It was true that great miracles of healing were taking place, but, at a price.

"Yes, I would like to be just like him", said Maun, "But, how can I? The sick just keep on coming. I cannot simply walk away".

"Yes, you can my son. You have already told us how Amyott has developed his healing powers. Could you not teach his brothers also? If we all trained others to take over our work, very soon it would be possible for you to leave. It's not as if you would be gone for good. You could return even stronger and with authority."

Maun was secretly relieved, for he had been feeling guilty about the strain his family were under and he wondered what would happen if for some reason his power was taken away? Better to take this golden opportunity offered by his family.

The brothers were devastated at the news, for excepting Maun himself, their lives had altered most. From being violent and aggressive young men, they had become the most gentle servants of Christ. However, they eventually became used to the idea and accepted that it was for the best.

The helpers decided that they would stay together and dedicate their work to Maun, but he would not hear of it - "*All work must be offered in the name of Jesus*" - he had emphaised. Well, they thought, if that is what Maun wanted, they would do their best to please him.

Amyott and his brothers, after their initial disappointment, took to their new role as principal healers and in order that they would be immediately be recognised, they had robes of dark reddish brown material spun. They also decided to call themselves, simply 'The Brothers'.

Eventually, Joseph decided they could delay no longer. He explained that his brother Martin was very old, indeed, he would be just a little surpised to find him still alive, although so far, he had not heard any news from Tours of his death, so he lived in hope.

Calim made enquiries regarding ships sailing for Gaul and discovered that a vessel was leaving within the month. The ship was not departing from Dunbriton, but from another port further east along the Clyde. As the ship was only docking to pick up a few passengers and supplies, they would be obliged to move into a hostel for at least one night, in order to be ready to embark at short notice.

Hanno packed all his records of the healings, which were now considerable, while Maun said goodbye to all his friends. He was about to ride to the farm to see Cedi, before leaving to spend some time with his grandparents at the villa, when a cart pulled up at the gate, containing Cedi, Eric, Anna and Sophie.

Maun told him, "I was about to make my way to the farm to see you Cedi. You have saved me a journey!". Cedi had his arm around Anna's shoulder and he excitedly told Maun that they planned to marry. They wanted the ceremony to take place in the old barn church before the building was demolished to make way for a larger one.

Maun wished them luck and told them how happy he was to see his friends together. However, he reassured them that the old church would be there for a long time, as the Brothers plan to build an abbey was still some distance in the future.

"You are indeed fortunate to have found your ideal partners. Not everyone is so lucky", said Maun, at the same time thinking to himself, 'If I feel a tiny spark of regret about becoming a priest, it is because I will not have the pleasure of marrying a beautiful young girl like Anna'. The thought passed quickly.

Joseph was taking his last climb up Bonfire Hill. He stood on the spot where he previously pleaded with the angels for Maun's life and where his beloved Alicia had appeared and kissed him. He put his hand to his lips at the memory, 'Was she watching him now?' he wondered. He looked around his valley for the last time. 'Now, I know why I had to come here, although it took long enough for me to find out.'

When he first arrived, he could never in his wildest dreams have guessed at the events which were to take place here. God most certainly works in strange and mysterious ways.

When Joseph came down from the hill, Maun was still saying goodbye to his all friends and even the man with the bossy wife turned up with several others.

Joseph called on him, "Come Maun. It is time we went" and with that, Maun mounted his horse. As he waved goodbye to the crowd that had gathered to see them off, he looked for the last time at the hills, surrounded in mist. They had been the first thing he had seen every morning on rising and they had also been the first landmark that he had recognised - even before he spotted Cedi - on the day he returned from his long journey home. Today, he thought that they looked sad, but whatever their mood, he had always loved them, even though sometimes they were covered in mist.

As they left, Alana, Clodus, Paulus, Bliss, the Brothers and the children of Bonavon all waved. Then Calim, Evan and Hanno mounted their horses and sped after Joseph and Maun.

CHAPTER XXVIII

THE PREDICTION

Moving into the villa was for Maun and his friends a wonderful experience. Not only were his grandparents there to spoil him, but there were servants galore to wait on their every need. Uncle Harran and his wife Elinor came - and all his relatives - who fussed around him asking questions. Evan enjoyed walking in the formal garden, without having to do any of the hard work, while Hanno studied the herb garden and made some notes. Joseph just relaxed and from time-to-time, he was spotted dozing off on one of the big couches; not that he would admit he was actually asleep - "Just resting my eyes", he would say if someone spoke to him.

Maun's cousins, Julia's daughters and Portia's two sons, despite all being a little younger than Maun, followed him wherever he went, asking questions. Helen and her sisters, Serena and Elisa were highly thought of by Conchessa and she had always admired their advanced reading skills. Maun wondered what she would say if she saw them follow him and hang on his every word, although he had to confess that the questions asked by the girls were not of academic subjects. Their first question had been, "What colour robe will you wear when you became a priest and will you wear a funny hat?".

He did not much like talking about himself and attempted to change the subject whenever possible, asking them about their work at the school. Young ladies from wealthy families did not usually work, but Harran insisted that his daughters and granddaughters had useful work to do.

His cousins thought Maun looked exactly as they imagined a disciple of Christ would. He was lean, selfless and shy, simple in his dress and he believed that cleanliness was vitally important. They admired him tremendously.

When Calpurnius saw his predicament, he called over to Maun, "What about that race you promised me?".

When Julia saw that Maun wanted to go with his father, she called out to her daughters, "Come on my beauties, you can see Maun again tomorrow. Let him go riding with his father. He won't have many more chances for a while".

When Calpurnius and Maun left the room, Joseph was still lounging on the couch, with Hanno trying to have a discussion with him about the records they kept of the healings. Because of Maun's difficulties, it was essential that he had evidence of his many successful spiritual achievements and be able to produce them. Joseph was warning Hanno that although he was anxious to keep records, they had to be accurate and show that the work done by Maun was neither exaggerated, nor toned down. Joseph emphasised that *"It had to be the truth",* which irritated Hanno slightly to think that Joseph should even think he would be guilty of either - but he understood.

Besides walking in the gardens, Evan enjoyed talking to the servants, visiting the stables and exploring the villa and the grounds. He also visited a tailor and bought himself a new tunic and coat. On his return Calim greeted him, "Did you find everything you wanted?" he asked.

"Yes Sir. I thought as everyone else was dressing up to travel, I might as well do the same."

Calim smiled and nodded. "Come, sit with me and have some refreshments. I have not had the opportunity to talk to you, there being so many people around these last few days." He rang the bell and a servant appeared, Calim ordering some wine for both of them. He continued, "I especially want to thank you Evan, for I have been told how you gave up your work in order to escort Maun home and protect him. We are all very grateful and appreciate how difficult a decision that must have been, considering you have a wife and family to return to".

"Well Sir. It was not too difficult, for I imagined one of my own sons in a similar situation to Maun's. I would hope that someone would take care of him. However, I must admit I am looking forward to seeing my family again."

"I do hope", said Calim, "That you all arrive in Gaul safely and you find your family well".

Evan added, "Yes Sir. I hope so too. It has been almost two years since I saw them".

The servant appeared with the wine and Calim poured two large glasses, handing one to Evan.

Evan asked, "Do you still preach at the Mission church in Dunbriton?".

"Not now, Evan", he replied. "I leave all that to the younger men who are inspired in that direction. I concentrate on my work with the Council, for I feel that it is important to take an interest in local politics, otherwise we would allow men who may be less than honest to have a hand in our affairs. Therefore, I insist on being present in the Council Chambers when votes are taken, for there are those among us who say one thing, but when it comes to the vote will cast it in their own self-interest."

"Nor do I interest myself in our shipyard. That is in the very capable hands of a man called Leelan and his sons, whose father was an old friend of my fathers. The old man's first wife and children were killed on the same day as my mother. They do a good job without our interference."

Evan was sympathetic, "I am sorry Sir. I had no idea that your mother had been killed. It must have been horrible for your family".

"Yes Evan. At the time it was totally destructive, to us as young boys and to my father and Leelan who was with us. I have dwelt on it many times. But, do you know what I think?" Evan looked puzzled. Calim continued, "As the years have passed and the older I become, I have observed that, evil very often walks hand in hand with great goodness".

"Really Sir?", said Evan, "What has led you to this belief?".

"Well. If that cruel and tragic war had not occurred, my father would never have become more than a builder of small craft. He would never have had the fire that encouraged him to build great ships, or to build this villa. I would never have met my dear wife Rhona, or acquired the power necessary to have a hand in the development of our town. There are Evan, thousands of men, women and children who are living better lives, having been educated at our Mission school."

Evan was thoughtful. "You know, Sir. There may be some truth in that. When I first saw Maun, my heart filled with pity for the poor pathetic boy. So mistreated, I would have gladly killed the people who had done this terrible thing to an innocent boy. But, within days, this boy had saved my life. Soon, pity turned to admiration for the way he held no bitterness against those responsible and admiration turned to love, just like I feel for my own sons. So, if Maun had not been taken into slavery, I would not be here now. Indeed, I would be somewhere at the bottom of the sea being eaten by the fish and my sons would be fatherless."

"Yes", said Calim, "That's exactly what I mean. Sometimes good comes from evil. At other times we must be careful not to let evil come out of our good intentions".

"I will remember to bear that in mind", said Evan.

At that moment Joseph arrived. "Am I interrupting your conversation?", he asked.

"No Joseph. We are discussing how evil might sometimes bring good to some people."

Joseph appeared not as surprised as Calim supposed he might be and said, "That has been the subject of much theological discussion. However, no one knows for sure, whether good would have come about in any other way? There is simply no way of proving or disproving it, although I am inclined to believe that God in his wisdom, works in mysterious ways."

Evan was having second thoughts. "No, I simply cannot accept that God would allow a frail and innocent boy like Maun to suffer the way he did, in order to save an old salt like me."

But, Joseph was deadly serious. "And why not", he said, "Did he not give his own beloved son, that others might live ...?".

Calpurnius and Maun rode along the banks of the Clyde and out into the countryside. They stopped to watch some retired Army officers falconing, but after a while Calpurnius sensed Maun was uneasy. He guessed that his sensitive son's sympathy lay with the birds, as he had a horror of living things being held captive, especially for the amusement of men.

To try to take his son's mind off the birds, Calpurnius suggested, "Since we are near to the house of my old tutor, Professor Theophilus, shall we call and see if he is at home?".

"Might as well", said Maun, "If we are so near" and they galloped towards the white stone house which came into view, then dismounting and tying their horses to a post. The professor must have seen them approach from a window, as he came rushing out to greet them, a wide smile across his now ageing face. Greeting them, he threw his arms around Calpurnius, "My dear boy come in".

Calpurnius introduced Maun, "This is my son, Sir". Maun noted that there was pride in his father's voice and that pleased him very much.

"I am so pleased you called. I have bean searching for an excuse to stop work and have a drink" and the professor called out to his servant to bring refreshments. However, when the servant arrived with a tray of fruit wine and some glasses,

Calpurnius was not surprised to see a beautiful young woman.

After the servant had left, Calpurnius said, "I hope we have not called at an inconvenient time?", noting the spread of documents on the table.

"No, no, my dear boy There is no one as important as one of my old pupils and nothing I like better than to hear of their progress."

"I am afraid Sir, that I have bean so busy with teaching - and a multitude of other works - to have kept up with my astral studies."

"Come now, Calpurnius, you must surely have completed your son's chart?"

"I must confess Sir. I have done nothing since I saw you last."

Theophilus made noises of displeasure. "We must put that right immediately. Now, remind me of your birthday, Maun".

"November, Sir ...", said Maun nervously.

Theophilus scanned the mountains of charts and scrolls stacked from floor to ceiling on shelves, then triumphantly retrieved one. "I've found your original." He placed a scroll on the table and unrolled it, "Ah! Yes!".

"This is yours, my boy. I see the Sun is placed at seventeen degrees of Scorpius."

Calpurnius interrupted his flow, "I must tell you Sir, that my son is something of a sceptic as far as study of the stars are concerned".

Maun winced. He hoped he was not going to get a lecture. He would not understand a word of it anyway. Theo's face looked pained, "Tsk! Tsk!", he said, shaking his head slowly from side-to-side. "Oh! My dear boy. I beg you not to be like these poor spiritually blind souls who believe in nothing, save what can be seen and felt in front of them. They can lift their faces to the Sun, feel its warmth and comforting glow, smell the sweetness of the flowers on a summer's day and then deny that the Sun has an effect on their lives! Without the Sun there would be no life upon earth at all."

"As for the Moon. The great tides of the oceans ebb and flow at her command. Many people take these great powers for granted. But the other planets are just as powerful."

"People throughout our world have studied the stars and their effects on the lives of mankind for more than four thousand years. That knowledge has been passed down through the centuries. Then my young friend, people who have lived on earth for only a few years try to tell me, *I am wrong!* How insulting to an intellect such as mine."

Maun tried to apologise. "Sir. It is not that I don't believe, so much as I don't understand. I cannot see how a star so far away, can have an effect on people."

Theo remembered that Calpurnius had told him of Maun's backwardness at reading and attempted to make amends. "My boy. On the very first page of the Jewish bible, it states 'God created the lights in the heavens to separate night from day, and to serve as signs both for festivals, seasons and years'. Besides, time and space to God is very different from what we perceive here on earth."

Theophilus studied the chart before him. "My boy. I see that you are about to embark on a long journey."

"Yes Sir," said Maun. He refrained from saying that he did not need the stars to tell him that - he already knew it.

Undaunted, Theophilus handed Calpurnius the chart and asked him what he made of it, pointing to some peculiar marks. Calpurnius examined it and then looked up at Maun and smiled, "My son. I see that a woman will come into your life and be a very strong influence upon it".

Maun secretly thought, 'Now that I do not believe. Has it not sunk into my father's head that I am going to Gaul to train as a priest?' - his expression, however, did not alter.

Then Calpurnius said, "This woman wears a crown". He looked up at his tutor for confirmation.

Theophilus glanced at the chart and smiled, "Carry on my boy. You are doing well".

Calpurnius continued, "I believe that this woman is young, yet has the wisdom of a sage. Her words and deeds will alter the way you think of yourself".

"Excellent", said Theophilus, "I see you have not lost any of your talent. The only thing I would add, is that the 'Crown' you speak of, is not one made of precious metals. It is a crown of wisdom and belongs to a higher realm. It is yet another sign of the wisdom of the woman. She has secret knowledge".

It was a pleasant journey back to the villa. They did not hurry, but allowed their horses to walk at a leisurely pace, father and son making the best of what little time they had left to spend together. It could be a week, or it could be only hours before the travellers would be called forward to join the ship. They reached the villa, servants coming out to take their horses from them and as they walked towards the entrance of the villa, Maun remarked, "You know father. I still cannot understand what you or Theophilus could see in that chart? It looked unintelligible to me".

Calpurnius smiled and led him to a garden seat, "Come and sit here a moment before we go inside, for I am sure that when we do, your mother and grandmother will not allow us another word. My son, I do not expect you to learn of the stars. It has taken me many years of study to achieve the little I know. A great deal of astrology is guesswork. Granted it is informed guesswork and based on sound principles, but so much depends on accurate timing. That is its weak point, for people can be careless about such things. However, given the correct time of, say, a birth, or an important occasion, the results are amazing".

"It is written in the Holy Book of the Jews, 'That whatsoever a person asks for in faith, shall be given unto him'. Many people imagine that this means God will pander to their greed and make them rich, or set them free. This belief creates many disappointments. I believe that it means whenever a person is open minded and curious enough to ask questions and truly wants to learn of spiritual matters, then God finds a way to answer them. That answer may come in a dream, or a meeting with a stranger who will give the answer. But, come it will. 'Seek and ye shall find', is not just a saying, or friendly advice. It is a universal and spiritual law, which must be obeyed."

"So, my son. You are a healer now of some reputation. Have you ever asked the question, *why you*? Have you never wondered why you have been chosen to heal."

"I don't think I have to ask, father", said Maun. "It is possible this work was given to me in exchange for my life. You see father, I died in captivity." Maun then told his father about seeing him pray by the roadside. Calpurnius was incredulous. Maun continued, "That was when I discovered how much you and mother loved me. After that, I could not get home fast enough".

"What in God's name did they do to you to kill you?"

Maun did not want his father to know every detail of his suffering, nor did he feel inclined to go through the memory again, so he said, "I became ill when the winter came".

"My poor boy", said Calpurnius, "What you have had to suffer! However, I am sure your future is going to be much better. Theophilus agrees with me that a lady will come into your life and make you very happy".

"Father", said Maun in an exasperated tone, "I tell you now I have no intentions of finding a lady companion. I fear I will be too busy; that is if God permits me to continue healing?".

"My son. Of one thing I am certain. For as long as you desire to heal the sick, I know God will supply the courage and the power. But, why are you so against a woman in your life? I fear that you might suffer loneliness."

Maun blushed, "Father. I fear I may be laughed at. I am not handsome to look at, like you, or good with words. My friends at school used to say, 'Why are you not handsome like your father? ... Why are you so different?'. I'm afraid Sir, I used to wonder about that myself. It was only when grandfather Joseph said I looked like him, that I could understand".

Calpurnius felt ashamed, for he used to ask himself the same question and had never considered Maun's feelings. "I am so sorry about that my son, for I would sever my right arm rather than hurt you. But, I must add that whether or not you want a woman companion in your life, if God thinks you require the assistance of a lady in your life, then you will just have to accept her. For you, my son, are the author of your own life. You have written her in. Therefore, you will have to accept her."

"I am afraid father, that I don't understand that?" said Maun.

Calpurnius answered as best he could. "My son. Being the sons of our great creator, we ourselves are creators. We create our future with our every thought. So, do not think yourself lowly. Think yourself that you will do your very best for your creator. Hold up your head and walk tall."

"Easier said than done, father", said Maun with a laugh, "Is that some of Theophilus's teaching?".

"Strangely enough Maun, that information came from your grandfather, Calim."

Maun was astounded, "Father, you have never spoken to me of such things before".

"I am sorry, my son", said Calpurnius, "But, you never expressed interest in the subject".

Maun thought for a moment. "Father, I admit that I never asked questions, but I did listen to you when you spoke to mother of the stars and planets and their influence on people. I was interested when you told mother that she was born under the sign of 'The pillars of the Temple' and how Alana was born under the sign of the virgin. I listened father, but never understood what you meant. The stars are so far away, it did not make sense to me".

"You have indeed been listening", said Calpurnius, "And I am not surprised you did not understand. Neither did I until Theophilus explained it and as often happens, once explained by a good teacher, the subject is made simple".

"You see Maun, astronomy and astrology, are part of the same science. However, astronomy is all about the stars, the ones that you can see on a clear night. The planets are different, in so far as they are wandering stars and, the very first astrologers were simple folks who slept under the night sky. They noticed how people born in different seasons behaved. It became obvious that those born in the spring-time - when everything in the countryside was new - were 'the pioneers' - always eager to move on to new pastures. They gave them a name to fit the character, which was the 'Ram'. However, the nearer they came to early summer, the character altered and the people became more stubborn. Their appearance also changed, most having thick necks and loud pleasant voices. They wanted to stay put and tend the land they had, so they were given the name of an animal with these tendencies - the 'Bull'."

"This did not all happen within a few years, but over centuries, until all of the signs were explored and named. Astrology has been studied now for thousands of years and it has developed into an art, as well as a science and has become the sister science of astronomy. However, it has more to do with the people of the earth; the seasons of the year and the effects of the wandering stars, rather than man's curiosity about how the universe was formed, which seems to be the astronomer's main interest."

"Do you think father, that grandfather Joseph and I are of the same sign, since we are so much alike?"

Calpurnius laughed, "Our grandfather Joseph has never disclosed his age, or his birthday to anyone - not even his daughter! However, some of the things he has done in his life, truly belong to the sign of the Ram. Who else - when his beloved wife died - would wrap his tiny babe of a few weeks in a sling around his neck and shoulder and set off on a journey of fifty miles to reach Tours, stopping only at inns to feed and clean her? Then, when he became a priest, he would travel into the most deprived and rough part of the town to seek converts. And, my dear son, your grandfather, believing that this part of the Empire was inhabited by pagans and heathens, who painted their faces blue, still came here".

Maun thought of something else. "What about when he took Paulus into the highlands and they were set upon."

"Oh! Yes", said Calpurnius, "How could I have forgotten. That was just a few months before you were born".

"I think we should go inside now, Maun. It is getting cold, besides your mother and grandmother will be getting worried."

Rhona and Conchessa were repairing clothes when they entered and Rhona asked, "Where have you two been?".

Calpurnius answered sheepishly, "We went to see my old tutor Theophilus".

"Say no more", said Rhona, "When you two get together, you forget to come

207

home. As for you young Maun, I thought you had more sense".

"Don't scold the boy, mother. It was entirely my fault", said Calpurnius with a smile.

Maun hoped that his father would not mention the chart, or anything about a woman entering his life. That would be too embarrassing, although he need not have worried - his father being the height of discretion.

The knowledge that Maun, Joseph, Evan and Hanno were leaving on the next ship, was constantly with Rhona and Conchessa. They dreaded the moment when they would be told of the ship's sighting and tried to keep it at the back of their minds, simply enjoying the last few days of having all the family together.

Conchessa missed Alana, she having been like a mother and a sister to her, but Alana was happy with Clodus and her children. She also missed Paulus, as he had been like an older brother, always there to help and protect her and she smiled at the thought of him, but he was happy with Bliss. Her family were grown up and had children of their own, making Paulus their grandfather, a now highly respected member of the community of Bonavon. She was very proud of him and his achievements.

The next few days passed pleasantly. Hanno, having packed all of his notes, spent his time wandering along the river bank, while Joseph walked and talked to Conchessa, telling her not to worry about them. Maun and his father grew very close and for the first time since he was small, Maun would seek out his father's company.

Then the news was brought to them. The ship that would take them to Gaul had been sighted and because the vessel was calling only to take on board fresh food and water, the travellers would have to move into the hostel by the dock, ready to leave on the next tide.

Everyone tried to hide their feelings, but Conchessa was especially upset. It was bad enough losing her son so soon after having him returned to her, now she was losing her father as well and she clung to Calpurnius for comfort. He was well aware of how distressed she was, for his own feelings were the same.

"Do not fret so much my love", he said, "I have been thinking. There is no good reason why you and I cannot go to Tours ourselves and visit Maun and your father. We are not needed here at the school as the Brothers have everything in hand. As for the Council, every other Councillor has taken long vacations. We could go in a few months, even sooner".

Conchessa's eyes widened and she looked up at her husband's now smiling face, "Are you serious? Do you really mean it?".

"Yes. I do mean it, for I will miss our son too." Calpurnius was pleased he'd thought of it, for Conchessa cheered up immediately.

"But, what of your father and mother Rhona. We cannot leave them so soon. They will feel left out of our plans."

"You're right", said Calpurnius, "It might be better if we say nothing of our intentions for a while".

PART IV

THE ROAD TO THE PRIESTHOOD

CHAPTER XXIX

SLAVE CHILDREN

Joseph, Maun, Hanno and Evan having said their goodbyes to everyone, moved into the hostel, not at the port at Dunbriton, but at another small port further east along the Clyde, just past the military base. Although, they could see the ship anchored off shore, they knew that they would have to stay at least one night in the less than hospitable hostel, with its uncomfortable bunks!

Maun's feelings were mixed. On the one hand, he regretted having to leave his parents, grandparents and all his family and friends, but on the other, it was going to be an exciting adventure to a strange country.

As he lay on the hard hostel bunk, his mind would not be still. He tossed and turned trying to settle, however, he knew from past experience, that he would not sleep. So, he got up, put on his big warm cloak with the hood - a gift from his grandmother - and tiptoed out of the dormitory, leaving his companions fast asleep.

He walked along the quay from one end to the other, stopping only to take in deep breaths of the cool night air. Reaching the far end of the quay, he was about to turn around, when he heard a noise - it sounded like a kitten mewing. He looked around, but saw nothing and he was about to walk away, when he heard the noise again, only this time louder. It sounded like a child. 'Surely, no infant would be out at this hour?', he thought. Then, he heard a noise like a key turning in a lock and then saw a glimmer of light as a door was opened in a small hut further along the road that led from the village.

Maun hid behind some boxes and watched. The door of the hut opened and as it did so, he watched as oil lamps placed along the rail of an old ship were lit, illuminating the deck and gangway. Then he heard voices coming from the hut and strange clanging noises.

What happened next, made Maun stare in disbelief. A woman came out of the hut followed by a row of small children. Each child was joined to the other by chains attached to an iron ring fixed around their necks. All of them had very fair hair and skin and although the children were not crying, they made choking noises. Maun was horrified and he could feel the anger rising within him.

As the pitiful procession left the hut, a man was last to leave, locking the door behind him and then following on behind. Maun was ready to accost him and as he was about to pass his hiding place, he stepped out in front of him, "Where are you taking these children?", he asked in a commanding voice.

The man was startled, believing no one was there to watch. Maun repeated, "Where are you taking these children? And why are they chained in that cruel way?". Maun called out to the woman, "Stop! Go no further". The man, having recovered his nerve, was about to tell Maun to 'mind his own business', when, suddenly he began to stare. For as Maun looked at him in anger, the rays shone around him, lighting up his face. The man, not understanding why, began to tremble uncontrollably.

The woman hurried over to see what was happening. She too became afraid. "I will ask you once more. Where are you taking these children?"

The woman replied, "We are taking them to Rome. The women of that town will pay a high price for one of these fair children".

Maun asked them, "Have you stolen these little ones?".

The man and the woman were adamant, "No sir. We have not stolen them. They are all bought and paid for. We have the receipts to prove it".

Maun was not satisfied, "Why have you chained them? That is most inhumane".

The man replied, "They are chained only to stop them running away on land. When they get on board, we will release them and they will be made comfortable. Sickly or weak children will not sell. It is in our interest to make sure they are well treated".

The woman added, "Sir. I can assure you. These children will thrive in the warm sunshine and fresh fruits of Rome. They will be well treated by their new mistresses".

Maun was inexperienced, but he did not trust these two. He remembered Amyott telling him how the light radiated from him when he healed the boy at Craiga and how they also heard a voice speak to them. He decided to frighten the slavers. He prayed and he heard a voice say, 'Allow the children to leave. Their destiny lies in Rome'.

But, he decided not to let these slavers get away with their diabolical trade. They needed to be taught a lesson and Maun took a step closer to them. They immediately stepped back, terrified expressions on their faces. He stared at them again, until he felt burning heat throughout his whole body and he knew that he was radiating light. Then he said slowly, "Do you know who I am?". The pair shook their heads from side to side. "I am the messenger of the Lord and I am sent to tell you to treat His children with kindness and love, for if you fail to do so and disobey my word, I will cast you both into hell."

The man and woman were clearly petrified at Maun's words and were ready to obey his every command. Maun asked the woman, "Is there a well nearby?".

She replied, "At the end of the lane".

Maun commanded her, "Go and fetch me some water in a vessel" and she obeyed immediately.

He turned to the man, "You, Sir. Remove their chains and bring the children to me".

The man protested, "I beg you, we have paid good money for them. We cannot afford to let them go".

But, Maun was stubborn, "I did not ask you to let them go. I said, *remove the chains*". The man brought the children forward; took the key from around his neck and with trembling hands proceeded to unlock the chains. The woman came back carrying a large pitcher of water.

Maun held his hands around the bruised and bleeding necks of each child, until they felt his soothing and healing touch. Tears filled his eyes as he looked at the wide-eyed and pathetic little faces; dressed in little more than a few rags. He blessed the water and gave each one a drink of it, then he made the sign of the cross on their brow and blessed them.

When he had healed and blessed each one, he asked the eldest of them, "Do you know where you are going?".

The boy answered, "Sir. I heard say we are being taken to Rome, a place far away".

"And are you willing to go?", Maun inquired.

"No Sir. But, we have no say. Our families are poor and need the money."

Maun then gathered the children around him and told them, "Be good children and believe that our Father in Heaven loves every one of you, so do not be afraid. Now go on your way".

The slavers were badly shaken, but even Maun was surprised when the woman came to him and asked him, 'Will you do for us the same as you did for the children?". So, he bade them kneel before him. He made the sign of the cross on their foreheads and placing his hands on their heads, he prayed for them and for the children. As they felt the power flowing from his hands, they said, "Sir. We promise to take good care of the children. It is in our interest that they remain in good health".

"So you have said", remarked Maun, "I say make sure that you do. For I tell you, that Our Lord God sees all and knows all. He will be watching your every move. Now go!". He watched as they walked up the gangway of the ship, each one then turning to look at him. After the gangway had been removed, Maun turned and walked away; back to the hostel and his hard bunk. He was amazed at the enormity of what he had just accomplished. The power he had been given was awesome! He knew that what he had done was inspired and he prayed and gave thanks.

Back in the hostel and amid the grunts and snores of his sleeping companions, he unpacked his favourite blanket - the one Evan had given him on the ship - wrapped it around his shoulders and got into the bunk and slept.

Within the hour, it was almost dawn, a messenger arriving to say that their ship was ready to board.

Evan struggled up, stretched out his arms and with a great loud yawn, announced that he had not slept a wink all night. Then, looking over at Maun curled up and sound asleep, said to Joseph, "Look at our lad there. I wish I could sleep like him".

Hanno gave Maun a shake and Joseph called out, "Come on my boy, look sharp, we are about to board the ship".

The vessel was in good condition and although their quarters were more comfortable than they expected, they were not luxurious and Joseph, recalling his journey of almost nineteen years before, hoped he would not be so sea-sick.

Evan was excited and in good humour. "Just think lad", he said to Maun, "I am on board ship as a passenger. I can watch other people work, for a change".

"And I", said Maun "Do not have to watch over any hounds! I wonder where she is now? She was a wonderful dog. Her puppies will have grown up now".

Evan could see Maun was anxious about the hounds and he said, "Never mind, Maun. When I get home and see Captain Bruner, I will ask him where he sold them and if he found them good homes?".

"Time has passed quickly", said Evan attempting to change the subject, "You have grown up and accomplished so much. You no longer look like the half-starved sparrow we took aboard at Hibernia. You are now a lean, but strong young man".

Maun shook his head sorrowfully, "I may look different, but in my heart I will be forever little Mauny".

"Give yourself time, lad", said Evan, "Do you remember our journey through the Highlands; when I attempted to educate you on your manhood? I should have added, some men mature faster than others. You are not quite eighteen and have a long way to go before you stop growing. You are as tall as your grandfather and your Ma had to stand on her toes to kiss you good bye".

"Yes, you are right, Evan. But, I was not only thinking of my height, but to the way I feel about myself in my head. I still feel like a boy."

Evan's response was to howl with laughter and when he stopped to take a breath, he said, "Lad. That is how we all feel. The trouble with you, is that you've been brought up in a family of teachers, Decurians and priests. Not many of us mortals have been born into such high company. So, my boy, don't be so hard on yourself".

After a moments silence, Evan leaned over and grinned as he said in Maun's ear, "By the way. You now have quite a few whiskers on your chin".

Maun laughed, "Have I really? I will soon have to buy myself a sharp razor".

They were standing by the rail of the ship looking into the water, when it began to move away from the dock. Hanno joined them and he looked happy. "Well", he said, "I wanted to travel and now here we are. This is my very first voyage in a large ship and I am looking forward to it".

Evan turned to him and said, "I have sailed on many a voyage - and some very long ones at that, to countries you never dreamed of - but, after so many, it just becomes hard work".

Hanno was not put off and replied, "I have rolled up all of our documents and packed them away for the duration of this voyage, but have kept this one roll of parchment, just in case. I have made up my mind to enjoy this trip".

Joseph had not returned on deck, so Maun decided to check on him and found him at prayer in his cabin. "I am sorry grandfather, I did not mean to interrupt you. I just came to see if you were well."

"Thank you, my boy. I am fine, just as long as no one mentions food!"

"Perhaps the cool air would make you feel better", said Maun.

"No. Thank you, my boy. I feel the cold a bit too much these days. I am no longer as fit and strong as I was in my younger days."

"Would you like to borrow my warm blanket?", asked Maun.

"That is very kind of you, my boy. I would like that very much." Maun put the blanket around Joseph's shoulders and in doing so, placed a hand on his back. "That feels wonderful. So comforting, Maun. I might be able to sleep now."

"I will call back when our meal is ready to see how you are", said Maun. Joseph raised his head and looked pale. "Sorry grandfather I forgot!"

Once outside the cabin door, Maun hesitated. For the first time he became very aware of Joseph's frail shoulders. He wondered if his grandfather was making this trip for the purpose of helping him become a priest? Or, was it the necessity to see his brother Martin and his old home for the last time? Perhaps, a bit of both!

Several days into their journey, the voyage passed without any mishaps and the weather had stayed fine. However, Maun was still anxious about Joseph and went below decks frequently to check on him. "Don't worry about me, my boy" said Joseph, "Everything is fine".

Not convinced, Maun told Joseph how Evan was enjoying himself watching the crew at work, the old man replying with a smile, "I can imagine how he feels after so many years at sea".

Then, remembering something said by the Captain of the ship, Maun told his grandfather, "Apparently we are calling at the next port to take another passenger on board". However, Joseph didn't seem interested. All he cared about was getting to Gaul as fast as he could!

Maun continued, "Apparently, there was a signal".

"A signal?", queried Joseph, "What kind of a signal?".

"I understand", said Maun, "That in the distance, there is a fire burning on top of a beacon hill. A single fire is the signal for the ship to call to embark a passenger; two fires mean danger and no fire at all means pass by as quickly as possible. The Captain told us he will use the opportunity to bring aboard more food and water".

Joseph turned his pale face towards Maun, who said, "Sorry grandfather. I forgot again!". Then he hurried away, calling back over his shoulder, "I will be on deck if you need me".

As they approached the port on the tip of the North Wales coast, the Captain unexpectedly announced that they would be spending a full day on shore, as a repair had to be made to the rigging.

Once on land, Joseph recovered quickly. The weather was still bright and dry and Hanno asked the innkeeper, "Was it safe to go exploring?".

"It is", was the answer, "Very safe. Indeed, I will tell you of a an interesting place to visit. However, it is quite a distance away. You will have to borrow my cart".

"What is this place?", asked Joseph.

The innkeeper answered, "It is a sacred place where the Druids gather. It is called the 'Eye of God'. It is believed that this island has the shape of God's head and where the sacred eye is, the Druids hold their secret meetings. The Druids - who teach the ancient religions - are very wise, although they do not put their wisdom in writing, but pass it to their novices only by word of mouth".

He continued, "The 'Sacred Eye' is not on the actual eye of the head, but here!" and he pointed to the spot between his eyebrows.

"Have you ever heard of Druids, grandfather?", asked Maun.

"Yes. I have, my boy, although not much. I do know that they worship natural things and see God in every living thing - like trees and plants. And I also heard that they do not have a hierarchy such as our Church."

"They elect a leader", added the innkeeper "And they also think that some plants have magic in them".

Maun was interested, that was until the innkeeper mentioned that the Druids also practised human sacrifice. "Are you teasing us?", asked Maun. "You mean, they actually kill their own people?"

"So I have heard", said the innkeeper.

The travellers spent an interesting day and they saw some pleasant scenery. However, since the 'Eye of God' was not marked on any map they had to use their imagination and after their journey of exploration, they crowded into the eating room at the inn, to be served with large bowls of stew.

The innkeeper obviously enjoyed company, the conversation eventually dwelling on ships and the sea, Joseph asked him if many strange ships arrived at the port? "Oh My! Yes!", he answered, looking grave. "Ships of all shapes and sizes arrive here - some barely seaworthy. The passengers come here, begging for food, then drift inland, never to be seen again. I believe some come from as far away as Iberia, although most are from across the sea in Hibernia. They have told of terrible hardship in that country. Kings and princes taking up arms against one another; constantly waging war. We have heard how families are broken up, as young children are obliged to take up arms, or work their fingers to the bone to provide their king or prince with the gold to buy arms."

Maun listened intently. The country they were talking about was where he had been held captive, although he had not given much thought to what the people had suffered themselves. He was now learning something of their mentality. He did not like them very much, but he was beginning to understand them.

The ship, with repairs now completed and with a new passenger aboard, set sail. The Captain introduced the new man as Brun Farra, a seed merchant on his way to Gaul to test the market there. He and Joseph, the latter always enthusiastic about plants, struck up an immediate friendship and they chatted endlessly.

Later, Maun would remark to Evan, how is it that since Brun came aboard, his grandfather had not complained of seasickness. "I expect", said Evan, "He still feels queasy? The test will come when the smell of our meal cooking in the galley reaches the deck!".

Maun also noted that his grandfather still had his blanket around his shoulders. He wondered if he would ever get it back - not that it mattered - his grandfather's comfort came first, although he was determined to heal him, if he was given the opportunity.

The ship sped along on a stiff breeze under full sail, when the Captain announced that because they were making such good time, they would - without a mishap - reach the next port of call the day after next. He told them, "This is a scheduled stop and we will spend some time there. If you like, you can stay in your quarters aboard ship - the crew will feed you well - or move into the inn, just as you please. I will be at home with my wife and children, as this next destination is our home port".

Evan was happy for the Captain, for he knew exactly what it felt like to arrive home after a long haul at sea. He thought to himself, 'It is getting on for two years since I have seen my wife and sons and I know that they would have grown some. Maybe, they won't remember me? Could be something awful might have happened to them? I dare not think about it'. These worries were always with him and one thing was certain, he was not going to sign on for another trip. He'd had enough of the sea. He was ready to settle down and be a father to his children and a husband to Margaretta. That is, if no tragedy had befallen them.

The Captain was right. As predicted, they spotted land within the two days and on the third sailed into a sheltered harbour. The Captain gave the crew instructions and cheerfully made his way to the gangway. Evan called, "Have a good leave … May you find your family in good health".

"Thank you, Evan. I will see you all in two days time."

It was Joseph who insisted that they move into the inn, saying "I must have some decent sleep in a bed that does not wobble from side-to-side and this is our last chance to walk on dry land, before the longest part of our journey to Gaul".

Brun decided he would stay on the ship and sleep in his tiny cabin.

Joseph, Maun, Hanno and Evan made their way to the inn, but found the building crowded with people. Joseph could hardly hide his disappointment when told there were no rooms available. "I don't understand this", said Evan, "Such a small harbour. Ours is the only sailing ship here, so where have all these people come from?".

There were several serving maids and no shortage of food and drink - but no rooms and Joseph asked the innkeeper why the inn was so full, surely it was unusual? He was informed that some pilgrims were on their way to a Holy place and one of them had twisted his foot, therefore, they could not move on. Indeed, they might even have to return home, their leader having gone to inquire about a carriage to do just that.

"Is that so", said Joseph with a sly grin, turning his head to look at his grandson. "Well, it just so happens that among my party of travellers we have a healer. He may well be able to put things right. Will you kindly inform the leader of the pilgrims of this when he returns."

"I will, Sir", said the innkeeper cheerfully, but Joseph wondered why he had given him a such strange look?

Turning away, he rejoined his grandson and his friends at their table, saying "It appears that the reason we cannot have a bed for the night is due to the inn being full of pilgrims on their way to a Holy place. They cannot move on because one of them has injured a foot. Turning to Maun, he said, "I'm sorry my son, I said that you might be able to help and asked the innkeeper to send the pilgrims' leader to see you when he comes back".

"That is interesting, grandfather", said Maun, "I wonder where this Holy place is they are aiming for?".

"Sorry Maun. I did not think to ask."

They did not hurry through their meal, neither were they keen to rush back on board the ship, or explore the very pretty town, for although it was bright outside, the wind was bitter cold and fit to take one's breath away. Not only that, the open log fire at the end of the room where they ate, was warm and comforting. Joseph's mind was set on a warm bed and unbroken sleep for the night and so they ordered some more wine - more to delay their departure, rather than quench their thirst.

219

Just then a young woman approached their table. She was very pretty, her cheeks red from the cold wind outside, her light brown shoulder length hair was windswept and she ran her fingers through it to take it out of her eyes. Underneath her woollen cloak she wore a pink dress, but within the folds of the skirt, the colour was dark red and it was plainly an old dress faded by the sun. Her light brown eyes were large, soft and warm and her lips turned up slightly at the corners which made her expression one of permanent happiness.

The four travellers looked at her curiously, wondering who she was and what she wanted of them? She appeared a little embarrassed, but eventually said, "The innkeeper told me that you may be able to help us? I am Flavia, the leader of the pilgrims".

Realisation dawned on Joseph, who immediately sprung to his feet, "My Dear, please forgive me. I was not expecting a beautiful young woman …!".

She ignored his compliment, saying "One of our men twisted his foot when he stumbled on a stone. It is most painful and if not healed we will have to return home. If your physician can help we would be most grateful, for if we do not leave soon, we will be late for the festival".

Maun stood up. "Madam", he said, "I am not a physician, but I may be able to heal your friend. If you will take me to him, I will do what I can".

She stared at him. The youngest of the four men at the table, he appeared the least likely be a healer. But, when he stood up and spoke to her, she smiled.

She could see how very pleasant he looked and the gentleness of his voice struck a chord with her. She said, "Thank you, Sir. If you come this way, I will take you to him". Maun followed her, Hanno falling in behind in order to make notes.

Julian sat on a chair, looking utterly miserable, his future wife Emma by his side comforting him. Not only was Julian in severe pain, he felt guilty for spoiling what had promised to be a wondrous pilgrimage. He looked up when Flavia introduced Maun to him, but it was clear he did not hold any hope of recovery.

Maun first knelt on the floor and removed the cold water pads which had been recommended by the innkeeper, then sat on a cushion which had been placed on the floor for him. He held Julian's foot between his hands and almost at once the tremendous power began to flow through him. He asked Julian, "Can you walk at all?".

"No Sir", he answered, "It is so painful, I fear it is broken".

"I do not think so", said Maun, "You will be fine and will soon be ready to continue on your pilgrimage". Maun could see in his mind's eye that a tiny bone had been displaced and he manipulated it back into position. As the healing was completed, he felt Flavia's eyes upon him and he looked up at her, but she was staring above his head, a far-away expression on her face.

Julian wiggled his toes and became very excited. "Look Emma. I can move my toes." He stood up and performed a little jig, delight spreading over his face. Without another word he ran out of the room and into the dining area of the inn where the other pilgrims waited. On seeing him walk and run, they all clapped their hands with pleasure.

Maun got up from the cushion and as he dusted his robe down, he became aware that Flavia was watching him. "Who are you?", she asked in a quiet voice.

Maun blushed, " My name is Maun".

"No. I don't mean that. I mean *who* are you to be able to work such miracles of healing? I only ever heard of one other man and he was killed many years ago."

"Do you speak of Jesus?", Maun asked her.

"Yes, I do. I am a Christian."

Maun smiled at her, "I am too. I am on my way to Tours to become a priest".

"Why go so far away?", asked Flavia, "Could you not study in this country?".

"I am going to Tours to please my grandfather. He has a brother there who he thinks could help me."

She gazed into his face, "If you will forgive me for saying this, I don't think there is anything they could teach you in Tours - or anywhere else - that could make you a better Holy man than you are already".

She took his hands in hers and held them, saying "The power in these hands belongs to Jesus, I am sure of it". She was still holding his hands and becoming aware of her actions, she made to let go, but Maun held on to one of her hands. There was a feeling of warmth and belonging together that was experienced by both and as they looked into each other's eyes, he realised that he was holding on to her hand more firmly and far longer than courtesy demanded and reluctantly loosened his grip.

Meanwhile, Julian was telling his fellow pilgrims how the pain had vanished and how wonderful he felt, "I could run to Avalon and back again", he boasted with a certain amount of exaggeration.

When Hanno reported to Joseph the success of the healing, Evan laughed, "We guessed as much when that young man came running towards his friends with the good news".

Hanno smiled a secret smile, "I think there has been another success. Maun and the young woman seem to have a lot to talk about. They were so engrossed with each other, they did not see me leave the room, or hear me speak to them".

Maun and Flavia did indeed have a lot to talk about. Never before in his entire life had he felt so much at one with another soul. "Can I ask you, Flavia", said Maun, "What makes this place Avalon worthy of your pilgrimage - especially in this cold weather?".

She looked at him askance, "Do you mean to tell me, that you, a Christian, have never heard of Avalon?".

"I am sorry, I haven't. I come from north Briton. It is a great distance away and I have never heard of Avalon, but I would be very pleased if you would tell me abut it."

"The story, as told to me", said Flavia, "Was that a kinsman of our Lord Jesus was a merchant in fine metals and came to these parts to trade. He was also a mystic and whilst here, he learned of the Zodiac carved out on the earth around Avalon. It is said that after this discovery, he brought Our Lord here with him, whether for company or to study the mysteries, we don't know for sure. But we can guess as to the truth".

"When Our Lord was crucified, his kin, who some say was his Uncle Joseph from

Arimathea, brought to Avalon the cup used at the last supper and placed it in the sacred well which lies at the foot of the hill. This hill is part of the sign of the 'Water Carrier' on the great Zodiac."

Maun was fascinated, "Could this be true? That Jesus actually walked here in this country? I wish my father was here".

Flavia asked him, "Why your father?".

Maun replied, "My father has studied the stars under the guidance of Professor Theophilus". Flavia looked surprised, "You mean, your father has never passed on to you any of his teaching?".

"Only a little", said Maun, "I doubt he knows of this Zodiac".

"I think", said Flavia, "That if your father has studied the stars, you can be sure he knows something. He must surely have heard of the tree?".

Maun looked puzzled and repeated, "Tree? What tree?".

"Why, the Holy Thorn Tree, of course. You have not been told of that either?". Maun shook his head. Flavia continued, "After Joseph from Arimathea concealed the chalice in the well, he climbed part of the way up the hill of the fish and stuck his staff into the ground. Then, he prayed that he would be given a sign to prove that Jesus was Lord of Pisces. That sign came when his walking stick burst into blossom and has done so every year since - once in summer and again around our Lord's birthday".

"This is wonderful", said Maun, "I would love to go there with you now - instead of Tours".

Flavia bowed her head, "I would also like you to come with us and one day we will meet there, I am sure, one day when you return home a priest".

Maun shook his head, "I don't know if I can become a priest? I doubt very much if I have enough love to spread around".

"Maun", she said, "Would you be alarmed if I told you that I have the gift of seeing into the future? I can assure you that you will become a priest - and a very good one. Do not doubt. I can see that you are very special".

They could hear chattering in the next room, then the door opened and Julian said, "Flavia. We are all ready to leave now".

Maun walked with them to the ferry boat that was to take them across the water to join the traders' caravan route to the east. He watched as they left the ferry on the opposite shore and saw them continue to wave as they dwindled in the distance. He also saw that just before they went out of sight, that Flavia turned around and waved.

When he arrived back at the inn, Joseph was in high spirits. He said, "Thank you, my boy. You will be pleased to hear that I have a bed for the night and I'm looking forward to a good night's sleep".

Evan was smirking at him, "So, my young friend. I suppose all we will hear from now on is how wonderful Madam Flavia is? And to think I believed you when you said you were not interested in women".

Maun blushed to the roots of his fair hair. "No, I won't, Evan. Although I admit I like her very much, it is very unlikely I will ever see her again."

Evan laughed heartily, "Don't be too sure of that, my lad. True love will always find a way".

After his two nights of sound sleep, Joseph was in good humour and had braced himself to face the next and longest voyage across the channel to Gaul.

They boarded the ship once more and were made welcome by the crew, the Captain arriving by carriage shortly after, gave the order to cast off.

Once out at sea, Joseph renewed his acquaintance with Brun, while Hanno transcribed his notes on the healing of Julian. Maun stood by the ship's rail day-dreaming and thinking of Flavia and the pilgrims on their long walk to Avalon. Evan was by now tired of the easy life and made friends with some members of the crew and offered the benefit of his experience - should it be required.

He spotted Maun standing by the rail and joined him, "You all right, lad?", he inquired.

Maun looked at him, partly pleased to see him, yet a little annoyed at having his day-dreams interrupted. "Yes. Thank you, Evan. I was just thinking about the pilgrims and wondering if they will be safe - it is a very long journey?"

"I know it is lad. While you and Hanno were in the other room healing Julian, your grandfather and I had a long talk with one of the other pilgrims. He told us that they hoped to join on to a traders' caravan to save them walking all the way. He also told me that Flavia had been married. Her husband had died several years before and left her a wealthy woman. He said that she had little interest in money, unless it was used to help the poor and the hungry."

"Did he say anything more of Flavia?", asked Maun curiously.

Evan smiled at him, "Am I right in thinking that you have taken more than a fancy to the lovely Flavia?".

Maun flushed with embarrassment and was on the point of denial, then thought better of it - Evan would know the truth anyway. So, after a moment, he said, "She is rather beautiful, don't you think?".

"Yes", said Evan, "Indeed she is and very brave. Shall I tell you something young Maun? If I'm not mistaken, she has taken a fancy to you".

Maun felt his heart pounding, "Why do you say that Evan?", he asked.

Evan could hardly hide his amusement, "Because lad, I saw how she looked at you when she said goodbye. I know that look. She was thinking, 'Come back soon' - I've seen it on the faces of our crew's wives when we sailed off to sea".

"I wish", said Maun, "I could have gone with them, for she told me some wonderful things about this place called Avalon. One day I will go there. I don't know when, but, one day for sure".

The ship made good time. There had been some heavy rain, but no storms and after a reasonably pleasant voyage, they arrived at their destination feeling relieved that the voyage was over and that they were none the worse for their journey.

Brun had made the journey before and knew where to hire a coach, which luckily could carry four passengers, Evan sitting up front with the coachman, both well wrapped up against the cold.

It was a long road to Tours and they had to stop several times to change horses and to eat and freshen up. Eventually, they arrived on ground which was familiar to Joseph and he was able to take them to the best inn that he could remember. In twenty years, the town had not altered much and he soon found his way around.

As soon as he was settled, Joseph set off to visit his brother and he was relieved to discover that he was still very much alive. It was over twenty years since they had seen one another and he hoped that Martin had not gone senile in his old age? He need not have worried. Martin still had his wits about him and upon his brother's entrance, he got up from his chair and met Joseph half way across the room. He said, "Little brother. How wonderful to see you. When did you arrive back in Gaul? Did the climate in north Briton not suit you?".

"I have been away over twenty years", said Joseph.

Martin looked incredulous, "I'm sorry little brother. Time passes so quickly. I lose track of it". Joseph noticed how Martin still lived frugally, a minimum of everything seemed to be his code to live by. After the considerable luxury he was used to at Bonavon, Martin's accommodation was sparse by comparison, although Joseph was pleased that he had relented a little with regard to servants. He assumed that the Church had insisted he have some help, for he was still very busy. His brother's list of engagements was lengthy and Joseph wondered how a man of his great age could cope.

He also began to feel guilty about taking up his time, but Martin seemed to be able to read his mind, saying "Come here little brother and let me give you a hug. Tell me again, why did you go to north Briton in the first place?".

Joseph smiled, "I was sent to convert the Highlanders".

"I remember now", said Martin, "And did you convert the Highlanders?".

"*Not one*", said Joseph, "Not a single one".

"So, little brother, on that score, you are a total failure."

'Afraid so", said Joseph.

Martin laughed, "Failure is good for the soul. It robs it of conceit, just so long as you have the occasional success".

Then Joseph got around to talking about why he had come, "Martin. I bring you news that will cheer you. My grandson is a healer of some reputation, he also sees visions just as you did in your younger days".

Martin's eyes lit up, "Have you brought him with you?".

"Not here", said Joseph, "He is back at the inn. I left him and his friends to rest. I wanted to see you before I contact the Church authorities about him becoming a priest. I believe he is so powerful, he needs the protection only the Church can give him. There is one difficulty to be surmounted, my grandson is unable to read or write well. We do not understand it, for he is especially bright in every other way".

"Do not worry, my little brother. If God wills that your grandson becomes a priest, nothing will get in his way."

Joseph was grateful for these encouraging words and said, "Now, I must not detain you further Martin. I know you are busy".

A servant arrived and Martin instructed him to make sure that when his great nephew arrived, he would be admitted right away. As Joseph was about to leave, Martin gripped his arm, "Don't forget little brother, bring him soon".

Once outside, Joseph breathed a sigh of relief, then he smiled to himself at being referred to as "little brother', for Martin was grown up when he was born and on the few occasions they had met, he had never called him by any other name. Indeed, Joseph wondered if Martin knew what his name was? 'Well', he thought, 'What's in a name?'. Martin knew and remembered him and that was all that mattered.

Joseph and Hanno kept their appointment with the members of the Church hierarchy, composed of several priests and officials and at least one Bishop, with Hanno carrying with him his notes on Maun's healing miracles, in order to persuade the authorities that Maun would make an excellent priest. They were to be disappointed. They were told that people turned up daily claiming to perform all kinds of miracles and every one, so far, had been proven to be false. Although Hanno protested that his documents had been meticulously kept, a very haughty priest told him, "Of course, these so-called records could be pure fiction. You have no actual proof that any of it is true".

Hanno was shocked that this committee of church officials could be so sceptical and mistrusting. Joseph was so angry that he told them, "I am ashamed that you dare to call us deceitful. However, it is not possible for us to make anyone sick in order to prove my grandson's power to heal" and with that he stood up, saying, "Come Hanno".

However, the Bishop, who had remained silent during the interview, then addressed them, "Please Father Joseph, do not be offended. Try to understand our position. We must be very careful not to be fooled by bogus claims of sainthood. We have been made a laughing stock on more than one occasion in the past and one man even tried to persuade us that he was our blessed Lord reborn. When we asked him to talk to us of his wisdom, experience and miracles, all he could do was babble gibberish! Now, I am sure that your grandson is all you claim him to be and we ask only that you bring us face to face with someone that he has actually healed".

Joseph and Hanno looked at each other and said, "Evan!".

"Who is this Evan you speak of ... Is he here?"

"Yes, your Grace. He was the first person to be healed by my grandson and he is with him now."

"Then", said the Bishop, "We will make an appointment to interview him very soon. You will be informed when this is to take place".

Meanwhile, Evan and Maun occupied themselves exploring the town, although Maun had noticed that Evan was very quiet, as though his thoughts were elsewhere. He asked, "What ails you Evan? Are you ill?".

"Oh! No lad. Not ill," said Evan.

"Then, what is the matter? You have not even teased me once today."

Evan smiled at him, "If you must know lad, I am home-sick".

"I'm sorry, Evan. I should have guessed. There is no reason now why you cannot go home. You have fulfilled your promise to see me home to Bonavon long ago. However, it is such a long way to Russia".

"No no, lad", said Evan, "I was born in Russia, but my home is here in Gaul. I married my Margaretta when my ship was docked at the port of Nanmentium. It is not too far away, maybe a few days ride, or sail along the river".

"Then, you must leave as soon as possible. Grandfather would be most upset if he thought you were unhappy and we must speak to him as soon as we get back to the inn, not to ask his permission or anything you understand, but I know he has your wages in his possession."

"Wages?", repeated Evan, "I'm not due any wages".

"Yes you are", said Maun, "Grandfather did not mention he was carrying gold with him, as he thought if you and Hanno knew, it would make you nervous. I know because I overheard my father and grandfather discuss it before we left".

"I'm sure I would be grateful for some money to take home", said Evan, "A sailor's pay is not much. If Margaretta's mother did not have a guest house, I don't know how we would have managed".

When Joseph and Hanno returned, Maun wasted no time in telling them that Evan was home-sick, Joseph saying how sorry he was for being so thoughtless. He continued, "However Evan, there is only one reason why you cannot go as soon as you are ready. You have been asked to testify to Maun's healing power before the committee. It seems that our word is not good enough. They want to talk to you as the only witness we have to Maun's healing powers".

Evan was astounded, "You mean that all these records and the sacred word of a priest are not enough? That is the most ridiculous thing I have ever heard. I will most certainly give witness and only when I have done so, will I think of leaving".

Joseph thanked him, " Bless you Evan. You have done well".

Joseph then addressed Maun, "I have spoken to Martin, your great uncle. He is most impressed with what I have told him about you and he is very anxious to see you."

Evan prepared himself to give a good account of Maun's work and although he knew that his every word would be questioned, he had no doubts. At the hearing itself, he told them everything that had happened, from the moment he first met Maun on the quay at Hibernia and gave an excellent account of his own healing. For good measure, Evan told them about the hound and her pups, the reaction from one member to that information, being to snigger ... "Impressed as you were with the hound and her pups, we do not think we can take seriously *the healing of a dog*".

Evan could feel anger rising, "Good Sirs. Trivial as it may sound to you, these animals were of high value and of great importance to our Captain and crew, for they were our wages!".

Sensing Evan's mood, the committee stopped laughing, one member asking, "You are very sure that this young man saved your life?".

"I know it", Evan replied. "I have been to sea for over twenty years and seen several men die of poisoning. I was certain that I would die too and I was very much afraid. Not only has Maun saved my life, but I have been witness to many more miraculous healings he has performed. I know that our friend Hanno has kept notes on each one and I beg you good sirs, to believe every word."

Evan's interview was long and he was relieved when it was over. When he walked from the dark Abbey, he was glad to breath fresh air again and he thought, 'Why

Joseph wants Maun to spend his time in a place like that, I will never know? His wonderful talent will be wasted'.

On the same day as Evan's interview, Maun went to see his great uncle Martin, who on seeing him, said "Come closer, my boy and let me look at you". Maun stepped forward a pace. "Well bless my soul", said Martin, "You look just like your grandfather did at your age" and he instructed his servant to bring a large chair and place it behind Maun for him to sit down. Maun glanced around, then sat down nervously, a bit closer to the awesome and ageing Martin than he would have chosen.

"Now, my son. I want you to tell me all about it."

"About what, uncle?".

Martin furrowed his brow, "Why, about how you were given this gift to heal, of course".

Maun told him everything, from being taken captive, until he reached the Lorne. Martin appeared not to have heard him, for he said, "Tell me again, please", Maun duly obliging. But, again Martin asked him to go through it once more. 'This could go on all day', thought Maun', 'I think my great uncle is a bit deaf'.

But, just then Martin opened his eyes and looked at him, "My son. Don't you think there is something strange about your story?".

Maun was puzzled, "Strange, Sir? Why no. I have told you the truth".

"No! No!", said Martin with slight irritation, "I believe every word you have spoken, but my son, do you not think it is strange that you are shown a ship by this angelic being? You escape and are able to walk or run many miles to reach it, then the only transaction to take place is two kegs of wine for a hound?".

Maun butted in, "But Sir. It is possible there was other trade before I arrived".

Martin ignored him and continued, "Then you reached a very small port in the Highlands - in enemy country. You tell me that the ship unloaded bales of material; sacks of nuts, seeds, boxes of Samian ware, iron pots and pans and countless other commodities. Do you not think that strange?".

"I confess Sir, at the time, I was not in a fit state to give it much thought. All I thought of was getting home to my mother and father in order to assure them that I was safe, for as I related to you, I was shown how they were both suffering."

"My son", said Martin, "I do not question your word or your motives, but I have good reason to acquaint myself with the facts. Allow me to explain".

"Some years ago, I was preaching by the coast. People gathered around me to listen, but when I finished my talk, everyone drifted away. I hoped to ponder on my words, but one man still stood there looking at me as though in a trance. I went over to him and asked if he had a problem? Perhaps, I could help him?"

"He seemed to shake himself out of his thoughtful state, saying 'Sir. Your words were like music to my ears, for I have long thought along these very same lines'. He continued, 'You spoke Sir, of the Baptism of each soul, but can I ask you about my ship'. The man bowed his head, then raised it again to look into my eyes. He said, 'It is new. Just like a new baby. I would like you to baptise my crew and bless my new ship. We are going to launch it on the new tide'."

"'Yes Sir, I want you, if you will, to bless my crew and my ship and give it a name'."

"How could I refuse Maun? I had just spent some time attempting to convince everyone how essential it was to be baptised. So, I decided to do what he asked. After all, if it made them better Christians, what harm could it do? He invited me aboard his brand new trader and offered me some refreshment, for which I was most grateful. I asked him what name he had selected for his ship … I could hardly say 'I bless this nameless ship'!".

The man laughed, "Indeed no. Please, will *you* choose a suitable name".

"Well Maun, I was at a loss for a name. Then, I happened to look at another ship in dock. There was a sailor repairing some rigging and as I watched him, I saw sweat fall from his brow on to the sail and it reminded me of the story of our own Saint Veronica."

Maun looked puzzled and Martin smiled, for he remembered what Joseph had told him about Maun not being a great scholar. "My Son. Do you know what a Sudarium is?". Maun could not be absolutely sure, although he could hazard a guess. Martin continued, "It is part of a garment worn by ladies. A three-cornered cloth that can be worn tied around the neck like a collar, or around the waist. It is not so much a fashion accessory, as a useful piece of equipment. When necessary, it can be removed, for instance and used to clean childrens' noses or dry the owner's hands after washing".

"The story goes, that on the dreadful day when our blessed Lord Jesus was forced to carry his own cross on a pathway up to the hill of his crucifixion, the blood from his wounds and sweat from his brow, were running into his eyes. A lady, among those watching, removed her Sudarium and fought her way through the crowd and wiped the blood, sweat and tears from his eyes. This lady was named Veronica."

"When she later examined her Sudarium, she found that the blood and sweat had left an imprint of our Lord's face upon it. Ever since then, that particular Sudarium has been called 'The Veronica'. Thus, I suggested this name to the owner of the new ship and he readily agreed."

"First of all, I baptised every crew member, then in a special ceremony of naming, I blessed the new ship and the *Veronica* was born."

"Now Maun. I have a strong feeling that the ship that came to your rescue, was that same ship." Maun remembered two things, Evan had called his ship affectionately 'The old sweat rag' and he had noticed on the vessel a crest - *S.V.S. Sudius.*

Martin smiled and said, "That is close enough. Glory be to God".

"You see Maun, some time after this event, word reached me that after several very unlucky accidents at sea, there was a rumour going around that it was unlucky to take a woman aboard ship. I wondered if the *Veronica* would be lucky enough to have a crew that were not superstitious? It would be the Captain's choice to alter the name to suit his crew."

"Have you grasped the meaning of what I am saying, my son? That the *Veronica* was sent by God to bring you home. I believe he has saved you for a special purpose. Our Father God has plans for you. Keep your faith strong and love your God with all your heart and soul."

Maun raised his eyes to face the eager face of Martin, "Yes Sir. I know that. I know that he wants me for some purpose or other. Why I wonder, for I am plain, uneducated and not wholly without sin?".

Martin's servant arrived to announce that his next appointment had arrived and he had brought with him Maun's cloak and placed it around his shoulders. But, as Maun made to leave, Martin called him back and indicated for him to move a little closer, as though to whisper to him. Speaking softly into his ear, he said "Maun my son. You are not plain. You are beautiful to all who have the eyes to see."

Maun said, "Goodbye" to his uncle and hurried away..

As he made his way back to the inn, he remembered that Evan would be leaving soon to go home to his family. 'I will miss him very much', thought Maun. He wondered how Evan would travel, 'Would he go by boat along the river or hire a coach and horses?'. Now that his interview with the committee was over, he could leave at the next opportune moment.

When Maun arrived back at the inn, Joseph informed him that he had been given work to do in the Abbey and that he had also been given a small house near to the Abbey grounds. He would be moving out of the inn within the next few days. Maun's thoughts were on Evan. "Grandfather. I've been thinking about Evan going home and I would like to go with him. He has told me that it will only take him a few days to get there and so far there has been nothing for me to do here".

"I cannot think of any good reason why not", said Joseph, "But, you realise my boy, that you would have to return alone?".

"Yes grandfather. I know that, but as the committee have not asked to see me and Hanno has a mountain of records to read to them and now I learn that you will be at work in the Abbey, I can't see what difference it would make. I also know that Evan is anxious to get home."

That evening, Joseph asked Maun to come to his room. "Come in, my boy. I need you as a witness". He then took from his travelling satchel, a large leather pouch, the contents of which he poured onto a table. Maun's eyes opened wide, for the coins were pure gold, shining in the light of an oil lamp. Joseph divided the coins into four piles and then he then took a smaller pouch from his satchel and placed inside one of the piles of coins.

Pointing to the pouch, Joseph said, "This is Evan's wages. Your father gave me this gold before we left home with instructions to pay it out on reaching our destination".

Maun pointed to another pile and asked, "Would this pile be mine, grandfather?".
"Yes, my boy. It is."

Maun then took several coins from his own pile and added them to Evan's pouch. "That is all very well, my boy", said Joseph, "But you have to live too".

"Evan needs it more than I, grandfather. He has a wife and family and he deserves it."

When Maun had gone to fetch Evan, Joseph took another new pouch from his satchel and put Hanno's share in. He then did the same as Maun had done, he took some from his own share and added them to Hanno's pouch. Hanno's skill at keeping the records of Maun's healings was the work of a genius, he had worked tirelessly and never ever suggested any kind of payment and he deserved a reward.

Evan, his spirits lifted at the thought of going home, was in a cheerful mood when Maun caught up with him in the eating house. 'Come lad, have a drink with your old friend.'

"I just came to deliver a message", said Maun, "Grandfather wishes to see you in his room". "Right lad. I'll come now. I probably had enough to eat and drink anyway."

As they walked together towards the inn, Maun said, "Can I ask a favour of you, Evan?".

"You may ask me anything lad. Anything your little heart desires. Just so long as it does not cost a lot of money."

"Why Evan?", asked Maun, "Don't you have any money to spare?".

"I have a little", answered Evan, "But I don't want to go home empty handed".

Maun was pleased to see that Evan was his old self again and he said, "When you go home, can I come with you? Grandfather is working. Hanno is reading to the Committee. With you gone, I will have nothing to do and no one to talk to. I am going to miss you very much."

Evan was surprised, "Won't they need you?".

"Hanno does not think so. It seems they question everything. He is very patient with them, although for how long, I would not like to say."

Evan laughed, "I can imagine. They are a stiff-necked bunch these churchmen. Never had a lot of time for them myself. Are you sure lad, you are doing the right thing? I would not like to think of you growing into one of them".

"I won't, Evan. Grandfather wants me to preach the word of Jesus. I agree that I should not imagine that I am in any way special. When I heal I do so in his name and not in mine."

"Be careful lad. Not too much humility. Your Lord Jesus cannot do without the devotion of selfless people like you. You, my lad could do very well without those dismal, pious and self-righteous, so-called servants of the Lord."

"They are not all like that, Evan", said Maun, "My grandfather isn't".

Evan thought he might have offended Maun and he said, "I agree, but then your grandfather was married. It makes a difference to a man to have a wife to love him and give him children and to welcome him home when his work is finished. I have always found that men who live for themselves, I'm afraid, become inward-looking and rather pathetic characters".

Maun studied Evan's face, "Do you really think so, Evan? They are supposed to be servants of Christ and his children".

"Humm", said Evan, with an expression of doubt, "Just you be careful!".

"You have not answered my question yet, Evan."

"What question was that, lad?"

"When you leave, can I come with you?"

"I will be honoured for you to come with me, providing your grandfather is in agreement."

"Thank you Evan. It will be just like old times. Don't forget grandfather is waiting for you", said Maun.

"No lad. I am on my way."

Maun did not accompany Evan. He thought Evan might be embarrassed to accept payment with him present and besides, it was not his business.

Evan tapped on Joseph's door and walked in, "You wish to see me Father Joseph?"

"Yes Evan. I wish to tell you that I … we will all miss you very much when you leave us, especially Maun. Come here my son, I have something for you." Joseph picked up the pouch and handed it to Evan. "You will need this to get you started in your new life, for I feel sure you will not want to go back to sea."

Evan took the pouch, "Thank you Father, every little helps".

"Oh!", said Joseph, "Don't thank me. Calpurnius gave it into my keeping for you when we reached our destination. The coins were divided into four, witnessed by Maun. I think you will be pleased".

Evan opened the pouch and looked in. When he saw the shiny coins, he looked up at Joseph in stunned disbelief. "They are gold! They are real gold! There is a fortune in here, more than I ever earned in all of my years at sea. I cannot accept all this Father, guarding Maun was a pleasure, not work."

Joseph spoke more forcefully, "Evan … Take it. Maun's family are exceedingly rich. They are grateful to you for bringing their beloved son home to them. They can well afford it. So, please take the money, with their blessings and with mine".

Maun arrived, "Have you asked grandfather, yet Evan?". His forthcoming journey home had slipped Evan's mind in the excitement of finding himself a wealthy man and Maun had to remind him, "Have you asked grandfather about me coming with you, Evan?".

Evan looked at Joseph, "Do we have your permission, Father Joseph, for Maun to travel with me when I leave?".

"Yes. It is fine by me, Evan. He is now old enough to make up his own mind."

Evan was in buoyant mood and said laughingly, "Let us go to the eating house, Maun. I am in need of a drink".

Joseph picked up the coins belonging to Hanno and went to look for him. He found him in his room, still working. "Stop writing for a moment, my son. I want to give you this."

He handed the pouch to Hanno, who took it from him almost absent-mindedly, with a careless, "Thank you". He placed the pouch on the side of his writing table and carried on talking, "I get so angry with this Committee, Father Joseph. Nothing seems to please them. You would think that Maun, being kin to Bishop Martin, they would be more ready to take account of that and believe that Maun is special. But, I actually believe that it counts against him! They question and criticise everything".

"Yes, I know", said Joseph, "But you must remember that men of the Church, are men like any other, although some believe themselves to be superior. They can be mistrusting, sceptical and at times, downright foolish. But, they have been given a task and they are sticking to the rules".

Hanno was surprised that Joseph agreed with him. He had expected him to be more supportive of his fellow priests and, perhaps, offering some spiritual reason for their attitude.

"To tell you the truth, Father. I have made up my mind to be blunt with them and tell them right out, that should they refuse to accept Maun into the Church, they will be the losers. Maun is so powerful, a new religion could be built up around him and his work."

Joseph agreed, "Yes, my son. That is a strong possibility. You know Hanno, in my time, I have seen the most overdressed, bejewelled and pious of preachers rub their hands together in glee at the mention of Church revenue, the sound of coins dropping into the offertory, music to their ears. I also believe that I was sent to the north of Briton because I chose to work amongst the poor of this city. It was said to me on many occasions, 'The rich also need to hear God's word, my son'. I thought then that what they should have said, if they had been honest, was 'Work on the rich and persuade them to part with their money'".

"Yet, my son. God works in mysterious ways, for now I am in no doubt that it was God's will that I went to Britain. If I had not gone, Maun would never have been born and we would not be here."

Hanno agreed, "Yes, Father Joseph. I do understand that and I also am well aware that Church buildings need repairs, which cost money and even if priests were not paid, they still have to eat". "Yes, my friend", said Joseph, "But, if too much thought is on finance, there is little time left over for faith."

Hanno had been amused to see Joseph angry, as it did not come easily to him to speak ill of anyone, let alone of his beloved Church. "Father Joseph", said Hanno, "That is the first time I have ever heard you utter words of criticism".

Joseph shrugged his shoulders, "To be truthful my son, it was a strange feeling and one I did not particularly enjoy and I am sorry for allowing myself to indulge in anger, for I know it to be a fruitless exercise. I know also that most people within our Church do their very best with the qualities they have and in their own way, obey God's will".

"I suppose my son, that I too am just a man like any other."

"Oh! No", said Hanno, "A man? Yes! But, not like any other man I have ever known".

Joseph had observed that the money pouch was still on the writing table and as he left, he said, "Do not forget to put your money in a safe place".

But Hanno's thoughts were on a plan forming in his mind.

Joseph was about to close the door behind him, when he heard the pouch fall on the floor. He expected some reaction from Hanno at the sight of the gold coins, but there was no sound and curious, he opened the door again. He saw Hanno kneeling on the floor staring at the pouch and the few spilled coins and looking up at Joseph, he said "Father. Did I hear you correctly? Did you say that this was my wages? Or, am I mistaken and you have appointed me treasurer of the Abbey?".

"No, my son, you heard correctly. These gold coins are a gift from Calpurnius."

Hanno protested, "But Father, there is a fortune here".

"Yes", said Joseph, "There is, however, it is but a fraction of the value Calpurnius placed on the safe return of his only son. Accept this reward gladly, you have been the most loyal of friends and Maun is devoted to you. He knows and understands well the work you have done on his behalf and as far as he is concerned, you have earned and deserve every dennarius".

"I don't know how to thank you, for this money will secure my future."

Joseph changed the subject, "Maun and Evan have gone to the hostelry to talk over their plans for their journey to Nanmentium. I am sure they would like you to join them for a farewell drink before they leave".

"I will go now", said Hanno, "Will you Father, take care of my money until I return?".

Evan and Maun were in deep discussion deciding on their mode of travel, when Hanno arrived. Evan welcomed him and offered to buy him a glass of wine, which he accepted. Hanno said, "Well, my friends, what have you decided?".

"After much discussion, we have decided to follow the river on foot."

Hanno was surprised, "Have you considered sailing along the river?".

"We have thought of every mode of travel possible. However, there are few boats that sail in the winter months and the coach is much too bumpy. We are leaving in the morning. Margaretta has waited for me for almost two years now, another day or two won't matter. Besides, I don't want to have to change one of my coins. I want to be able to give them to my wife, as they are. Perhaps, they will make up for the time I have been away. If we grow tired during the journey, we will lodge at an inn."

Hanno wished them a safe journey and told them to take great care. He also added, "And you young Maun, return safely".

Hanno hurried back to his room. A plan had formed in his mind, based on Joseph's words, 'That priests and bishops were men with human failings'.

Hanno was due to meet the committee again in the morning, to read one more episode of their travels through the Highlands. The next healing recorded dealt with the farmer who had fallen from a ladder, but Hanno did not consider this to be dramatic enough for his purpose. Instead, he chose the next incident he had recorded - the story of the rough men at Craiga.

Hanno was a proud man, his origins coming from a race of people with a long history of great wisdom and selfless service to the peoples of the Highlands and he was tired of being servile to this committee of self-righteous sceptics.

Setting too, he re-arranged his script, making the words sound even more dramatic, without indulging in exaggeration or lies - just the simple truth - but just a little altered. 'Yes', he thought, 'That will do very well'.

The next morning, he made his way to the Abbey and as on every other occasion, he was kept waiting in a draughty corridor before he was called before the committee. When at last he was admitted to the chamber, he was again kept waiting until they were ready to listen to the next miracle. Before he could start reading, he had to wait for the signal to begin, normally a careless wave of the hand.

Eventually he was given the go-ahead and he started to read from his records.

He spoke about how the men had entered the inn, scattering pots and salvers and frightening the people who ran away. Hanno, looking up from his records, said "My friend Maun subdued them with one look, then healed the boy with the deformed foot, before their eyes. After that experience, they followed us. When we reached Bonavon they caught up with us and offered themselves in service to Maun and to the people".

Hanno spoke about the scene around Maun's home, the crowds waiting to be healed and the great joy as they walked unaided, or upright where before they had been bent and crippled.

Hanno described how gifts were brought, by both rich and poor leaving precious gifts or money ... "But, my friend Maun would have none of it, insisting that their need was greater than his. However, one very wealthy patron handed over a fortune in gold, he was so grateful to Maun for healing his small son".

Hanno described how the people bowed before Maun, but he told them, "Address your prayers and devotions to our Lord Jesus. Not to me!".

One member of the Committee asked, "Did he return *all* of these gifts? Did he keep *nothing?*". "Yes he did", said Hanno, "He gave back everything. However, the wealthy merchant insisted that I keep the gold to pay my Lord Maun's expenses".

As he spoke Hanno, took from his belt a bulging money pouch, at the bottom of which he had previously placed coins of little value, on top of which he had placed gold coins. Putting the bulging pouch on the table before him, he opened it slowly, tipping out several of the shiny gold coins. Discerning an intake of breath from several members of the committee, he carefully poured out several more, making sure as he did so that he held on tightly to the coins of low value. With his eyes on the faces of the committee, he poured out a few more, other members strained their necks to get a better view of the shiny gold coins.

'Joseph was right', he thought, 'The pouch still looked half full and there was no reason why the committee should not assume that all the coins were gold'. Hanno began to pick the gold coins up and return them to the pouch, when one of the priests asked, "Does not that gold belong to the Church, as it was given for work done in the name of our Lord Jesus?". The Bishop glared at the speaker.

But, Hanno seized on the opportunity to say his piece, "Indeed no, sir. This gold was given to my friend and master Maun, who I and many others will follow and serve for as long as he wills. That he has chosen to serve Jesus through becoming a priest of this church, is of no advancement to him whatsoever. I believe that he is too good, too powerful and too wonderful a soul to be shackled to this establishment".

Hanno continued, "I have come before you now several times, reading extracts from these records of Maun's work and the miracles he has performed. I have suffered your criticism and your disbelief. I do not wish for the great nephew of our beloved Bishop Martin and the most powerful healer since the Lord Jesus Christ, to suffer the indignity that you seem only to offer".

Collecting his scrolls and his pouch of gold, he said, "I will trouble you gentlemen no further". He bowed and stepped back two paces - as was his custom - and left. The Committee stood stony faced and silent.

As he walked away from the Abbey, he wondered what Joseph would say about what he had done, 'Would he be angry? Or, would he be pleased?'.

Too late now. The deed was done. He was not particularly pleased or proud of himself, for he had lied in saying that the gold had been given to Maun. He hated liars, believing that they debased themselves and rendered themselves hollow and untrustworthy. Lies were designed to deceive and were a dangerous practice, no honourable man would ever indulge in and he was a most honourable man. However, he felt that a point had to be made and he argued with himself that there were occasions when it was expedient to bend the truth a little. Besides, he had secretly enjoyed seeing that self-righteous and smug committee being taken down a peg or two.

Hanno need not have worried, Joseph understood perfectly, "My son. I too have lied by omission. Therefore, I am in no position to judge you. I too would have enjoyed that committee's discomforture. Indeed Hanno, I have been wondering if I have been wise in bringing Maun here, knowing his lack of ability to read and placing him in situations where he may be ridiculed? However, anyone who has witnessed his work, could not fail to ask why the Holy Church would reject him? We will just have to put our faith in God's hands and see what happens. But now, with Evan and Maun away and myself back at work, what will you do by yourself, my boy?".

"Don't worry about me, Father", said Hanno, "I have it in mind to find a home of my own. It seems as if we will be here some time and I would like to come and go as I please and be more fastidious in what I eat. Then, perhaps, when Maun returns, he will wish to join me. I hope and pray he is safe. Nanmentium is a very long way away".

Meanwhile, Evan and Maun had covered a fair distance, although compared with the struggle through the Highlands, this was an easy and pleasant walk. They had managed to get a lift for part of the journey on a merchant's cart, but, despite this, Maun's feet were hurting and Evan's stomach was howling for want of food and he said, "We will eat and rest at the first inn we come across".

"I hope it will be soon", said Maun, "I did think we would have found somewhere before now. We have passed several villages on the banks of the river and if we had spoken to the people, I feel sure they would have gladly given us some refreshments".

Evan looked at him, "You are a trusting soul Maun. Strangers are seldom trusted by people in small villages. If they had decided we were robbers, we could have been attacked, killed and ended up floating down the river. You cannot be too careful!".

Maun laughed at Evan, "I think we are safe enough, but I will bow to your superior wisdom in such matters".

Within the hour they came upon a hostelry next to a jetty. The owner - a jolly man, rotund in stature - welcoming them. His wife although straight-faced, had a dry sense of humour. They had two daughters, who introduced themselves as Cressida and Vilma.

Cressida was pleased to tell them all about their business and she said, "We make some money in the summertime - when people like to cross the river to see what it was like on the other side - but, in the winter, business is bad".

"My sister Vilma and I clean and serve, mother does all the cooking, while father supervises from his chair."

Their father protested, "Now, my dears", he said, "You know I do my fair share". However, glances from his womenfolk threw grave doubts on his claim.

Madam appeared from the kitchen area and asked Evan and Maun what they would like for their supper and mentioned some mouth-watering dishes that she was willing to prepare for them. But, Evan was in a hurry to eat and suggested some scrambled eggs, with bread and butter and some wine.

The cook looked relieved and she told them that while they were waiting for the food, they were welcome to soak their tired feet, which after their long walk, should be very restful. She also suggested that her daughters would be glad to give them a massage with their special foot balm. Maun declined the offer of the massage, but was glad to bathe his feet in warm water. Evan accepted the foot massage. The reasons being that he could not reach his own feet! Maun was amused when Evan discovered he was ticklish and could not stop laughing. Cressida and Vilma had one foot each and could hardly keep them still enough. When Madam called to say that supper was ready, they quickly dried them and hurried away to help their mother.

They ate their eggs by scooping it onto rather stodgy bread, but despite this, the food tasted all the better, because they were so hungry. The inn was fresh and clean, so they decided to rest for the night before setting off refreshed in the morning. Evan inquired of their hosts if rooms were available and was told that there were several which they could choose from.

Their host invited them to join him for a drink before they retired and for all his teasing, it was clear that his life was centred on his womenfolk. He enjoyed making fun of his daughters' unmarried status and was much amused by their embarrassment.

Both young women resembled their father in having pleasant, round faces, but both worked too hard to put on the extra weight carried by their father.

Evan and Maun slept soundly, waking up refreshed and ready for the day's walk ahead of them. They enjoyed a good breakfast of bread and cheese followed by a large jar of warm milk and feeling more than satisfied, they paid for their board, added a substantial tip for Cressida and Velma for the foot massage and waved good bye.

After several miles of walking at a cracking pace, Evan was beginning to think he had been too ambitious as the walk, although pleasant enough, was taking too long and he wished he had accepted advice and bought a horse. But, his desire to see Margaretta's face when he presented her with the pouch of gold coins, was overpowering. The fact that she would never have to work again, brought a smile to his face and they would now to be able go and visit friends in another town, or visit special places of interest. He smiled to himself, 'We will plod on. Perhaps, we will get another lift on a wagon?'. He was reluctant to spend his money for another reason, for he knew that once strangers spotted that a person had plenty of money to flash around, one became vulnerable to robbers. Better to appear poor and helpless!

'Oh! Well', he thought, 'Too late now to change. We are now about half way home'. However, he soon started to get tired and irritable again.

Maun sensed Evan's mood and decided to engage him in conversation, "Did you think Cressida and Vilma were very pretty?", he asked.

Evan slowed down to listen, "Yes, I did. I thought they were both very handsome young ladies. Why do you ask, lad?".

"Well, I was thinking that there are beautiful ladies who seem to be admired, yet shunned and some who are not quite so good looking, who are sought after."

"Well", said Evan, "The same goes for men too. I don't think looks are everything. Personality is more important. My Margaretta is very beautiful and I'll never know why she chose me - but she did".

Evan gave Maun a suspicious look, "What brought on this conversation, lad? Are you trying to tell me something?".

"Well, it's like this, Evan. I thought Velma was very beautiful, but her face could not occupy my thoughts like another."

Evan could not resist the temptation to tease the innocent and unworldly Maun, "Oh! Yes? So who could this lady be who occupies your mind then? Could it be Barney's daughter Mora, who followed you out to the stream to talk to you, so early in the morning. Or, your old friend Anna who pretended to be sick, so that you might heal her? Or, was it your beautiful cousin Helen who rushed to open doors for you?".

Maun was exasperated, "You know well enough who I admire most. I told you on the ship coming from Britain".

Evan smiled at him, "I remember now. It's the pilgrim - the lovely Lady Flavia. Yes lad, I knew all the time it was she. Your face shows pleasure whenever her name is mentioned".

"Regarding your earlier question about why some good looking women are not pursued, I always think that women are like flowers. Some are like rosebuds, newly opened, fresh and pink. Others are like lillies, tall and majestic. They all have their own beauty. It depends on what attracts a man. Now, your Lady Flavia is like an orchid; strange, mysterious and very desirable. She is also attracted to you lad, I could see how she looked at you."

Maun seemed doubtful, "What could she ever see in me?".

"I will tell you what she sees in you", said Evan, "She sees a young man with an extraordinary gift, who is clean, pure and innocent. Free of greed and lust and unspoiled by cruel treatment and other misfortunes life has thrown at you. Don't ever try to be like other men, who want to crush and spoil the beauty to be found around us in this world."

"You do surprise me sometimes, Evan", said Maun, "I never once heard you talk of flowers and women".

Now it was Evan's turn to be embarrassed, "Well, lad. It is probably because I have the face of a woman in my mind and in my heart. It is a beautiful face and I have stayed away from it for far too long. That is why I am now growing impatient. So, let us move on quickly".

A few miles further on, they came upon what at first sight looked like a farm, but the closer they got to the spot, the more they realised it was a place where horses were broken. They reached the gate and stood there watching, as several men held onto ropes attached around the neck of the biggest and most beautiful stallion they had ever seen. "Isn't he a beauty?", said Evan.

The men whipped the horse, which made the most awful noises and protested by kicking out and struggling against the ties. Neither Evan or Maun liked what they saw, although they understood that to subdue animals to serve man, was common practice. Suddenly, the horse kicked out and caught one of the men in the ribs. He fell to the ground screaming with pain and holding his chest, writhing in agony. With one man less holding the ropes, the magnificent animal struggled against and overpowered the remaining men, who were forced to let go the ropes altogether, the stallion now free, jumped a high fence with the greatest of ease, before disappearing into the distance, clean out of sight.

The injured man still lay on the ground, refusing to let anyone to touch him and Maun forced his slim body through the fence, running to the man's aid. Evan tried to follow him, but had to climb over the top, lest he got stuck.

Maun approached the man, saying "Please Sir. I beg you, try to keep still for one moment".

But, the injured man was in too much pain, crying out, "No! No! Don't touch me".

Maun reassured him, "I promise I will not touch or move you. Allow me to help you".

All the other men stood around watching, not knowing what to do, Evan arrived breathless and knelt on the ground opposite Maun, for he knew that Maun could use his energy to help heal the man.

Maun was holding the man's hands and gradually the patient became quiet. He then placed his hands on where he had seen the horse kick, realising at once that several ribs were broken. He knew that the longer he held his hands in place, the more the ribs would be healed. He said, "You are fine now, but lie still for a moment before you try to get up. Don't worry, your life is not in danger. Go to your bed and rest for a while and all will be well".

The men who were watching were fascinated, "How did you do that?", asked one of them.

"Your friend was afraid", replied Maun, "He has only a few bruises. Please take him to where he can rest. He will recover very soon".

But, to everyone's surprise - with the exception of Maun - the injured man got up by himself. He looked at Maun with a strange expression on his face, "I don't know what you did boy, but it sure as hell worked".

The men offered Evan and Maun some food and drink, but both politely declined their offer, saying "We have just eaten, thank you", then said good-bye and continued on their way. "You know what?", said Evan, "I am starving, but I could not have eaten in that place. I did not like the feel of it".

"Nor did I", agreed Maun, "It looked like they were breaking horses for the Army".

"You could be right, lad. It is a cruel trade and I'm pretty sure there must be a more humane way."

Food became the subject of conversation for the next few miles and they discussed what they would have at the very next eating house or inn they came to. Suddenly, Maun stopped. He pointed to a nearby meadow saying, "Look Evan! Look there!".

Evan peered into the distance, but could see nothing.

"Under the tree", said Maun still pointing. Then Evan saw the great stallion nibbling the grass, the ropes still hanging from the noble neck. Maun began to walk towards the horse.

"You're not going near it!", yelled Evan, "It's wild. You could get killed if he kicked you like he did the breaker", but Maun was already half way across the meadow. Evan put his hands over his eyes, then opened his fingers a little to peep and saw Maun reach within a few yards of the horse, then standing still to see what the horse's reaction would be. Maun himself sent silent prayers into the ether, hoping his angelic friends would hear and come to his aid.

The stallion raised his head and looked at him, then started to walk towards him. Maun turned to walk back to Evan, who was now half-hiding behind a tree, the stallion following like a lamb. "Look Evan", called Maun, "We are friends".

As Maun and the horse reached Evan, he said, "Now that you have caught him, what do you intend doing with him?".

"I don't know yet", said Maun, "Although I do know where I am not taking him, that is back to where he escaped from. Look Evan, what they have done to him. The whips have cut into his flesh".

"You are right lad, besides they could kill him for being too dangerous and, perhaps, he is, so please be careful."

Evan searched through his satchel and found his razor, "See if this will cut through the ropes. We cannot leave them trailing like that". The horse was still, as although he knew he was with friends.

They continued on their journey, walking faster than before, just a little afraid that the owners of the stallion would catch up with them and accuse them of theft. They need not have feared - no one came.

Soon they spotted the buildings of the old town of Julianus in the distance and for Evan, this was a welcome sight. He said, "I hope they have a bath house. I don't want to arrive home stinking of sweat and covered in dust".

"I will stay out of town", said Maun "And take care of the horse".

"That would be best lad. We don't know how 'Dancing Willie' will behave with other horses or people."

"Dancing Willie?", repeated Maun.

Evan smiled, "Have you not noticed how he dances when he stops walking - as though he cannot bear to be still".

'When you have had your bath Evan, will you bring me something to eat."

"I will that lad. What would you like?"

"Some fresh bread and cheese, or maybe an apple?"

"I will do my best, lad."

Within the hour, they were just outside the town and Maun found a good spot to wait. There was a stream, a stone on which to sit and a nice patch of sweet grass for the horse to nibble.

"Will you take care of my money for me, lad. I don't want to take this into town." He took only enough for what he planned to buy and went off. He called back, "I will be as quick as I can be". Maun unrolled his warm blanket and placed it on the flat stone. He was pleased enough to rest his feet, for they were hot and tired and he closed his eyes and sighed with relief. Then thoughts entered his head, 'Why had this supposed wild animal attached itself to them? … Surely this was a most unusual thing'. Immediately he began to feel distant. A mist formed around him and he became aware of a voice. Not a human voice, just vivid thoughts, that were not his own. That he was about to learn something important regarding his work, there was no doubt! So, he waited and listened. Soon the voice spoke again, 'The Dancer is a gift for one you will meet soon, a good man of military bearing. You will give him the Dancer free of charge'.

Maun was puzzled, 'Please tell me more. How will I know this soldier and where will I meet him?'. There was no reply and Maun began to get more than a little frustrated, 'How can it be that these messengers can give me the name of the horse, yet fail to relate the name of the soldier? There are some things I will never understand about heaven'. Then he heard the voice again plainly say, 'He will wear a flower', a slight hesitation then, 'Have perfect faith, beloved. Trust us'. Maun smiled, yet felt mildly chastised for his lack of faith.

He walked over to Dancer and said, "My friend, it seems that you belong to another. Whoever he is, he is a very lucky man". Dancer snorted and nodded his head up and down.

Maun decided to stretch his legs, Dancer following his every step.

Evan returned, fresh and clean and stinking of perfume. "Oh!", said Maun, "I think I preferred the way you smelled before. Still I expect it will wear off a bit".

"Less of your insolence, young Maun. This bath cost me a fortune. It's not that bad, is it?"

"Not really, Evan. But, I think Margaretta will smell you before she sees you."

"It will wear off long before we get home. While I remember lad, there is a stable yard just inside town. I think we should have Dancing Willie shod before we go on any further. My home is almost within our sights. Another day might be enough. So, let us see to him, then we can be on our way again."

The three of them walked into town and found a blacksmith and with Maun standing within the sight of Dancer, the stallion behaved perfectly.

A mile or so on and Dancer stopped and refused to move. Evan said, "What ever is the matter with him?". Then, he noticed that they had stopped by a large stone that could be a convenient mounting block. "You know, lad. I think he wants you to get on his back." So, Maun climbed up and very carefully sat on Dancer's back.

What happened next frightened Evan. Dancer took off at top speed and ran like the wind, far into the distance, with Maun hanging on around his neck for dear life. Evan shouted, "Come back. Come back", but there was no sight of horse and rider. Evan was terrified, "What have I done? How can I face Father Joseph and say I allowed his grandson to mount a wild stallion?".

Just then, Dancer and Maun came back into view. They were travelling at full gallop and came to a stop within a few strides of the white-faced, ghostly-looking

Evan. "Are you all right lad?", he asked with a tremor in his voice.

"That was wonderful", said Maun when he eventually caught his breath.

"Get off, lad - in case he decides to take off again!"

"He won't, Evan. He just wanted to show us how grateful he is to be free."

The three of them went on their way.

CHAPTER XXX

BACK AT TOURS

Joseph was working in the Abbey, when he was approached by the most senior member of the committee. "Good day, Father Joseph. I have been looking for you". Joseph simply bowed his head briefly. He did not speak, but his gesture said, 'You have found me'.

"Your scribe I feel, is rather annoyed with the committee and has, indeed, declined our offer to restart his readings."

"Oh!", said Joseph - as though having heard this for the first time - "That does sadden me, for our scribe has kept meticulous records of all healings performed by my grandson and he is devoted to him. I find it hard to believe that he would do anything so foolish; unless of course he did not feel there was any progress to be made".

The Bishop continued, "No Father. It is not your scribe that has acted foolishly, but rather one or two of our young priests, who were a little overcome at the sight of so much gold and allowed their avarice to show. Mind you, not that I blame them, for they see in monetary gifts the opportunity to treat themselves to a little luxury in their frugal lives. A cell with a hard bed is not a lot to look forward to at the end of a hard day's work!".

A look at Joseph's face inclined him to add, "Of course Father, you know all about that yourself".

Joseph turned to face the Bishop, "Your Grace, my grandson did not ask to come here. On seeing his great gifts to heal, I believed that he belonged to Our Holy Church. I thought - rather foolishly perhaps - that he and the Church would benefit from his training and give him the authority necessary for his great work. I now think I was wrong and such training might spoil his natural ability. I apologise for wasting the committee's time".

The Bishop was most gracious, "Father Joseph, please reconsider. At least allow us to meet with your grandson once again, that we may be in a better position to judge".

"I am sorry", said Joseph, "My grandson is away at the moment, but he should return in a week or two. Had he held any hope of being accepted, he would not have gone away".

"Then, please Father Joseph, inform us immediately he returns". The Bishop then bid him good-day and left.

Joseph finished his work in a hurry and hoping no one would delay his departure by asking questions, he went in search of Hanno. He found him in the hostelry deep in conversation with Brun Farrar. They were discussing, not only the flavour of herbs in cooking, but their healing qualities, as well as the dangers from some plants.

When Joseph arrived, he spoke to Brun in greeting, then turned to Hanno, "I had to tell you right away, my son. Your little deception worked. I have been approached by the Bishop and been asked to take Maun to see him as soon as he returns".

Brun smiled at him, "Father Joseph. Master Hanno has told me a little of your efforts to get your grandson into training for the priesthood. I remember seeing him on the ship coming over from Briton and on the coach to here. A very gentle boy. I hope they don't try to make him conform too much".

Joseph answered him, "I know exactly what you mean Brun. That worries me too and I will be keeping a watchful eye on him at all times".

CHAPTER XXXI

MARGARETTA

Evan and Maun had made excellent progress. They had met a wool trader who gave them a lift on the back of his wagon. They hitched Dancer to a convenient hook on the back and relaxed for the last mile or so, until they reached Nanmentium. A short walk and they reached Evan's home.

For some reason, the nearer they got to his home, the more nervous Evan became, "Suppose lad, Margaretta has tired of waiting for me and no longer wants me back?".

Maun shook his head, "Evan", he said, "You have not been away all that long. I am sure everything is as you left it and you will be made welcome. It is entirely possible that Margaretta has been wondering if you have been faithful".

"*Me? Unfaithful!*", yelled Evan, "Margaretta would never think *me* unfaithful!".

Maun laughed at him, "Then, why Evan, should you think that of Margaretta? Is she less honourable than you?".

Evan was annoyed with himself, "Take no notice of me, lad. It's just that everything is going too well. We are so near now. I always worry when things go too well. I reckon I am just an old fool. I am glad you came with me, lad. I always imagined you meeting my sons Adam and Karl. You will get along with them, just fine".

The house stood back off the main street. It had clearly seen better days, but still looked sturdy and imposing, if a little old-fashioned.

"You go on in, Evan. I will wait here with Dancer."

"No! No lad, you come on in with me."

Just then a young man appeared from one of the outbuildings. "Papa?", he called, "Is it really you?".

Evan's face lit up with sheer joy, "Adam, my boy".

They hugged, then Adam called out, "Mama! Come quickly! Pa is home". Evan, with his arm around his son's shoulder, walked towards the door, expecting Margaretta to open it and come out. However, when the door opened, it was Karl who came out first. He held the door open for his mother.

Maun sensed that there was something strange about their behaviour, but said nothing. She did not run into his arms, but waited until Evan reached her, although Maun was relieved that she appeared happy enough to see him. She was indeed as pretty as Evan had said, although to Maun, she looked quite old. 'Why', he thought, 'She must be at least as old as my own mother!'.

Having held on to his wife, tears of relief and pleasure on his face, Evan then asked Adam to show Maun where to stable Dancer, then to bring his friend inside the house.

Adam obeyed, "Yes, Pa". He went to Maun, "Come, I will show you where your horse can rest. I expect he is in need of water and some hay".

There was room for several horses, but only one stall was occupied and Adam said, "That's Tsarina. She is now more a pet, than a working horse. There are so many new inns and boarding houses built nearer to the dock, we don't seem to get the custom we used to. Tsarina is not used to company".

Maun told Adam how pleased his father was to be home at last. He went on to say, "He was miserable knowing he was so near home, yet not wanting to offend anyone by leaving us".

Adam laughed, "That sounds like Pa, but I am afraid he is not going to be happy for long".

"Why is that?", asked Maun, "Your mother seemed very pleased to see him".

"Indeed she is", replied Adam, "She has shed many a tear over him, worrying if he would ever come home. However, he is about to find out that years of hard work and worry has ruined her health. It will not take him long to discover how very sick she is".

Maun was content to wait to be asked to use his power to heal Margaretta. It is a universal law, that those with any supernatural power do not use it until invited to do so. For there are cripples who may believe that they are repaying a debt for past evil deeds; and some who enjoy their illness, or at least the sympathy and attention it may bring them. He was certain Margaretta's illness was genuine and that very soon, she would approach him.

They had settled Dancer in his stall, Maun patting his nose and telling him to behave himself and he would be back later to sleep in the stable with him - Dancer snorted.

Evan was so happy at first, that he had not noticed Margaretta's stiff movements, or that Karl was performing the duties of a hostess; cooking the meal and pouring the wine, while Margaretta remained seated. He just thought that she had trained the boys well.

"I am home for good now and I tell you my dear, I am not the same man who left here two years ago. So much has happened to change my life and I have a surprise for all of you, that will change all of our lives." He produced the pouch of gold coins and made his way towards Margaretta, saying, "Hold out your hands, my love". She was slow to do so and Evan took her hands in his and turned them over. His plan was to pour the gold in her palms, but then he saw her hands. The hands that were at one time her pride and joy; now swollen at the joints, her fingers twisted to the side.

"What in God's name has happened here?" He stood looking at them, shocked. But, then his numbed brain began to work. He had seen hands like that before and Maun had healed them. He looked around and saw Karl watching him, his face full of sorrow. "Where is Maun?", he asked, perhaps a little more sharply than intended, for his feelings were of anger as well as anguish.

"He is in the stable with Adam, Pa. Shall I go and get him?"

Evan paused for a moment before saying, "No, my son. It is for us to go to Maun. Come let us help your mother".

Adam and Maun were about to leave the stable and make their way into the house, when the door opened and Karl holding it open, waited for his father and mother to slowly follow. Adam wondered why they had come, but said nothing and Karl, following instructions, placed a stool among the straw for his mother to sit on.

Maun could see the look of pain and guilt on Evan's face, so he said, "Evan. Do for me and Margaretta as you have done for so many others. Help me".

Maun and Evan sat either side of Margaretta, Adam standing behind his mother to support her back, placing his hands on her shoulders. Karl sat at her feet. Maun took her free hand and held it between his own. Almost at once, the atmosphere in the stable became strange. There was a light that did not stem from the dull oil lamp, yet its source could not be detected.

Adam became aware of faces watching them. They were all around them, as though taking part in some wonderful occasion. He was not afraid, but full of wonder. Karl watched his mother's face and saw the weary lines of pain fade away. Evan had seen it all before, many times. He knew that Maun's power would heal his beloved Margaretta, but he was still angry with himself for leaving her. He thought, 'Suppose he had died? What would have happened to her?'. It did not bear thinking about.

When Maun began to feel the power fade, he silently gave thanks. Until Margaretta spoke, it was as although they had forgotten why they were there, they were so enthralled. She looked into Evan's eyes and said, "My dearest. The pain has left me".

Maun took her hand again, but this time he kissed it, saying "Madam Margaretta. I have heard so much about you. Ever since I knew your husband, he has never stopped talking about you".

She smiled at him, "Yes and I have heard all about you as well. Captain Bruner came to deliver some gifts and told us how a young man had saved my husband's life. Now you have saved mine - it seems".

"I owe you a double debt of gratitude."

"You owe me nothing, Madam", said Maun, "It is I who owe Evan. He took care of me on a very difficult journey, for which I am most grateful".

Evan said, "Come into the house everyone, now we can celebrate". Adam was holding his mother's hand and looking at it, a puzzled expression on his face. He helped her up, but realised that she was so light, it was clear that it was not only her hands that had been healed. Her health had been completely restored.

Once inside the house, Evan announced that he had a wonderful surprise for the family. He again reached into his satchel and produced the pouch of gold coins, which he proceeded to pour on to the table. "Where did you get all that, Pa?", his sons asked him.

"Never mind about that now. We will talk about that another time. But, it is all ours. We are going to enjoy the rest of our lives. No more scrimping and saving. Bring out the wine, Adam", he commanded with a flourish.

Adam reluctantly tore himself away from the pile of gold, "I've never seen so much money all at once", he said, as he went to get the wine.

The meal was almost ready. Now Margaretta was helping her son and she brought out their best tableware, her pleasure at performing this simple act without pain was a great joy to her.

Maun had known that there was some reason why he had to accompany Evan home, the feeling had grown as they got nearer. He prayed silently, thanking God for the gift to heal and being able to bring comfort to so many people, especially Margaretta, for he knew how much she meant to his friend.

The celebrations went on for several hours, until Maun said how tired he was from his long walk, besides the wine had made him sleepy. He went to the stable and slept for what seemed hours and strangely enough, Dancer never made a sound.

He was awakened in the morning by Adam who brought him a glass of milk. When Adam had first met Maun, he had been jealous of this boy who his father thought so highly of. But, now he knew why. After the previous evening, when he witnessed the healing of his mother - and he had seen for himself those angelic faces looking on - he wanted to know more about Maun. He also knew why his father had become so fond of him, for he was not as other young men of his age. He looked younger and more delicate, although not in a feminine sort of way. 'Perhaps, refined is the word that most suits him', thought Adam.

The next few days were blissfully happy for Maun. He rode Dancer around the old town and through the beautiful countryside, Adam riding beside him on Tsarina. For the very first time in his adult life, he felt free of his responsibilities and his worries about becoming a priest were left back at Tours.

As they rode along, Adam pointed out places of interest and they bought trinkets at a market and ate at one of the most expensive inns. There was no doubt that a solid bond of friendship had formed between them.

On the morning of Maun's seventh day at Nanmentium, he announced that it was time he went back to Tours, as his grandfather would be worried. On hearing these words, Adam's heart sank. Maun had introduced him to another side of his life he was unaware existed. For the last two years of his father's absence, he had watched his mother suffer and become more and more dependent on him and his brother Karl. They both had to grow up quickly and do all the work in the boarding house and take care of the guests (not that there were many of them). But, for two young boys, it had beeen difficult, there being no time for fun, friends, or for that matter, to find romance.

Being the eldest brother, he had to take important decisions and do the accounts, Karl doing the cooking under verbal instructions from his mother. Now that his father was home for good - and his mother's health restored - where did that leave him? He had considered joining the Army and also given a lot of thought about going to sea like his father. But, he had decided against all of these options, for he had seen what worry was caused to the wives of sailors, as one day, he hoped, he would meet the woman of his dreams.

It had been a truly wonderful day when he came out of the stable and saw his father. Then, he had witnessed his mother being healed. That was indeed as near to a miracle as one gets, but his outstanding memory was of seeing those wonderful angels standing around. The love and compassion that flowed from them was unbelievable. The atmosphere had been breathtakingly mystical. Now that Maun had announced his imminent departure, Adam wondered, 'What will I do without Maun around? To think I was jealous of him when I saw how much father cared about him - now I realise why'.

Adam knew in those moments of reflection, that he wanted to follow Maun. He wanted to learn more about that other world he had glimpsed and he wanted to be part of his healing mission, but first he would have to ask his father.

Evan was a little disappointed at first, for he had dreamed of being at home with all of his family together, intending to make up for lost time. It was Margaretta who did not hesitate, "Let Adam go with our blessing. He has been head of this household for a long time. Now that you are home, there is no room for two masters in any one home. He wants to go with Maun. Better he goes with him, than wait until he is driven out to join the Army, or something worse".

Evan sighed, but he knew she was right - she always was.

Later, when he had time to think about it a bit longer, he was pleased, for he was worried about Maun going back to Tours alone. It was a long journey and Maun was completely inexperienced in any kind of self defence.

Then, Evan thought about his younger son Karl, he would miss his older brother. Again, Margaretta reassured him that Karl would be fine. He would take over Adam's place in the household; move into his larger room, have the full attention of both parents and now that they did not have to worry about being short of money, he could go out with his friends. Evan put his arm around his wife's shoulder and gave her a squeeze, "And my love, no more work for you. From now on, it is an easy life without worries".

Next morning, Dancer and Tsarina were saddled. With saddle-bags packed, Adam and Maun waved good bye. It was not easy for either of them. Adam had just had his father returned to him, while Maun would miss Evan, for he had been his protector and companion through the most difficult times of his life.

They did not hang around long, once they were ready, that would have been too painful. Margaretta wept, Evan comforting her, "Don't worry, my love They will have a wonderful time. I know they will".

Maun and Adam did not hurry. They travelled at an easy pace, stopping often to rest the horses. They ate and slept at every respectable inn, one of these being 'The Ferry Boat Inn'. Cressida and Vilma were overjoyed to see Maun again, but wanted to know where his big friend was? When told that Adam was Evan's son, they fussed around him, offering extra food and wine, as well as their famous foot bath and massage treatment. However, as they both were on horseback and had not suffered sore or tired feet, they declined the offer graciously. Adam whispered to Maun, "We had better be careful, or these two will have us drunk, then anything could happen!".

Maun laughed, "I don't think so. We are safe enough. They only want us to feel welcome".

Adam was doubtful, "You can think what you like Maun. I am going to bolt my bedroom door this night".

Maun was right. They went to their rooms and slept soundly until morning. It was Cressida and Vilma's mother, who gave them breakfast and packed them some food for the journey home. She explained that her two daughters had gone to market, but that they had asked her, "To wish you both a safe journey home".

Adam was disappointed, "I was quite looking forward to being fussed over again at breakfast". Maun was amused, "It is your own fault", he told him, "You should not have bolted your bedroom door last night!", they both laughed.

They arrived back in Tours early the following evening. Joseph had requested the innkeeper to inform him as soon as his grandson returned, so while Maun and Adam were taking the horses to the stables, a messenger was sent to Joseph with the news. When they returned to the inn, having seen to Dancer and Tsarina and given the stable-hand a good tip for taking special care of them, Joseph was waiting inside to greet him with a hug saying, "My boy! Thank God you are safe".

Maun introduced Adam, Joseph gripping his hand warmly, "It is a great pleasure to meet the son of our dear friend, Evan", he said.

As they sat at a table, waiting for their meal to be served, Joseph told Maun all that had transpired during his absence, "So, my boy. The Bishop wishes to see you".

"Not tonight, grandfather I hope", said Maun.

"No, my boy. Not tonight."

CHAPTER XXXII

THE NOVICE

Maun lay on his hard bed in his cell at the Abbey school. He had been there for several weeks and hated every moment of his life as a novice priest.

His fellow students were offhand; they gathered in small groups to study, but he was never invited to join them. He was ignored, even when he asked a simple question. The food was plain and tasteless, nor was there sufficient to sustain a sparrow.

To make matters worse, he knew that Hanno and Adam were spending a lot of time at the flat fields, racing Dancer against some of the Army officers' horses.

Maun had visited Hanno and Adam during his brief periods of free time and they had boasted how Dancer had won almost every race and how exciting it was, crowds of soldiers and others gathering to watch and cheering Dancer on.

"Has anyone offered to buy him?", asked Maun.

"Not yet", answered Hanno, "Though he has many admirers".

Maun sighed, "I miss all of you so much - and I miss Dancer. Don't forget, if anyone offers to buy him, he is not for sale! However, if someone makes an offer who is wearing a flower, come for me. That is the only clear instruction I have".

Hanno could sense Maun's misery. He said, "Yes Maun. We do understand. If anyone shows an interest, we will send for you, so that you can see him for yourself".

Maun forced a smile, "Thanks. Now I had better get back before I am missed". When he had gone, Hanno and Adam felt very guilty. They thought they were cheering him up talking about Dancer's triumph, but all they had done was to make him realise what he was missing.

Maun lay on his bed thinking of his friends up at the fields having a wonderful time, 'I don't think I can stick this out. I will have to speak to my grandfather'. With a rare show of ill temper, he tossed his scroll down and was about to utter some words unworthy of a man of God, when suddenly he heard someone in the corridor outside call out. Next, he heard the sickening thud of a body hitting the stone floor.

Maun was up and through the door in seconds. Brother Christophus lay face down, blood pouring from a head wound. A tooth had been knocked out and lay about an arm's length away, his nose also appeared to be broken. Maun knelt down and gathered the Brother in his arms and he was in the process of wiping the blood from his face with the sleeve of his white robe, when some of the other Brothers gathered around him. He asked them to fetch a damp cloth from his cell and when they brought it, Maun cleaned the injured brother's face.

As he did so, the wounds did not appear to be as bad as first thought and after spotting the missing tooth, Maun reached out and picked it up. He opened the blood-filled mouth of Christophus and pressed the tooth back into its socket. The watching Brothers muttered between themselves as they looked on fascinated. Another damp cloth was brought and Maun gently washed the face clean, only a faint scar on the side of the head now visible. Brother Christophus groaned and opened his eyes. He looked up at Maun and said, "Oh! It's you". He sounded most surprised and and not a little disappointed.

Maun asked the other Brothers to help Christophus back to his room, so that he could rest a while and when they were out of sight, Maun went back into his own cell. The sleeve and front of his novice's robe was covered in blood and as he poured some water into a bowl to try wash the sleeve, the water turned pink, making it look worse. In the end, he put his stained robe to soak in the bowl of water and put on his other robe, the one Captain Bruner had bought for him. He immediately felt relaxed and comfortable - more like his old self.

Kneeling by the side of his bed, he thanked God for his gift to heal and asked forgiveness for his ungraciousness. Then, a knock at the door interrupted his prayers. He called out, "Enter. The door is open". Maun looked up to see Brother Christophus enter, followed by several of his companions, all looking somewhat subdued. "Can I help you?", asked Maun.

"We have come to thank you for what you did for Brother Christophus. We have never seen anything like that in our lives. We would like you to listen to what Brother Christophus has told us happened to him."

Maun nodded and Christophus began to speak, "I was hurrying along the corridor, when my sandal caught on a raised stone slab. I stumbled forward and could not save myself. My head hit the pillar with great force and I fell, knocking my head for a second time on the stone floor. I imagine that I was unconscious. Then I had a dream. A man in a white robe came towards me, he picked me up and said, 'Do not worry. You will be well. My servant will heal you'. I opened my eyes and there you were. I could hardly believe my eyes. When I was taken back to my room, Brother Damian told me about the tooth. I felt around my mouth and could find no trace of a loose or missing tooth".

"We want to say how sorry we are to have been so off-hand with you. It was extreme bad manners on our part, but we heard that you were kin to Bishop Martin and receiving special treatment."

Maun thought of the trouble Hanno had gone to and the amount of persuading his grandfather had done in order to get him accepted and wished with all his heart and soul every day that they had not tried so hard. Now he discovered that his fellow Brothers were off hand and unfriendly because they thought he was receiving special treatment! 'In what way?', he wondered.

Maun bowed his head. After any healing, when he had been in the company of his angels, he felt mellow and almost intoxicated with compassion, so he replied simply, " I am sorry if my own nervousness made me appear unapproachable".

Then he changed the subject by asking Christophus, "How you feel now?".

"Thank you, Brother Maun. I feel very well", then he added, "Is there anything I can do for you?". Maun asked him if he knew where he could get his robe washed? The Brothers smiled, "Allow us to take care of that". He handed them the bowl of pink water containing the robe and they left, walking backwards, as though keeping him in view for as long as they could. Maun followed them to the door and then closed it when they were out of his cell.

He lay on his bed again, with the comforting feeling of knowing that he was able to do his work for God. He was relaxed to the point of sleep, when a face came into view out of the mist. His heart began to beat faster, for it was the lovely face of Flavia. 'How did you get here?', he whispered in his thoughts, 'I pray you have not died to earth life'.

She smiled at him, 'I was thinking of you Maun and became aware of your unhappiness. Then I saw you in my mind sitting with the Brother and waited for you until you were alone. I am waiting for you to come home'. Then her face began to fade into the mist, with the words, 'Think of me, Maun'.

'As if I needed to be told', he thought, 'She is in my heart and my mind constantly, like the missing half of myself'.

'Oh! My good Lord', he thought, knowing that she longed for him too, made his life the sweeter. 'I cannot return to her a failure. She is expecting me to return a priest of the Holy Church of our Lord Jesus. I must work harder and achieve my goal'. He corrected that statement, 'Achieve my *grandfather's* goal!'.

CHAPTER XXXIII

JOSHUA AND MAX

About a week later, Maun received a note, informing him that a young cavalry officer was showing interest in Dancer and could he try to get to the flat fields that evening. Maun did not fully understand the note, but guessed that it was from Hanno and could only mean one thing, his presence was required.

This would mean missing an important lecture, but he hoped he would not be missed. There was no time to change out of his novices robe, so he hurried along the road to Hanno's house.

"It's like this, Maun", said Hanno, "An old soldier has approached us and asked if Dancer was for sale? Not for himself, but for his officer who is in the Third Legion, his horse had to be put down when it became lame. This servant said that his officer was a good man who treated him well, although of late, he'd suffered many misfortunes and had become deeply depressed. Tonight, he hopes to persuade the officer to come to the flat fields and see Dancer race. So, Maun, I thought I had better let you know, just in case he turns up wearing a flower".

Maun laughed, "I know it sounds silly, but it's all I've got to go on. I must be sure that I give Dancer to the right person".

"Adam is at the stable now grooming Dancer, making him look his best. We have to meet him, before going to the flat field for the racing."

Hanno, Adam and Maun set off, Maun was excited. At last he would see Dancer race. However, he also felt guilty at missing his lecture and wondered what his tutor would say to him - something unpleasant, no doubt!

Adam rode Dancer, whilst Hanno and Maun rode in a buggy drawn by Tsarina. The usual crowd of young officers were there with their servants acting as grooms and there were crowds of local people, making bets and generally having a day's sport. The officers waved to Adam in greeting, no doubt, hoping for a race later on. There was great excitement and lots of shouting and cheering, as a race was just ending.

The servant arrived and told them that his officer had promised to come along later, "I told him that the horse may be for sale to the right person and he was interested, well, at least as interested in the horse, as he has been in anything of late. It seems everything is a great effort to him".

"I do hope he comes", said Hanno, "We have gone to great trouble to get the owner here".

"Have you, really?", said the servant, "Where is he?".

Hanno introduced Maun, the servant introducing himself as Max. He said, "I am most surprised to see that you are the owner, Sir. It never occurred to me that a *Patris* would be in a position to own a horse? I assumed they were all too poor!".

Maun smiled at him, "I don't really own him. I am holding him in trust for the real owner". Hanno nudged Adam and asked him, "What name did he call Maun?".

Adam informed him that 'Patris' was the name that some military men called their priest, "It means 'Father of the church', in one of the many natural languages of the soldiers".

Max asked them not to let Dancer race before his officer arrived, "For I am sure that as soon as he sees him race, he will be unable to resist him".

They reluctantly allowed two races to pass and still the prospective owner did not show up.

Adam took Dancer forward for the next race and Maun found himself a good spot to watch. Four horses were lined up. There was silence as everyone waited with baited breath, then the flag dropped and they were off. The horses had to run the full length of the field, turn and run back again. Maun cheered with the crowd as the excitement grew. Dancer won by a length.

This was the first time Maun had seen him race. They were so busy cheering and shouting, they did not notice that Max had been joined by his officer. He brought him over and introduced him as Major Joshua and Maun could see how proud Max was of him - his pride more like that of a father than a servant.

Maun liked Joshua on sight. He bore an uncanny resemblance to his father Calpurnius and he hoped that he would be the one to receive Dancer. However, there was no trace of a flower. "Did you see the race?", asked Hanno.

"Yes, I did", said Joshua, "Dancer is even better than Max described. I would love to ride him, if you would allow me?".

"Of course, you may", said Hanno, "Once he has rested for a little while".

But, however much Maun wanted Joshua to be the new owner, without a flower, he would not let him have Dancer. Hanno knew how much trust Maun placed on guidance from 'those on a higher plain' and felt sorry for both Max and Joshua.

Adam returned leading a sweating and very proud horse.

When Dancer had cooled down and recovered, Joshua again asked if he could ride him, "Not in a race, just around the field for a little while". Maun nodded agreement, but he was worried. How was he going to explain to Joshua that he could not have Dancer?

As Adam brought Dancer forward for Joshua to mount, Max came up behind him and took his cloak from him and there, revealed high on his shoulder, was a tattoo of a flower.

Maun uttered an almost silent, "Thank God"; Hanno a great sigh of relief.

They all watched Josh and Dancer canter around the field. "They look well together" said Max and everyone agreed.

Joshua returned, looking very happy, "He is a wonderful animal and I would be very proud to own him. If he is for sale, I would like very much to buy him".

Maun said, "I am sorry Major Joshua. Dancer is not for sale". They all looked at Maun in surprise, Max and Joshua's faces expressing deep disappointment. Then Maun added, "No, he is not for sale. He is a gift to you. You are to have him without charge".

"But! Why?", said Joshua, "When I am willing to pay".

Maun replied, "Because Joshua, he is not ours to sell. He was directed to us to

256

hold in trust for one who wore a flower. He is a gift especially for you, from one who has passed from this world, but who has not forgotten a promise".

"That cannot be", said Joshua, "I do not believe in Heaven; spirits of the dead, nor do I believe there is a God. The world is too cruel a place".

Maun bowed his head, for he remembered a time when he was of the same opinion. He simply replied, "Because you do not believe in God, it does not follow that God does not believe in you. Tell me truthfully. Is there no one who once promised you a wonderful horse?".

Joshua's face drained of colour. Maun continued, "Tell me, Joshua. Why do you have that tattoo on your shoulder?".

"You mean this rose?", queried Joshua, " It is my mark of identification should I be killed in battle".

Maun asked him, "Do all soldiers have a flower?".

"Oh! No", said Joshua, "Some have animal heads or birds; some have their names. I can assure you no other soldier would have a flower".

"Then, why have you chosen one?"

Joshua was surprised at being asked so many questions, "Because it is supposed to be a rose - not that it looks much like one! The tattooist was not very good at his art. I have a rose because my mother's name was Rosa".

Joshua sat on the edge of Adam's buggy. He appeared to be in some distress and tried to compose himself, then he told them the story of his early life.

"I was an only child. Never knew my father. Mother said he died, but I had doubts about that. She was a wonderful mother who spent her life teaching children to sing and dance. She was always happy and one day she took me to see a family, who had a pony for sale. 'Do you like him?', she asked. 'Yes mama', I said, 'He is beautiful'. 'Then my pet, you shall have him.' We took the pony home and I spent many happy hours riding and grooming him."

"One day mother said, 'When you have grown up, I will buy you a horse, the best one I can find. One that can run like the wind and who will take you anywhere you want to go'."

"That was not to be. My mother died, why, or of what disease, I never knew. I was sent to her only relative, an older brother, who although not an evil man, was as mean, as she was generous. He was given everything of value that my mother owned and he sold my pony - he said that 'it cost too much to feed'. My life became very unhappy. Everything had a price. Happiness had no value for my uncle and as soon as I was old enough to work, I had to do so and give him every little coin I earned. I made up my mind that I would leave home as soon as I was able to support myself and I joined the Army whilst still a boy. I decided then, that there was no God, or he would not have taken my mother away. Since then, I have seen nothing to make me alter my mind. Now this has happened! Do you think my mother will forgive me for my disbelief?"

Maun answered him, "Death is no barrier to love. She will always love you and forgive you anything".

"How is it", asked Joshua, "That you were entrusted to deliver Dancer to me? I am a cavalry officer. Why was he not delivered in the course of my work?".

Maun shrugged modestly, "Because, Sir. You would never have known it was your mother who sent him. She is anxious that you know she still watches over you".

Joshua then looked at his servant Max, "Is that also why I was given the most loyal and fatherly of servants to care for me?".

Max, who had been following the proceedings intently, said, "Need you ask, Josh?". Then, he said to Maun, "You have given him much more than a horse this day". And to Joshua, he said, "Come, Sir. Let us take this wonderful creature home. Both you and Dancer have had a busy day".

Hanno, Adam and Maun watched as Max and Joshua led Dancer away towards the military camp. They were sad to see him go, for it meant the end of their sport. However, it had been fun while it lasted and it was also with a sense of relief that this particular work was completed, as they had never laid claim to Dancer, always being aware that he belonged to another.

CHAPTER XXXIV

BROTHER DANIEL

Joseph was working in the Abbey; cleaning and filling the oil lamps; polishing silver and welcoming visitors. He had just finished dusting various nooks and crannies and as he pottered, he was turning over in his mind the events that had brought him back to Gaul. It was true that he wanted his grandson to receive the authority and support of the Holy Church, but there was another reason. For, when he was a young man, he had required help and on that occasion he had turned to his older half-brother and he had helped unstintingly.

While he was working in north Briton, he had thought of Martin and realised that he was - if still alive - getting very old. He had thought at the time, 'I would like to be there, if Martin needs me'.

That was a joke, he thought cynically, 'Here I am, working in the Abbey, too frail and cold to work outside, while Martin - in his eighties - is still receiving famous people; still travelling around to many different towns, visiting other churches and advising them on how to settle disputes. Me, I have had the very best of everything this past twenty years or so, while Martin has been living his frugal existence and still managing to do more work than me'.

'If only I did not feel the cold so much, although I must admit that since that dear lady, who is my neighbour wove me that woollen shift to wear under my robe and those woollen slippers that go under my boots, it has made a difference - I have felt more comfortable.'

Joseph was miles away, allowing those idle thought to pass through his mind, when suddenly, he heard a voice say, "Father Joseph". He forced himself to look up and pay attention. Hurrying towards him was the bishop in charge of the novices. Joseph bowed a little, to acknowledge his presence, "Good-day, your Grace", he said.

The bishop motioned him to come and sit beside him, "Father Joseph", he said, "I have come to tell you that you were right all along ...". Joseph could not think what he meant, but waited for him to continue, "...Your grandson's written work ...".

"Oh!", said Joseph (butting in), "Is it improving?".

The bishop laughed, "Good gracious! No. My dear Joseph, I have an eight year old nephew who can write better than Brother Maun ...", then added sarcastically, "... Standing on his head!".

Joseph winced and thought he had better be quiet and listen.

"I am so sorry Father Joseph for being so cruelly blunt", said the bishop, "But, there is little improvement in Brother Maun's writing skills. However, there have been developments in other ways, which we must not ignore".

Joseph looked up into the bishop's face and repeated, "Developments?".

"Yes", said the bishop, "Important developments".

"Last week, I had to go home for a few days. Before I left, I was called upon to give the last rites to young Brother Daniel. He had a disease of the lungs. When I saw him, he was in a bad way and I did not think he would last the day. I returned to the Abbey school this morning and asked about Brother Daniel's funeral? No one seemed to know what I was talking about, so Father Joseph, I went along to his quarters to see for myself. As I approached, I saw coming towards me none other than Brother Daniel, looking a picture of robust health. I called him over and congratulated him on his rapid recovery and asked him what medication the physician had given him to bring about his miraculous recovery? To which he replied, 'I had no medicine at all. Brother Maun came and put his hands on my throat and chest'."

"Brother Daniel then informed me of several more miraculous healings that had taken place, all attributed to Brother Maun. He described them to me in detail. They were all unbelievably spectacular."

"I have deliberated on this and have decided to consult with my superiors. I have in mind a plan to put to them, that Brother Maun should learn by rote the essential services, then he should be allowed to go forward in his healing ministry with our blessings."

Joseph smiled, "Thank God for common sense - at last".

CHAPTER XXXV

CONCHESSA AND CALPURNIUS

Conchessa had kept herself busy, in an attempt not to think of her father and son so far away. She took on extra work teaching at Calim and Harran's school, which had grown bigger every year and Harran was now considering building an even bigger school in a village not too far away, called 'Glasco' (which means 'The green place').

Recently Leelan (the youngest son of old Hoel's friend), had extended the shipbuilding yard, which had attracted young men into the district. As the aim of Harran and Calim was to educate the people of the border, they had big plans for the new school.

When not teaching, Conchessa visited her friends at Bonavon. The little ones she had taught there, were now grown up and had families of their own. She liked going there to relive her fond memories and visit Alana and Clodus, also Paulus and Bliss and their ever expanding families.

The Abbey was still in the early stages of being built and although progress was slow, local men and women were being educated and employed and that pleased her.

However, she longed to see her father and her son again. She had tried to be patient for Calpurnius's sake, being tempted many times to remind him of his promise, but she had held back, knowing that he always endeavoured to keep his word and his promises.

So, it was a surprise to her one evening, when Calim and Rhona asked them to come into their quarters. "What is it? Is something wrong?", Calpurnius asked.

"No! No! Nothing is wrong, my son. Your mother and I have been thinking. Why don't you take Conchessa and go to Gaul and see for yourself what is going on there? I am sure you both must be as anxious as we are."

This was music to Conchessa's ears. She looked at Calpurnius and he too was delighted, but he protested, "What of you father and you mother? How would you manage?".

Calim put his arm around his wife's shoulder, "Would you just listen to the boy. He thinks we cannot manage without him". Then turning to his son, he said, "We have a legion of servants to run the house and estate. There are thousands of past pupils who would love to have the opportunity to teach - all of them perfectly qualified. There is absolutely nothing to stop you. We have been wondering why you have not suggested it yourselves?".

"There is a new ship in the yard. It has just been completed and it is of the very latest design. We will go to the yard tomorrow and speak to young Leelan, then we will visit the docks and select the most experienced crew available. The ship and crew could be ready in a month or two, that will give you time to get ready

261

and decide what servants you wish to take with you."

Calpurnius was still worried, "But, father. I thought you had a customer for the new ship?".

"Yes. We did, my son", said Calim, "But alas, the customer had to cancel the order due to his financial problems. Now don't worry. Your uncle Harran and I have discussed it and decided that you and Conchessa should have the use of it. You, my boy, have always been a hard worker and contributed to the design of all of our most successful ships. You have never asked for any reward. Nor have you ever claimed anything that you have not earned. So, take the use of it with our blessings".

The new ship did not even have a name, but after some deliberation among the family members, they settled for the *Leelan*, as a tribute to the family who had worked and managed the shipyard for so many years.

They hired several more crew than were really necessary. There were so many eager applicants, all very able and willing, that Calpurnius and Conchessa decided not to take any of the household servants with them, except for one maid for Conchessa.

The ship was painted and a family crest fitted to the bow, composed of a shield divided into three parts: one part contained a tree, to represent the wood used in their trade; the second part depicted a small ship and the third - and largest section in the centre of the shield - contained the sign of the 'Cross'.

Within two months, the *Leelan* was ready and packed with stores and Calpurnius and Conchessa set sail for Gaul.

Joseph, Hanno and Adam worked with Maun, reading aloud to him his vows and instructions, until he was word perfect. Although exceptionally bright, Maun's reading and writing difficulties were not due to lack of intelligence, but perhaps more with poor eye-sight. It had always been a puzzle to Joseph, since Maun was the child of the brilliant Calpurnius and his daughter Conchessa - who was a gifted teacher and Joseph had often thought to himself, 'How unfortunate for Maun to have inherited my own problem of word-blindness'. Even so, Maun's difficulties were much greater than his had been.

Joseph was excited, for he had at last achieved what he had set out to do, to see his beloved grandson acknowledged by the Holy Church. He believed in his heart, that this was what God wanted of him. He also knew in his heart that as soon as Maun was ordained, he would leave Tours and return to Dunbriton. He was dreading breaking the news to Maun that he would not be going back with him. It would break his heart to see Maun go, but he could not face any more cold sea journeys. He thought to himself, 'My travelling days are well and truly over and besides, it is better to stay here in my comfortable little house, with my housekeeper to take care of me, than suffer the long journey back to north Briton and allow my daughter to watch me slowly die. Nor, do these young people want me holding them back'.

He began to wonder what he could give Maun for a gift after his ordination? This he knew would not be an easy task, for Maun was not given to wearing jewellery - not even a crucifix. He had always expressed the opinion that he would rather advertise his Christian belief by his words and deeds. He had also related to Joseph that he would rather celebrate his Lord's life as a living heavenly being, radiant with light and love for all mankind, than be constantly reminded of his cruel death.

'So, what could he get him for a gift? No point in getting a prayer book he could not read. This is going to prove difficult', he thought.

Some days later, he was walking home as quickly as he could. It was cold for early autumn and Madam Leoni (his most valued housekeeper) had said she would make him something hot for his supper.

As he hurried along, he could almost smell his meal, when he heard a voice say, "Father Joseph? Would you be *the* Father Joseph of Bonavon?". He stopped and looked around. Standing a few yards away, was a tall young man in military uniform, who said "Can I have a word Father?".

Joseph was puzzled. Not many used his title now-a-days, especially here in Gaul, 'Who could this be?' he wondered. "Yes, of course you may young man, but not here in the street. Come with me to my home, it is not far away."

"Why, thank you Father", said the young man as he followed him.

Once inside, Joseph hung his cloak on a hook behind the door and offered to do likewise for his guest. As the young man removed his Army cloak with its high collar and revealed his face, Joseph stopped in his tracks, "Well! Bless my soul, you look very much like a dear old friend of mine."

The young man looked at his feet and shuffled a little, then said, "Would that friend be Commander Antonius Gaius?".

"Why, yes", said Joseph, "Would you be his son?".

"No Sir", replied Antonius, "I am his grandson. My grandmother has told me how much I resemble him. She also told me that he died in a far country and that a priest by the name of Joseph of Bonavon had been responsible for making sure that she received his legacy to her, without which she would not have survived".

Joseph's memory was not as good as it used to be, but he remembered his quandary in writing to more than one woman, none of whom Gaius was actually married to. So, he had written to each as though they were the only one and the legacy had been shared equally between them. Joseph coughed, attempting to hide his thoughts.

Luckily at that point, Madam Leoni made a timely entrance with their supper. She was a pleasant woman of mature years and having outlived her family, she was grateful for her new job, which gave her a good living, someone to talk to and who made few demands, only that she keep the house warm and a hot meal on the table.

She had chanced to speak to Joseph one day in the Abbey and seen how very cold he was, so she had woven him a woollen undergarment, just like the one she wore herself. She had taken it to him and how pleased he had been. He went to her house to thank her and when he saw how poor she was, he offered her the job as his housekeeper.

Placing a large tureen of thick stew on the table, along with two bowls and spoons and a few chunks of coarse bread, she watched as they devoured their first helping. During a more leisurely second helping, Joseph asked the young man his name and he replied, "I am Sir, Antonius Gaius, named after the grandfather I never knew. That, Father Joseph, is why I had to come and see you. I want to know everything you can tell me about the man whose name I bear".

Joseph had to think fast. This young man obviously hero-worshipped his grandfather and he would have to be careful what he told him. "How did you know where to find me?", inquired Joseph, "For I have not been back in Tours for very long?".

Antonius recounted how he was up at the flat fields, watching his fellow officers race their horses against a superb stallion owned by a civilian, who some said was a priest of the Church. Antonius continued, "On making further inquiries, I learned that the owner was the grandson of Father Joseph at the Abbey, who had not long returned from missionary work in north Briton. I guessed that you could be the Joseph of Bonavon, the man who wrote to my grandmother".

"After my father died, I went to see my grandmother and asked if I could look at the document that informed her of my grandfather's death. She said that the letter had given her great comfort, for it proved that he had not forgotten her after all. She was so proud that you found him a fine man who had become a Christian, not simply in name like others, but a man whose words and actions became thoughtful, kind and loving."

"The letter also explained that a vault had to be opened and she would 'in due course receive the contents', as her husband had willed. The letter was signed, 'Joseph of Bonavon' - I took a chance, Sir."

"So, you can see Father, why I had to find you. I want to know as much about him as possible and you are the only one who can tell me."

Joseph was kind to young Antonius. He related story after story of his old friend's adventures, making sure not to mention Gaius's more unpleasant side to his nature, or the fact that his grandparents were not married.

"Despite having a difficult and unpopular job, your grandfather became sensitive and caring of his men and truly repented for any unhappiness that he may have caused in the past."

Then the young Antonius said, "Father, it has been such a pleasure to meet you and I am so very pleased that you were with him at the end of his life and made sure he had a Christian burial at Alcluid. I will cherish that knowledge. Now I must go, Sir. I have taken up so much of your valuable time. I thank you for all the information you have given me, stories I could not have heard from any other than your good self".

Joseph would have loved him to stay longer, but had to confess to being tired. "Come again," he called out as Antonius left.

His mind was still full of his life in Dunbriton and as he climbed into bed, he began to reminisce about the day of his daughter's marriage to Calpurnius.

What an exciting day that had been. He remembered with pleasure, the enormous amounts of wonderful food and wine; the beautiful gowns worn by the ladies; the little children in their angelic tunics and the robes designed especially for the men, in vibrant shades of blues and greens.

How could he ever forget that thrilling moment when the Commander approached him and asked if he could tell him more about Jesus.

Suddenly, Joseph sat bolt upright, 'My Robe!'. He jumped out of bed, just as fast as his creaking knees would allow and going to a secret box, he retrieved a key which he used to open his travelling trunk. Reaching underneath some of his valuables, he pulled out a parcel, which was wrapped in lengths of muslin, all the time praying that no moths had found it. Some of the dried herbs he had packed in it to keep it fresh - like the twigs of lavender - fell to the ground as he unwound it. Finally, there it was, as fresh as the day it had been made.

He held it up against himself. It seemed longer than he remembered, but he thought to himself, 'It will fit Maun perfectly and won't he look handsome in it, the peacock blue against his fair hair?". He felt enormous relief, for now he had a gift for Maun that would be useful. After carefully rewrapping the robe in the muslin and putting it back in his trunk, he climbed back into bed, hoping to get some sleep. However his mind was now active. There was something young Antonius had said that was puzzling him. At the time it had struck him, but as the conversation proceeded, he had let the remark go - now he remembered.

'How was it Antonius knew that his grandfather was buried near to Alcluid? He was quite sure he had not mentioned that in his letter, simply stating that it was 'a Christian grave'.'

He thought to himself, that boy is the double of the Commander and could be easily mistaken for him. The only differences he observed being a more kindly speaking voice and refined manners. The Commander had neither.

The more he thought along those lines, the more he believed that young Antonius was the Commander reborn. His interest in a man he had never met; his military career; his appearance and his use of the name 'Alcluid' - that was a local name for 'the rock in the Clyde' - a name the Commander had used. Joseph had preferred to use the name Dunbriton, which means 'the fortress of the Britons. 'Perhaps I'm wrong, I suppose I could be mistaken. It is a long time ago, but still, why not?'.

Joseph believed wholeheartedly that life was life. It could not die, or be killed. The body was but a temporary home for the light of the soul and when it was damaged beyond repair, the soul took flight, only to return when the opportunity arose to receive it into a new experience, or one that would allow the soul to right the wrongs of the past. For that reason, the soul almost always returned to the same family, for that is where it could continue, where it left off.

However, that was not a law.

He had his own experience of Ysu. That had been vivid and he had no doubts about that. However, he was aware that his version of rebirth was over simplified. In his conversations on the subject with Calpurnius, he learned that planetary influences were more important than ever imagined by anyone upon earth. "We are", said Calpurnius, "Reborn within a certain set of planetary forces, which we ourselves have created over many lifetimes; by our every thought; word and action. When we pass from this world, we do so under that planetary configuration that is our very own".

'Frankly', thought Joseph, 'It is all too deep for me. I know that I will die one day. I do not want to know the hour or day it will happen'.

'Oh! Dear me! All these thoughts going around in my head. When that happens I have awful trouble getting to sleep.'

'The best thing I can do now is, to make sure I think of pleasant things - like Maun in my blue robe' and with that thought, he smiled to himself and snuggled down.

CHAPTER XXXVI

FLAVIA

Flavia had been a natural mystic for as long as she could remember and had suffered for it. Some people had thought her insane; an idiot, for appearing to converse with herself and it had taken hard work and concentration to train herself to recognise the difference between those who were of this world and those who had passed from it.

Her mother Jess was helpful, although at first when Flavia started to talk to her invisible friends, she was alarmed and frightened and she did not know what to do to save her little daughter from ridicule. At first, she had laughed and tried to convince Flavia that she was imagining things, then she explained that other people could not see her friends and were afraid. But, Flavia did not understand, because she could not tell the difference.

Then, Jess began to listen to what was being said and realised that far from being an idiot, her little girl was very special!

As Flavia grew up, she became aware of other souls who came to talk to her. They were very different in how they dressed and spoke to her. Their words were silent, but were impressed in her mind. She saw them only on special occasions - when she needed to know how to handle a problem. When they did appear, it was briefly and she would catch a glimpse of a flowing cloak or a golden crown, just enough to let her know that they were present.

She was very pleased when they came, for they made her feel good about herself. They gave her advice about her life and told her many secrets about life on earth.

She was told how God's commandments were not simply advice for living a good life, they were universal and spiritual laws that each soul must pursue and live up to, in order to be able to return to their high estate.

They also told her that men or women should never blame anyone but themselves when things appear to go wrong, then added that man had achieved a level of wisdom when he realised that no other person owed him anything, 'Your life is yours, to seek and find. To learn and to achieve without causing suffering to another living being'.

On another occasion, when she had been taunted in the street and ignored by those she had thought were friendly, she had returned home in tears and gone to her bed sobbing. Then, one of her guardians appeared. He wore a golden robe, his face was beautiful and full of compassion. She looked at him through her tears, then she heard his words, 'You must not worry about these souls so lacking in truth. For I tell you now, that there is a reason for their behaviour. It is for your protection. You are being saved for another. One who will need your light and wisdom'.

Flavia grew into a lovely young woman, shy and lacking in confidence, but very serene and wise. However the people of her village were slow to forget and she still had the reputation for being 'odd'. No young man of marrying age wanted to become involved with the 'village idiot' and this hurt her a lot. However, she understood their blindness and forgave them, knowing the spiritual reasons behind their behaviour.

When she was about sixteen, Jess her mother, was offered work in the house of the governor of the district - the Lord Probius - as housekeeper. She was offered quarters within the house and told she could bring her daughter with her. It meant moving several miles away and Jess was pleased about that, for it was an opportunity to get her daughter away from the taunts of the local youths.

CHAPTER XXXVII

PROBIUS - LORD OF THE DISTRICT

The Lord Probius was handsome for his age, a widower and a good hard working man. But, one thing was lacking in his life - a son - and he longed for a boy child that would grow up to inherit his estate. His first wife bore him a daughter - Sarah - who now lived with his dead wife's parents. Fond of her as he was, she was not a son. He married again, a handsome woman of a good family and despite the ten years they were together, she died childless. How could it be that the poverty stricken 'young sprouts' of the district could produce sons like rabbits, unlike him who could give a son everything, including a title and wealth. It just was not fair.

His assistant and steward suggested that he search for a young woman not yet spoken for from among the poorer classes, who would be more likely to conceive a son. In sheer desperation, Probius reluctantly agreed and the steward called at the village where Jess and Flavia lived and on the pretext of searching for a housekeeper, he interviewed Jess. As soon as he discovered she had an unmarried daughter who looked very presentable, he chose her.

Probius felt guilty about using people, so when Jess arrived with Flavia at the big house, he gave the order that they must be well treated; given the best of everything; food and quarters and the girl must not be made to work too hard. When he first caught a glimpse of Flavia, he loved her, she was so beautiful. He could not believe she was an unspoken-for virgin and he wondered, 'What were the young men of her village thinking about?'. He decided not to rush things. He had waited so long, he could wait another few months in order to get to know her.

He made no advances towards Flavia until he was sure he would not be rebuffed. Flavia grew fond of him too, for he was the kindly father she never had and a deep understanding of each other's problems developed between them.

It came as no surprise to Jess when after only a few months, Probius came to her and asked for her daughter's hand in marriage.

She puzzled over why he bothered to ask her, as Flavia was now old enough to make up her own mind? Jess was pleased though, for in asking her, it showed something of this man's honourable character, that he considered and respected her feelings. Besides, this may be the only proposal of marriage her daughter would ever receive.

Flavia accepted his proposal, believing that this man Probius was the one that her guardians had spoken of. He was special and he needed her.

Probius came to love Flavia as he never loved before and took her with him on his travels and meetings around the countryside.

It was on one of these journeys that she learned of 'Avalon' and heard the story of the visit to these parts of a man they called 'Joseph of Aramathea', who many years before brought his nephew the Lord Jesus himself to this country. The story of how Joseph of Aramathea, a Holy man, trained in the mysteries, who set out to learn of the Zodiac carved out of the earth, hundreds or even thousands of years before.

Many years later, when Jesus was killed, Joseph returned to Avalon and placed his staff on the hill which in the ancient Zodiac represents the sign of Pisces. This was the sign the mystics knew would rule over the affairs of the earth for the next two thousand years. Joseph believed that the teachings of Jesus indicated that he was Lord of that sign and the staff he placed on the hill was a test to confirm this knowledge. When the staff took root and burst into bloom near to the birthday of Jesus, Joseph, knew he was right. He built a church nearby and settled down with - it was said - thirteen members of the Holy family, whose descendants still live in our country.

Flavia, as expected, became pregnant and amid great happiness and excitement, gave birth to a baby boy, a son for Probius. His dream had come true. However, his dream was short lived. Within six months, the baby died in his sleep.

Probius, believing he was being punished by the Gods, shut himself away and Flavia heart-broken, blamed herself. She had lost her baby and now she was losing her husband as well. She went to see him and pleaded with him, "We could try again?".

"But", he told her, "It is too late. I am too old. Don't feel bad my dearest. You have given me more happiness than I ever knew before and I did have a son. But, you are much too beautiful to be tied to an old man like me".

Flavia protested, "No! You don't understand. I love you".

Probius took her hand in his and spoke softly to her, "You are young and I am about to leave this world. I want you to bring Sarah back from her grandparents to help you. I have divided my wealth fairly between you. Use your share to do good in the village and to take care of the poor. I know that you have it in your heart to do that and let Sarah care for her grandparents".

Probius died within days and Flavia was broken-hearted - going to her bedchamber distraught. Then, remembering her guardians, she sat up. Drawing her knees up to her chin, first she prayed, then she called out in anger, "Why did he have to die? You promised me a life with someone special, then you take him away". Tears of deep sorrow flowed down her cheeks and on to her bedcovers.

Then she became aware of the presence of her guardian. He drew close to her, so that she could plainly see him. His words filled her mind.

"Blessed child. We have not broken our promise. Probius merely prepared you for what is to come. He is not the one we spoke of. There is another who needs you. One with whom you will share the rest of your life. Believe that your greatest happiness lies ahead. Go now and begin to serve."

Flavia realised that her life had altered dramatically through her short life with Probius. He had made her grow up into a mature woman; gave her opportunities to learn of many things during her travels with him and she had learned to govern the estate and handle money wisely. Now, she had the authority to take care of the poor. Her gentle nature and desire to help in any way, made her a respected and honoured mistress of the estate. Since the passing of Probius, she had developed her powerful intuition and her childhood as the village idiot ensured her great compassion for those less fortunate. She never would forget the pain inflicted by the thoughtless actions and words of others.

Over the next three years, she became highly respected for her hard work as manager, councillor and solver of everyone's problems and her devotion to duty.

Sarah and her grandparents moved into the house, Jess welcoming them and their company, for it could get lonely in the big house whilst Flavia was working.

Sarah's grandparents were not too happy when they heard that their deceased daughter's husband, was taking yet another wife in order to have a son, as they thought that their granddaughter would lose her share of his estate, in favour of his new wife. However, they had long since changed their minds, for when they came to know Flavia, it was plain that Sarah would be treated fairly and receive her full entitlement.

One of the farm workers - Julian - had become a devout Christian and had heard of the story of Jesus having visited Avalon. Remembering that the Lord Probius had taken Flavia there, he was forever asking her questions, "What was it like? How long did it take to get there? Did you feel his presence there?". Since Flavia was not then such a devout Christian, she did not know how to answer him, but one day after his endless questioning, she rashly promised to lead him and his future wife Emma on a pilgrimage. No sooner had she said it, than she regretted it. It was a long way away and she simply could not spare the time away from the estate. Surprisingly, when she mentioned it to Jess, she thought it was a good idea. "You work too hard. It will do you good to get away. I will be fine, now that Sarah and her grandparents are here to keep me company."

It seemed to Flavia that it was some kind of conspiracy to get rid of her and she felt sure that the farm manager would say he could not do without her. He didn't! He even asked how he could help her! "Don't worry", he said, "Everything will continue the same as usual until you come back".

So, Christmas was chosen as the best time to arrive in Avalon. Julian and Emma were all excited, Flavia having told them that it was the best time to be there. People from far off places gathered there to celebrate both Christmas and Yuletide, the ancient festival that said goodbye to the shortest day of the year and welcomed the return of the Sun to the north.

The time came to leave and all the preparations had been made. They would walk five or six miles north west, then spend the night at the inn, then hope to join a caravan on the traders' route east.

She chose an old red dress to travel in, which had deep folds and the extra material would keep her warm. She would also wear her thick woollen cloak and soft leather boots that were specially made for comfort. She was not looking forward to this long journey, as it would remind her of the time she spent there with her husband.

Now she came to think about it, those years were buried deep in the past and it had been some time now since she had given thought to the man who was responsible for her being here. She put it down to keeping herself busy.

It puzzled her how she appeared to be being pushed into this pilgrimage against her will. Excuses she made were all brushed aside, until she gave up looking for more.

The day came, bright and sunny, but breezy with a nip in the air and they met at the small temple in the village which once honoured another god. Now, it had been transformed into a Christian meeting room - with Julian in charge.

He asked for God's blessings on the pilgrimage and for their safety on the way. Each one carried a small amount of food, some water and some money to spend.

They set off at a fair pace and covered several miles. They were within a few miles of the inn, when Julian screamed and sat on the ground, rolling about in agony. He had half stepped on a rock and twisted his foot. He cried out, "I think it is broken - I heard it crack". He moaned and Emma began to panic.

They could not go back, they could only go on, somehow.

The other two men put Julian's arms around their necks, to enable him to hop along on one foot, but it quickly became obvious that this was not satisfactory. So, the men crossed their arms and held hands and carried him, stopping often to rest. By the time they reached the inn, they were exhausted and instead of having a meal and moving on, they were forced to book rooms for the night, the men in one room, ladies in another. Unfortunately, Julian could not get up the stairs and had to sit in the innkeeper's own comfortable armchair at the back of the inn, where he had to stay all night with his foot propped up on a cushion.

When morning came, they held a meeting to discuss whether they should all go home, or wait until Julian's foot healed? They all agreed that they would stay together and if Julian and Emma were forced to return home, they would all go and the pilgrimage would have to wait until the following year. Julian was so disappointed.

Next morning, Flavia decided to walk into the village to inquire at the stables if there was a coach to take them home? She stepped from the inn and stopped for a few minutes to watch a ship arrive. It was an exciting scene, with a lot of men shouting instructions to one another. She watched the gangway being placed in position and passengers begin to descend, before hurrying towards her intended destination.

At the stables, she learned that the only coach to go anywhere near their village, did not leave for another three days. She'd had a strange feeling inside about this pilgrimage, 'What are we to do now?', she asked herself, 'Staying at the inn for several days will use up all our money. Well, when all else fails - pray!'.

As she walked back towards the inn, she called out to her guardians, 'Where are you when I need you? We have prepared for this trip for such a long time. Julian and the others will be so disappointed'.

She entered the now crowded inn and was making her way towards the back room where Julian and Emma waited, when the innkeeper called her over, "Madam. You are in luck. There is a healer amongst the ship's passengers who says he might be able to help you". He pointed to Joseph.

She had approached him, then there was that embarrassing scene, where she had to introduce herself.

But, then Maun had stood up and said he would help. He was the youngest of the four men who sat together and the most unlikely to be the healer, she had thought.

Suddenly for Flavia, her perception of the scene around her changed. It was as though a fragment of the sun had floated down to earth and lodged in her heart. She felt glowing in a light that held only herself and Maun. The rest of the people and the inn fell into deep shadow and she heard a voice say, "I will take you to him". Then she realised that the voice was her own. This feeling had started when Maun began to speak. His voice was so soft; so beautiful and his smile so warm. She then took him to Julian, who was still propped up in the innkeeper's chair. He had not slept well and looked very unhappy.

Flavia had put her arm around him and said, "Help has come. You will soon be well". Maun knelt down and removed the cold water pad from Julian's foot.

This feeling of light was still with her. She felt strange and unreal. 'My God! What is happening to me here?' Then, she realised she could see two bright figures on either side of Maun. As she watched fascinated, another figure entered her vision and she recognised him as her own guardian. He smiled at her, then held out his right hand to Maun and his left hand to her. Then, he clasped both hands together. His message was crystal clear.

Flavia remembered that day vividly. Even as she had led the pilgrims away and sailed over the water on the ferry boat that would take them to join the traders' caravan. She was still glowing at the memory of Julian's healing and meeting Maun. There was not a shadow of a doubt that they would meet again. A powerful link had been forged between them.

The pilgrimage had been a great success. Julian was thrilled with the healing and enjoyed the whole event. He kept saying, "Isn't it wonderful? To think I might have had to return home".

They had managed to get taken a good part of the way on the back of a cart which followed the mules with their heavy back packs of clay and metals, Flavia felt sorry for them, having to carry so much.

Most of the trade in the South West was transported by ship, however some traders were afraid of the sea, as so many ships were lost and so many people drowned. Instead, mule trains were a common sight and were used by the civilian traders as well as the Army.

At Avalon, they had held hands and meditated around the 'Holy Thorn Tree' and collected some fallen leaves to take home as momentos. They attended a Christian service in a church built on the site of Joseph of Aramathea's original and they sang hymns around an open-air log fire.

Flavia knew that she would meet Maun again - but when? She would have to be patient. Training for the priesthood took a long time. She had waited patiently, believing and trusting her guardians.

It was, therefore, unexpected when after less than two years, she began to feel that Maun was preparing to come home. The vision of the church at Avalon kept coming into her mind and as the days passed, the compulsion to prepare for the journey became stronger. She knew for certain he would be there for the coming Christmas and she had thought about him constantly, wondering how he was and sometimes she could pick up his thoughts. There was also the time when she was aware of his unhappiness, then found she could see him healing a young Brother who seemed to be losing a lot of blood. She had even managed to speak to him on that occasion, however, that did not happen often, but that they were in harmony with one another, was clear.

She called on Julian and Emma, who had since married and had their first child, saying "I know that you are unable to come with me. But, perhaps one or two of your friends would like to come".

Julian suggested Rebecca, the young woman who worked at the poultry farm, "She was sorry she could not come last time and, perhaps, Sholto - he is very keen! If you like Flavia, I will ask around".

Only five were free to go, the others being committed one way or another. Five was enough. Three women and two men and plans were made.

She had seen on her travels, that enterprising people created for their comfort, covered wagons. She had also seen these at the end of the wagon trains and guessed that the men took turns sleeping in them. Remembering the trouble they had on their previous pilgrimage - when Julian had to be carried - Flavia decided they would have their own transport and she consulted the estate coachman and asked if he could convert one of the large farm wagons.

He was enthusiastic and accepted the challenge, some of the farm workers also keen to help. Soft beaten leather was chosen to cover the roof arches, being warm and weatherproof and the floor was covered by a straw filled mattress. Soft cushions were placed around the inside to give extra comfort and there was sufficient space for extra clothes, blankets, food and drink.

Jess had been told about the pilgrimage and had prepared herself mentally for Flavia's departure. Although she did not want her to go, she had always wanted the best for her daughter. Flavia had told her about Maun and Jess understood that he was very special to her and that she cared very much for him. Jess knew if all went well with this meeting, she may never see her daughter again, but fortunately, Sarah and her grandparents would be pleased to run the estate in Flavia's absence.

The day came when the wagon was ready. They were given the biggest and strongest horse and everything was packed for the long journey.

They waved goodbye to their families and they set off.

CHAPTER XXXVIII

EVAN AND MARGARETTA

With their new found wealth, Evan, Margaretta and Karl were enjoying life and Evan was busy supervising the reconstruction of the boarding house, much to the irritation of the professional craftsmen.

Margaretta was cooking and delighted in being able to lift her heavy cooking pots, their home being a hive of industry.

Young Karl was making up for lost time, going out and about with his friends. It was wonderful to have his mother well again and his father at home permanently, although he missed his brother Adam. However, there were compensations.

He had been walking by the docks with his friends, when he stopped to watch a ship in the harbour. "Would you look at that?", said one of his friends, "That is what I would call a real ship" and they stood watching it for some time.

Margaretta put the food on the table, smiling cheerfully. Expecting praise for her efforts, she was not disappointed, Evan and Karl remarking on the aroma, then on the taste and then asked for seconds.

However, it was not until after their meal that Karl mentioned the ship. Evan was only mildly interested, until Karl mentioned the three symbols on the shield - a tree, a ship and …! At this point, Evan held up his hand, "Don't tell me. The third portion has a Christian cross".

Evan, deep in thought, after a pause continued, "What you saw, my son was the family crest of Maun's grandparents. It means that the ship was built at their yard. I must go and see it for myself. It is possible that one or two of his family will be on board. Come, my son. Show me where this ship is".

They hurried down to the dock and made their way to where Karl had seen the vessel. Much to their disappointment, the ship was not in sight. Not to be put off, Evan went to see the harbour master. "Yes Sir", he said, "The ship sailed not half an hour ago. It came from north Briton. The men told me that the owner's son was aboard and that they were on their way to Tours".

Evan's heart was pounding and by the time they arrived home, he had made up his mind and said to Margaretta, "How would you like to go to Tours and meet Calpurnius and see Adam and Maun again?".

Margaretta asked him, "What about the house and the repairs?".

"Never mind about that. We will leave that to the professionals." He laughed, "I think they will cheer when I tell them I am going away for a while. Get your best dress ready. We will leave in the morning".

CHAPTER XXXIX

ORDINATION

Rome, at this time, was being threatened by hoards of warriors from the east. The Pope was either in hiding, or travelling in Gaul. However, despite these difficulties, somehow his ring seal of approval for the ordination of seven young novice priests was obtained.

Joseph thought it a coincidence that six of the seven novices happened to be those whom Maun had healed, the seventh being Maun himself. 'I am getting cynical in my old age'," he thought, 'Strange though, how they managed to find His Holiness at a time like this'.

Stranger still was why these young men who were Maun's staunchest supporters, were also being ordained. He was aware that people who had received healing from Maun developed their own special gifts, however, working in the Abbey as he did, he knew of the constant stream of sick, crippled and downright weary souls who came in search of the novice priests who healed.

The bishops - and other members of the Church hierarchy - did not take kindly to their easy going and peaceful routine of the Abbey being disrupted by these unwelcome visitors.

The ordination of the novices seemed to Joseph to have been arranged with undue haste. His suspicions would not go away, however, he decided to be philosophical, 'What does it matter? I don't care how, or why. The only thing that matters is that we have achieved what we set out to achieve. This time next week, my grandson will be a priest of the Holy Church where he belongs'.

Maun had worked hard, memorising his responses and every service and sermon that a priest should know. He was now word perfect.

He sat with his grandfather enjoying Madam Leoni's excellent fruit bread and drinking diluted wine. "Are you nervous my boy?", Joseph asked him.

"No Sir. Not of making my vows. Although I am worried about falling on my face!"

Joseph laughed, "You do not have to fall very hard. Just think, my son. You will soon be Father Maun".

"Grandfather", said Maun, "Is there any rule that says I must be addressed as Father?".

Joseph was perplexed, "I don't know Maun, although 'Father' is not spoken the same in other languages. Therefore, to answer your question, I would have to say no, there is no rule. But, why do you ask?".

"Grandfather, you and other priests I know, have worked endlessly for the honour of your title. Your experience is vast and I feel inadequate. That I love our Lord Jesus and believe his miracles and his teachings, I have no doubts. However, I have reservations regarding the many rituals and the dressing up in expensive robes. Did our Lord not say that these things were meaningless and that what mattered to God was the quality of the human soul?"

"I agree wholeheartedly, Maun", said Joseph, "However, Christianity is a religious order and members need to be able to recognise each other; also for people who come to us for help, or seek our advice, it is important they know they are speaking to an official priest. Our dressing up, as you call it, is our uniform. Just like your Army friends, Joshua and Max find it necessary to recognise their more senior officers. So, for these reasons alone, these robes are useful."

Joseph studied his grandson's unhappy face and said, "I suppose my son, you can call yourself by another name if you wish to do so, just so long as the meaning is the same and people are aware of who and what you are".

"Have you a name in mind, my boy?".

Maun looked Joseph in the eye and said, "I have been for many months now, referred to as Patris by those in the military. I am told it means Father of the Church. I have grown accustomed to it and feel that it suits me better".

"Well", said Joseph, "The meaning does appear to be the same. So, if that is what pleases you my son, so be it. However, I do not think you should act on that until you are back in your own country".

"Are you offended grandfather?", asked Maun, "That I should chose to be different".

"Bless your heart, my son. It would take more than that to offend me. Shall I tell you something Maun? I have my individual thoughts also that I usually keep to myself. I have inquired into other faiths and what I have seen has distressed me, for I have found fanatics leading the pathetic; whose individual beauty and unique gifts are buried in a deep sea of conformity. I, my son, welcome your individuality."

"So, my boy, may you always do and say what you feel to be right for those who come to you for help, regardless of the rules."

Maun hugged his grandfather, "I hoped you would approve and say something like that".

CHAPTER XL

THE ARRIVAL OF CONCHESSA
AND CALPURNIUS

Joseph was as usual going about his duties in an automatic manner, his mind occupied by thoughts of events that had happened in his life. So engrossed was he, that at times he spoke out loud. He hoped no one was around to hear his mutterings, or if there were people around, they would think he was at prayer and take no notice.

Suddenly and unexpectedly, he heard a familiar voice, "Father! Father!". He turned around to see Conchessa hurrying towards him, with Calpurnius following and trying to keep up with her. She rushed into his arms and hugged him so tight, "Oh father, it is wonderful to see you again. You look so well - Gaul must agree with you".

Before he could reply, she asked, "Where is Maun? Is he well?".

"Allow me to get my breath back and I will tell you", said Joseph, "You have arrived just in time. Maun is to be ordained in a few days. He is well and he will be overjoyed to see you both".

Joseph spoke to one of the other priests on duty, "Should anyone be looking for me, will you please tell them I have been called away on an important matter".

"Now, come with me to my home and my housekeeper will make you something to eat."

They walked the short distance to his home and Madam Leoni was happy to meet Joseph's family. There was plenty of prepared food and Conchessa and Calpurnius wanted to hear all the news about their son.

Joseph told them everything he could remember. He had to think hard, as his memory was not quite as sharp as it used to be, but he was able to satisfy their immediate curiosity. "When we have had our meal, we will go to see him. He will be so pleased to see you both. I know he has missed you very much."

When Calpurnius saw Maun, he was overjoyed, "My son. Look how you have grown. You look so well and happy".

"Having you both here has made me happier still", said Maun, "It is so good to see you. Now you must tell me all that has been happening at home".

They told him all about the ship and how they had put off coming in case grandfather Calim needed them, when all the time Calim and Rhona were wondering why they had not made up their minds sooner.

They talked about everything, except Maun's impending ordination.

CHAPTER XLI

PRIESTHOOD

The air in the Abbey was heavy with the pungent smell of incense and burning oil and the chanting of the monks and the Brothers created an atmosphere that was spellbinding. Conchessa and Calpurnius were discretely seated at the back of the Abbey, but they were surprised when Joseph brought some young men to join them. Then, a wonderful surprise, as three more visitors turned up. One they knew was Evan and they guessed that those who were with him were Margaretta and Karl, moments later they were joined by Hanno and Adam.

The ceremony was spectacular. There was not a sound to be heard, other than the voice of the Archbishop and the responses of the young men taking their vows.

The ceremony seemed to go on and on, but when it was over, the guests were pleased to get out into the fresh air. Joseph hurried towards them and introduced Joshua and Max, then the mystery guest, who the others did not know. "I would like you all to meet Antonius Gaius, grandson of our dear friend", which meant nothing to Maun or his friends. However, Calpurnius and Conchessa remembered well the presence of 'Antonius the first' at the port of Dunbriton on the day Joseph and Conchessa arrived and later as the honoured guest at their marriage. They were thrilled to meet him and showed great interest in the young Antonius, relating to him different stories about his grandfather, which Joseph had forgotten.

All of the guests returned to the Hanno's house, where he had arranged food and wine for everyone. Meanwhile, Joseph having collected his small parcel from his private cupboard within the Abbey, waited for Maun to come and join him, then they both followed the others.

Calpurnius said, "I had expected to meet Bishop Martin, having heard so much about the famous Martin from Father Joseph". He was disappointed when told that Martin had been called away to Poitou.

"Seems they have some trouble to sort out there … Hopefully, you will still be here when he returns", said Hanno.

It was an emotional gathering. Evan knew that his son would be leaving with Maun and going to north Briton and that he might never see him again. The three soldiers - Joshua, Max and Antonius - expected to go to war at any time and Joseph knew that this was the very last time he would ever see his beloved daughter and her husband. He knew that he was going to have to break the news to them that he was going to stay behind in Gaul - he'd had enough of these long, cold sea journeys.

He had thought it over very carefully and decided he did not want to return to Bonavon. His work there was finished and it was now time to get back to being an ordinary priest of the Abbey. Besides, these young men did not want him slowing them down.

His eyes wandered over to his daughter and her husband. There was another reason for not leaving. He did not want his beloved daughter to watch him slowly die. 'No, much better if I stay here in my cosy little house with my housekeeper to take care of me.'

His eyes wandered over to his grandson who was talking to Max and Joshua. Joshua was looking into Maun's face in admiration and hanging on his every word; Calpurnius and Antonius were laughing, while his daughter was talking to Margaretta. He felt a lump in his throat as he looked around at all his family and friends, knowing that this was the very last time he would see them. Pulling himself together, he thought, 'I had better cheer up or I shall burst into tears.' So, he stood up, "May I have your attention, please". Everyone stopped talking.

"My dear friends. It is indeed a joy to see my family and friends together, all enjoying this momentous occasion." Joseph then realised that he could not say what he intended, that he was not going back with them, so instead, he said, "I have a gift for my grandson. It is an unusual one, for he is not an easy person to obtain a gift for".

He then produced the parcel and gave it to Maun. Everyone looked on curiously while Maun unrolled the lengths of material. Finally, the robe emerged, Maun was speechless. Recovering, he said, "It is beautiful grandfather", as he held it up in front of him, "It fits perfectly! Thank you grandfather, I like it very much and I will keep it for special occasions".

Whilst they were all admiring the robe, Calpurnius said, "I recognise that robe! Is that not the one you wore to marry us, Father?".

"Yes, indeed it is", said Joseph, "I have kept it safe all these years. Many times I would have given it to the poor, but could not bring myself to do so. It holds such happy memories".

The celebrations went on until dusk and it was time for Joshua, Max and Antonius to return to camp, everyone following them out into the yard to say goodbye. Evan went over to Dancer to renew his acquaintance with his old friend. The stallion on seeing him, began to jump about a little. "Look", called Evan highly pleased, "He remembers me!".

Maun did not like the thought of his friends going to war - or Dancer come to that. He thought, 'He is such a brave young horse, he had suffered enough'. However, he had a strong feeling that his friends and Dancer would survive.

As they rode away, he called out, "Good luck".

They called back, "God bless you, Patris".

"What now?", asked Evan, once they were all back inside the house, "Are you going to stay in Gaul, or are you going back to north Briton?".

"We are going home", said Maun, "Back to see how the work progresses at Bonavon. From then on, we will have to trust in God to direct us".

"However, before that, I have an appointment to keep at Avalon."

Joseph, Evan and Hanno exchanged knowing glances, but said nothing, however Calpurnius responded immediately, "Avalon? Where is Avalon? What is so special there to make us stray from our journey home".

Maun went into some detail about Joseph of Aramathea and the sacred thorn tree, but when he described the signs of the ancient Zodiac which were cut into the earth, Calpurnius was immediately sold on the idea.

Evan smiled to himself and thought, 'So, my lad has not forgotten his pretty pilgrim. I hope she has not forgotten him'.

Joseph then broke the news that he would not be going back with them and as expected Conchessa was very upset and not a little hurt. Joseph explained, "My dear daughter. My work there finished on the day Maun returned home and the brothers took over at the school. What would I do there now? I have unfinished work to do here in Tours. Our Lord was right when he said, 'The poor are always with us'. Working here in the Abbey and walking in the town, I can see that the need is greater here".

The next day, Evan, Margaretta and Karl went home and the day after, Calpurnius, Conchessa Maun, Hanno and Adam all said goodbye to Joseph and set sail for Avalon.

Joseph returned to his little house, feeling empty inside, yet relieved that he could now get on with his own life. As he opened the door, the aroma of his hot supper filled his nostrils and he took a deep breath, hung his cloak on the hook behind the door and warmed his hands by the fire. He sighed and thought to himself, 'Yes. I have done the right thing. I have not deserted my grandson, or my beloved daughter. I will pray for them - it worked once before'.

Flavia and her five companions were well on their way, the road now becoming familiar, this being the third time she had made the pilgrimage.

Now that they had the wagon, they could take turns to rest or sit up front watching the scenery pass them by and although they would not need to sleep overnight at the inn, they decided to call in and have a good meal.

Flavia wanted to stand where Maun stood when she first saw him, although she was pleased that the others were not aware of the significance of her plan, as she thought it would allow her to feel a little closer to him and maybe, relive in her mind, the experience of two years before. Of one thing she was certain, he had not forgotten her, indeed the more she thought of him, the clearer she could see him in her mind's eye. The picture she received was of him waiting for her at the entrance to St. Joseph's church in Avalon.

The inn was empty and as no ships were due for a day or two, the innkeeper was only too eager to please them, providing a good meal and allowing them to hire a room to freshen up before they moved on.

It was a happy trip. Caradoc played a flute, while the others sang at the top of their voices and they were so busy that the entire journey seemed much shorter.

They had travelled for about a day and a half, when in the distance, they first saw the distinctive shape of Tor Hill come into view. Suddenly, the horse pulling their wagon, reared-up and then whinnied, before finally stopping completely. It did not take long for them to discover the reason why. In front, straddling the road, some rough-looking men stood wielding clubs. One of the men immediately grabbed the nervous horse's reins and began to lead him with the wagon and the terrified passengers into a nearby wooded enclosure.

CHAPTER XLII

REFUGEES

The *Leelan* sailed along the channel towards the lower Severn, to an old harbour once used by the Army, this being as far east as a vessel of its size could sail. The local people had been watching the ship approach for some time and had paddled out in their small craft to greet them. They were met enthusiastically by the Captain and crew, who proudly showed enthralled visitors around. To be on such a modern ship was exciting and they eagerly examined everything.

Calpurnius inquired of the villagers how far it was to Avalon and was pleased to hear that it was only about twelve miles away and for a small fee, they could be taken there.

On dry land, all five of them waited while a wagon was brought out of its shelter. It was one reserved for special occasions, brightly painted with exotic flowers and birds decorating the whole wagon and despite being open to the elements, was comfortable enough to ride in, with padded seats and back rests. They found that their driver was helpful, giving them information about the Yuletide celebrations, however, he knew nothing of Christmas - or of ancient legends.

Before leaving, Calpurnius gave the *Leelan's* crew instructions, "If we are not back in a week's time, come and look for us" (this was meant as a joke, for they intended only to stay a few days). It had been arranged that the driver and the wagon would wait in Avalon to bring them back to the *Leelan,* when they had seen everything they wanted to see and Maun had met up with his friends again. So, the journey began and wrapped up well against the chilly weather, they set off.

Maun had been very excited at the thought of seeing Flavia and he was curious about Avalon. 'Would it live up to his expectations?', he wondered. He would have to wait and see. For the last two years, he had been certain of seeing Flavia again - here in Avalon - but right now, in this wagon, he developed an odd feeling in the pit of his stomach, the feeling that all was not well. He felt sure Flavia was trying to communicate with him, but the message was confused and it worried him.

They were all pleasantly surprised, when on reaching Avalon, they found the small town extremely busy. There were food stalls all along the streets, each giving out a different and tantalising smell; roasting meat, baked bread and sweet cakes, apples and pressed apple juice, milk, boiled eggs. The whole centre of the town was alive and vibrant, with hundreds of visitors and performing artists giving it a festival atmosphere and they were glad that they had decided to come.

Walking down the centre of the street, they were entertained by jugglers, tight rope walkers, men on stilts and dancers, but Maun and Hanno were concentrating on searching the faces in the crowd in the hope of spotting a familiar one. There were none. As they slowly passed along the rows of stalls, each one selling different wares, Calpurnius and Conchessa bought some sweet cakes wrapped in leaves from one of the stallholders, then sharing them with the others, until at the end of the road they came upon the church of St. Joseph. A round building, with pillars at either side of the double doors, they entered the building and gave thanks for their safe journey and asked that the remainder of their voyage north would be equally uneventful. Calpurnius asked the preacher about the story of Joseph of Aramathea, the priest being only too willing to relate all he knew, including the story of the Chalice in the well. Fascinated by this, Calpurnius and Conchessa wanted to visit it right away, but Maun said, "Please go, but I must wait by the church in case my friends arrive".

Maun waited patiently, not wandering anywhere out of sight of the church doorway, his uneasiness growing. He paced unconsciously, praying all the time that Flavia would turn up and thinking of the consequences if she didn't and he thought, 'I will never see her again. Oh Lord, please guide her here ... *please!*'.

Hanno and Adam arrived, Hanno told him, "I've been looking around to see if I recognised any of the pilgrims, but so far, no luck. Why don't you come and see the dancers, Patris? There are men along there with antlers on their heads and some with bells on their legs".

"If the pilgrims turn up, they will come looking for you."

"I had better not," said Maun, "But, you go and enjoy yourselves. Please, don't worry about me, there is a lot for me to see waiting here".

"Are you sure? We don't like to leave you here alone."

Maun forced a smile, "I'm fine. Please go".

The longer he waited, the more worried he became. He could hear the music of the dancers, the drum beat, the weird pipe and the bells, then he saw his parents coming towards him. "Still no sign of your friends, my dear", said Conchessa, "How disappointing for you".

"I think we should return to the ship", said Calpurnius, "There is not one room to be had at any of the inns. As expected, they are full and if we want to rest tonight, we had better start back now. I am sorry my son, your friends have not arrived. Perhaps, they have been delayed? It will begin to get dark soon. We had better find our wagon and get back to the *Leelan*. Your mother is tired".

It was with a heavy heart that Maun agreed to go with them and then Hanno nudged him, "Patris! Look, there."

Standing between the pillars of the Temple, was a lone figure of a woman in a long cloak, the hood covering most of her face. Maun's heart began to pound. He walked cautiously towards her, his hands trembling as he slowly lifted the hood from her face. There was a lump in his throat as he whispered her name, "Flavia".

He was shocked at her thin and tired face and as he put his arms around her and held her close. He kissed her cheek then spoke softly, "What in God's name has happened to you?".

She held on to him for a few moments before speaking, "My dearest. You must come with me. There is a great deal of healing work to be done".

"On our way here two days ago, we were captured by men who we thought were bandits, But, it happened that they were people in trouble - they were all sick and starving. We did what we could for them, but it was not enough. If you and your family have any money, I beg of you that you buy as much food and blankets as you can and come with me."

Calpurnius and Conchessa had been watching their son take this woman in his arms and embrace her. It was so unexpected, they stood with their mouths open, astounded at the sight. Hanno was amused by their expressions and Calpurnius, seeing Hanno's grin, turned to him and said, "You knew about this?".

"Yes", replied Hanno, "But, it was not for me to tell you about it, for if she had not turned up, Maun would have been embarrassed".

Just then, Maun brought Flavia over to them. He still had his arm around her as he introduced her to his parents, "Mama and Papa. This is Flavia". The way he looked at her, left his parents in no doubt about his feelings for this young woman.

He wasted no time in advising his parents of what Flavia had just told him about being taken by bandits and how it had been discovered that the men and their families were in trouble. He said, "They have escaped from somewhere and have nothing, save what they have on their backs. They are in desperate need of help and healing".

Calpurnius immediately began organising a shopping spree; all the food and drink they could carry and all the blankets and skins they could pack into the wagon that brought them, the driver being only too willing to lend a hand.

Flavia then made a sign and her covered wagon came into view from around the back of the temple, one of the older male refugees in charge. By now it was dusk and they knew they had to hurry.

Arriving at the ruins of what had been once a substantial house, Flavia was assisted down from her wagon by Maun. "This is where they are", she told him, hurrying to what had been the front of the building and opened the rickety door, they all went inside.

Shocked at seeing the state of the women and children, Calpurnius began immediately to supervise the unloading of the food and blankets from the wagons.

But, Flavia said to Maun, "Allow the others to take care of these things. You must heal". Maun nodded and went with her to one side of the ruin. Here they found some remains of what had been a high wall, which would at least give some shelter from the elements.

Flavia said, "Wait here, Maun and I will bring those most in need" and within moments, she returned with a mother and child, who both looked miserable and half starved. Adam followed her bringing two lamps.

"Perhaps, they should eat first?", said Maun.

"They have just eaten", replied Flavia, "It will take more than a meal to help them!".

Maun took the baby boy in his arms and held him, stroking the his head and face. He was well aware of the power flowing from his hands into the baby, when suddenly it began to cry. Not the sickly whimper as before, but a loud bellow. Flavia smiled and took it from him.

The baby's mother held out her arms to take her baby back, but Flavia held on to him and instead, took the mother's arm and placed her in front of Maun. The woman was very weak and walked as though she found difficulty in breathing.

Maun put his hands on her back and around her shoulders and soon her breathing eased and she stood up straight. The mother then took her baby back from Flavia and walked away. Word soon spread and within seconds everyone had gathered around to watch. Flavia continued to bring the sick before him and he healed them.

CHAPTER XLIII

NEXT DAY

The food that they had brought from Avalon was almost finished, so Calpurnius and one of the refugees, who appeared to be the leader, took the horse and wagon and went into town to buy more. It was then Calpurnius realised that he understood the language the man spoke, not everything, but enough to communicate a little. It was the language of Hibernia, although the accent was slightly different to that of the refugees who arrived in the north.

He learned that these people had been robbed by their landlord, until they had nothing left for themselves. A merchant, who traded in gold and silver and who often crossed the sea to Briton, took pity on them and had promised to take them away to another country. They had gathered their belongings together and went to the harbour, where they boarded a boat that was waiting. Then, word was received that the merchant and his small crew had been arrested and their gold and silver seized. They were advised to cast off and sail away, which they did, only to discover that in their haste, they had not taken on board any food or water, nor was there a sailor on board who could guide the vessel to where they were supposed to go.

It was sheer luck that within four days they spotted land, the boat eventually going aground on a deserted beach. They were cold hungry and some very ill, but somehow they managed to reach the deserted and ruined house. All they had to eat was leaves and grass and they had been forced to drink from puddles of rainwater. The men went in search of anything they could find to improve their lot and on reaching the road and seeing the wagon approach, they had decided to take it into the wood and off the road.

"We did not mean any harm, but were afraid, for we did not know whether we were in a friendly country or not, We were very lucky, for as soon as the young women saw our difficulties, they did all that they could to help. The men lit a fire and the women gave us everything they had, even their own food. They saved our lives."

On their return to the camp, they found everyone working and trying to rebuild as much of the house as possible, in order to make room under cover for everyone.

Calpurnius looked around for his wife; he had bought her some sweet cakes in town, knowing how much she liked them. Then he heard childrens' laughter coming from the building and looking inside, he saw that Conchessa was surrounded by children. She was brushing the hair of one little girl, while singing to them. He was so very proud of her and he thought, 'She still has that wonderful affinity with little children, even after all these years'.

They all worked hard in order to help the refugees settle in their new country, but at the end of two weeks, Calpurnius decided it was time for them to get back to the *Leelan* and continue their voyage home. Their wagon driver had been back to the ship several times to advise the Captain of everything that was happening and to collect Conchessa's maidservant, as well as fresh clothes. Individual members of the crew with special skills also came to help and Conchessa's maidservant, who assumed she would be tending her mistress, found herself helping her to care for the children, a situation she was not too pleased about (not after the cleanliness of the ship). She was overjoyed when Calpurnius said, "Only one more week, so let us work to that end".

The pilgrims were also planning to leave. Their covered wagon was cleaned, the straw mattress hung out to air and food and drink stored for the journey.

They did not need to be told that their Mistress Flavia would not be going back with them, for they had watched her and Maun working as one and knew they would not part. But, they were just a little surprised, when Rebecca said, "When you get home, please tell everyone that I am going to stay with Flavia as her companion". Flavia had never had a personal maid and what she could not do for herself, her mother Jess had always been on hand to help. Now Rebecca had volunteered her services, that would mean only four of them on the road home - there would be more space for them to spread out!

Rebecca had been upset when she heard that the pilgrims were planning to return home and she went to see Flavia and asked her to employ her as a companion, or even a maid servant, so that she could be near Hanno. Flavia was not surprised, for she had noticed there was a growing attraction between them. However, they were both very shy and proud people and they had never spoken or even acknowledged one another and neither had experienced romance.

Rebecca was tall and elegant and had always considered her stature a drawback to romance, living as she did in a community of small to average size people. Then she saw Hanno, the tall foreigner, who was not only good-looking, but was also very intelligent. She made up her mind that he was the only man for her.

As for Hanno, he had in the past, always given the impression that he was not interested in women (not that he was ever other than polite and considerate towards them). He seemed unwilling to become involved, as though he feared he would be distracted from his work. However, when he saw Rebecca moving gracefully amongst the refugees, caring and compassionate, his resolve vanished.

When he heard that the pilgrims were going home earlier than planned, he panicked. He realised that if he let her go now, he would never see her again. He went to see Maun and found him talking to Flavia in the now restored part of the building. However, when Flavia saw how anxious Hanno looked, she left.

"Are you well, Hanno?", asked Maun.

Hanno was trembling. He did not answer the question. Instead he asked, "Is it true the pilgrims are going home ... I just heard from Calpurnius ....?".

"Why yes", replied Maun, "They will leave in a day or so".

Hanno was flustered, quite unlike his normal unflappable self, "You are not allowing Flavia to go away?".

"No. I am not", said Maun, "She is coming with me to Bonavon".

Then Hanno blurted out, "Maun. I don't want Becky to go".

It was at this point Maun realised that Hanno did not know that Becky had already made arrangements to be Flavia's companion. Remembering the many times Hanno had laughed when Evan had teased him in the past, he decided to enjoy just a little sweet revenge. Maun shook his head, "This could be difficult, my friend. You see, Flavia has already chosen one of the pilgrims to be her companion and I understand plans have already been made".

Hanno's heart sank, "Which one Maun? Which of the pilgrims did Flavia choose?".

"You know, I have quite forgotten", said Maun (trying to sound convincing), "If you wait here a moment, I will go and ask her".

Maun went outside and called to Flavia, then said loud enough for Hanno to hear, "Who is the young lady who is to come with us?".

Flavia eyed him with suspicion, "You know very …". She got no further.

Maun said quietly, "I know who she is", then he smiled and pointing back into the building, he whispered, "But, he does not!".

Flavia glanced in and saw Hanno pacing about inside, "Oh! Maun. You are wicked. Go at once and put him out of his misery. l will go and get Becky".

Maun returned inside, "You are in luck Hanno. Flavia has chosen Becky".

Hanno slumped onto a vacant seat, "Thank God! I don't know what I would have done if she had left without knowing how I feel about her".

Maun laughed out loud, "Hanno, everyone knows how you feel about Becky". Hanno looked up at him, a puzzled and embarrassed expression on his face.

"My friend", said Maun, "When a superior and dignified personage, such as yourself, walks into a wall, making his nose bleed; trips over children playing in the grass and falls flat on his face; tries to feed his stew into his ear, allowing it to fall down the front of his tunic, all because he cannot take his eyes from a young lady, his friends begin to suspect that his feelings for her are rather special".

Hanno said, "So, you knew all the time? And Rebecca's passage on the *Leelan* has already been arranged?". Maun nodded.

"And you have been teasing me?"

Maun smiled, "Don't you think it is time you spoke to Becky?".

"I would love to Maun", said Hanno, "But, I am unaccustomed to these feelings. When I get close to her, my courage fails me".

"Well, my dear friend. You will have to make an effort, for on our ship there are few places to hide. If it is any consolation, she feels the same way about you."

Hanno looked relieved, "Are you sure Maun?".

"Yes, my friend. I am very sure. But, why don't you ask her yourself?"

Just then, Flavia came in leading Becky by the hand. She led her to stand in front of Hanno, then without a word spoken, Maun and Flavia left.

Hanno and Becky were nervous and stood for several moments in silence, then in a voice trembling with emotion, Hanno said, "My nose has almost healed".

Becky raised her eyes up to look at him, then smiled, "I'm glad its better".

"And I have almost removed the food marks from my tunic!" They both laughed at the memory of the incident.

Then Hanno said, "I am so glad Flavia chose you to be her companion. I must remember to thank her".

"Yes", said Rebecca, "Although, until I spoke to her, she was unaware she required one".

Hanno shook his head, "What a blathering idiot I am! All of my life I have been proud of my gift for words, but when it really mattered, to communicate with the only lady I have ever wanted, I could not bring myself to say a single one".

Rebecca slowly leaned forward and kissed him on the cheek, "Words are not always necessary. Your actions spoke to me louder than any words ever could".

CHAPTER XLIV

GOING HOME

The weather was good, with not a single cloud to spoil a clear blue sky and it was time for the *Leelan* to set sail once more. They were going home at last.

Calpurnius called a conference with the Captain and crew in order to plan the voyage; which ports to call at to pick up fresh supplies of food and fresh water; what meals the cook should prepare for everyone and most important of all, to work out the mens' pay which they would all receive the moment the ship docked at the port of Dunbriton.

The Captain beamed with pleasure, "Sir", he said addressing Calpurnius, "This voyage has been the ultimate dream of every retired sailor. That a wealthy ship owner would one day arrive at the port and invite him to be the Captain of a brand new ship of the latest design and tell him he can select his own crew. We have loved every moment of this grand adventure and we will all be sorry when it is over. You have given us wonderful memories to talk about and enjoy in our old age".

He looked around proudly at his crew, who all agreed, then he added, "And we are going to be paid for the privilege".

Calpurnius replied, "You have all been a most excellent, versatile and professional crew, who have never quibbled or quarrelled. Every one of you did your very best to make our voyage special; each one of you working way beyond your official duties and what could have been a dull voyage was made extra special by the food our cook provided. I thank you all on behalf of the owners of the Hoel Shipyard and the Leelan family, who built this wonderful ship. Finally, on behalf of all the passengers, God bless you".

Taking his leave of the Captain, Calpurnius went to the galley and poured some apple juice into a glass, adding a spoonful of honey, before giving it a stir. He then made his way to his cabin, where he found Conchessa curled up in her small bunk, fast asleep. Giving here a gentle shake, he said, "Wake up sleepy-head. I've brought you a drink".

Conchessa opened one eye and in a weak voice, said "Let me sleep. I am so tired".

Calpurnius laughed, "If you sleep all day, you won't sleep tonight. Now sip your drink and wake up". As she opened both eyes and struggled to sit up, he said, "I am lonely without you to talk to".

"I am sorry Cal, but I am washed out. I feel that I could sleep amid a class of four-year-old children! Where are the others? Where is Maun?"

Calpurnius grinned, "Well my dear. On the way here I spied Maun and Flavia in a sheltered nook by the galley and I had to struggle over Rebecca and Hanno sitting on the steps outside our cabin".

"Oh!", she said smiling, "And what of Adam. Is he not lonely without his friends?".

"Far from it", said Calpurnius, "He is in love with the ship. I watched him earlier working with the crew and enjoying every moment of it - I expect it is in his blood!".

"I am glad we are taking Maun home with us", said Calpurnius, "Mother and father will be so pleased to see him. They suffered so much when he was taken - it hit them hard".

Conchessa nudged her husband, "I wonder what they will say when they see he has a woman with him?".

"I expect", said Calpurnius, "They will be as surprised as I was when he met her at Avalon and kissed her. I was never so surprised in my life before, more so, because of what he said to me on the day he left with your father. He clearly never expected to meet anyone who would love him. Or that he would love someone like Flavia. He was resigned to a life of loneliness".

"Well", said Conchessa, "That goes to show that God has other plans for our son. We may yet become grandparents!".

Calpurnius's mood changed. He stood up and looking down at his wife and said, "In all seriousness, don't count on that, my dear, for I feel it in my bones that God's plans for our son and his chosen, do not include children".

Conchessa's face fell, "Oh! Cal. Don't say that. I have my heart set on a grandchild".

Conchessa lay down again on the bunk, "What makes you think that, Cal?".

"Our son has far too much work to do", said Calpurnius, "Flavia is a helpmate, a very sensitive young woman. I believe she has been sent to give him courage and companionship - nothing more. I hope I am wrong, but we will just have to wait and see".

Conchessa pulled the covers over her and closed her eyes, "I am so tired, Cal". He sat for a while just watching her. For the few weeks they had spent at the camp with the refugees, she had worked very hard. Every bit as hard as the younger women, neither expecting or given any concession for her age or position. He had watched as she took charge of the little children; playing games, teaching them language, clearing their hair of infestations. She seemed tireless.

Then, one day she had approached him carrying a pair of sheers, "Here, Cal take these and cut my hair off - to here", she said, pointing at her shoulder.

He hesitated, "Why", he asked?, "What is the matter with it?".

She gave him a thunderous look, "It is full of creepy crawlies!".

Calpurnius protested, "I expect Hanno could make up a herbal mixture to get rid of them?".

"That would take too long. Just do what I ask and cut it. Well, what are you waiting for?", she said impatiently.

"Right. I'll do it! I'll do it!", said Calpurnius.

When he had cut off a long hank of her soft brown hair, he held it up and admired it, then spoke with some regret, "I think I will keep this as a memento".

"Oh! No you won't. You will put it on the fire. Go on then," she said impatiently, "Get on with it".

He realised for the first time that his wife had a voice of command that would have put the late and great Commander Gaius to shame. "All right! All right! I'm going" and as he threw the hank of hair on to the fire, he heard it sizzle.

He wondered from where this new and ferocious character had come from? Surely, this was not his sweet and gentle wife?

When he returned to her, she was in the process of sticking her head in a bucket of cold water, although pulling it out quickly! Gasping for breath, she said, "That is freezing!". He laughed at her, but at the same time offered her a drying cloth, which she wrapped around her head turban-like.

She smiled at him, then began to laugh, "Don't look so shocked, my love. It is the only way to get rid of them".

"But, why did I have to do that?", he asked, "Where is that timid maid of yours?".

"She asked to go back to the ship", replied Conchessa, "It was a mistake to bring her. She has led a sheltered life at the villa". Conchessa undid the turban, moved nearer to the fire and combed her now short hair into a simple style.

"You suit it", he said, trying to sound convincing, "It's ... er ...um ... different".

"I don't care how it looks, Cal. I could not stand it any longer. I would have worn my fingers down scratching."

That had happened days before, now he stood in their small cabin looking down at her. She was snuggled down under the covers and had reverted to her usual more gentle self, although it had puzzled him where that other side of her personality had come from. Then, he remembered how Joseph had told him of her determination to accompany him to north Briton, even though they had been led to believe that the natives ran about naked and painted their bodies blue. Their chances of survival were, they believed nil - yet she came.

Calpurnius conjured up a mental picture of the young Conchessa ordering the painted savages around, the natives running away terrified of this little woman. He smiled at the thought. She opened one eye again, "What are you grinning at, Cal? What amuses you so?".

"Nothing, my dear. You go back to sleep. I will find Adam and we will raid the galley" and with a self-pitying glance he left.

The voyage home was uneventful, in so far as it was safe and smooth sailing and the relationships of Maun and Flavia, Hanno and Rebecca and even the long-married Calpurnius and Conchessa grew stronger in every respect.

For the young people, living in such close proximity, there was the risk of becoming over-familiar, or tiring of each other's company; there being no escape in the confined space of the ship. However, that did not happen.

Maun and Flavia discussing plans for their work and how they would listen to and be guided by those above in charge of the healing mission. They seemed to become as one person, acting and speaking with one voice.

Hanno and Rebecca made plans to marry as soon as they settled, either at the villa or Bonavon; they were not quite sure where they would be working from.

Calpurnius and Conchessa had always been in love, but they had seen each other in a new and more powerful light. She saw him take charge of the refugees and earn their respect. The value of his knowledge of a strange language made so much difference. He was a natural leader, yet with dignity and consideration for everyone. He saw her rise to the occasion, taking charge of the children. She fed them, dressed them, played games with them and sang them to sleep, while their parents rested and recovered from their trauma.

The *Leelan* was sighted entering the mouth of the Clyde, word soon reaching Calim, who was delighted and relieved. He sent word to every member of the family to come to the villa, ready to welcome Calpurnius and Conchessa home.

As the ship came into the harbour, Calim, Harran, Clodus, Sergaeus and Paulus were all on the quay waiting and as soon as the ship had docked, they all went on board. Calim was grateful to see his son, but when he saw Maun, he was overcome. He hugged him, "My boy. Your grandmother will be overjoyed to see you".

Then, Maun brought Flavia forward and said, "Grandfather. I would like you to meet Flavia".

Calim was surprised, but too happy to judge the situation. He took her hand in his and said, " I am so pleased to meet you, my dear".

There was a lot of back-slapping and hugging before they left the ship and took their seats in the waiting carriages, Calpurnius and Adam being the last passengers to disembark from the *Leelan*. The crew would stay on board another week to clean up and make the vessel like new again, ready to be sold. They were happy, yet that happiness was tinged with regret.

The ladies all waited on the wide steps of the villa, ears alert for the first sound of horses' hooves on the driveway, followed by the coachman's voice shouting, "Make way! Make way!". Rhona could hardly contain her excitement as she paced up and down.

Many times she regretted her part in asking her son to go to Gaul. He had never before in his life travelled further than the professor's house in Glasco. Suppose something happened to him and his dear wife? She would never have forgiven herself. Now, they were home, 'Thank God!'.

Then the carriages came into view, the first passengers she saw being Maun and Flavia. Although confused for a moment, she recognised her grandson and she called out, "My blessed Lord! It is Maun" and she waved her arms about as though she could not wait for them to get out of the carriage.

Stepping quickly down from the coach, Maun rushed into her arms, it was all too much for Rhona and she wept. Maun held her, "Grandmother, I thought you would be pleased to see me?" and he smiled at her.

She looked into his face, "My darling boy. I could not be happier, but I have been so worried about all my family. We live in such dreadful times".

Calpurnius came and put his arms around her, "What are you doing with that stick, mama? Can't I leave you for a little while before you hurt yourself?".

Calim joined them, "Are you happy now, my love? You have your son, your grandson and your old man to fuss over".

He put her arm in his and helped her walk into one of the reception rooms, her walking stick tap-tapping on the marble floor. When she had calmed down a little, Maun brought Flavia to see her, saying, "Grandmother. I want you to meet Flavia".

Rhona could see clearly by the expression on her grandson's face, that Flavia was someone very special to him and sitting beside Rhona, Flavia said, "Madam Rhona, Maun has told me all about you and I have so looked forward to meeting you".

Rhona searched her face, "Thank you, my dear. It is a pleasure to meet a dear friend of my grandson. Thank you for coming".

There was a great deal of talking and hugging, all the family gathered to eat and drink, the servants flitting around happily, bringing jugs of wine and platters of food. They too sensed the joyfulness of the occasion and felt part of it, Rhona having always been a good employer. She could have had slaves - any number would have been pleased to live and work in the villa without payment because of its grandeur - but, Rhona was a Christian and remembered that every man or woman should be worthy of their hire. She also ensured that her servants always had money to spend when they went to town.

It was Elinor, the wife of Harran who welcomed the other guests and took them in turn to see Rhona, who seemed to be overcome by all the excitement. When she saw Hanno again, she remembered him and on hearing that he had brought his intended wife - and planned to marry her soon - she said, "All this happiness and a marriage to look forward to. It is so wonderful".

Harran asked, "Where is Julia, Sergaeus and our granddaughters?".

Elinor replied, "They will be along presently. Sergaeus has taken the carriage to fetch them".

At that moment, Sergaeus's carriage returned and three beautiful young women ran into the house, calling "Where is he? Where is Maun ?". They ran towards him and taking hold of his arms, dragged him away.

Maun and Flavia had been talking to Calim, when the three boisterous cousins ran towards him, calling out, "Come, Maun and tell us all about Gaul ... Are you a real priest? ... Can you marry people? ... Have you a uniform? ... What colour is it?" and if Flavia was jealous, she did not show it, except perhaps for the high colour on her cheeks. She simply smiled at Calim and looked surprised. He sensed her feelings, "Take no notice of his cousins. They have always thought him wonderful, especially Helen. But, I think he finds them a little too excitable for his quiet taste".

Calim led Flavia to meet Portia and Markus and they explained that their two sons were in school and would not arrive until later. Markus remarked to Calim that he must not let Rhona get too excited, "As she may fall over - it will do her no good to break a bone - although except for her stiffness, she was quite well for her age".

Paulus was there to greet his sister, Conchessa saying, "Hello, big brother. How is Bliss and all of your family?".

Paulus was now nearly fifty years old and was looking his age. He replied, "She stayed at home, Conchessa. If all of them had come, there would have been no room for anyone else. But, I had to come to make sure you arrived. Perhaps, you and Calpurnius will come to Bonavon to see us? There have been many changes there".

"I will", said Conchessa.

Alana returned from checking the beds for everyone. She looked at Conchessa, turning her head from side to side, "Tell me Conchessa. Why are you wearing that white scarf around your head?".

Conchessa laughed, "You might as well know" and with that she removed the scarf, revealing her short hair.

Alana said, "What have you done to your hair?".

Rhona looked shocked.

"My husband cut it", said Conchessa.

"You wicked boy", said Rhona, "Why did you do such a thing?".

"Because, I made him. It was an emergency. But, please do not worry, it will grow again".

Calpurnius then told everyone about the refugees and how they had become involved with them. "That, my dear mama, is how Conchessa lost her hair. She took over the care of the little children without thinking about herself."

Harran remarked that refugees were pouring into the town, "They are in such poor condition. I don't know what is going on in that country over the sea, but it must be bad to make so many people flee from their homes".

"I hear they have even got as far as Bonavon. We will all have to pay the Brothers a visit. I understand they are having some difficulty in coping with the situation. I was told, Maun, that they were praying for your return."

"Then, we must go as soon as possible", said Maun.

Eventually the celebrations ended and Calim took Rhona's arm in order to escort her to their quarters. But Maun took her other arm and said to his grandfather, "Allow me the honour, grandfather". Calim smiled and let her go.

Once in her bedroom, Maun said to her, "Grandmother. Where does it hurt most?".

"My darling", said Rhona, "There is not a bone in my body that does not ache".

Maun said, "Then sit on your wicker chair and I will give you some of my strength". He then stood behind her and placed his hands on her shoulders, then ran his hands down her arms to her hands.

Having held her hands, he then bent over and placed them on her knees, while he stroked her head. Rhona raised her hand and touched his, "You have such warm and soothing hands, my darling. I feel better already". After a moment's silence, she continued, "When you move around the country, my dear, please be very careful." Rhona sounded anxious.

"Grandmother, don't worry about me. I always feel protected when I am working."

"By the way", said Rhona, looking around at him, "I like your young lady. I was watching her when she thought no one was looking her way. She could not take her eyes from you".

Maun flushed, "Yes, I know grandmother. I love her too. We are two of a kind. I was very fortunate in meeting her. Father might say that I should thank my lucky stars".

She laughed at him, "I think he would say, that in a past life, you must have done something to please God. Or, that you were twin souls".

The following day, they made their way to Bonavon in the company of Alana,

Clodus and Paulus, Amyott was at the gate to meet them. "Thank God. My prayers have been answered. We need you, Maun. Need your power. It has been very difficult keeping faith, when all around us seems to be falling apart. There are so many strangers who have no respect for our way of life. They move in and take what they want, without fear of redress."

Maun said, "Don't worry, Amyott. They are from places where no one has ever shown them respect, only fear. We must try to be patient. Are there those among them who need to be healed?".

"I have heard", said Amyott, "That some of them are in a poor health".

"Then", said Maun, "We must hold a healing service and use gentle persuasion to bring them a more peaceful way of thinking, although it might take more than one meeting to allow the word to filter through to those most in need".

Amyott was pleased and said, "I prayed that you would come, for we have so much work to do and cannot get on with it. Our time is taken up trying to keep the village in order. Progress on the Abbey has been delayed and although we would have liked to have shown you a building almost complete, I am afraid, it is more-or-less as you saw it last. It is fortunate, indeed, that we decided to keep Father Joseph's Barn church".

Word was passed around, "Bring out those who are sick - see them healed by faith in our Lord Jesus".

Crowds gathered. Those who knew Maun sat patiently waiting, while the strangers mocked and whistled. They were in the yard of what had been Maun's childhood home and he was not a little hurt and offended at the desecration, but he prayed silently, asking that this meeting would be the beginning of a new life for those who had been so physically and mentally ill treated.

Flavia came to him, "Are you ready, my love? Do not forget Maun. You have the power. *Use it!*".

He raised his hand and pointing at the disbelievers, said in a slightly raised voice, "Be silent!".

At once there was silence. The healing continued; those who were brought forward by Flavia and Adam were healed miraculously.

Soon Flavia moved among the strangers and chose one of the men and he reluctantly went with her. Maun blessed him and healed him of infected boils around his neck.

The meeting went on for several more hours without a heckle or whistle.

When the service of healing was over, they sang a hymn of thankfulness. As Maun made to turn away, Adam hurried towards him, "Patris. You must release their tongues. You bade them be silent. Now they are dumb".

Once again, Maun was astounded at the extent of his power. He raised his eyes and pointing to the silent strangers, said "You may speak now. God be with all of you".

Some of them coughed and then fled, only to return within the hour to offer to help in any way they could. Amyott was happy, "We, of the village, would be grateful, if all of the rubbish spilled was gathered up and burnt". So, his wishes were carried out. The stinking puss and blood stained rags once used as bandages and the walking sticks used by the lame were set alight, the villagers singing as they piled the rubbish on the fire.

Amongst the crowd was another stranger, a sour-faced and sinister-looking individual, who showed no emotion when he witnessed the miracles of healing, but once out of sight, made notes of the events. However, Calpurnius - who had witnessed this - also made notes and he warned his son, "Be careful. You are being spied upon. Give no one reason to accuse you of false practice".

When they arrived back at the villa, Rhona met them on the steps, this time without her walking stick.

That first day at Bonavon would become a pattern for all other healing services.

CHAPTER XLV

BOOTS AND TURNIPS

Sergaeus and his nephew Beran - son of Portia and Markus - were still land agents for Harran and travelled long distances attempting to collect taxes from those who lived on Harran's land. They were aware of the severe difficulties now facing many of the people who once worked for the Army, such as the villagers who had once made boots and other leather goods who were now redundant; some trying to make a living making boots of a different style for the local people who could not afford to buy them; farmers who once sold a whole field of turnips to the Army, now watched them rot in the ground. "The people of those places are failing fast", Sergaeus told the family, "They need help badly".

It was decided that if Maun had to go to such remote places to work, it would be no use whatsoever depending on charity and that he and his helpers would need a comfortable place to sleep, as he could not complete the journey there and back in one day, as well as hold healing services which could last several hours.

So, Calim arranged to have two large tents made of the most weatherproof material available and provided a coach large enough to take four passengers. His plan was that the men should ride their own horses, the ladies having to share the coach carrying the tents, which would be stored on the roof. However, until such time as the tents were ready, meetings would have to held nearer to home.

They did not have long to wait. Within a few weeks, the tents were ready and a journey of some distance was planned.

At the villa, neither Maun and Flavia or Hanno and Rebecca had much time together. Their quarters being at opposite ends of the villa and when they did meet, they were either working or eating in the large dining room.

Hanno asked Maun to make arrangements for his marriage to Rebecca, however, as they had been very busy, Maun promised that their next trip would be the last for a few weeks and on their return, he would be happy to perform the ceremony.

The meeting was the largest ever, crowds were pouring in from miles around, unfortunately Rebecca had became sick just as she was about to enter the coach. She insisted Hanno should not remain with her, but go with Maun as arranged. Conchessa also backed out, saying that she had to catch up with household duties. This meant that Flavia would be the only woman present and she knew she could not let Maun down, as he relied on her.

The healing went on for hours. as did the screams of delight as one person after another was healed. Even when there were no more patients waiting to be healed, the crowds gathered around Maun asking questions, reluctant to let him go.

He blessed them and told them to look within themselves, saying "Each one of you have gifts to develop and use".

Calpurnius came then and told the crowd that it was time for them to leave, as the weather was changing, "Please go to your homes now. It is not fit to be out". However, they still did not leave, but gathered around the ritual fire, burning rubbish and discarded crutches.

Despite the crowd's obvious reluctance, Calpurnius asked Maun to hurry saying, "The weather is breaking".

It had been a bright and sunny day for early spring, but the sun had now set and a breeze began to blow and it became bitterly cold. Flavia was already settled in the coach and the men were already astride their horses, when Maun came running towards them and mounted his horse. Sergaeus called out, "Its already getting dark. A frost is beginning to form on the ground and I doubt we will make it home tonight. Better, if we find a sheltered place to camp. It is too dangerous to go on".

They had not travelled far before they found such a place, a hill that would shelter them from the east wind. Calpurnius tried to light a fire, but the wood was too damp to light from his flint sticks, so he went to the carriage and wrenching off the back of the seat, chopped it into tiny splinters. Within a short time, these caught alight and the fire blazed.

They erected one of the tents by the light of the moon and laid the other one on the ground to provide a dry floor. The horses were tethered to a tree close to the hill and provided with some protection from the weather in the lee of the carriage, but as extra protection, Sergaeus also put on their long horse coats.

There was still one problem - Flavia. Calpurnius, after apologising for ruining the inside of the coach - where she might have been able to sleep - and for using the second tent as a groundsheet, arranged for a rope to be strung across a section of the tent and a curtain of blankets to offer her privacy. She didn't appear to mind and said she would be comfortable enough in her small partition and safe from wild animals.

There was ample bedding and in addition to having their own bedrolls, there were sheepskins and blankets. Before making their own beds, they first ensured that Flavia had enough covers. The tent was warm and comfortable and they sat inside while Calpurnius brought from the fire a jug of warm ale, to which he added a large spoonful of honey and poured each of them a measure. Feeling content, they retired to bed and everyone, including Flavia, soon drifted off to sleep.

However, as the night went on, the wind changed direction. The fire was almost out and it became bitterly cold, although the men were warm enough huddled together, Flavia woke up, freezing cold. She did not know what to do and as she would not enter the mens' section of the tent, she stayed in her bed shivering. At one point, she must have made a sound and Maun on hearing her immediately jumped out of his bed and went to her. He asked anxiously, "What ever is the matter, Flavia?".

"Oh! Maun ... I think I will die of cold."

He hurried back to his bed, picked the lot up and carried it through the partition. Remaking her bed using all of his bedding, he then got in between the covers and holding out his hand to her, he said, "Come. We will keep each other warm". Flavia immediately did as she was bid, but she was well aware of the situation.

Calpurnius woke up when he heard Maun move around. He also heard Flavia say, "I think I will die of cold", so he also got up, pulled on a large wide brimmed hat and wrapping himself in an extra blanket went outside. He went to the carriage and wrenching off the other seat, he tossed it into the dying embers. Almost at once the fire came to life again, Calpurnius then put on the wood that he had left to dry. Very soon the fire began to throw off some heat.

Maun and Flavia were soon warm and comfortable and fell asleep, but after a few hours, Maun awoke.

Aware of the soft and warm body of Flavia next to him, he wanted to love her, 'But, how could he?'. He had come to her bed uninvited in order to heal her and he would not take advantage of his power, or of her trust in him.

Having wrestled with his conscience, he withdrew his arm from around her and turned away. With that, Flavia woke up and raising herself on one elbow, she leaned over him. She put her hand on his face and when she felt his mouth she brushed her lips over his. He felt her warm breath now in his ear, "Maun", she whispered, "Do not deny our love. Do not deny me".

With that, he turned to face her and embraced her and they loved each other.

Outside, Calpurnius first talked to the horses, then scouted around to find more fallen branches to burn on the fire. Taking the keg of ale, he poured some into a pot and put it to warm beside the fire, then he sat on a log to think.

Knowing that his son was with Flavia, both pleased and puzzled him. He remembered Maun saying that he did not ever expect to meet any one who would love him, but if he did, he would have to give her all of his attention - all that a wife deserved. 'So, what now?', Calpurnius wondered, 'Would Maun give up the Church for Flavia? Or, would he break her heart?'. All he wanted for his son was his happiness, but not with a guilty conscience, which it seemed he would have, whatever he decided.

Dawn broke and Calpurnius got up from the fire and went inside the tent. The men were still snoring, their breathing deep and regular. He was loath to wake them up, as he wanted Maun to get up first, knowing that he would not want Flavia to be embarrassed. He reluctantly peeped behind the partition and saw Maun's fair head on his pillow and Flavia's soft brown hair on his shoulder. He whispered Maun's name, then closed the curtain again.

Outside once more, Calpurnius poured himself another jar of the ale, 'This will keep me awake', he thought. He then became aware of someone behind him and turned around to see Maun, who sat on the log beside him. "Is Flavia well now? I heard her call out in the night and saw you go to her."

"Yes, father. She is fine."

After a moment, Calpurnius glanced in Maun's direction and asked him, "Do you, my son, intend to marry Flavia?".

"I don't know, father. The only thing I do know is, that Flavia is part of my life and part of my healing ministry. Without her, there is neither. If the Church does not like it, that is their loss."

Calpurnius was struck by Maun's strong words. He had not expected such a reaction to his question. He continued, "Do you remember Professor Theophilus, Maun?".

"Of course I do, father. We went to see him before I left with grandfather for Gaul. He drew a star chart for me."

"And, do you remember what he told you about your future?", asked Calpurnius.

"Yes, I do father. He said something about a woman being a part of my life, not that I believed a word of it at that time."

"Well, my son. The professor is a widely travelled man and has studied in many countries; especially among the Jews and Arabs and he has studied their customs and way of life. He once told me that our Lord Jesus was a married man and the father of several children."

Maun turned to stare at his father in amazement, "Really, father - did you believe him?".

"I saw no reason to disbelieve him", said Calpurnius, "How could I argue with him? I had no way of knowing for sure one way or the other. He was told that according to Jewish custom, the story of the wedding at Cana would not have been written otherwise. In this story, Mary his mother, was told of the wine shortage. According to custom, this would have been wrong, unless Jesus was the bridegroom. There are other stories of his children escaping to Gaul after the crucifixion. So my son, take of this as you will. I merely pass on the words of Theophilus for you to ponder over".

"Why father, is this information concealed? It seems ludicrous to fill our heads with lies for no logical purpose. They tell us that to lie is to sin!"

"I am not the one to answer that, my son. You will have to ask your bishop when you next see him. It is, perhaps, possible that it has something to do with a total male dominated hierarchy that fear the power of female sensitivity. For, that women are more aware of the world of angels, I have not the shadow of a doubt."

"Yes. You are right about that father", said Maun, "It is Flavia's sensitivity that makes the healing of so many sick people possible in such a short time. Without her, I would be worn out".

Calpurnius smiled, "For that reason Maun, I think God brought you two together. So my boy, you must do as you will. Whatever that is, you will always have my support".

"Also, do not forget the influence of the stars. I do not think God put them there to ornament the sky! They are there to make us raise our thoughts."

At that moment, Hanno came out of the tent yawning and stretching his arms, Calpurnius getting up from the log, leaving his place by the fire for him. "Sleep well Hanno?", he asked.

"I think I did", replied Hanno, "Don't remember much about it, although l did wake up once and saw that your bed was gone, Maun and your father's was empty. Did you go somewhere?".

"No. We were here. Father has been taking care of the horses and keeping the fire going."

Maun hoped Hanno would not ask any more questions and fortunately, his curiosity seemed satisfied, "Don't forget, Maun. You promised to marry Rebecca and me soon after we return home. *It is urgent, Maun*".

"Why the hurry, my friend? You are not going away anywhere, are you?"

Hanno looked at him sideways and wondered if Maun was teasing him? Surely, he must have guessed that Rebecca was already carrying his child. Although early days yet, Hanno wanted the marriage performed for Rebecca's sake - to make her feel more secure and happy.

Maun was pretty slow at catching on, but then he remembered Rebecca's sickness the previous morning and it finally penetrated. 'I'm a prize idiot', he thought, 'Hanno must think me even more stupid than before'. So he said, "I will arrange the ceremony the moment we arrive home".

"We don't want your little one born out of wedlock, do we?".

Hanno smiled and said, "Thank you Maun. I knew you would understand".

On their arrival back at the villa, they found everyone waiting anxiously for them and Rhona said, "Thank God you are all home and safe. When the weather changed, we began to worry. Are you sure all of you are well ?".

Calpurnius laughed, "Mama", he said, "The only thing to suffer any misfortune, was father's carriage. I'm afraid we had to use the seats to light the fire - it was the only dry wood available".

"To save your lives, you could have burnt the whole thing", said Calim, "We are so grateful to have you all home again". Then he said, "Your mother worries so much".

Rhona turned to glare at him, "And I suppose you were not in the least worried?".

While Hanno, Sergaeus, Adam and Clodus were folding the large tents, Rebecca - who was watching Hanno from a window - saw Maun help Flavia down from the front of the carriage. She appeared to be well wrapped up against the cold. Rebecca could see that Maun was holding on to Flavia and she watched as they looked into each other's eyes for several moments before he let her go. Rebecca thought, 'Hardship has made them grow closer together', then her attention turned again to Hanno.

CHAPTER XLVI

THE MARRIAGE OF HANNO AND REBECCA

Maun was not looking forward to Hanno's marriage ceremony, as he disliked formal occasions, where he had to memorise the part. His uncle Harran, or even Calim, performed almost all of the Christian baptisms, marriages and funerals in the town, although now that he was a priest of the Holy Church, they had hinted that he should take his turn. Despite this, he managed to get away with it, because of the amount of work he did at his healing services and the time he spent away from home. However, Hanno was his special friend and he had promised him.

He struggled to revise the service from the written word. It was a waste of time and Flavia had to read it out to him several times before he became more confident. "Don't worry so much", she told him, "You will be fine".

But, he did worry, for it was one thing to go amongst strangers and allow the power of the Almighty to guide you through healings and inspired words of wisdom - the poor souls who were sick were not out to check on his grammar! It was quite another thing to stand before a congregation of people who are educated and who will pick up on every mistake. That he would find this marriage ceremony a bit of an ordeal, was an understatement.

On the big day, everyone was exquisitely dressed in their finest clothes. Fortunately for Maun, it was decided to have the wedding in the family temple within the villa estate, the guest list being fairly small. In spite of his revision and going over time and time again the actual service, he was still very nervous, so much so, that his mind went blank.

He went to look for Flavia and spotted her talking to his grandmother Rhona. He had never seen Flavia dressed up for a special occasion and he stopped in his tracks and stared at her. She was dressed in a beautiful gown of pale lilac, her hair garlanded with flowers and she looked so small and delicate and very beautiful. She spotted him standing by the door and went over to him, "What is it, Maun? You're not still worried about the service? You will be fine".

He looked doubtful, "Will you stand close by where I can see you?".

She raised her hand to touch his face, "Don't I always?".

He was wearing his grandfather Joseph's blue robe and had taken great care over his cleanliness and appearance. Picking a tiny speck of lavender from his robe, she took a step back and said, admiringly, "You look wonderful, Maun! So handsome and dignified".

Realising how much he relied on her and how very much he loved her, he bent down and whispered in her ear, "I wish with all my heart that it was you and I being wed".

She placed her arm around his neck and spoke softly in his ear, "My love, don't you know? We are already married, made one before our God. There never were two people more married than you and I".

Still basking in the glow of Flavia's words, he went before the congregation with confidence, his uncle Harran and his grandfather Calim in attendance on either side of him. As Hanno and Rebecca came before him, his nervousness vanished, but he could see that Hanno's hands were trembling and his eyes had a glazed look. Maun felt great compassion for his friend and immediately forgot his own problems.

He set about putting his friend at ease and went on to deliver the ceremony with great sensitivity. His voice was soft, mellow and beautiful and word perfect.

However, there was one more slight difficulty to overcome. Calim had written the 'Certificate of Marriage' on a parchment scroll, couched in the following terms: 'This is to certify that a marriage has taken place, this day the ninth day of February in the year of our Lord four hundred and two, between Master Hanno of Baccara and Rebecca of Probius'. At the bottom Calim had left a space ... followed by the words 'Signature of Officiating Priest'.

The ceremony almost over, Hanno watched anxiously as Calim placed the scroll in front of Maun and Harran gave him a stylus to write his signature.

Taking a deep breath, Maun bent over the scroll and wrote, very slowly, in the place specified, everyone who knew of his difficulty with writing, holding their breath.

He then raised the stylus and looking anxious, handed the scroll to Hanno, who after inspecting the document, raised his eyes to meet Maun's and said, "It is perfect, Maun. Just perfect". In the space allowed the signature, Maun had written, 'Patrick Mun' and not Patris Maun, but it was near enough and for Maun, close to a miracle.

The celebrations began with everyone hurrying towards the villa to eat and drink. Flavia was waiting for Maun and when he arrived, she said, "I told you everything would be fine. You were wonderful. Your grandmother was crying - as well as your mother!".

Maun, with a puzzled expression, asked her, "And you think that is a good thing?".

"Oh! Yes", said Flavia, "Women always cry at weddings - they are so very special".

CHAPTER XLVII

THE YEARS PASS

Two years on and Maun, now affectionately known as Patrick by some, was still working hard in the Strathclyde area. When not taking mass with the monks at Bonavon, or preaching at the Mission at Dunbriton, he would be with the many members of his family and, perhaps, one or two of the Brothers, visiting a town where they had been requested to hold a service of healing.

Over the last two years, the healings had become grand, colourful and often spectacular affairs and although prayer, healing and thanksgiving was the purpose of the occasion, the evening usually ended with a powerful carnival-like atmosphere. Anyone who could play anything resembling a musical instrument would be there, ready and waiting for the evening celebrations and once the fire was ablaze, they danced around singing and dancing; drinking wine and ale and getting very merry. It also was the norm for people attending to wear colourful clothes, to match the party atmosphere.

While all this was going on, the tents would be dismantled and packed on top of the coach and the luggage stashed inside. By the time the music stopped and the party was over, Patrick and his family would be on their way home, however, if they were too far away from home, they slept in the tents and made their way home next morning.

Because of the hard work carried out by Patrick Mun and his family, the area of Strathclyde remained quite peaceful, for under their influence, many people were united; there was no discrimination, anyone chosen - either by Flavia or Adam - being healed.

Hanno, when not working with Patrick, spent his time at Bonavon, for he had been dismayed to discover that the Brothers had neglected the herb garden, in favour of growing more and more vegetables. So, he often went there to work, taking with him his wife Rebecca and his small son Phillipe. Sometimes, if the weather was not too good, they would ask Conchessa to look after Phillipe and this was a task Conchessa loved, for he was a delightful little boy and she adored him. She wished that he was her grandson.

Her resentment towards Flavia was growing. She blamed her for not wanting to marry her son officially and being unwilling to have his child, despite the fact that Calpurnius had told her that they lay down together.

Something in her mind told her she was being unreasonable, but as she watched Rebecca in the garden playing with Philipe, her bitterness grew out of all proportion. It even crossed her mind that Flavia must know some trick that prostitutes use to prevent conceiving a child. She could not confide in Calpurnius, for he admired Flavia almost as much as he did his son.

For some time now, she had made excuses not to go with them on their travels, the wonder of seeing sick and crippled people healed miraculously and crowds adore her son being outweighed by the cold reality of the situation - either baking under the hot sun, or freezing in the open air. However, as much as she preferred to stay in the warmth of the villa with its underfloor heating, the truth of the matter was that her love of little Phillipe and her desire for a grandchild was uppermost in her mind.

As she stood by her window, watching Rebecca play with her son, she calmed herself down and casually walked into the garden, smiling and friendly. She sat down beside Rebecca and remarked on how beautiful Phillipe was; and how much he had grown. Rebecca smiled with pride, saying, "Yes he is, Madam Conchessa and he is so bright. He can already say many words!".

Conchessa could hide her feelings no longer and she blurted out, "I wish Phillipe was my grandson, for I doubt very much Flavia will give me one".

Something in Conchessa's voice alerted Rebecca to the realisation that all was not well. It dawned on her that no one had told Conchessa anything about Flavia; her life or her circumstances. While she considered what to do, she rang the bell for Phillipe's nurse and when she arrived, she said "Will you kindly take Phillipe and put him down to rest for a while?".

When they were out of sight, she said, "Madam Conchessa, I am ashamed. I have let you down. I have been so tied up with my own affairs, my marriage and the birth of Phillipe that I have neglected to give you information that I should have shared with you long ago".

Conchessa turned her face away and bit her lip. Her impulse was to get up and run away, but she wanted to hear what Rebecca had to say, so she waited, although she was not quite prepared for what followed.

"Madam Conchessa. Flavia is so much like you and I am sure that is one of the reasons Maun loved her on sight."

Conchessa turned her head slowly to face Rebecca and frowning a little repeated, "Like me?".

"Yes Madam. Just like you. She looks like you. She works hard like you. She married a wealthy man like you and she had a son also. Unfortunately, her son died and her husband also. The birth was a difficult one and had not her husband been a wealthy man and could afford the most skilled physician, she also would not have survived. She confided in me that since that day, she has not seen any monthly sign of fertility."

Conchessa sat quietly and listened while Rebecca continued to tell her all about Flavia's work and service to the people of their village, especially to the poor and her kindness to the family of her husband's first wife.

"I tell you, Madam Conchessa. When Maun takes her home next year to visit her mother Jess and they enter our village, everyone will turn out to welcome them and it will be her name they will call out, for she is *their* Lady Flavia."

Conchessa stood up slowly. She said, "Thank you my dear for confiding in me", then she walked away, her face ashen as she went to her quarters. Once inside her bedroom, she sat on her wicker chair beside her bed, staring into space, but after a few moments, she whispered, "What have I done? While my son loves a woman because she reminds him of me. I have … Oh! God … What have I become? How would I have felt if Madam Rhona had thought of me, as I have Flavia? What would Calpurnius think of me if he knew? He would hate me and rightly so".

She began to sob uncontrollably. The more she condemned herself, the more she cried, until her cries became moans of despair, the sound of a soul in torment, being torn apart by guilt.

A housemaid happened to pass Conchessa's door and heard the strange noises. Realising something was wrong, she hurried to the villa's west wing, to the quarters of Rhona and Calim. She knocked on the door, calling out, "Madam Rhona! Come quickly. Something is wrong with Madam Conchessa!".

Rhona came out of her room looking anxious, "What is the matter, girl?".

"It is Madam Conchessa."

Rhona followed the maid to Conchessa's room. She could hear the moans for herself and not bothering to knock, she went straight in. Rhona turned to the maid, "Hurry and send the messenger to fetch Doctor Markus. He will know what to do".

Rhona sat on the bed beside Conchessa, "Come my dear. Come to your mama Rhona. There is nothing surely to upset you like this? Is it Calpurnius? Has he said something to upset you?". There was no response from Conchessa. She was inconsolable, her body heaving as she sobbed. Rhona decided to simply sit by her bed, talk to her and wait for Markus to come.

Markus arrived within the half hour. He felt Conchessa's forehead and looked into her eyes, then after a few more tests, signalled to Rhona to go outside the room. Following her, he said "She seems to be in some kind of shock - like soldiers after a battle! Could she have seen or heard something that would bring this on?".

Rhona shook her head, "No, Markus. Nothing I know of".

"I will give her a sedative to calm her down, then she might sleep it off, but make sure she is not left alone."

Markus lifted Conchessa into a sitting position, Rhona holding her while he poured the sedative into a spoon and tipped it into Conchessa's mouth. It had a bitter taste, yet Conchessa did not seem to notice. She was cold and shivery, so Rhona put her under the covers, adding another, before finally tucking her in. Rhona then sat on the wicker chair beside the bed and held Conchessa's hand.

Markus's potion worked and soon Conchessa was asleep, Rhona herself also nodding off.

By afternoon, Conchessa began to stir and when she saw Rhona asleep beside her, memories of what happened earlier came back. She was feeling relaxed, at least her body was, but she had trouble putting her thoughts in order.

Waking up, Rhona saw Conchessa's eyes open and she bent over towards her, "How do you feel now, my dear?".

Conchessa looked into her concerned face and said, "Thank you, Mother Rhona. I am better now".

'Thank God', said Rhona, "I was so worried about you".

She was desperate to ask her daughter-in-law what had brought on the attack, but was afraid it might start her off again.

"Mother Rhona, do you like me?", Conchessa's eyes anxiously searched her face.

"Why, of course I do", answered Rhona, "I have, ever since the first day you arrived here. I thought at the time, what a lovely innocent young lady - just right for my son".

This statement might have been enough to start Conchessa off again, but she had no tears left and the sedative was still having an effect, "Mother Rhona. I have been very cruel and unkind to Flavia. I have hated her; blaming her for not having a child, one that would be our grandchild".

Rhona had heard enough. She had guessed the truth anyway. She said, "Is that all? Good grief! I thought something awful had happened". She shook her head from side to side, "My darling, I think you try too hard to be perfect and no one ever is. We all have faults. It sometimes comes as a shock to discover that what we think is wrong in our character, is not at all what others think".

"Now. I always thought that you did not have enough fire in you. I would have preferred you to come right out and say what you thought was wrong. That you seldom enquired into anyone's business or criticised them, that I thought was a fault in you, for I never knew what you were thinking. I had to accept you the way you were and hoped that you would accept me along with my imperfections."

"Mother Rhona. Please, don't tell Calpurnius! I would be so ashamed."

Rhona touched her hand reassuringly, "I won't say a word and if Markus says anything, we will say it was something you ate at breakfast. You know my dear, one thing I don't like, are wives who tell their husbands every little thing and worry them half to death". She spoke with exaggerated gestures in an attempt to make Conchessa laugh. It worked and Conchessa smiled.

"Now, my dear daughter; if we want to get you well before the gang return, let's start with a freshen up and a nice hot drink. You know Conchessa, life is too short by far. Try to be at peace with yourself."

Several hours later, the horses with their riders returned. Rhona and Conchessa were watching from the window and they knew the routine. The grooms would come and take the horses, while Maun helped Flavia from her carriage. She, in turn, would collect her bag of personal things and come into the house. She would bathe, put on a fresh robe, then meet the men again in the dining room for their supper. This was Rhona's treat, for it was not easy to find time to eat while working and they would have had nothing, apart from a very quick snack and sometimes, even that would have been given away, so they were usually starving when they got home.

Conchessa was calm now, although she did not know what she was going to say to Flavia, having ignored her on previous occasions. They were all discussing the triumphs of their day; not in a boasting way, but in awe of the miracles they had witnessed. While Calpurnius, Sergaes and Adam talked, Hanno, Maun and Flavia ate, seldom entering into the conversation. When Conchessa entered, Calpurnius went to her, saying, "You are up late my dear?".

"Yes", said Conchessa, "I waited up to see all of you".

"Come mama, sit with us and have some supper", said Maun.

She took a deep breath, closed her eyes for a moment as though to utter a short prayer and went to sit with them. She asked, "Have you been very busy today, then?".

"Unfortunately, yes mama. It seems there is no end to illness and suffering."

Sergaeus agreed, "There was some fine work done this day. At this moment, there are people sound asleep and without pain, perhaps for the first time in their lives".

Sergaeus finished his supper, saying "Well! I had better get off home. Julia and Helen will be waiting up for me to tell them everything that happened".

Adam followed, "Good night everyone and thank you Madam Rhona for the wonderful supper. And thank you Madam Conchessa. It was a pleasant surprise to see you".

Calpurnius put his empty plate down, saying, "That was most enjoyable, mama. Thank you". He held his arm for Conchessa to take hold of, but Rhona gave her a look to remind her why she was there.

Taking her arm away from Calpurnius, Conchessa walked over to Maun and Flavia. She kissed her son, saying "Good-night my darling", then without hesitation, she kissed Flavia on the cheek, saying to her softly, "Thank you for taking such good care of him".

When Calpurnius and Conchessa left, Hanno thanked Rhona, "If it were not for your special supper Madam Rhona, I might starve! Rebecca is so tired running after Phillipe, she sleeps at every opportunity".

Rhona said, "Good night my dears" and left.

Now on their own, Flavia looked up at Maun, "How strange Maun. I could have sworn your mother did not like me?".

"I think, my love", said Maun, "That the only person in the world mama does not like, is herself".

CHAPTER XLVIII

FLAVIA'S REVELATION

From then, on Conchessa made a vow to go with her family to the healing services and get to know Flavia better. She also desired to grow closer to her son.

As she watched them at work, her heart filled with pride and she thought, 'How could I have been so blind? They are perfect for each other'. It was now clear to her that he could never have healed so many people, without her special gift of knowing who were genuinely sick and those who were pretending, in order to get attention.

On one particular evening when the meeting was almost over, Maun was giving a blessing to several people who had waited. Flavia, no longer required, went to the tent to get her shawl and she was surprised to find Conchessa there, resting on some cushions. "Are you well Madam Conchessa?", she inquired.

"Yes my dear, I am fine. Just a little cold", said Conchessa, "I find the evening chill penetrating, but I did stay and watch longer than I intended. I had almost forgotten how wonderful and fascinating these meetings were, the crowds love him so".

Flavia agreed, "Yes madam. It has been a great success.

There was silence for a few moments, then Flavia said in a slightly distant voice, "Madam Conchessa. You and Master Calpurnius think always of your son as one who happens to have this wonderful gift to heal - that is, of course, true. But, it is not how I see him. All of my childhood, I was considered a fool because I could see people no one else could. As I grew up, my gift - although at times I thought it a curse - developed and I could see beings from higher realms".

Flavia raised her eyes to face Conchessa, then continued, "I see Maun as he truly is. He, Madam Conchessa, is a Prince of Heaven, one who has so much compassion for the suffering souls upon earth, that he sought permission to be born again in order to serve and heal. I tell you now Madam, that in order for this to happen, suitable parents had to be found, parents of special wisdom and light who would raise this soul to manhood with love and tenderness. He is so refined, that the harshness of life at times is unbearable for him. Only you and Master Calpurnius, as well as his grandparents - especially his grandfather Joseph - were suitable for this task. You are all very special people. But, now he is a man. He has to live and work as a man". Conchessa could only sit and stare. Flavia continued, "Some nights, when we are away from home, when the crowds have gone and everything is quiet, he comes to this tent and rests against these cushions, just as you do now. I watch him in the glow of the lamp and see him as he truly is. Adorned in his spiritual robes of palest green, a band of gold around his waist and a crown of gold around his head. His beautiful delicate and ageless face, makes me want to love and protect him".

"Long before I met Maun, I was told by one of his kind, that I was being prepared to serve and assist a great soul with his work. That I now do this, is my life's work and my great joy. But, he grows stronger now. He has to, for Madam, I tell you that he has to accomplish in this life, all that it would take an ordinary man a thousand lifetimes to achieve."

Conchessa was speechless. She stared at Flavia in disbelief. Then, what she had just heard slowly sank into her consciousness and with it came understanding of the strange little boy who was her son. She felt a warm glow of admiration for the young woman before her. She heard herself say, "Maun is very lucky to have you. He loves you very much".

Flavia bowed her head again for a moment before saying, " Yes, madam Conchessa. I know and I love him also".

"Is Maun aware of what you have told me?", asked Conchessa.

"At this time Madam, I think not. He is much too modest to accept this concept of himself. However, given time he will begin to perceive the truth of it.

Conchessa was still puzzled. She said, "I often wonder why he had to suffer so much. He was hardly strong enough".

"It is difficult to understand", said Flavia. "But when we are born to earth, a door is closed to our heavenly knowledge. This is to allow us freedom to live, pursue and achieve in our own right and in most cases that door to heaven is only opened again to allow us to re-enter when we die to the world. There are, however, times when a soul is so near to death, that the door is partly opened and when he eventually recovers, he is blessed with beautiful memories of that higher state of being. This is what happened to Maun. In that state of blissfulness between life and death, he was shown the plan for his service to mankind. He has more power than he is willing to admit to, because he is too cautious to put it to the test. One day I fear he will have to".

Another year on, Maun and his companions were still working hard, often returning to places already visited to check on the progress and well-being of the people. Very often, they came across camps of refugees newly arrived from Hibernia and Maun had by now become more familiar with their language. They were always exceedingly grateful for his help and astounded at his power to heal. Although not everyone required healing, they were uplifted and made stronger by his presence.

Always there were young men and women who wanted to follow him, but he told them, "Think very carefully before you leave your loved ones. God would not thank you for following him and leaving your little ones in mortal danger. Far better you stay with them, for all that is required of you, is that you love and care for one another. That was our Lord Jesus Christ's last commandment".

CHAPTER XLIX

JESS

The time for them to prepare to leave drew near. Maun had promised Flavia that he would take her to visit Jess. Adam also was anxious to see his parents and his brother and Maun himself wanted to check up on his grandfather Joseph, who was never far from his thoughts. He also had, what was for him, the rather unpleasant task of reporting to his bishop.

The day came when the three of them sailed away, but with the promise that they would return the moment their business was completed.

Their first port of call was in the west corner of Britain, where he had first met Flavia. This was an exciting and nostalgic visit for them. They were received, with cries of delight from everyone, especially Jess. Flavia showed Maun and Adam around the estate and for the first time Maun realised just how much she had given up to stay with him. He was aware she had given up her home, but the vastness of the estate was a revelation to him. He was even more shocked when he found out that the main reason for the visit, was to sign documents, handing her share of the estate to Sarah and her farm manager husband, in return for them caring for Jess.

This visit ended all too soon. It was a happy time for Maun and he enjoyed visiting Julien's little temple on the estate, which he blessed at Flavia's request Their ship was due and it was with regret that they had to leave, but with the promise that, if they could, they would return one day.

CHAPTER L

VISIT TO EVAN AND JOSEPH

Their journey to Gaul was pleasant enough. So much depended on the weather and that was fair; the beds and the food could have been better, still they got there safe and sound and that was what mattered.

Evan and Margaretta were delighted to see their eldest son again, as well as Maun. Margaretta had not met Flavia before, although she had heard about her from Evan. Having hugged the breath out of them, Evan asked to be told everything that had happened since he had last seen them.

Margaretta and Flavia were very soon the best of friends and Adam told his parents that he would be staying with them, while Maun and Flavia went on to Tours to see Joseph. That pleased them very much.

Evan, Margaretta and Karl were now enjoying a more relaxed and comfortable lifestyle, thanks to the gold coins Evan had earned. They rode around in a new carriage; walked by the riverbank and had time to meet friends and relatives. Young Karl soon tired of roaming around with friends of his own age. It had been a novelty at first, but he had responsibilities and had to grow up fast. Now, his friends seemed rather immature and Karl decided to adopt a more responsible attitude, which pleased his parents no end and despite his father's money, he resolved to earn his keep by taking charge of the horses and stables.

Before they left, Maun told Adam that this would be a good opportunity for him to discover whether he wanted to stay at home, or continue serving at the healing meetings. Adam replied, "Do you imagine I could be happy doing anything else?".

"That is good", said Maun, "Because I cannot imagine our meetings without your special gifts. It is doubtful we could manage without you".

"When you both get to Tours", said Evan, "Tell Joseph how I think of him often. How I remember our stay at Bonavon together and our adventures on our way here".

"I will", said Maun, as he and Flavia boarded their carriage.

They had waited with Evan for a day and a night, before they set off for Tours.

The road was bumpy and in places down right uncomfortable, but Maun and Flavia loved every moment, for they were alone. No one to watch their every move. No one spying on them. No animals nuzzling their way into their tent and taking their food. They stopped at good inns, with comfortable beds and this was the nearest thing to heaven on earth for both of them. To be by themselves where no one recognised them; to be able to go out walking, just a short walk while waiting for a change of carriage. It was a joy and if they had not been on their way to see Joseph, they would have taken even more time over it.

But, Maun was anxious to see his grandfather. There was a bond between them that spanned distance; a love so deep, it was beyond human experience.

The innkeeper at Tours had been warned more than a month before by Joseph that his grandson was due and would he please send for him the moment he arrived. So, when the carriage stopped at the door of the inn, they were recognised by the innkeeper and a messenger was sent to the Abbey with the news.

Joseph was overjoyed and he excused himself from his duties, saying that he had important business to attend to.

As he hurried towards the inn, he thanked God for his grandson's safe journey. There was danger on the roads and disease was rife. It was a constant worry when those you loved had to travel great distances, so this was an occasion for celebration.

Maun and Flavia had hardly walked upstairs to their room, when Joseph came in. "My boy! My dear boy! Let me look at you".

Maun was pleased to see his grandfather looking so fit and said, "Madam Leoni must be taking good care of you - you look so well. Come up to our room grandfather and we can talk while we take off our shoes. I feel as though I have walked all the way here!".

"Tell me all the news from home … How is your Mother? … Are you alone? … Where is your friend Adam?"They were still talking when the innkeeper sent news that their meal was ready and he had also provided one for Joseph.

Joseph, Maun and Flavia enjoyed their meal, but Flavia was tired from the long journey and asked to be excused. She went to their bedroom, leaving them still talking. The innkeeper sent Joseph and Maun glass after glass of wine and they were so engrossed in their conversation, they failed to notice that the wine was undiluted. So, when Maun said he would walk Joseph back to his house and stood up, he realised that something was wrong. "Are you all right, grandfather?", he asked.

"Why certainly, my boy. I feel fine." However, once outside in the fresh night air, he was not so sure and Maun had to put an arm around his grandfather and help him back to his house. On the way, they had staggered, almost falling over and giggling uncontrollably. When they eventually reached the house, Madam Leoni was not too pleased - she had waited for Joseph, keeping the fire going and his now ruined supper, hot.

"You are both intoxicated!", she said, "Men of the Church and you are both drunk".

Joseph looked her straight in the eye and said, "Intoxillic … Intoxi … I have never in all my life been intoxilicated".

"Well, you are now", said madam, "*Very intoxicated*". Joseph and Maun looked into each other's faces and began to laugh again. "I am going to bed", announced Madam Leoni, "Some people need to sleep".

Maun helped Joseph into bed. He wanted to go back to the inn and Flavia, but the wine and the night air had played tricks with his senses. He had to admit to feeling a bit odd, so he lay on the couch and slept.

It was almost dawn when he woke up. Madam Leoni came into the room and enquired, "Is father Joseph all right?".

"I do hope so", said Maun, "We did not realise that the wine was so strong. I am so sorry Madam for allowing you to worry so much".

"Do not concern yourself, Patris. When I saw you help him into the house, I thought he had been taken ill. I was so worried. But, when I saw that you were laughing, I was so relieved."

"You must have had an uncomfortable night on that old couch. I expect you will want to get back to the inn and get some sleep", said Madam Leoni, "If you want to leave, I will take care of Father Joseph".

Maun was grateful, "Thank you, Madam. Will you tell my grandfather that we will call on him tomorrow evening".

Maun hurried through the semi-dark streets of Tours back to the inn. He saw that the wash-house at the back of the inn was open and always particular about his cleanliness, he went in and washed away the smell of the wine.

He crept into the bedroom, with his boots in one hand and his outer robe over his arm, thinking that it was almost time to get up. As he got into bed, Flavia put an arm around him, then drew back quickly, "You are wet and cold! Where have you been?".

He related how he had to take Joseph home and how they got into trouble from Madam Leoni. Flavia said, "Poor Joseph and I suppose he has to work in the Abbey today? I hope he will be well enough?".

Maun's visit to see his bishop was a disappointment. The only one available to see him was unknown to him and it had been a waste of time. He had to explain who he was and where he came from. The old bishop having been told everything about him, seemed to forget almost at once and kept asking the same questions. Maun was relieved when the interview was over and so it seemed, was the bishop.

Surprisingly, Joseph was not too distressed after his excessive wine consumption. After his usual day at the Abbey, he was well enough to entertain Maun and Flavia that evening, however, he did not offer them any wine.

The travellers left Joseph in good spirits and at Nanmentium, they called to see Evan again and pick up Adam. He was ready and waiting and told them, "I have loved being home, but missed very much the excitement of our work".

Evan, Margaretta and Karl saw them off at the docks. There were tears in their eyes, but it had been wonderful to have Adam home and know that he was happy in his work.

CHAPTER LI

MORE REFUGEES

They were welcomed home by everyone, every member of the family turning up to see them and inquire about Joseph. Conchessa especially was pleased to hear that her father was well and in good spirits.

While they had been away, many more refugees had arrived in Dunbriton, however, with help and advice from their fellow countrymen already settled, there had not been too much trouble.

Calim, who had memories of the warlike nature of the Hibernians, was not at all pleased at the vast number of new arrivals and complained, "It's not that I have anything against ordinary folks trying to make a better life for themselves in another country. Indeed I welcome them. But, not all of these refugees are ordinary people. Some have held high office and are partly to blame for the difficulties in their own country. Now, they have turned up here and brought with them their bigotry, stupidity and evil ways and think they should be given special treatment! They have some strange notion that the people of Briton owe them a living. The people of this country have fought hard for peace and we want it to stay that way. If I could, I would put all of them in a ship and send them back to where they came from".

Rhona whispered to Maun, "Take Flavia by the hand and follow me". He did as he was bid and followed her along the wide corridor that led to the west wing and her quarters. On the way, she said, "As your grandfather is excited by his favourite subject, I thought it a good time to make our escape".

They stopped outside a large door, which she opened and went through, beckoning them to follow her. Rhona said, "These are my guest rooms. While you are both my guests, you will consider these apartments your home. When you arrived here before, Alana did not expect four extra guests and was unprepared and unsure of your relationships". Then grinning, she looked from Maun to Flavia and back again, "I think we are quite sure of your relationship now".

Maun and Flavia were just a little embarrassed, but Maun said, "Thank you, grandmother. We appreciate your thoughtfulness and all your hard work. But, are you quite sure we won't disturb you when we arrive home late?".

"My boy, have you forgotten that I always wait up for my children to come home?"

"No, grandmother. How could I possibly forget your wonderful suppers."

"Right", said Rhona, "Now that you know where your quarters are, we shall return to the family and pray that your grandfather has changed the subject of his conversation".

Within a few days, they were back at work; Maun preaching at the Mission temple in Dunbriton and saying mass for the Brothers at Bonavon. However, no large or grand healing meetings were planned for a few weeks, which left time for him to show Flavia around the town as they had travelled to Bonavon not only to serve, but to visit friends. They also spent time at the homes of Maun's uncles, Harran and Sergaeus and his daughters. Flavia was not quite so much in awe of them now, being more certain of her own place within the family and in Maun's heart.

There was also time to spend with his father, Calpurnius and talk to him of his many interests. Maun asked him why he had not become a confirmed Christian? "I know that you do believe father, but you are not so strong in your faith as either of my grandfathers or uncle Harran. Is it because of the teaching of Professor Theophilus?".

Calpurnius was surprised at this question, "What ever gave you that idea, my son? I have always marvelled at the teachings of Jesus. His words are so full of common sense, something I find sadly lacking in some other religious orders".

"The way I see it Maun, is that Jesus has taught a way of life. He has informed us of a loving God who is a Father to the children of the earth. I believe that. There is nothing Theophilus or anyone else can teach that can alter that."

"Theophilus and I have discussed, science, politics and the writings of the great Greek philosophers. Still I find nothing to contradict my Christian beliefs. Indeed, the opposite is true. As for the study of the stars, 'Was it not made plain that Jesus was born under a large star that hung in the sky for many days and led three astrologer kings to his birthplace'."

"I believe, my son, that it is wise to learn as much as possible about the world we live in. Those who believe in Jesus and bow to faith alone, have nothing to fear, although I think that those of us who explore the unknown, may indeed be answering silent, but perceptible instructions from those in one of the many planes of being, mentioned by Jesus himself. We, as human beings, must look for and expect to receive inspiration from on high, for in that way progress may be made. You never know Maun, perhaps one day, someone will invent a carriage that won't need a horse to pull it. If that should ever happen, it will be due to science and faith, not faith alone."

Maun laughed, "I cannot imagine a carriage moving along by itself!".

"Neither can I, my son. Yet, we see every day heavy cargo ships sailing along on nothing more than invisible wind in their sails. Makes you think, does it not?"

"We, as human beings, must keep our minds open and receptive to new ideas. I believe that it is an insult to God and his messengers for us to turn a deaf ear to their instructions. Prayer, my boy is thanking God for the many blessings he has bestowed upon us and for answered prayers."

"But, did not Jesus tell us to pray in private and God would answer us in private; to be still and know that he is God?".

"I believe in that stillness, Maun. To me, it is the most satisfying and renewing experience." Maun smiled at his father. He remembered sitting on a rock waiting for Evan to return from his bath in the old town of Julianus and how he had heard the instructions on how to deliver Dancer. He had heard the words clearly, yet without human sound, so he knew exactly what his father meant.

Calpurnius continued, "I truly believe Maun, that the day will come when each soul upon earth must be personally responsible for the evolution of their own souls. That they must listen to all information available and make up their own minds. God has created us individuals, each one of us unique".

"To some of us, Christianity is a revelation. To others, merely a lesson on our way through life and to some, it is a ploy to stop them robbing and cheating their fellow man."

"What seems obvious to me, is that people cannot expect to reach Heaven on the coat-tails of their teachers, or on the say-so of another. If they have lied and cheated they have to atone for that, despite what Jesus had to say about him taking the sins of the world upon his shoulders."

"There are sins and there are evil sins. No one who has given the matter much thought, would expect our Lord to take upon himself the evils of the world. I see you - Flavia and Adam - working with and healing the sick. I see those who are crippled, come before you Maun, carrying with them the result of every sin they have ever committed, through many lifetimes. When you heal them, you awaken the part of them that is God, that part of them that they buried deep through fear and ignorance. They are then able to forgive themselves."

"Father", said Maun, "I cannot find fault in anything you have said - I never could".

The time arrived for a healing rally to be held, the location of which was some distance away and for which they would require the carriage. Fortunately, Calim had had the whole thing renovated; new seats inside and fresh paint outside. It looked brand new. Calim said, "Please take care of the carriage, I cannot afford to have it completely renovated every time you use it!".

Calpurnius knew that his father was joking, so he replied, "I will, father. I will take particular care of it this time - we will take some dry firewood with us!".

Calim laughed, "I only wish I could come with you, but my days of sleeping on the ground are over. I'm afraid I enjoy my creature comforts too much to go gallivanting around out in the night air, besides, who would keep your mother company and help her with the supper?". He then asked how many men were going with them to help and was a large crowd expected?

Calpurnius told him, "We are not sure just how many will turn up? Sergaeus and Berin were in the district last week and they spoke to the head man and he nailed some posters around the village. However, it has been so long since we have held a healing meeting, we wonder if the people will have forgotten the purpose of them?".

"How many helpers are going with you?", Calim repeated.

Calpurnius thought about it, "Well, there is Sergaeus; his nephew Berin; some young volunteers from the Mission temple; Adam of course; Conchessa and myself".

"Do you think there are enough men to control a crowd?"

Calpurnius laughed, "Father, if no one in the village can read, there will be no one there to control".

The appointed meeting place was in a field by the river Clyde and when they arrived, there was not a soul in sight. They looked at one another, "Are you sure Sergaeus, we are in the right place?". Sergaeus and Berin were adamant that it was, so the tents were put up and a fire lit.

"Perhaps, we are just a bit early. Take advantage of the peace and quiet and rest a while", Calpurnius told them.

They did not rest for long. Suddenly, people began to arrive from every direction, even from small craft being rowed along the river. Soon, they were all seated on the grass, eagerly waiting for the show to begin. Calpurnius announced himself and explained what the procedures were, then took his place at the side of the crowd to watch out for any troublemakers, or for anyone who required help.

Adam and Flavia walked amongst the people, choosing those whom they sensed were in greatest need. An elderly man, in agony with toothache; a youth with a cough. Then, Calpurnius spotted the spy and he thought to himself, 'Who could mistake that miserable face?'.

He went to talk to Sergaeus and point out their unwelcome visitor. Sergaeus remarked, "Do you mean that tall man in the black cloak; the one Flavia is now approaching?".

Calpurnius turned around to see Flavia stand before the spy and offer him her hand. He appeared even more sour than usual and it seemed as if he was reluctant to go with her. However, with all eyes upon him, he relented and followed her.

Maun and Adam asked him to lie down on a blanket, where both placed their hands high on his stomach. They spent some time with him, then he was helped to his feet by Adam and Maun and escorted back to where he had been standing. Calpurnius noticed that the man did not wait around, quickly disappearing out of sight.

After two hours of hard work, the meeting ended. The people had not forgotten the rituals, a fire being lit to burn the discarded bandages, walking sticks and anything else lying around. Musical instruments were then produced and soon the dancing and drinking began.

As Maun listened to the music, suddenly it sounded familiar, yet he could not remember where he had first heard it. He looked around for Flavia, but couldn't see her. He made his way to the tent and as he opened the flap to enter, he saw her. She was swaying to the music and wearing his new robe, the one his grandmother Rhona had had made for him and which he had considered a little too ornate for a man.

She became aware of him watching her and stopped dancing. Embarrassed she started to remove the robe. "Don't take it off, Flavia. It suits you. I didn't know you could dance", he said as he approached her.

"I'm not very good at it", said Flavia, "It's only what I have seen others do".

Suddenly, he remembered where he had heard the music. He went over to her and took her arms and put them around his neck. He held her waist. He then began to imitate the dance he had seen on the quay at the Lorne many years before.

Flavia eyed him curiously, "Where did you ever learn such a dance as this?".

"When Evan and I left the ship at the Lorne, there were women there who danced with the sailors. Evan said it was a 'choose your partner for the evening dance', but I didn't feel like dancing one dance, let alone dance all evening!".

Flavia began to giggle. He felt hurt, "What is it you find so amusing?".

Flavia sat on the stool and looked up at him, " Oh! Maun. You are so innocent. Those women were prostitutes. They were not selecting dancing partners, they were choosing go to bed partners".

Maun was stunned, "Oh my good Lord! What would have happened if I had asked one of them to dance? You know, I often wondered why Evan gave me such a long explanation as to why he could not dance. He kept saying that he was a happily married man. I wondered what that had to do with him not being able to dance".

Flavia noticed that Maun's face had gone very pale, "I should not worry about it, my love. You were very young at the time".

Maun smiled, "Come, let us dance now". He took her by the hand and led her out of the tent towards the dancers, where they joined with them. They were not very good to start with, but soon got the hang of it.

Calpurnius was surprised and pleased to see his son dancing with Flavia, but when he looked around the happy, clapping crowd, there was the spy watching - no doubt, making mental notes.

It was a very successful event and as usual, there were many enquiries from young men anxious to join with them. They received the usual reply, "If you have family, take care of them before planning to take care of others. If you have no one to care for, then you may join the Brotherhood. It will not be an easy life, but one that will bring satisfaction and contentment".

Within the Brotherhood, they were taught to be self sufficient; they learned to farm poultry, grow food and herbs, bake bread, also to read and write Latin and to pray. Maun, his family and friends worked very hard, guiding these young men to become responsible citizens.

Flavia concentrated on helping the women and their children, giving them advice on how to feed their little ones. It seemed strange to her, that so many mothers imagined that small babies did not need to be fed solid food for the first year of their lives. For some that was fine, but for other mothers who were malnourished, it was a disaster and she wondered that so many babies lived as long as they did.

CHAPTER LII

SEVERAL YEARS ON

Over the following years, many new monasteries were built, although at that time, the Brothers were not as disciplined as they were to become much later.

They could leave if they so desired, although very few chose to do so.

By now, everyone knew Maun as Patrick, even some members of his family.

One day, Conchessa told her son that she was becoming worried about her father, "I just feel that something is wrong". Maun had had similar thoughts, although he had been so busy, they had been put to the back of his mind. Now obliged to give it some thought, he put it to Flavia that they should leave right away for Tours. Indeed, the worry over his grandfather became very strong.

When he broke the news to his parents, his father did not want him to go, but his mother Conchessa, who had confessed to the same feelings of foreboding about her father, convinced Calpurnius that their son should go. She also hinted that she would like to see her father as well.

Calpurnius was not pleased, "I could not bear for both of you to be away; my mother and father are now old and frail. It is my place to be here and I need you with me Conchessa".

She agreed, "If something is wrong with my father, Maun is the one to be able to help him. I would only be in the way".

"Your father is right, Maun. There is far too much work to be done at the villa. Your grandmother Rhona needs my help, as she can no longer cope."

"Indeed", said Calpurnius, "I talked with father recently, Maun and he has made up his mind to hand the villa over to uncle Harran. Since Portia and Markus's son Berin married, there are now fourteen members in his family. The house they live in once belonged to your aunt Elinor's parents. When Harran and Elinor could have shared the villa, she turned it down, saying she wanted to live in her own home. However, it is now rather small for such a large family. Father would like to move to Bonavon, as he feels Conchessa would be happier being close to her brother Paulus and her dear friend Alana".

"Of course my son", said Calpurnius, "You and Flavia will always have a home with us, wherever we are".

Maun seemed depressed. He told Flavia, "I cannot envisage the villa without my grandparents Calim and Rhona. I fear that a move to another place would not be good for them. They are so used to being the centre of the family, it could mean the end for them".

Flavia tried to comfort him, "Don't worry, Maun. It is their choice and they will still be with your father and mother, who I expect will make them very comfortable. Unfortunately, we have to make the journey to Gaul and thankfully, leave your family in good hands".

CHAPTER LIII

THE PASSING OF JOSEPH

When Patrick, Flavia and Adam arrived at Tours, they went straight to Joseph's house. At first, they thought they had made a mistake, for it was Joseph who answered the door. They were very pleased to see him walking around, but when he spoke, they realised how weak his voice was and his eyes were sunken in dark sockets. It was plain he was very ill.

"You received my message then?", he said looking up at his grandson from his armchair, into which he had sunk back into the very moment he let them in.

"We did indeed, grandfather and my mother also. She became most anxious that I came to see you right away. Now I see you up and about and seemingly quite well".

Joseph smiled at him, "My boy. It is a sham for the benefit of my housekeeper, who tends to fuss over me. At this moment, she has gone to church to pray for me, although I am supposed to believe she has gone to market".

"Now, listen to me carefully, for I have little time left. My time has come to leave this earth, with maybe only a few short hours left to talk to you. I hear my name being called, so do not worry about me. I have no fear of passing from this earth. I have done so many times in the past and will no doubt do so again."

"You my son, have a special mission. I see you working in a foreign country. I must tell you, not to worry. You will be protected on all sides."

"Now, my boy. I have that gold your father gave us. I had little use for it, except to help some of the poor of the town and my dear housekeeper, Madam Leoni. The remainder you must take. You will need it in the future, for you will not have your grandparent's great wealth coming to you. That will go to your father and mother, who in turn will give most to the Brothers for their great work. You will not be there, so you must take my share and use it to give yourself and your beautiful companion some semblance of comfort."

Patrick had listened carefully, for Joseph's voice was weak and he spoke slowly and breathlessly. He was attempting to say everything he needed to, before he forgot, or it was too late.

From then on, Joseph became weaker, until he sank into unconsciousness. The following day, he passed away peacefully.

The service in the Abbey did Joseph credit. The bishop said what a good man he was; a wonderful servant of Christ and his Holy Church. That would have pleased Joseph.

The day after the funeral, Patrick went to see the bishop. He was pleased to find that this bishop was one who he got on well with and not the absent-minded one he'd seen the last time he was here. The bishop said how much his grandfather would be missed. He also remarked on how similar Joseph and Patrick were to the

Bishop Martin. The bishop said, "All three of you have cared little for wealth. Martin found God in poverty; Joseph found his God in bringing the poor to Christ and you Father Maun, although brought up surrounded in wealth, have shown little regard for it, choosing the simple life".

The bishop then gave him a strange look, saying, "There is a difference though. For unlike Martin, I understand you have chosen to keep a woman in your camp? It has been reported that you were seen laughing and cavorting with a woman after a service of healing".

From the bishop's expression, he clearly expected Patrick to show surprise that he had been found out, but Patrick remained calm. He looked the bishop straight in the eye and said, "Your inquisitor was spotted amongst the sick at the healing meetings!". Patrick then smiled, saying "He stood out like a goose amongst the gulls. Not a very good spy. The lady he referred to is the Lady Flavia of Protius! She is my wife; my companion and helpmate and without her by my side, there would be no healing mission. I depend on her good judgement; her compassion when dealing with the women and children. She is a gentle soul, with the gift of spiritual insight, which compliments the work I do".

"Yes", said the bishop, "I guessed as much. However, you do realise that unless you cease to be associated with her, you will never be considered for promotion".

Patrick could feel the anger rising in his heart, but managed to control himself. "What Sir, do I care for rules and regulations created by men? I have and always will, listen only to God."

The bishop grinned from ear to ear, as he said, "Father Patrick, I was not criticising you. I sought only to acquaint you with the facts. I am well aware that you came to the Church reluctantly to please your grandfather and apart for your love of a woman, you have worked tirelessly to promote the Church in every other way".

The bishop continued, "I know that the Church asks too much of its servants. I have always wondered why we are forbidden to marry? Rendered emasculated and impotent! What good can come of it? Why would our loving Father in Heaven forbid his servants the joy of fatherhood; the bringing of a child into the world, when he himself sent his own son here, it is a joy given to the poorest of men! It has never made sense to me. There have been times, many times, when I have yearned for the tender and loving touch of a woman; but alas, the only woman ever to hold me and say that she loved me, was my mother when I was about seven years of age!".

The bishop sighed at his memory, then continued, "I admire your work and your courage, Father Patrick. I know also that you came to the Church reluctantly to please your grandfather. It may be tempting for you to disregard it, now that your grandfather has passed on, but I beg you to stay with us; for of all the Church's shortcomings, your grandfather Joseph was right. It is a refuge from a world of pain. A place of quietude to a weary soul and for some, a magnificent source of enlightenment". Patrick agreed by nodding his head.

"I wish you well, as you continue your healing ministry", said the bishop. Patrick thanked him, bowed and left.

As he walked back to Joseph's house, he felt different. He remembered once telling Evan that he still felt like a boy, but not now. Suddenly, he felt older, more mature. He had faced the bishop on more equal terms; he actually felt a bit sorry for him. He had often wondered what his reaction would be if he were ever challenged about having a wife? Now, he knew and he was proud at his response. It may have been the loss of his grandfather, combined with having to see the bishop, but whatever caused it to happen, the *boy* Maun had finally gone. In his place was the *man* - much older and wiser.

He opened the door of his grandfather's house and went in. Flavia was comforting Madam Leoni, whose eyes were red and swollen. "Don't be sad, Madam", said Patrick, "You know that my grandfather would not want you unhappy. He lived a life doing good and our Father God will love him for it".

"I know. I know", whispered Madam Leoni through her tears, "But, I will miss him so much".

"Yes", said Patrick, "I know how you feel. I will miss him too. No matter how much we know of God's Heaven and his care of our souls, it is the personality we miss; his warmth and compassion. We must not, however, keep calling him back with our grief".

Madam Leoni put her hand on Patrick's arm, "Do you know that he loved you most of all?".

"Yes, I did", replied Patrick, "And I loved him. He was my guide; my protector and my teacher. And he altered peoples' lives for the better".

Madam Leoni nodded sadly, "I must go to the Abbey and offer a prayer for him" and she put on her cloak and left.

Flavia asked him how his meeting with the bishop had gone? He did not reply, but he went to her and enfolding her in his arms, he held her for several moments, before saying, "How long is it since I told you how much I love you - and need you?".

She was a little puzzled, "You told me yesterday, my dearest?".

"Well, I will tell you again. You are my life and my love and I am honoured that you have chosen to stay with me."

Flavia's cheeks flushed, "I am where I belong and I will be here for as long as you need me".

CHAPTER LIV

ADAM'S CHANGE OF HEART

When Madam Leoni arrived at the Abbey, she knelt to pray. She did not notice Adam, who was on his knees by the alter. In the years he had travelled with Patrick and Flavia and despite all the wonders he had seen, there had been times when he longed to be with his family. The memories of his mother walking up and down on the dock watching for his father's ship to come home; the tears she shed, worrying as to whether he was dead or alive. The whole family missed him so much.

So, as he knelt, he asked for guidance, "Please tell me Lord, what do you want of me?". He waited for an answer and eventually it came.

He met Madam Leoni as he left the Abbey and taking her arm, he walked her back to the house. Flavia had already set the table, ready for Madam to serve the meal she had prepared earlier and they ate quietly, only Madam Leoni's sniffs into a piece of linen, breaking the silence.

After they had finished the meal and Madam Leoni was clearing the dishes away, Adam said, "I have something to tell both of you. I'm not returning to north Briton with you. I have decided to stay here in Tours and become a priest like you and serve God in my own town of Nanmentium".

He looked from Patrick to Flavia to see how they were taking the news and could see that they were speechless and taken completely by surprise. Adam continued, "I have heard you Patrick, tell thousands of people over the years, that they should stay with their families to love and support them. I know that you were right. I miss my family more than I can say and I don't want to cause them any more worry. However, it was the atmosphere in the Abbey that started me off in this turn of thought. It may have been the incense; or, the chanting of the monks - I don't know, but something stirred in my soul. My dear friends, I owe you everything. I have seen so many wondrous miracles, can you blame me for wanting some of my own?"

Patrick and Flavia understood, "My friend", said Patrick, "I know only too well the value of a loving family and know that your power of seeing visions has grown. You will make a wonderful priest and Evan and Margareta will be delighted that you will be staying in Gaul. We will call on our way home and tell them the news".

Evan was sorry to hear of the death of Joseph; a man he admired greatly. However, on being told of Adam's decision to become a priest, neither he or Margaretta were surprised, for since the evening when he helped Maun in the healing of Margaretta, there had been a change in Adam. He had been awakened to visions of another world; one of other beings of light and love. That he had decided to serve the Church in his own home town was, however, news that pleased them very much.

Patrick and Flavia enjoyed their few days as the honoured guests of Evan and

Margaretta, while waiting for the departure of their ship to north Britain. They had been pleased to find that Karl had married and was now the proud father of a daughter, now two years old, the pride and joy of her grandparents.

On the day they had to leave, they were driven in style to the docks in Evan's carriage. Evan and Margaretta waited until the ship was untied from its mooring and set sail, both waving until the vessel was almost out of sight.

Margaretta gave Evan a rag to wipe his eyes, "You are a big softie, Evan. Patrick is as happy now as I have ever seen him, so why are you so sad?".

Evan dabbed his eyes, "I know", he said, "It's just that every time I see him, I am reminded of the first time I saw him, standing by our ship at the dock in Hibernia; little more than walking bones. How could one human being treat a young boy so cruelly? This Jesus he loves so much, has exacted a high price for saving his life".

Margaretta placed her hand on his arm, "Was it not Jesus who gave him his wonderful gift to heal, a gift both you and I are grateful for? If it were not for Jesus, we would not be here".

"Yes, you are right, my dear. We would not be here to enjoy these happy years, or know our little granddaughter. Yet, I still think he carries a heavy burden".

"Don't worry", said Margaretta, "I am sure Jesus will take good care of him".

Patrick and Flavia watched Evan and Margaretta until they were dots in the distance, before looking for a suitable place to shelter. It was not easy; the wind was howling and the rain pounding the deck and for the second time in Patrick Mun's life, he found himself at sea in a violent storm. With an extraordinary amount of good luck, the ship was blown towards a sheltered cove, although not without some damage to the side of the ship.

The passengers and crew were frightened and soaked to the skin but, surprisingly, no one was injured. The inhabitants were used to shipwrecks, being partially surrounded by jagged outcrops of rock. With the arrival of the damaged vessel, the locals turned out in force to help them and they were all taken to the nearest inn, where an assortment of dry clothes and covers had been quickly collected together. Although the inn was very small, Patrick and Flavia found a corner near the fire and tried to make themselves comfortable.

Next morning, despite an improvement in the weather, they learned that it would be some weeks before the ship could be repaired.

They enjoyed the inhabitants kind hospitality and did not complain about any of the inconvenience. Indeed, the local people seemed to enjoy their visitors company; they were friendly and talkative and when a member of the crew mentioned that Patrick was a priest, the word went around that the ship was saved because God took care of his servants. After that, they came to him with their problems.

He was not called upon to heal anyone, but when he saw anyone looking worried, he would go to them and when the opportunity arose, he would touch their arm, or shake them by the hand. He knew that they were being helped, for he felt the healing power leave his body.

The ship was soon repaired, albeit temporarily, the Captain making it plain, that he would be sailing to his home port to make more substantial repairs, before embarking on the remainder of the journey to the north.

After several weeks, the ship was ready to sail; every islander turning out to wave good-bye and although the passengers were pleased to be on their way again, they were grateful for the kindness and hospitality that had been shown to them.

The home port happened to be on the lower Severn and Flavia was delighted to recognise the small town she had passed through on several occasions on her way to Avalon. She asked Patrick, if they could go there to pass the time until the work on the ship was completed? Patrick enquired of the Captain how long they expected to be tied up for and when he received the reply, "Perhaps, two weeks?", Patrick agreed to go to Avalon.

They hired a buggy and driver and set off happily; making plans to visit their old friends they had made some years before.

On the way, they noticed an extraordinary number of funeral pyres, then a whole line of coffins being wheeled to a burial ground. He asked the driver if he knew why this could be, "Why are so many people dying?". He was told that there was an epidemic of a disease which had been called the 'burning disease'.

This disease apparently was no respecter of age or station; everyone, from babies to the elderly - it made no difference. One day they would be about their work, the next they become ill, death swiftly following. The driver told them that the epidemic had been raging for some time, although it now seemed to have burnt itself out.

They moved on to the best travellers' inn they could find and ate well, before deciding to go and see if their friends were still where they left them. They were delighted to find that they were and it was wonderful to see how well they were and how they had progressed. The house that once was their emergency shelter, was now the village hall and surrounded by new homes.

They had also grown in numbers and the young boys whom they had helped, were now tall and healthy young men. They clearly remembered the horrendous escape they made in the ill-prepared boat; the travellers who gave up their wagon and food to help them and the man who had healed them. Over the years, their parents had never stopped singing the praises of the strangers who had helped them settle in this strange country and when they saw Patrick again, they were thrilled and could not take their eyes from him.

Three young men were introduced to Patrick as Kevan, Sheran and Raig and before Patrick and Flavia returned to the inn, the three asked if they would return to their village and teach them their faith? An invitation such as this, Patrick could not refuse and he and Flavia visited the new village on several days, until eventually, the three young men pleaded with Patrick to be allowed to go with him and become his disciples. The young mens' parents were in full agreement and plans for them to accompany Patrick and Flavia were made.

After a visit to the church and another to the sacred well, Flavia began to pack their satchels ready to leave. They were talking about arriving back at the villa and wondered if his grandparents had moved to a smaller house, as Calim had said he would? Patrick, said laughing, "Where are we going to make our home? We may have to build a house of our own?".

Flavia, also laughing, said "I would love that. Just you and I together".

He turned to smile at her and saw she was sitting on the bed holding her head. She looked up at him and said, "Maun, "I don't feel very well".

Hurrying to her, he helped her lie down and as he held her, he realised she was very hot to his touch and he said, "I will get some cold water and bathe your head" and with that, he ran outside to the water tank and soaked a cloth.

Sheran and Kevan were sitting on the grass opposite the inn. Patrick called out to them and at his call, they immediately came over, Patrick anxiously telling them, "Flavia is ill! Will you fetch a physician?".

Some time later, Kevan's mother arrived at the house, saying, "No physician will come. It is the burning disease, There is nothing to be done". She indicated to her son and Sheran that they must leave and reluctantly, they left the inn. However, they did not go far, but sat on the grass where Patrick had found them and where they intended to remain.

Patrick sat beside his beloved wife using all the power he could to try to heal her, but nothing worked. He could not believe that God had let him down at this crucial time and he kept hoping Flavia would recover as suddenly as she had become ill. Sitting on a stool beside the bed with his arm around her, he prayed.

For two days he bathed her in cool water and from time to time she seemed to rally, only to sink again into delirium. On the third day, Patrick knew that their struggle was over. The fever had gone, but so had her will to live. Her breathing was shallow and as she lay with his arm around her, she opened her eyes and whispered in a voice only just audible, "You must go to Rome". These were her last words before she died.

Patrick, exhausted and distraught, could not believe that this had happened to them and he wished with all his heart that he had died with her; for he could not envisage his life without her.

Kevan's mother returned, bringing with her the priest from St Joseph's church. Whilst she and the innkeeper's wife prepared the body for burial, the priest attempted to comfort Patrick, but to no avail. However, he stood up and going to his satchel, took out his robe, the one that Flavia had danced in and loved so much and wrapped it around her body lovingly.

For several days after she was laid to rest in a grave by the edge of the apple orchard, he did not wash or shave, nor cared if he lived or died.

Raig had gone home, his faith in Patrick's miraculous healings severely dented, Kevan and Sheran continued to wait patiently on the grass opposite the inn for Patrick to recover. Kevan frequently went into the inn to speak to the innkeeper's wife, who had said she would keep him informed if he showed any sign of recovery.

After several days, Patrick finally emerged and strode off aimlessly, Kevan nudged Sheran and jumping to their feet, they followed him. They did not get too close to him, but followed and watched, for they suspected he might try to end his own life. But, Patrick stopped by the sacred well and drank some of the cool water from cupped hands, then splashed some on his face. Continuing his walk, he started to climb the Tor and went right to the top. Once there, he stopped and looked around at the scenery; the hills behind him and before him, the marshes. He glanced upwards at the milky-white sky, feeling cold, empty and helpless, then anger filled him. He shook his fists at the sky and yelled, " Why? Why have you done this to me? Have I not done everything you ever asked of me? Why have you taken my beloved?".

He sat down on the grass and having cried until no tears were left, he stared once again into space.

Suddenly, he became aware of thick black clouds rolling towards him. Never having seen anything like this before, he could only sit and watch as the blackness enfolded him. He lay back on the grass watching and wondering what it all meant. when in the far distance, he saw a tiny movement, like the fluttering wings of a bee. It seemed to be coming closer and as it did, he could make out that the movement was a wheel. Closer and closer it came; bright yellow he thought, until it got really close, then he could see that it was bright shining gold. The wheel was not like any he had seen on a wagon. This one had handles on, like the steering wheel on the new ships. It came so close; so big that the hub hovered above him.

The next thing Patrick knew, he was standing in the middle of a room. He had been in one something like it before. It was so light, yet there was no trace of a lamp. The walls were opaque. He then became aware of a presence behind him and speaking over his shoulder, a voice saying, "Watch and listen".

One of the walls cleared and Patrick watched as every life he had lived paraded before him; from his arrival through the heavenly gate of Arcturus as an infant spirit; to his life this day. Several caught his attention. One where he saw himself in conversation with Jesus and another as an old man named Maun, who converted two young boys by the side of the river Clyde. Patrick recognised his grandfather Calim and his uncle Harran as the boys. He saw the light gather around them, as they touched the tiny scrap of the robe that had once belonged to Jesus. That had been one of his greatest pleasures.

As old Maun, he had stayed close to the boys, until he was satisfied they had absorbed all he had to teach them. After that, he had waited at the port of Dunbriton, for a ship to take him home to Gaul. He knew that his life was near its end, for he was very tired, yet satisfied that he had completed his task. He had died on the ship; the crew promptly disposing of his body over the side and throwing his satchel in after him; and with it his cedar box containing the scrap of Jesus's robe.

The visions continued and Patrick was given information on the purpose of his life and work. "But, why?", he asked, "Did I have to endure so much humiliation and suffering?".

The voice replied, "Those who are born to earth, agree to live and abide by the laws of that planet". Throughout the review, he was aware of the presence of Flavia always near to him; in some lives she was his mother, but in most, she had been his closest companion and lover.

When finally the review was over, the voice indicated for him to walk through an archway into another room. Unlike the one he had just left, this one was full of people; beautiful beings of light and the feelings of purest love and compassion filled him. A lady approached him and took his hand. Recognition dawned, for as he looked into her enormous blue eyes, he saw the angel that had lived as his grandmother Rhona. She took his hand and led him to a dais, where another figure lay as though asleep. His heart leapt as he saw that it was Flavia.

He went to her, bent over and kissed her and as he did so, she opened her eyes, smiled at him and said, "Why are you here Maun?. You are to go to Rome".

"I know, my love. I am on my way."

But, the voice said, "Wait! You have a new and more powerful guide who wishes to go with you". A door opened and through it came a being of tremendous light and power. Patrick caught his breath as he recognised the soul that had been his great uncle Martin; not now old, but as a young warrior for Christ. Then the voice said, "You know now that your power was subdued to allow Flavia to return. You would have held on to her and the plan could not have gone forward; but your power has been returned to you three-fold. You are to fear nothing. For no enemy can hold, or harm you".

He turned again to look at Flavia saying, "I wish you were coming with me".

"Don't worry", she said, "I will join you as soon as I can. Now, don't forget Rome!".

"I won't forget, my love." He then felt himself being drawn backwards. He looked up to glimpse Flavia one more time and was surprised to see another heavenly being turn around and smile at him. 'It can't be?', he thought, 'Not Conchessa, my mother?'. He knew then that his mother's earth life was over as well as his grandmother's.

On the hillside, Kevan and Sheran stood looking down at Patrick, who was mumbling, "I am on my way" - they really thought he had gone mad, but then Patrick's eyes opened. He looked up at the two disciples who had remained loyal, then held up his arms for them to pull him to his feet. He looked around at the scene once more. The colours seemed more vivid; the sky was blue and the world seemed a more beautiful place. He was still dirty and unshaven, but his eyes were no longer red from grief, but shining, like two pale green diamonds. He put his arms around the shoulders of Keevan and Sheran and said, "How would you both like to escort me to Rome?".

CHAPTER LV

ROME

Rome was a crowded city. Patrick did not expect to see Pope Celestine at short notice, so he had a message written by a professional scribe, stating that Patrick Mun of Bonavon, north Briton requested an audience and handed it to the gatekeeper. Expecting to wait for days, if not weeks or months, he and his friends went exploring the city. When they arrived back at their lodgings, they were met by an anxious landlord who told them that no sooner had they left, than a guard of his Holiness came looking for them, "You are to report tomorrow at noon and his Holiness will give you an audience".

Patrick brushed his best clothes and had his hair trimmed, satisfied he looked presentable, he went to the palace. He was shown into a waiting room and was surprised to see one other person waiting. He was wondering which one of them Celestine would see first, when one of the guards called both of them forward and they were taken before the Pope.

"Father Patrick", said Celestine, "Meet Paulinius. He has been working in Hibernia for some time. Unfortunately, that country is not acquainted with Latin and his task was almost impossible. I have been given to understand that you have some understanding of the language of that country and it is my wish that you should take his place there. For many years, we have prayed that the whole of the Britannic islands be Christianised; we fear that with the withdrawal of the Roman forces and peoples from surrounding countries pouring in to fill the vacuum, wars will destroy all the good works already done. Therefore, I am sending you to Hibernia and Paulinius will go to north east Briton to Caladonia, where he may find the people there more receptive, having been exposed to Roman influence".

Patrick and Paulinius waited in Rome only long enough for robes to be created and soon, at a ceremony within the Vatican, Patrick was anointed bishop. He was proud to have bestowed on him the rank he felt he deserved, but he kept thinking, 'If only I could have Flavia returned to me in the flesh'. The thought of her and her promise that she would join him as soon as she could, gave him a warm glow and he knew that it would be her spiritual presence he would become aware of. However, knowing that nothing could ever harm her where she was now, was a blessing, as he never, ever again, wanted to see her suffer as she did on this earth.

Paulinius and Patrick prepared for their journey to north Britain. Patrick wanted to see his family and inform them of Joseph's death and his assignment to Hibernia and Paulinius had suggested that he go with him to Dunbriton and find an escort and interpreter there to help with any language problems. He'd learned a valuable lesson on the lack of ability to communicate and he did not intend to make the same mistake twice. He already had a companion who acted as his servant, but he spoke only Latin and would not be of assistance on that score.

Their journey to Dunbriton was long and tiresome, but eventually they reached their destination.

At the port, they hired horses and rode immediately to the villa. When it came into view, memories of his happy times spent here with his grandmother, made him smile, even though he knew that she was no longer there. However, he was looking forward to seeing his grandfather Calim and his father.

It was a surprise when a servant said she would inform the Mistress of the house and Helen came into the room. When she saw that the visitor was Patrick, she rushed into his arms in tears, "If only you had not gone away, Patrick. I have bad news for you. Our parents are all dead. Your mother and mine; my father Sergaeus, grandfather Calim and Doctor Markus".

"What has happened to them? Who has done this terrible thing?", Patrick asked.

"Not who", she replied, "But, what? It was a disease that came upon our country. People died after a short but violent illness; they became very hot and seemed to burn out".

Patrick slumped on one of the large well-worn couches and put his hand to his head. Suddenly, he looked up and spoke, "My father? You have not mentioned my father, or my uncle Paulus".

"Your uncle is also dead", said Helen, "But your father is alive, but it may have been better for him had he died". Helen continued, "It came to our attention that people were suffering; so many dying and children roaming the streets crying for their parents, without food or shelter. Our parents and our grandparents decided to go and help them. They went to the Brothers and bought medicines. Armed with bundles of herbs and mixtures, they went to where they were told the illness was. When some time passed, the Brothers became worried, for they expected one or two of them to return for more medication. So, when no one came, several of the Brothers went in search of them. When they finally found the village where they had been working, they learned that our families had worked hard, helped many people and found homes for the orphan children, but one by one, they caught the disease and died. The Brothers were then taken to a house and shown the one survivor. It was your father, Calpurnius. He was in a dreadful state; no longer aware of who he was. The Brothers took him to Bonavon to nurse him back to health, but the last I heard of him, there had been no improvement in his condition".

"I must go to him", said Patrick.

Helen protested, "You and your friends have travelled a long way; please take some food before you leave on yet another journey". He was impatient to go, but looked at his hungry and tired companions and agreed they should have food and drink.

Helen rang the bell and servants soon brought refreshments. They ate hurriedly, not wanting to delay Patrick from seeing his father. They appreciated that he was anxious to get away and although he tried to hide his impatience, he was not very successful and having eaten and drank, they were soon on their way. Patrick was aware of the familiar landscape of his home territory, but all he could think of was reaching Bonavon and seeing his father.

One of the Brothers, working near the gate of the Abbey, saw the five riders approach and recognised Patrick as the leader. He welcomed him and the others, but was worried about breaking the bad news about Calpurnius.

Patrick sensed his unease, guessing the reason. He said, "Thank you Brother for your welcome. I have been informed by my cousin that you have saved my father's life. Is he here?".

The Brother breathed a sigh of relief, "Yes, he is. I will take you to him, but I must first inform Brother Amyott of your arrival. He will want to tell you everything himself". Patrick nodded graciously and followed him, Paulinius and the others doing likewise.

Amyott emerged from his office and looking unhappy, said "I wish Patrick, we had better news for you. I must warn you that we are very worried about your father. Come, I will take you to him".

They walked behind the Abbey and crossed the main road to the fields, where the Brothers were gathering vegetables for the evening meal. Standing watching them, without expression or interest, was Calpurnius. He was dressed in the dark red robe of the Brothers; a rope was tied around his waist, the other end of which was tied around the waist of Brother Shonus. Patrick's heart sank, "Why is my father tethered like a dog?", he asked.

Amyott replied, "It is necessary Patrick to save him from wandering away. We were afraid he might fall into the river".

Patrick called out, "Papa! It is me, Maun" as he walked towards the little group of workers, who by now were all looking in his direction. That is everyone, except Calpurnius, who was standing still as though he had not heard anything. Patrick called out again, "Papa! Look, it is me, Maun". But, there was no response from Calpurnius, not a flicker of recognition crossed his face.

Patrick summed up every iota of healing power he could muster and hugged his father, holding him firmly. After a little while, the onlookers saw Calpurnius raise his arms and place them around his son's waist and then rest his head on his shoulder. This was the first time he had shown the slightest change of action or expression. As father and son stood in the vegetable patch in a steady embrace, Calpurnius began to cry, Patrick then slowly leading him back towards his companions, asked "May I take him to his quarters, Amyott?".

"Most certainly" he replied, "But, they are not as your father has been used to all of his life. He has to share with the Brothers, for we have had to watch his every move - for his own safety".

"I appreciate all you have done for my father. He is all the close family I have left and I am extremely grateful. Is there somewhere else I can take my father to sit with him?"

"Yes", replied Amyott, "The office is free. You may take him there a while".

Patrick said, "Before I go, may I introduce to you Bishop Paulinius and our companions and friends. They have expressed a wish to see the Abbey and grounds".

Amyott bowed, "Indeed, Patrick. That will be my pleasure".

Seated in the office, Patrick was facing his father, smiling at him, when

Calpurnius said with the utmost difficulty, "Mauny, is it really you? I thought you were dead".

"No! Not me. I have been to Rome, where I met His holiness Pope Celestine and would you believe it father, he has made me a bishop!"

"You, my son? A bishop?", Calpurnius forced a weak smile.

Patrick smiled back, "Yes father. I am". Patrick looked around the office. This was the house where he was born, although the beautiful wall decorations were now sadly faded and dirty.

Calpurnius broke the momentary silence by saying, "Have you been told of your dear mother's death?".

"Yes, I have", replied Patrick, "But, I knew that before I came home. Father, I had the most amazing experience. After my own Flavia died, I was taken to a place, I can only describe as Heaven, where I saw her again, in the company of grandmother Rhona and my mother. Believe me father, they are all young, beautiful and safe in our Father God's care".

"You saw her? You saw your mother? Did she say anything to you?"

It was tempting to tell a small lie, for Conchessa had only smiled and thinking he was on safe ground, Patrick simply said, "Mother conveyed to me that she is happy and loves you very much". With that, Calpurnius seemed to brighten up considerably.

"What do you want to do, father? I mean, would you like to move back into the villa, where Helen and her family would love to take care of you? Or, live with the Brothers? Or, if you like, come with me to Hibernia, where Celestine has seen fit to send me on a mission?".

"My son. I do not want to cause offence to anyone, but given the choice, I would like a little comfort in my old age. Kind as the Brothers are, they live a frugal life and now that the villa is in uncle Harran's family, I would not feel right. As for travelling to another country with you", Calpurnius shook his head slowly, "No, my son. I never did take to any other country. I like my home too much".

"Father, do you recognise the building where we sit now?"

Calpurnius slowly looked around him, "It seems familiar".

"It should", said Patrick, "This was our home. I was born in the next room. We gave it to the Brothers when we moved to the villa. Would you like it back?".

"We could not do that, Mauny. We could not ask for a gift to be returned."

"No, father", said Patrick, "I agree. But, we could buy it back?".

"No, my son. I have no money left, or if I have, I do not know what has become of it."

"But, father", said Patrick, "I have money. Lots of it and I have no intention of taking any of it to Hibernia."

The longer Calpurnius was in Patrick's company, the stronger he became and for the next three months they were inseparable. The Brothers were delighted to sell the farmhouse back and with the gold they received, they could afford to build a larger dormitory for the new Brothers and many other things they had wished for. They even promised to restore the farmhouse to its former glory.

Calpurnius watched his home spring back to life; with the vibrant colours he had originally painted and it seemed to everyone that as the farmhouse came back to its original state, so did Calpurnius.

During the three months that Patrick had worked with his father and the Brothers, Paulinius had interviewed several men to find one who would be a good guide and interpreter. He had been told that the people of Caledonia had been influenced in some measure by the Army. He had learned a lesson once, as to the folly of going into a strange country ill-prepared and misunderstood, so as well as searching for a guide, he took lessons on the language of the Caledonians from Amyott's younger brother.

The time came when Paulinius could delay his assignment no longer and preparations were made for a farewell celebration. Patrick would provide a service of healing, while Paulinius would follow that with a service of thanksgiving and finally, they would process through the village, blessing it as they went.

Patrick had not performed a healing service since before Flavia died and he had left for Rome. He wondered how he would manage without her and her wonderful spiritual vision? Nor, did he have Adam, whose contribution was always a tower of strength. He was on his own and he prayed for guidance.

Paulinius had never seen anything like it in his life before, "Where have all these people come from? Not from this small village alone, surely?". The crowds poured in and sat patiently around the yard of the farmhouse, the air filled with excitement.

Paulinius could hear snatches of conversation, "The moment we heard Patrick Mun was home, we had to come … We have walked ten miles to get here … We could not bring our child he is much too sick, but we have brought his clothes for Patrick to touch and bless, we know that it will work just as well".

When Patrick and Calpurnius came out of the farmhouse, the atmosphere was so exciting, it was tangible. Patrick looked around at all of them; their expectations of him were high - perhaps, too high! 'Where, my Father God, do I begin?', he asked himself. Then he saw it. A bright light hovered above the head of a child in his mother's arms and he heard Flavia's voice say, "We are here. Continue".

Paulinius stood watching as, one after the other were healed of their sickness or injury and waited while Patrick blessed clothes and shawls belonging to others too weak to attend. He had not heard of Patrick until he met him in Rome and he could not understand why this man of miracles had not been promoted bishop long before himself? He felt that he had witnessed the Lord at work.

The healing service over, everyone crowded into the still unfinished Abbey for the thanksgiving service to be taken by Paulinius. After what he had just witnessed, it crossed his mind that his mass might be a bit of an anti-climax, however, he need not have been so concerned, for after the wonderful healing service and the excitement of it all, he spoke with softness and utmost calm and the people relaxed and enjoyed it.

On the very last evening of Patrick's visit to Bonavon, Clodus and Alana came to see Calpurnius and they were happy to find him so well. They had tried to persuade him to live with them when the Brothers brought him home, but he did not know them and reluctantly they had to allow the Brothers to nurse him back to health. Now, they were chatting away about old times, Patrick looking on, amused and pleased to see them so happy.

Becoming aware of activity in the yard, he went to the window and peeped through. Outside people scurried about, entering the church carrying various sized dishes. The old church was being used as a dormitory for new monks, so Patrick was curious as to what was going on? He asked Clodus if he knew why the Brothers were working so late? Clodus laughed, "You might as well know, Patrick. The Brothers and the people of the village are preparing a farewell meal for you and Paulinius - everyone is coming. Why do you think we are here? It is to occupy you and your father until they are ready for us".

Patrick sniffed, "I can smell cooking now. Where is Paulinius and our friends? Is it not a surprise for them also?".

Clodus replied, "No Patrick, the surprise is just for you. Paulinius and your friends are helping to cook".

"Paulinius cook?", he exclaimed in surprise, "I look forward to this meal!".

There came a knock at the door and when Patrick answered it, several children stood looking up at him. Together, they said in chorus, "You are to come with us" and took him by the hands and pulled him towards the old church. Calpurnius, Clodus and Alana followed and they were all very amused.

When Patrick saw what they had done to the church, he was thrilled. It was clean and decorated with small trees and flowers and trestle tables were stacked with a variety of delicious food.

Now that all of the people who came from far away to be healed were making their way home, it was a sea of familiar faces that looked up at him from their places at the tables. He could see Cedi, his brother Eric and their wives, Anna and Sophie and their children, Victor and his family were nearby. He also recognised the people who had been the slave children, now very proud and respectable tradesmen. Another quick glance around the tables and he could see Hanno and Rebecca and guessed that the two very tall young men standing by the door were Phillipp and his younger brother. He also saw Clodus and Alana surrounded by young people and he guessed that they were their grandchildren.

Amyott, who was sitting between Patrick and Paulinius, stood up, raising his hands to indicate that they were ready to start the meal. He then said grace, after which everyone began to eat. It did not take too long for the piles of food to be demolished, Patrick and Paulinius having had a taste of every dish, so as not to offend anyone who had lovingly prepared it. Paulinius confessed to baking the fruit bread, "It is my speciality", he said with pride.

When the tables were cleared, everyone remained sitting on the benches and Amyott leaned over to whisper in Patrick's ear, "They are waiting for you to address them".

So, he stood up and cleared his throat a little, "This night has been for me a truly wonderful surprise. I look around this old church that was my grandfather's pride and joy and I see so many familiar faces of my friends and family. My grandfather Joseph would have loved to see it like this and he would have loved to see all of you too, just as I do now. Tomorrow, Bishop Paulinius leaves for Caledonia and I also leave for Hibernia on the instructions of Celestine, the Bishop of Rome. His hope is that wars between the Highlanders, the Irish and the Britons will end if Christianity is taken to these places. We will take with us the happy memories of this very special evening, spent with so many wonderful friends. All of you will be in my prayers, wherever I go".

Everyone raised their voices, calling out, "And you will be in ours also".

Paulinius stood, "My friends. May I add my thanks to all of you for allowing me your hospitality and providing me with an interpreter and guide; who is your own brother Gilles. I am, indeed, grateful to him and others for teaching me the language that will help me with my work. May I bless each one of you by saying, *Go forward in your lives with wisdom in your minds. Love in your hearts and truth on your lips; and no harm will ever touch your souls*".

The tables were quickly removed. Music began to play and the dancing began, Patrick joining hands with the children and dancing with them.

He slept in the small room that had been his when a child. When he awoke early to prepare for his journey, he automatically went to the window to look up at the hills and then across at the stables, as he had always done. Memories flooded back, not all of them pleasant, but he remembered his golden pony he had first seen through this small window and the happy days spent riding with his father.

Looking now at the stables, he saw Kevan and Sheran bring out the horses ready for their journey. He wished he did not have to go - not today, anyway. He had danced the night before with the children, displaying less dignity than, perhaps, was expected of him. Still it was fun, nobody seemed to mind, although Paulinius raised an eyebrow before deciding to join in.

He dressed, then went to say good-bye to his father. He found him already having breakfast and waiting for him to eat with him. " Don't you worry about me, my son", said Calpurnius, "I have my home and good servants to take care of me; my friends to entertain me and the Brothers have promised to take care of my soul, *What more could any man ask?*".

Patrick laughed, "I'm sure we could think of something, if we tried hard enough. But, if you are content father, then so am I".

He then went to see Kevan and Sheran and asked if they had eaten? "No. We have not", they replied, "But, we have a box of food left over from last evening. We can stop on the way and eat and drink at the spring".

Paulinius came hurrying towards them, "Goodbye my friends. God bless you and good luck. Thanks to you, I now have the opportunity to succeed. I know you will fare much better in Hibernia than I".

"We will have to wait and see about that", said Patrick modestly, "Goodbye and good luck to you also".

In spite of the early hour, most of the villagers were out to see them leave, some weeping as they rode off.

EPILOGUE

Hibernia - or Ireland as it was now called - held no terror for Patrick. In his heart he knew exactly what had to be done and he was conscious of the great spiritual power within him. Anyone who came within arm's length of him became aware of it; they felt he was special and were compelled to follow him.

With the help of Keven, Sheran and his many followers, they set up monasteries to teach men how to grow food, tend animals and care for the land. Patrick taught them that in order to be free of tyranical rulers, they had to be strong, self-sufficient and educated.

Over the following years, he travelled through several kingdoms preaching the word of Jesus and gaining followers. Rulers sent sons or officials to arrest him, but after meeting him, they all returned to their masters to say that Patrick had moved on, taking with him even more followers and in some cases, very often the rulers' own sons.

One day, a mysterious stranger approached Patrick and asked him to return to Avalon with him. Patrick did not want to go, memories of Flavia's death there still lingered and he was making good progress in Ireland. However, he was persuaded by Kevan and Sheran, who were homesick and longed to see their parents once more. "Besides", they said, "You have many workers and followers to carry on here, while we are away". Patrick was now convinced and so they crossed the water to Avalon.

Once there, Kevan and Sheran went to see their parents and although they did not want to leave Patrick with the stranger, he insisted he would be safe and so arranged to meet them in two days at the inn in the town.

The mysterious stranger led Patrick to a house some distance away, where he introduced him to a group of men, who told him, "We have heard of you, from time to time and know about your miraculous powers of healing". Patrick thought that they were going to ask him to heal one of their number, but they didn't. Instead, the leader of the group said, "Have you heard the story of Joseph of Aramathea bringing thirteen members of our Lord's family to Avalon?".

"Yes, I have indeed", said Patrick.

The leader of the group continued, "We - my friends and I - are the descendants of that thirteen. There are many more of us scattered around the country, but always thirteen of us remain in Avalon. We meet and pray every day. We have been told that you, on the orders of Pope Celestine, have a mission to convert Ireland to Christianity? Well, my friend, we also have orders from a higher authority".

Patrick was puzzled, "What authority on earth could be higher than the Pope?".

The mystery man continued, "It is our task to ensure, using all of our skills, that certain members of our Holy family are chosen to ascend the royal throne of this country. These Britannic islands have always been sacred; called long ago the 'white isles', or the sacred isles. We must ensure they remain sacred. That is why it is essential that the country's rulers are chosen with the utmost care".

"Word came to us of your great spiritual power and we have need of that power now. We need confirmation of our latest instructions, that is why we have brought you here. We wish you to join with us in deep prayer, believing that because you are true to Christ, we can be certain of the truth and quality of our instructions."

Patrick realised that they wanted him to sit in silence with them, however, he asked them why they had asked him? He was not one of this sacred family, "Was there no one of their own Order to sit with them?".

"But, my son", said the old man with the pointed beard, "Are you not aware that you are a child come to earth through Arcturus?".

Patrick raised his head, as the memory of his heavenly dream returned, "Yes Sir. I do know that. Tell me how can I help?".

Patrick stayed with the family and was able to re-assure them of their destiny. Two days later, before he left, he asked the old man his name? "It is not the name I was baptised with", he replied, "But, one I inherited and will pass on. It is Artura".

"Please Patrick, come back and sit with us again. I have never felt the power of the kingdom so strong. I trust that you felt it too?"

"Yes, I did", said Patrick, "And I will return when I can".

From there, he went to Flavia's grave. In as much as he knew that her soul was safe and she was happy, he missed her presence; her voice, her loving touch. He could bear the pain no longer and went to the inn to meet Kevan and Sheran, who said, "We are relieved to see you Patrick. We were so worried about you being with that strange character".

"Bless you both for caring so much, but I was quite safe", said Patrick.

They wasted no time in returning to Ireland and Patrick, now almost fifty, allowed his beard to grow; partly because shaving was time-consuming and uncomfortable.

He spent a lot of time in the fields teaching his novice monks to care for the animals. He laid paticular emphasis on treating all of them with the utmost gentleness and kindness, insisting that the animals would respond to this, by being more healthy and contented.

Regardless of his status, he was never one to shirk work and was often found helping out with the dirtiest and more unpleasant tasks.

On such a day, Kevan came hurrying towards him, "There is a deputation to see you, my Lord and they are not at all happy".

Patrick stood up and leaving the others to see to a lamb which had just been born, he asked, "What do they want?".

"They did not say, my Lord", replied Kevan.

"Humm", said Patrick, "Give me a moment to wash my hands. Tell them I will be along presently".

It was a bitter cold morning and Patrick had to break the ice in the leather bucket of water before plunging his hands in to wash them. He wrapped his heavy cloak around his shoulders and went to meet them.

Before him stood several men, very similar in appearance; olive tinted skin with very dark hair. Kevan was right, they were more than a little aggrieved. They waited, ready with a mental list of complaints. Patrick invited them into the Abbey church where it was just a fraction warmer. The men wasted no time. "Sir", said one, "Everyone is praising your good works, but good works for some has meant misery for us. When our masters were convinced by your preaching that slavery

352

was bad and unchristian, they gave us our freedom. At first, we thought it was wonderful, but now we find ourselves without a roof over our heads and with the marks of slavery upon us, no one will employ us. Our women and children are starving and have no warm clothes in this cold weather".

Before Patrick could say a word, another of the men spoke, "We have been told how you were born to a rich nobleman and it is easy to see that you are not concerned with our troubles. For years we have worked and suffered; seen our fellow slaves die from hard work and lack of care. Now we are no better off". The others mumbled their agreement.

Kevan, Sheran and some of the other monks gathered around as they sensed the ex-slaves were becoming more and more angry. They wondered why Patrick did not hold up his hand in front of them, as he usually did with irate people to calm them down. That, usually brought about a more calm and peaceful situation. But, Patrick simply stood there looking very sad. A tear started to roll down one of his cheeks.

The monks wondered why Patrick allowed this verbal abuse to continue. It seemed to them that he was absorbing all of their bitterness into himself. When they stopped shouting, only then did he hold both hands up to bless them, but, immediately after, he slowly began to remove his cloak. Then he removed his thick woollen robe. Standing in his long sleeveless undergarment, he turned side-ways. There for everyone to clearly see, was the hideous red snake-like scar; the mark of a slave, standing out against his very white skin.

Those gathered before him gazed in disbelief, Kevan and Sheran no less than the others, for they had never been told of his early life. Patrick picked up his robe and put it back on, then one-by-one, the monks and the former slaves fell to their knees; some begging forgiveness, others beginning to sob.

"Please stand", said Patrick, "The floor is much too cold to kneel on".

He then asked them where their women and children were? When told they were hiding in the woods, he gave orders for them to be brought to the Abbey church. A fire was lit and food prepared, enough to feed all of the freed slaves, their women and children.

Word was sent to the women of the Order of the Sisters of Mary, to come and take the mothers and children and give them beds for the night.

Patrick's orders were to take Christianity to Hibernia. He knew that to confine his efforts to the male population and create monks of them all, would hardly allow Christianity to grow and prosper amongst the people. The women and children were just as important, which was why he always encouraged any monks who wished to marry to do so. He also permitted them to keep their work in the Abbey farm or any of the number of trades available and paid them a fair wage.

So, when women pleaded with him to make room for them, he suggested they should have their own Order. And so the Order of the Sisters of Mary was created.

Unlike his great uncle Martin, of whom it was said, disliked women and felt uncomfortable in their company, Patrick was fond of them. He saw in some the beauty and dignity of his grandmother Rhona; in others the shy vulnerability of his dear mother Conchessa. Others, he could associate with the women in his family and those he had met during his life. He was happy to talk to them about their work or listen to their problems.

He often put this knowledge to use and when one of the Sisters confided in him that she would prefer to work in the kitchens, he saw a vision of Barney's wife with her serious Saturnian face. The only sign of pleasure, being a slight curl at the corner of her lip, he asked her, "Are you sure Sister, would you not prefer to work with the children?".

She had replied, "Oh! No, my Lord Bishop. I really do like to cook". However, Patrick had his doubts? He remembered well Barney's wife's burnt buns, which were even too unpalatable for his good friend Evan - he of the hearty appetite!

With this recollection in mind, he said, "I think Sister, it is only fair that you should try for a week or so to see how you get along". He watched the Sister's lip curl up at the corner at his words - so he knew she was pleased. However, when she had left, he said to himself, 'I hope I will not live to regret that decision'.

Patrick's association with the monks and Sisters was always warm and friendly, yet he never got too close to anyone in particular, as he was aware that even in the most spiritual of societies there was the possibility of jealousy raising its ugly head if favouritism was shown. A lesson he had learned from Brother Christophus, in Tours, many years before.

There was an endless stream of homeless people coming to join them. When they learned a trade they moved on, so when the former slaves asked him if they could be taught the trade of blacksmith - as they would like to start their own businesses in other towns - he was happy for them. The Brothers spent months teaching them the trade and they were filled with gratitude and profuse in their praise and thanks. One of the new blacksmiths asked, "If there is anything we can do for you, my Lord Bishop, you only have to ask".

Patrick thought for a moment, then said, "Yes. There is something you can do for me".

"Name it", said the blacksmith, "Anything you want, it will be our pleasure to do".

Patrick told them, "Wherever you work in your trade, you are bound to find slave branding irons - they do not melt away! I ask all of you to reforge these irons into something of usefulness or beauty, for I would be happy to see the end of them and ensure that slavery never returns to this country".

"We will do that with great pleasure", the blacksmith said. "Indeed, my Lord Bishop, I make you a promise. We will rid this country of these snake irons, for you and for ourselves. We will offer a price for every one brought to us. That should get rid of a good number."

Patrick nodded and smiled, "I think, my friends that in reforging these objects of pain and horror, you will find that your grievances will disappear and you will be happier".

"Yes, my Lord Bishop. We do believe you are right", said the blacksmiths.

The monks of Patrick's Abbey remained faithful into their old age and protected him from all intrusion. There were those who tried to get close to him, so many, they would have drained him of all his energy; for this reason Patrick was jealously guarded. Unfortunately, this led to misrepresentation and he was often wrongly portrayed as being distant and excessively religious.

In truth, he was much loved, for he was kind, compassionate and always fair-minded. He worried about the poor and their conditions of life, often asking how they kept warm in cold weather and would ask those who could weave to make blankets for them, for which he would pay.

He spoke little of his personal life or of his past. Rarely did he reveal his innermost feelings. There was never a man so sensitive, yet so brave. He would challenge any man who hurt another for any unjust reason and win; such was his 'wondrous spiritual power'. Despite his age, he retained a certain youthful, unworldly charm and sense of humour.

Most of all, Patrick's love for Jesus was strong. He was often found deep in meditation, just before those who were sick or injured were brought before him. He never failed to heal them.

Patrick never again visited his old home at Bonavon and it was some years before he sent a party of monks to visit the Brothers there, in order to see how a long established monastery was organised. On their return, they reported that his father Calpurnius had passed away peacefully in his sleep several years before, at a ripe old age, surrounded by his many friends.

There was more bad news. The monks recounted how the country was now overrun by members of the Scotti tribe, a wild and aggressive race of people from Ireland, who had moved to the islands off the coast of Briton and who had now infiltrated every town and village in the Strathclyde region. They were not the only ones, as from the east had come people from over the sea and it seemed as though everyone wanted a share of the land vacated by the Roman Army. However, one good piece of news, was that none of those newcomers had interfered with either the monasteries or the academy at Glasco. It was hard to believe that these wild people appeared to appreciate that education and religion was an acceptable part of life, or perhaps, they were simply afraid of them.

Until the Romans arrived, the people of the Clyde valley were originally of the same race as those in Wales and the south west corner of Briton. Then, after several hundred years of intermarriage, they had become an amicable mixture.

Patrick was always proud to call himself a Roman Briton, even though his grandfather Joseph and his mother came from Gaul. The reason for this being that both his paternal great grandfathers were Romans who had married local Celtic women and in their homes, the Roman way of life was upheld.

Patrick did visit Avalon again, in order to meet and talk with Artura. He learned more about the ancient people who created the zodiac carved into the earth and was astonished to discover some of the mysteries of time and space.

How he wished he had leaned these things many years before, for now he was old and was aware that death could not be far away, not many men lived for so long. His ability to heal himself when in the process of healing others was the most likely reason for his longevity, but now he was becoming tired and sometimes confused. He began to spend more and more time in his dreams and visions than in the real world, but what dreams and visions they were! In them, he rode his golden pony along the banks of the Avon Tibernae and laughed and chatted with his grandfather Joseph and his father Calpurnius.

But, best of all, he could be with his beloved wife, Flavia. They could stroll hand-in-hand through scented gardens, or stand at the summit of the Tor at Avalon and admire the view - how he hated it when they woke him up! 'Why could they not let him sleep', he wondered? 'He had never felt so tired'.

His fellow priests, monks and Sisters were worried. They wanted to know where he would prefer his last resting place to be, but he never stayed awake long enough for them to ask him. They would have to guess and they pondered on whether to arrange for him to be taken to his home at Bonavon Tibernae, to rest beside his father, or to Avalon, a place he loved and of which he had many happy memories? Or, their third choice - simply bury him in the place he had called home for the past forty years - right here in Armagh?

The latter would be the easiest option, except for one thing. There was a lucrative trade in relics and Patrick was a prime target for these unspeakable grave robbers. For those who loved him, it was unbearable for them to think of their sainted Patrick being dug up and cut into pieces, to be sold in markets by evil, irreverent men.

One cold and blustery day in March, Patrick did not wake up. He had passed away in the night. Those who waited by his bedside did not notice right away and it was not until morning that they realised his breathing had stopped and he was cold to the touch.

By now they had agreed a devious plan to fool the relic hunters.

They held an elaborate funeral service, the most senior Archbishop in the country eulogising over the body. The Archbishop described what an extraordinary life Patrick had led; how many people he had healed and how many he had brought back to life from the brink of death. The monks prayed, the Sisters of Mary wept and the thousands who came to pay their respects wailed, as the coffin was lowered into the grave. After the service, guards were placed around the grave and a vigil kept, anyone found nearby being stopped and asked to state their business.

Only, it was not Patrick in the grave, but an elderly monk who had died the day before him.

Patrick's body was still hidden in the monastery. wrapped in the finest linen and placed inside a oak casket, the body then being taken to a secret place for a private burial. There, ten men and three women stood around a newly dug grave, each one of them vowing before God, never to speak of Patrick's final resting place.

None of them ever did.